God's Plot & Man's Stories

God's Plot & Man's Stories

Studies in the Fictional Imagination from Milton to Fielding

Leopold Damrosch, Jr.

The University of Chicago Press • Chicago and London

LEOPOLD DAMROSCH, JR., is professor of English at the University of Maryland. He is the author of *Samuel Johnson and the Tragic Sense, The Uses of Johnson's Criticism,* and *Symbol and Truth in Blake's Myth.*

The University of Chicago Press, Chicago 60637
The University of Chicago Press, Ltd., London
© 1985 by The University of Chicago
All rights reserved. Published 1985
Printed in the United States of America

94 93 92 91 90 89 88 87 86 85   5 4 3 2 1

Library of Congress Cataloging in Publication Data

Damrosch, Leopold.
  God's plot and man's stories.

  Includes bibliographical references and index.
  1. English fiction—18th century—History and
criticism. 2. English fiction—Early modern, 1500–1700—
History and criticism. 3. Puritanism in literature.
4. Christianity in literature. 5. Fiction—Stories,
plots, etc. 6. Milton, John, 1608–1674. Paradise lost.
I. Title.
PR858.P8D3 1985   823'.4'09382   84-8754
ISBN 0-226-13579-9

For Joyce

"Which were it toilsome, yet with thee were sweet."

Paradise Lost *IV.438*

Frontispiece to Genesis in Luther's Bible (Wittenberg, 1545), by Lucas Cranach the Elder. By permission of the Folger Shakespeare Library, Washington, D.C.

Contents

Preface

Spellings have been modernized throughout because modern editions exist for some but not all of the writers whom I quote, and in any case these editions are inconsistent in their practice. It seemed absurd to choke Bunyan's colloquial fluency with capitals and italics while allowing Milton greater ease because his editors (and translators of his Latin works) modernize while Bunyan's and Defoe's do not. In the notes I have attempted to acknowledge fully my extensive debts to other writers, but no debates or investigations are carried on there. When not otherwise indicated, translations from French and German are my own.

During the years that this book has been in progress, I have benefited immeasurably from the conversation and critical advice of colleagues, students, and other friends. I wish I could thank everyone whose thinking stimulated or corrected my own, but memory is untrustworthy and it would be invidious to mention some names and not others. I can at least record my special gratitude to everyone who read portions of the manuscript (some long ago in versions now drastically altered). During the years I was at the University of Virgina, these included Peter Carlton, Vera Camden, Craig Davis, Frans De Bruyn, Alan Howard, Alan Jacobs, David Levin, Michael Moses, William Rowland, Regina Schwartz, and James Turner; and I want especially to record my gratitude for the combative and generous intelligence of William Kerrigan. Discussions at the English Institute in 1980, where I presented a paper on Bunyan and Defoe, helped me to define my approach. At the University of Ottawa, where I spent a very rewarding year in 1980–81, I was grateful for the advice of many people, in particular Dennis Danielson, Ina Ferris, Linda and Gary Hauck, John Hill, David Jeffrey, and Michael Keefer. Friends elsewhere gave me valuable criticisms: Stephen Greenblatt, Mary Poovey, John Rumrich, and John Stevenson. And above all, I have had the happy advantage of a brother, David Damrosch, and a wife, Joyce Van Dyke, who combine imagination and critical insight with affection, and have made the final draft much better than it would otherwise have been.

In addition, the suggestions of two anonymous readers for the University of Chicago Press were welcome aids to eleventh-hour revision. At the eleventh hour and fifty-ninth minute, lecture audiences at Stanford University and the University of California at Berkeley helped me to clarify the argument of my chapter on *Clarissa*. Carol Sapora, at the University of Maryland, verified references with good will and good judgment.

I am most grateful for two sources of institutional support during the years of research and writing. A summer grant from the National Endowment for the Humanities in 1978 allowed me to launch the project, and an associateship in the Center for Advanced Studies at the University of Virginia, from 1981 to 1983, gave me time for writing by reducing my teaching duties.

1

Doctrine and Fiction

The Novelty of the Novel

Whether or not the novel "rose" in the eighteenth century, the fiction of Defoe and Richardson certainly signals something new, and many reasons have been advanced to explain it: a new reading public based in an ascendant middle-class culture, a new interest in the individual, a new concern for everyday experience described in everyday language. A number of scholars have thought in addition that the first English novels had a good deal to do with Puritanism, either as a faith or as a social ideology. I want to pursue that connection, but in a different and (I hope) more searching way. Whether Puritanism has been understood doctrinally or sociologically, it has been invoked mainly as a uniform "background" against which to interpret *Robinson Crusoe* or *Clarissa,* and has been treated as less complex than the novels themselves. I want to show that it was quite extraordinarily complex, and that its complexities are an important source of the special energies of the first novels. But more than that, Puritanism is of great interest in itself. Both in what it asserted and in what it tried to resist in modern culture, it gave imaginative shape to attitudes that remain potent to this day.

The present book is not a source-study and it is not a poetics of narrative. Rather, it is an attempt to understand how particular narratives, at a crucial period in the history of Western culture, both embodied and questioned the religious ideas that their authors and readers held. Such a study has much to do with the "rise of the novel," but it is not offered as causal explanation, if indeed (which I doubt) so complex a development can ever be referred to distinct "causes." And it has much to do with the theory of fiction, but it is not in itself a

theory of fiction. Rather, I want to explore and celebrate the uniqueness of certain masterpieces, and to try to expose some of the deep
assumptions from which they draw their special power. My theme is
the tension between invented narratives and the divine structure of
meaning that human life was supposed to embody. In principle,
God's plot—I borrow the phrase from the seventeenth-century
preacher Thomas Shepard[1]—must be wholly congruent with man's
stories, but in practice that congruence grew increasingly problematic, as traditional ways of thinking about existence bent and altered under the insistent pressure of the modern world.

Every masterpiece is *sui generis.* By virtue of the ways in which it
embodies its questions it answers them differently from other works
even by the same author, let alone by his contemporaries. In Mark
Schorer's phrase, technique is discovery.[2] But technique is rarely an
end in itself: it develops in order to solve issues that go far beyond the
devices of story-telling, and what is discovered is not so much new
kinds of technique as new ways of posing the perennial human questions. My concern is just as much with the ideas themselves as with
their fictional embodiment. I am deeply interested in the question
"How did the novel begin?" but also in the question "How did Christian belief express itself at the beginning of the modern era?" My
subject is the fictional development of religious ideas and values; I am
interested in where Milton was going as well as in where Defoe came
from.

Here let me state my fundamental assumption: the eighteenth-century novel was very much a novel of ideas. It did not simply illustrate
or allude to ideas; it embodied them, tested them, and fought with
them. Specifically, the early novel had much to do with a tension in
the central doctrines and narrative modes of Christianity. These began to be tested in new ways even in the didactic narratives of Milton
and Bunyan, and their urgent revaluation informed the fundamental
structure of *Robinson Crusoe* and *Clarissa.* The greatest novel of the
eighteenth century, *Tom Jones,* was conceived in explicit opposition to
the Puritan novel, inverting its assumptions but responding to the
same cultural tension. When the tension waned in the later eighteenth
century, so did the novel; narratives went on being written, but far
less interesting ones, with the exception (which proves the rule) of the
remarkable anti-novel *Tristram Shandy.* Only with Austen and Scott,
and with that flawed work of genius, Godwin's *Caleb Williams,* was the
novel reborn as a great literary form, and then on very different
terms.

The conservative humanists Pope and Swift, who tended to despise
the new novelists ("Earless on high stood unabash'd Defoe," Pope
wrote in *The Dunciad*), were bitterly antiheroic and anti-epic in their
critique of the political and social order. But at the same time they

accepted that order as the only possible structure of reality in this world, and were notably vague about the nature of God's activity in it. Ethically they were earnest Christians, but the metaphysical aspect of religion—which had been absolutely central throughout the seventeenth century—was dismissed to the periphery of attention, either because it encouraged idiosyncrasy and fanaticism (Swift's *Tale of a Tub*), because it raised questions that were too deep for human comprehension (Swift's sermon on the Trinity), or because the Augustan ideal of harmonizing opposites was committed to blurring philosophical distinctions (Pope's *Essay on Man*). It was the novelists, in contrast to Pope and Swift, who kept religious concerns at the center of their art, but they did so in remarkable feats of transposition; the implications of religious doctrine were reimagined, and covertly tested, in what purport to be merely mimetic tales about ordinary life. Groping toward a poetics of its own, the new genre was peculiarly open to the fundamental aesthetic questions: not only the nuances of "realism" or "point of view" that have interested modern critics, but also the ultimate problem of the relation of fiction to truth, and the role of the author who perpetrates that fiction while claiming to tell the truth.

The Significance of Puritanism

To a large extent, the Puritan contribution to English literature has been undervalued because it was unattractive to opponents who lived to write the story. As Macaulay said in a similar connection, "The friends of liberty labored under the disadvantage of which the lion in the fable complained so bitterly. Though they were the conquerors, their enemies were the painters."[3] In addition, however, the Puritan contribution has been undervalued because it has been construed in needlessly simple terms, as a minority group's moral orientation that furnished some didactic themes for early fiction but was left behind as soon as fiction emerged from its naive childhood. I propose here to try to get behind the didactic themes and to ponder the deeper implications of the Christian myth as men and women, in the later seventeenth century, sought to live it.

From the Renaissance onward, Christianity found itself under attack from within and without. From within, the unity of Catholicism fragmented into the proliferating churches and sects of Protestantism, an evolution during whose course every possible variation and heresy was put forward and opposed. From without, skepticism gained increasingly in strength until, during the Enlightenment, it threatened to take over European culture at large. A faith under attack has to defend itself, and theodicy became a central genre of apologetics. *Paradise Lost* was written "to justify the ways of God to men," which is an admission that many people felt that God's ways needed justifying.

In one sense the members of the various Puritan groups were firm in their belief, and hence among the last to feel the breath of change. But in another sense they were the most vulnerable, perilously exposed in the strenuousness and complexity of their faith. Their special preoccupations made them keen analysts of the self, peculiarly alert to its frustrations, deceptions, and yearnings for wholeness. The affinity between Puritan individualism and the novel is deep and significant, but far from simple: the point of contact is not so much that the individual is valued, as that the nakedness of separate individuality forces one to *examine* one's worth (or lack of it) in the largest possible context. What Puritan psychology tended to produce was a paradoxical union of self-analysis and self-abnegation. The outward-looking expression of self is a common theme (perhaps indeed the major theme) in Renaissance literature, where the drama is filled with it. But only a genius like Shakespeare could combine the external manifestation of self with a Montaigne-like inwardness, and even Hamlet remains mysterious because dramatic: he has that within which passes show, and no critic can hope to pluck out the heart of his mystery. For the Puritans the self is all-important not because it *is* one's self but because it represents the sole battleground of the war between good and evil. "For what is a man profited if he shall gain the whole world and lose his own soul?" (Matt. 16:26). But the self is duplicitous and complex, requiring the most stringent analysis, and its duplicity makes it impossible for direct introspection like Montaigne's to yield trustworthy results. The truth can only emerge from a sustained scrutiny of behavior over a period of time, and thus the need for temporal narrative is born. The narratives that were based on this search for the self gave it a primacy that the ideal of self-abnegation ought logically to contradict; as their enemies saw clearly, to study the self so intently, even while accusing it, is in a sense to glorify it, and so in a sense the Puritans were supreme egotists.

If one translates these considerations into specifically religious terms, what gives Puritan psychology its extraordinary power—and its significance as a basis for fiction—is the way in which it locates the self in a universe controlled by a mysterious and inexorable Providence. The relevance of Puritanism to the novel does not really lie in particular doctrinal points which the novelists inculcate, especially if these are mechanically deduced by the modern scholar from routine sermons and tracts—from what Rosemond Tuve, in another context, called "neat little packages of dried meanings."[4] The relevance of Puritanism lies rather in the peculiar power, as a basis for fiction, of a faith that sees human life as a narrative invented by God but interpreted by human beings. Studying the story of his own life, the

Puritan seeks to discern what Shepard called "God's plot," implying by "plot" a stratagem or manipulative program that has much in common with plot as literary critics understand it. A novelist like Defoe, imitating the Puritan autobiographer, simulates this search for clues to the divine narration. But since Defoe is the narrator of a story invented by himself, he is plunged into the deep paradoxes of a creator who pretends to create nothing, an inventor of plot who pretends that his plot was planted by the Almighty.

As with plot, so with language. Puritans believed that only the simplest and most transparent words could convey spiritual truth, yet they were keenly aware of the opacity of speech and of the unbridgeable gap between signs and the ultimate reality toward which they gesture. In a world emptied of sacramental immediacy, all signs are doubtful and potentially meretricious. Here too Puritan writing leads directly to the ambiguities of novelistic narration. At a time when religious explanations were under increasing strain, the intransigence and absoluteness of the Puritan position exposed implications of the central Christian paradoxes which the authors themselves might have preferred to leave in obscurity. As the unintended ironies of *Robinson Crusoe* abundantly make clear, one outcome of this confrontation was the development of "a sort of man-made religion"[5] which retained the old framework but adapted it drastically to satisfy the demands of an increasingly secular world.

Myth and Novel

That the novel somehow replaced or superseded religious narrative has long seemed plausible. Frank Kermode rightly observes that literary fiction appeared at just the time when revelation was losing its authority. But it need not follow, as Kermode claims, that the openness of fiction ought to be contrasted with the rigidity of myth.[6] For the Christian myth (as Kermode's own later work recognizes) was itself peculiarly problematic and open to interpretation, and the first novels grew directly from the struggle to reconcile tensions which the myth could no longer hold in harmonious suspension. Far from being the stable "background" against which literary scholars like to place works of fiction, Christianity is paradoxical at its very heart. In many periods, of course, its paradoxes have been felt as life-giving rather than troubling, but from the Reformation onward they were held up to increasingly disturbing scrutiny, and disputed points of doctrine fueled conflicts in which a great deal of real blood was shed. Moreover, Christianity, unlike most world religions, has always been remarkably propositional. In addition to paying allegiance to a culture and its deity, the believer must assent to a number of highly specific beliefs, and these vary disconcertingly (in interpretation if not in verbal form) from sect to sect. It is quite true that the ordinary believer may know and care very little about theology. Nevertheless theology is not an accidental accretion but a necessary attempt to make sense of dogmas that lay claim to truth. And even the most casual believer, in the seventeenth century at least, could hardly avoid catechisms and creeds. Puritanism developed during an era of extraordinary strain, when the unity of Western culture was breaking up violently, and when the cognitive order was likewise breaking up in every domain— scientific, philosophical, and political. Each sect claimed to be the True Church, and had to defend its ideas about man and the universe against the drastically different ideas of its opponents.

Christianity, with its complex union of Hebrew faith and Greek philosophy, has always sought to mediate powerful tensions. While the Reformers (particularly Calvin) gave these a logical structure that exacerbated their ability to generate anxiety, the paradoxes had always been there, as Tertullian's famous *certum est, quia impossibile est* suggests. Tertullian made his statement in unflinching response to Marcion's argument that the doctrine of the incarnation makes no sense, since an unchanging and perfect God cannot transform himself into a limited and imperfect man. But this is the central doctrine of Christianity, and as Tertullian saw very clearly, it has to be accepted whether it makes sense or not. Christian theologians in most periods have therefore insisted on the element of mystery and strangeness in their faith.

For our purposes two corollaries need to be noticed, one negative and one positive. Negatively, Christianity is in trouble (except in periods when its rightness is taken as self-evident) if it attempts to defend its logic in terms appropriate to other modes of thinking. We shall return to this point when we consider Milton's justification of God in *Paradise Lost*. Tertullian himself ran into deep difficulties, as Bernard Williams observes:

> Marcion had said that if God had been incarnated, he would have changed; but change involves losing some attributes and gaining others, and God cannot do this. Tertullian briskly replied that what Marcion had said was true of temporal objects, but God is not a temporal object, and that therefore what Marcion said did not apply. But this is to counter one's opponent's move by smashing up the chessboard.[7]

The real force of Tertullian's position must be that a word like "change" loses its familiar meanings—becomes, in human terms, incomprehensible—when applied to God. Hence the paradox.

This leads to the second and positive point, that a paradox may seem potent rather than trivial if it is embedded in a context of authority, sustained either by the impressiveness of the person who utters it or by the impressiveness of other statements with which it is joined. As Williams points out, the speaker of a paradox is in a strong position because he obviously knows he is speaking paradoxically, so that anyone who objects "is like a man who has missed the point of a joke or an ironical remark or an imaginative comparison, and insists on taking it literally" (p. 190). Hence the special affinity of paradox with myth and art, in which Christian beliefs have been characteristically expressed from the parables of Christ onward. But whereas the *Divine Comedy* can assume the Christian myth to be absolute and invulnerable, *Paradise Lost* must treat it as embattled and problematical. This is not in the least to suggest that Milton's faith was weaker than Dante's, only that the faith of his contemporaries was more troubled than that of Dante's contemporaries, so that the myth had to examine and translate itself in ways that exposed its paradoxes to unprecedented threat.

Paul Ricoeur writes eloquently of the tendency of rational *gnosis* to cripple myth, but also of the irreversible drive of the human mind to seek *gnosis*.[8] During the Renaissance it was still possible for fable to be seen as confirming myth; on a system of analogy drawn from Platonism, fictive images in this world could mirror eternal realities. But by the end of the seventeenth century, fiction and its symbols were under massive attack. Pope, leaving his youthful pastorals behind, "stooped to truth, and moralized his song."[9] Dryden and Swift jeered at the Puritan tendency to detect emblems in everyday phenomena, and Puritans themselves grew increasingly anxious about the scope and limits of symbolic interpretation, claiming to read the Bible literally and preferring veracious narratives to mere fictions. But mythic significance could not be reduced either to logic or to plain speaking, and in the novels of Defoe and Richardson the mimetic setting, as we shall see, allowed the fundamental paradoxes to reappear with exceptional vividness.

It will be apparent that I am using the word "myth" to refer to the total structure of meaning that a culture accepts, which in the case of Christianity is a body of narratives and prophecies, from Genesis down to Revelation, that are interpreted through theological exegesis and also through other narratives. Thus I do not mean by "myth" any single story, like the Greek "fables" that Milton alludes to in *Paradise Lost*. But I do not mean by it, either, the structural armature that Northrop Frye elaborates for literature out of his wonderful medley of folktales, parables, and romances, where fisher-kings and foundling babies turn up over and over again. Tom Jones is a foundling, but I would not wish to assimilate him freely to Perdita, let alone to Oedipus or Moses. Fielding's romance is very different from the older kinds, complicated as it is by pressure from two extremes: on the one hand, the demand that the new genre describe "reality" mimetically; on the other, the demand that the events of a mimetic reality be shown to mirror the benevolence of divine Providence. It is in this latter sense—in appealing, however obliquely and playfully, to Christianity as a structure of meaning—that *Tom Jones* grounds itself upon the Christian myth.

When the myth itself is under strain, its tensions are particularly visible in narratives that purport to reflect the coherence of reality. Theologians and preachers could continue simply to assert the old doctrines, but it is never enough for a narrative to assert; it must dramatize convincingly. And this means that the inner logic of a fiction often goes beyond, or even contradicts, what its author intended to "say." Literary scholars of a historicist bent have been loath to abandon the goal of reconstructing precisely what an author intended, and have usually equated his meaning with that of some larger cultural institution. But this is to mistake the slipperiness of meaning. Individually, no author will succeed, even if he wants to, in perfectly embodying a set of doctrines in his art. As René Girard says, "It is quite possible that the novelist's abstract vocabulary and even his 'ideas' do not always reflect him accurately."[10] And culturally, no body of ideas or attitudes is sufficiently coherent to serve as the unified "background" that scholars seek. This is particularly true when, as is usually the case, the scholar combines close study of a particular text with enormous generalizations about its background.

Moreover, the energy that motivates a great literary work is seldom a desire to corroborate some comfortable and secure body of ideas. On the contrary, it is precisely the rifting and disturbance in belief that give rise to great literature. Theologians tend to be wiser on this point than literary scholars. As H. Richard Niebuhr says, the nostalgia for medieval or Puritan or Victorian piety is really an emotional reaction against the modern world, a longing for "the security of the closed society with its social confidence and social loyalty." He goes on to observe that the religious systems themselves have never been as integrated as nostalgia might wish.

> They are not like plants that have grown out of a single seed, but more like forests with trees and undergrowth of many origins. They are not like persons with definable bodies, minds, and intentions. Their doctrines and thoughts have an even more manifold origin than those of any individual and are brought into coherent order far less frequently than happens in the case of persons.[11]

In considering Bunyan or Defoe we have to distinguish between their dual roles as Puritan readers and Puritan authors. The Puritan reader expects pious lessons when he reads, and when he writes he will certainly try to enforce such lessons. But the Puritan author is, as it were, an author before he is a Puritan: however predictable the minor writers in any tradition may be, the great writer follows out the imaginative logic of his invented fiction, which includes the suspended dilemmas that it exposes and tries to mediate. The modern scholar who reconstructs the pious lesson is certainly finding what is really there. But much more is there as well, both in the fiction and in the turbulent faith from which it springs.

At the extreme, such considerations may seem to invite the free-wheeling license associated with deconstruction, but I am not arguing that there are no controls on interpretation, only that interpretation must confront the rifting that literature attempts to repair. Nietzsche, the patron of deconstruction, said that man builds his imaginative world in the gap or lacuna of what he lacks: "Er baut seine Welt in diese Lücke hinein."[12] It is precisely there—in what is not clearly defined, and even rejected as inimical—that we need to look for the pressure that generates a masterpiece. This insight can be duplicated in much less alarming thinkers than Nietzsche. According to the philosopher Stuart Hampshire, "The significance of a writer, whether poet or philosopher or historian, and that which makes him worthy of study now, commonly does not reside principally in the conscious intention behind his work, but rather in the precise nature, as we can now see it, of the conflicts and the imaginative inconsistencies in his work." To this Edward Said adds, persuasively enough, that unconscious intentions are still intentions, and that these too have their method, even when it is at odds with the consciously intended one.[13] And Wolfgang Iser, in his phenomenology of reading, holds that literature is built upon whatever system its author accepts but is motivated by the need to answer the unanswered questions of that system: "Through it, we can reconstruct whatever was concealed or ignored by the philosophy or ideology of the day, precisely because these neutralized or negated aspects of reality form the focal point of the literary work."[14] I would add only that in the most interesting works, the questions resist answers and may be unanswerable.

What gives the first novels their special interest, in this connection, is their claim to recreate literal reality without fabulous or artificial shaping. As Watt has shown, they presented particularized characters with ordinary rather than symbolic names, located them in precise contexts of space and time, and described them in referential language that avoided figurative playfulness.[15] This commitment to a version of lived experience represented a truly radical departure from earlier literary modes. What is more, it had continually to be renewed, for each new literary solution soon collapsed into familiarity, and what began as a breakthrough in realism came to look like "mere fiction."

Hence, as Warner Berthoff says, the history of the novel is a history of reactions, of anti-novels that strive against their predecessors to achieve "a wider or a more intense truthfulness."[16] Even if we confine our interest to literary technique, the novel must be seen as a continual effort of reconstruction. Berthoff suggests that each attempt at richer truthfulness goes back to myth, in whose large structures the aspiration to recreate reality can find an adequate basis. But this means that pure mimesis is an impossibility. There can be no mimesis without meaning, however tacit or implicit, and all meaning is to some degree allegorical since it requires that one thing represent another. Throughout this book we shall be concerned with the constant tension between the poles of allegory and mimesis. *The Pilgrim's Progress* is an allegory that keeps turning into a novel in spite of itself, and *Robinson Crusoe* a novel that intermittently tries to revert into allegory. C. S. Lewis speaks of the sixteenth century as the locus of "the difficult process by which Europe became conscious of fiction as an activity distinct from history on the one hand and from lying on the other."[17] That process was by no means finished by the eighteenth century, and indeed it underlies everything discussed in this book.

There is a further disjuncture between novel and myth. Not only does myth impose meaning upon naive imitation, it also imposes atemporal structures upon temporal ones. All novels take place in time, even when the linear sequence is disturbed by flashbacks and scrambled chronologies. But myths, though they may contain historical sequence as the Bible does, tend to place temporal development in a larger context of eternal recurrence. Even in *Paradise Lost,* which openly embraces the paradox of time and eternity, this doubleness generates complications. And in the novel it is far more perplexing, because the special vocation of the novel is to describe what happened once only, in a specific time and place, to specific people, while the vocation of myth is to describe what always happens. The Bible tells a sequential story, but it *contains* it, and declares that when Christ comes again "there should be time no longer" (Rev. 10:6). And as soon as Christian interpreters began to read the Bible typologically, events lost their uniqueness, spatial patterns replacing temporal sequence. Human events in the Bible are aspects of universal recurrence, so that, for example, the story of Abraham and Isaac, though represented as entirely "real," is significant above all as an anticipation of Christ's sacrifice.

The ultimate gap between myth and novel resides in the fictitiousness of fiction. When a myth is alive it is perceived as anonymous and decisive. Much of modern literature, contrariwise, exemplifies the difficulty of inventing a myth that is known to be invented. Puritan writers devoted arduous effort to understanding the problem of freedom in a universe controlled by an all-knowing and all-disposing

God, and novelists in the Puritan tradition had to face the further paradoxes involved in fictionalizing such a universe. Creators who mimic the only true Creator, they present imaginary events that imitate the real events ordained by the Almighty. Ideally their art should resemble the dance of the heavenly bodies which Milton invokes as an analogy for heavenly art:

> Mystical dance, which yonder starry sphere
> Of planets and of fixed in all her wheels
> Resembles nearest, mazes intricate,
> Eccentric, intervolved, yet regular
> Then most, when most irregular they seem.[18]

As in Ptolemaic astronomy, apparent disorder resolves into order when the complex hidden laws are known. Eighteenth-century fiction, until the time of Sterne at least, aspired to mirror this order. But Milton's achievement, resting as it did on the one definitive myth available to his culture, proved unrepeatable. The eighteenth century came too late for comprehensive embodiment of the Christian myth, and too early for Romantic appreciation of the psychological and cultural bases of imaginative experience (one consequence of which would be to reduce Christianity to the status of a myth like any other). Most writers wanted to believe in the absolute coherence of events in actual life, and for them the contrived and artificial status of fable or story was a painful challenge.

In our own time the artifices of art are openly admired, and openly contrasted with the incoherence of a reality that no longer deserves to be imitated. "Real life," Frye claims in one of his celebrations of fictive pattern, "does not start or stop; it never ties up loose ends; it never manifests meaning or purpose except by blind accident; it is never comic or tragic, ironic or romantic, or anything else that has a shape."[19] For most writers of the seventeenth and eighteenth centuries this existential void would have been repellent and unacceptable. However painful life might be—Burke called it a tragedy, Swift a tragic farce—it nonetheless displayed the workmanship of the supreme author.

Frye says sardonically in another place, "In ordinary life a coincidence is a piece of design for which we can find no practical use. Hence, though coincidences certainly happen in ordinary life, they have no point there except to suggest that life at times is capable of forming rudimentary literary designs, thereby seeming to be almost on the point of making sense."[20] For the writers we will be studying, this formulation would need to be turned upside down: nothing in life is random and pointless, and it is literary works which struggle to emulate the coherence of reality. But this was more a matter of faith, or wish, than of certainty. Philosophers and ordinary people alike were growing deeply suspicious of claims for coherence, and since fiction was not yet prepared to revel in its fictiveness, the problem of structure produced deep uneasiness. Novels exhibit patterns of order, as well they might, since the novelists have put them there. But why should anyone regard these factitious patterns as evidence for the providential structure of reality?

Toward the end of *Paradise Lost* Michael tells Adam,

> Yet doubt not but in valley and in plain
> God is as here, and will be found alike
> Present, and of his presence many a sign
> Still following thee, still compassing thee round
> With goodness and paternal love, his face
> Express, and of his steps the track divine.
> (XI.349–54)

Once Adam and Eve are ejected from Eden (the "here" of which Michael speaks) man is condemned to search for God and meaning in signs and ambiguous tracks. The development of literary fiction mirrors that search and embodies its frustrations.

The Novel, Consciousness, and Society

It is usual to identify the novel as the genre peculiarly concerned with the experience of man in society, and for the great European novels of the nineteenth century this is certainly right. But when Lionel Trilling rebuked American fiction for neglecting society, he might easily have rebuked the eighteenth-century novel as well.[21] Society is present in these works, but in peculiar and oblique ways. Families are seldom sustaining and almost never intact, even when the protagonist does not run away from home. And society at large is a series of environments to be passed through or (as in *Clarissa*) rejected, not a structure of relationships and obligations to be accepted. Restoration comedy, for all its stylized artifice, accepts the pressure of social reality more fully than any great novel of the eighteenth century does. It is certainly true that, compared with the *Arcadia* or *The Faerie Queene,* the early novels situate people in society: "I was born in the year 1632, in the city of York, of a good family. . . ."[22] But compared with *Mansfield Park* or *Adam Bede* or *Barchester Towers,* they do not show the individual to be defined and directed by social position. On the contrary, these novels are about breaking *out* of one's position, achieving a radical self-definition against it or, as in the comic romance *Tom*

Jones, hitting the road in order to discover a true status that wholly reorders previous social relationships.

Whatever the novel may later have become, its origins—as our reflections on Puritan inwardness suggest—lie in the private experience of the individual who was faced not so much with society as with the ultimate order of the universe, of which society may or may not be a faithful mirror. By way of developing this theme I propose to look at Georg Lukács's brilliant *Theory of the Novel.* Lukács himself repudiated this work when he became a Marxist, since it is rooted in a Hegelian history of consciousness rather than in material conditions. But its virtues as well as faults are those of its theoretical consistency, and in addition to casting light on the status of the individual in the early novel, it offers a valuable model for thinking about the intimate relationship between ideas and literary forms.

The heart of Lukács's argument is the Romantic reinterpretation of the Fall of Man as the discovery of consciousness, the knowledge of good and evil that radically divides the self from an exteriorized realm of otherness. Philosophy is born of man's discovery of "transcendental homelessness," and this discovery imposes an intolerable awareness of psychic fragmentation.[23] Like many other thinkers in the German tradition, Lukács contrasts this alienated condition with a lost unity purportedly enjoyed by the ancient Greeks. The validity of the historical claim need not concern us here; at all events his formulation works well for the eighteenth century. In Lukács's aphorism, "The novel is the epic of a world that has been abandoned by God" (p. 88). One could add that the last of the epics was overtly dedicated to justifying the ways of God to men, many of whom had begun to doubt him; and when Fielding reinvented a special kind of epic, he did so in a comic and ironic mode that only confirms Lukács's claim.

The correspondence between microcosm and macrocosm had given way to a series of disparate heterocosms, aesthetic entities shaped by their authors in open opposition to any "real" world beyond them.[24] The split between inner and outer, even if an author seeks to deny it, tends increasingly to undermine mimesis. For as Lukács observes, the writer's sense of inner reality can never be fully integrated with the more abstract and conventional exterior reality that he is attempting to describe. The logic of this analysis leads to a surprising but compelling conclusion: the novel, far from occupying a position diametrically opposed to the subjective lyric, is in a certain sense its expanded expression, for the lyric impulse is the voice of the interior self. If the literary work possesses coherence and unity, it does so internally and by reflecting the consciousness that created it, not through simple fidelity to external truth. Lukács therefore concludes, "Art, the visionary reality of the world made to our measure, has thus become independent: it is no longer a copy, for all the models have gone; it is a created totality, for the natural unity of the metaphysical spheres has been destroyed forever" (p. 37).

Now, the novelists (always excepting Sterne) did not directly recognize this preoccupation. Only with Romantic philosophy and poetry did it become explicit. But they illustrate it implicitly, for their worlds of social "reality" are in fact imaginative constructs, and the source of those constructs is a quest for self-knowledge which—as the Puritan autobiographers knew—can never be finally successful. Diderot, that brilliant skeptic, said eloquently that Richardson "carries the torch to the bottom of the cavern. . . . He breathes upon the sublime phantom that presents itself at the entrance, and the hideous Moor whom it masked appears."[25] The Moor is human (not an impersonal id) but is ominous and uninterpretable, a dweller in the interior cavern who stands revealed when the sublime conventions of traditional art are stripped away.

The lyric may perhaps hope to allay this anxiety, for it glories in the subtleties of consciousness while transforming reality into a shape given by symbols that flow from within. But the eighteenth century was no age of lyric, and it is not surprising that many of its greatest successes were in prose forms that tried to avoid fiction-making altogether: Johnson's and Boswell's biographies, Gibbon's and Hume's histories, Burke's political jeremiads. As soon as an attempt was made to embody consciousness in narrative, the paradoxes of mimesis returned in full force, and imitation abruptly collapsed into irony. We see this clearly enough in Fielding, who may not have understood the full implications of what was happening, and still more clearly in Sterne, who certainly did understand.

Invoking Sterne in passing, Lukács emphasizes the affinity between ironic humor and subjective experience:

> The humorist's soul yearns for a more genuine substantiality than life can offer; and so he smashes all the forms and limits of life's fragile totality in order to reach the sole source of life, the pure, world-dominating "I." But as the objective world breaks down, so the subject, too, becomes a fragment; only the "I" continues to exist, but its existence is then lost in the insubstantiality of its self-created world of ruins. Such subjectivity wants to give form to everything, and precisely for this reason succeeds only in mirroring a segment of the world. (p. 53)

Tristram Shandy is no fluke, and the absence of other major novels in the second half of the century is no accident. Sterne's ironic anti-mimesis is a profound response to the paradoxes of fiction in his age.

Finally, it is well to remember that this inward tendency had long been potential in Western literature, above all in the plays of Shakespeare. What Lukács says of tragedy applies very exactly to *Hamlet:*

> Every tragic work must turn to silence without ever being understood, and no tragic deed can ever find a resonance that will adequately absorb it. . . . The language of the absolutely lonely man is lyrical, i.e. monological. . . . Loneliness has to become a problem unto itself, deepening and confusing the tragic problem and ultimately taking its place. Such loneliness is not simply the intoxication of a soul gripped by destiny and so made song; it is also the torment of a creature condemned to solitude and devoured by a longing for community. (p. 45)

We shall return to these pregnant remarks when we consider *Clarissa* as tragedy. Meanwhile it is worth emphasizing the crucial difference that emerges when the loneliness of a dramatic character is transposed into the loneliness of a novelistic one. When the novel is constructed around a central consciousness, incidents are of value—as in Puritan autobiography—if they assist the journey within, the carrying of the torch into the cavern. But the further in one gets, the more one becomes aware of emptiness, lack of power, and anxiety provoked by fear of exterior forces. In the traditional religious narratives with which we will begin our study, these forces are personified in God and Satan. In later narratives like *Robinson Crusoe* and *Clarissa* they are displaced on to other objects but retain the imaginative charge of their religious origins. And because the story is *narrated* and not simply *presented,* their status becomes intensely problematic: they cannot be left in mystery, but cry out to be explained and understood.

So the eighteenth-century novel can be seen as a disguised battlefield, a scene of deep if dimly understood movements, a reconceiving of essential questions about man and his fate. These movements were both generated and controlled by the suddenly urgent struggle of a religious myth that was losing its ontological certainty. But my essential premise—and I would not want to be misunderstood here— is that this was far from a simple rejection of the myth. On the contrary, the tangled development of the novel flows directly *from the myth itself,* dramatizing tensions that lie at its very heart. As Ernest Becker observes, modern ideas of psychology are a direct consequence of religious breakdown and the loss of the old unity: "Modern man became psychological because he became isolated from protective collective ideologies. He had to justify himself from within himself. But he also became psychological because modern thought itself evoked that way when it developed out of religion."[26] The story of the novel is an aspect of that development.

If the early novel has surprising affinities with lyric, that is not to deny its fundamental concern with the individual in society, only to stress that it is indeed the *individual* whose role is emphasized. The relation between Puritanism and individualism will occupy us repeatedly throughout this book, and is certainly not susceptible to simple causal demonstration. Recent research, indeed, suggests that individualism in some form, with its social and economic corollaries, was the norm in England in medieval times, long before any possible influence from Protestantism or modern capitalism.[27] But at all events, the narratives we shall be considering express a new *sense* of the individual, whose relation to society is unprecedentedly precarious. This is in part because Puritans, in their idealizing imaginations, tended to reject the world outright, defining nature as a fallen realm that cannot be man's true home. For as Jonathan Edwards said,

> Nature is a thing more constant and permanent than any of those things that are the foundation of carnal men's reformation and righteousness. When a natural man denies his lust, and lives a strict, religious life, and seems humble, painful, and earnest in religion, it is not natural; it is all a force against nature, as when a stone is violently thrown upwards; but that force will be gradually spent; yet nature will remain in its full strength, and so prevails again, and the stone returns downwards.[28]

Whereas a secularized radical like Rousseau (who was raised a Calvinist) might reject society but embrace nature, the Puritan was bound in theory to reject both.

Yet in practice most of them did not, and perhaps they can hardly be blamed for their apparent hypocrisy, participating as they did in an immense cultural shift from an other-worldly to a this-worldly religion. Robert Bellah observes that while primitive religions have tended to accept the world and to find symbolic means of integrating mankind into it, the great religions that began to emerge in the first millennium B.C.—in China and India as well as in the West—were characterized by a radical rejection of the world. Man and society were defined in negative terms, and a transcendental realm of value was dualistically opposed to the world men knew. Salvation in the "other" world, rather than integration with the familiar cosmos, became the chief good, and the individual was encouraged to distinguish his inner or "true" self from the empirical self trapped in the flux of daily experience.[29] But in Protestantism, paradoxically, emphasis on the radical self encouraged a return to this-worldliness, for it is entirely possible for this world to be the theater in which God commands his people to work out their salvation for themselves. Max Weber was surely right: Protestants who condemned the flesh also insisted on the ultimate significance of action in the realm of the flesh, both because God required man to labor in his vocation to restore a damaged world, and because he endowed each of the elect with faith (or grace) sufficient for the task. Puritan piety insisted on the importance of the individual even while condemning the sinful self, and demanded involvement in the world even while lamenting its submission to the Prince of Darkness.

Finally, the Puritans were exposed, more than other Protestants, in an ambiguous position both inside and outside of their society. We are all of us conditioned in countless ways by the attitudes of our group, as becomes obvious if one changes professions or goes to live in a foreign country. The Puritans were—and wanted to be—a foreign body within the British nation; yet their extreme individualism made it likely in addition that a Puritan would feel himself to be a foreign body within the Puritan group. The need of the individual to belong to a group is thus doubly tested in Puritanism. If the seventeenth century was an age of the anarchic will (one thinks of the protagonists of Jacobean drama, and of Milton's Satan) the eighteenth century strove mightily to tame the will and restore the damaged social fabric. Its dominant literary form, for several decades at least, was satire, whose mission was to ridicule eccentricity and confirm order. But the novel was born very differently from the experience of individuals who moved through society without ever being of it—the rootless adventurers of the picaresque, and the rootless pilgrims of Puritan tradition.

2

Puritan Experience and Art

Puritans and Puritanism

Except as a convenience of exposition, it makes more sense to talk about Puritans than Puritanism. In either case the term covers a range of interrelated possibilities, just as in Wittgenstein's principle of family resemblance no two members of a family look exactly alike but each shares certain features with certain others. It would be quite wrong, as recent scholars have pointed out, to assume that the Puritans were identical with other groups just because they seem to use the same language. They and their enemies alike recognized this phenomenon but saw it as a notorious scandal, Puritans and Anglicans regarding each other's use of similar terms as a hypocritical parody of truth.[1] The Puritans' contemporaries certainly thought they knew how to recognize them, and each sect or subgroup of Puritans, likewise, had a vivid sense of its own identity. But the pecularity of the tradition is that its tightly-knit groups were founded on a premise of absolute individuality, the nakedness of each soul before God. Considered collectively they exhibited aggressive confidence; considered individually they exhibited anxiety and alienation, or were warned by their pastors that not to exhibit these attitudes was an ominous sign.

Whatever their descendants may have become in the relaxed days of Nonconformity, Puritans of the seventeenth century were characterized by a special drivenness. Even the Georges, whose study of English Protestantism is filled with benign moderation, emphasize its "insecure, aggressive" quality, "the private gropings of sensitive men caught in an age of frightening tension and irresolvable conflict."[2] In the doctrines of Calvin, Michael Walzer has argued, Puritans found a discipline that could channel and relieve anxiety. Indeed the Calvinist "saint" became the prototype of the modern political activist, committed to a cause that transcended family and social bonds, and remarkably competent at altering the social order to embody his ideals. Discipline of the self, just as in later times with the Jacobins or the Bolsheviks, led to social discipline.[3] Militant Puritans exhibited the psychology of thought reform and totalism which later history has made familiar: love for the common cause, faith in a millenarian future, aspiration to selfless sainthood and martyrdom, and insistence on embodying theoretical principles in a way of life.[4] So we have the paradox that if we steep ourselves in Puritan religious writing, we get a picture of profound spiritual isolation, while if we consider the political scene we get a picture of highly efficient activists, brilliant and ruthless agents of change. No wonder their enemies thought them hypocritical.

Another way of addressing this paradox is to realize that Puritans lived an ambiguous double role as Puritans and as Englishmen. In his sociology of religion Peter Berger draws a contrast between *nomos,* the sense of total order in which a social system is felt to be congruent with ultimate values, and *anomie,* isolation and loss of meaning. Normally the linguistic and imaginative structure of a society serves to build up a sense of coherence, so that "to participate in the society is to share its 'knowledge,' that is, to co-inhabit its nomos."[5] But if the social order is under strain, smaller groups within it may struggle to define their own separate *nomoi,* even while they are branded by the culture at large as rebels and heretics.

Augustine, the favorite theologian of Puritanism, postulated a *nomos* in the Catholic Church which was coextensive with the Roman Empire, embracing many of the same human members, and yet was radically separate from it through allegiance to the other-worldly City of God. Puritans, however, tended to belong to sects rather than churches: you are *born into* a church (for instance the Church of England) but you *enter* a sect by undergoing conversion and passing special tests of membership. They were thus faced with a life of oppositions. First, they opposed the larger culture that branded them Puritans (originally a term of abuse, like "Quaker" and "Methodist"). And second, they claimed membership in one or another sectarian group that stood in opposition both to the culture as a whole and to other competing groups. Their ideal might be a reformed society in which every individual would be fully integrated, as in the *volonté générale* of Rousseau (who grew up in Calvinist Geneva). But their daily experience was of conflict and separation, and they were strongly drawn to the example of biblical prophets who stood out intransigently against their culture.[6]

Mary Douglas argues in a broadly based anthropological study that alienation from the social order regularly produces individualism,

glorification of inner experience, and rejection of mediating institutions and their rituals. These tendencies will be still more marked if
confirmed by political revolt: "A violent source of anti-ritualism is
opened up when persons are perceived to be behind the principles, or
benefiting from them."[7] That is exactly what happened with Puritanism, whose hatred of church ritual may seem pathological unless
we recognize the association of ritual, in the Puritan view, with corrupt institutions that falsely pretended to be the necessary link between man and God. This was in fact a logical extension of the
Protestant tendency to reject magic of all kinds, including the Catholic
sacraments. Man was now seen as inhabiting a desacralized or (in
Weber's famous phrase) a disenchanted world whose objects were
neutral rather than charged with sacramental significance.[8]

Thus the individual occupied an exposed and ambiguous position,
the implications of which differed according to personal temperament and historical circumstance. It was quite possible for someone
cut free from ritual to feel exhilaration in the face of a new openness.
But it was equally possible to feel anxiety and helplessness in the new-
ly desacralized world. Moreover, it is very difficult for human beings
to live for long without some form of ritual order, and the Puritans
were no exception. Puritanism was particularly attractive to uprooted
people (Hobbes's "masterless men") who were restive under social
controls which they could no longer internalize. But their successors
were bound to impose new structures and rules, as they notoriously
did in New England, often at great psychological cost, since the rules
had somehow to coexist with an ideology of freedom. Still it is also
true that they continued to reject ritual in worship and refused to see
it as confirming the larger *nomos* or English society. And this left their
imaginative world peculiarly vulnerable, for myth is normally an expression (or rationalization) of ritual. Instead of allowing myth to
arise from ritual and give it meaning, they had a myth ripped loose
from ritual and from the social order that the ritual attempts to symbolize. We shall return presently to the imaginative implications of the
nakedness of the Word.

Just as many Puritans were converts who chose that faith (though
of course they felt themselves irresistibly "elected" to it), so also there
were many who broke with it and embraced alternative structures of
explanation. And even at the height of their political power Puritans
were never a majority. But for those who could not escape or did not
want to, the Puritan symbolic system—as all contemporary observers
confirm—was exceptionally stylized and self-authenticating. It was a
world of meanings whose inhabitants saw themselves as initiates; the
fact that outsiders mocked it only proved that the outsiders were reprobate. Like other closed systems (those of Marxism and psycho-

analysis, for instance) it was self-justifying and magnificently defended, since it could not be criticized except through principles which it ruled inadmissible. In fact it was ideology as Althusser describes it, an unconscious structure of living as well as a conscious structure of thinking, which is perceived by its adherents as the "world" of reality itself.[9]

The power of this ideology, then, was twofold: inwardly, a radical analysis of the self, and outwardly, a radical critique of the social order. Another way of putting this would be to say that the Puritans saw themselves psychologically while their enemies saw them sociologically. In their own minds they were unique individuals, joined perhaps in brotherhood with others of the elect, but ultimately alone in direct relationship with God. In an English society where most of them felt marginal or outcast, status no longer mattered: a despised and ill-educated tinker like Bunyan could be a saint, and because he was a saint could be a powerful preacher and religious writer. On this interpretation, the Puritan was liberated from the structuring role-playing that society ordinarily demands, and could define himself as a *self* rather than as a tradesman, a father, an Anglican. But as their enemies never tired of pointing out, the Puritan subgroup was remarkably consistent in its behavioral peculiarities. Social psychology sees every person as learning a complex system of behavior, so that occupational training is not just the acquisition of skills but also a "novitiate" that instills the assumptions and expectations of a given group.[10] In just this way the Puritan saint learned to be a Puritan and a saint, and what looked from the inside like individualism looked from the outside like rigid conformism, albeit conformism to a rebelliously eccentric pattern.

Still, the willed exclusion of the Puritans from English society must not be underestimated. They did (as everyone must) belong to organizations which encouraged predictable roles and attitudes, but they did so by conscious choice and in deliberate contrast to the unchosen status of the ordinary person who was born an Englishman or Englishwoman and by simple extension became a member of the Church of England. The porter at the House Beautiful tells Christian in *The Pilgrim's Progress*, "I will call out one of the virgins of this place, who will, if she likes your talk, bring you in to the rest of the family, according to the rules of the House."[11] In exactly this way Bunyan's congregation at Bedford demanded an oral confession from every candidate for admission,[12] a procedure which modern writers sometimes describe as captious or bullying. In fact it was an essential act of mutual trust: the newcomer had to prove compatible with the group, and the basis for compatibility was a declaration of deep spiritual affinity, not just the wish to join a club.

The Puritans thus stood at once in *a* society and outside *the* society, able to see the larger culture with unusual clarity since they had only one foot in it. To put the same thing in theological terms, their theodicy was drastically different from that of the social whole, thereby contradicting the norm which sociologists describe:

> If theodicy in its metaphysical sense may be the submission to an inscrutable providence, there is also the social theodicy in which men submit to evil and suffering as it is inflicted by society. The two theodicies are not unrelated. It is in the name of the metaphysical judge that the empirical executioner brings down his sword.[13]

As it grew comfortable, Puritanism undoubtedly did tend to merge the two theodicies, but in its radical youth the movement defiantly separated them. Just because it followed an all-powerful God of justice whose will could not be questioned, it was free to question the cruelty of men who inflicted suffering in his name. The logic of Puritanism, whether politically revolutionary or mystically quietist, was to cast doubt upon the whole structure of social authority.

During the course of this book we shall often have occasion to recall the social identity of Puritans, but from this point forward our emphasis will be on the individual: the consequences of Puritan attitudes in the lives of particular men and women, and in the literary works in which they tried to come to terms with their condition. Bunyan's Christian abandons his family and sets out on a perilous journey with the anguished cry, "What shall I do to be saved?" Bunyan and many others had temperaments in which religion burned, in William James's words, "not as a dull habit, but as an acute fever."[14] It is true that such persons often described their experiences conventionally, and from the outside their expectations may seem self-fulfilling. As Haller says, "With the most anxious curiosity, they looked into their own most secret thoughts for signs that the grace of God was at its work of regeneration, and what they so urgently looked for they naturally saw."[15] But Haller surely overstates the optimistic side when he represents Puritanism as a guarantor of courage and success. For Puritan doctrine, especially when embraced by troubled souls, ensured that few could be certain of the salvation they so desperately sought. Burton, Locke, and Swift all described Puritan "enthusiasts" as melancholics, or as we would say, neurotics. We shall return later to the phenomenon of inner anxiety producing outward confidence, but first we need to look closely at the psychological basis of Puritan belief and experience, and its inseparable relation to the stern theology in which it found expression.

Guilt and Accusation

When the church and its comforting structure of ritual are removed, then the forces of good and evil contract their activity into the individual soul, and the psyche is potentially open to intolerable strain. Any thoughtful Puritan was necessarily a psychologist. And this was no merely theoretical matter, but a confrontation with turbulent impulses that could neither be ignored nor escaped.

The fundamental premise of the Augustinian tradition is the burden of guilt. Guilt is not a hypothesis or a doctrinal conclusion, but an existential fact. Many men and women in every age have been little troubled by guilt or have found ways of mitigating its discomforts. Such people have seldom, in the spiritual sense, been Puritans. To be a believing Puritan was to feel guilty; or, since so many notable Puritans were converts to their faith, one might say that to be oppressed by guilt made one a strong candidate for becoming a Puritan. In Paul Ricoeur's phenomenology of religious symbolism, sin is a state of having breached a personal bond of loyalty to God, with the consequent loss of integrity that is perceived as "alienation from oneself." Guilt goes further: it is an internalization of judgment that laments "the evil use of liberty" as the cause of inner dividedness and anguish.[16] Persons suffering from guilt of this type are afflicted by a strong sense of determinism. They feel themselves controlled by forces which they want to repudiate, yet they feel also that those forces could not enjoy mastery unless the self had somehow acquiesced.

When Augustine was a Manichee he could dispose of the problem of guilt, for evil impulses merely reflected the material element into which his soul was temporarily plunged, irrelevant to the true self that awaited reunion with the divine. But Manichaeism—though he never fully escaped its dualism—failed to satisfy him, partly for intellectual reasons but above all because his conviction of guilt (or the anxiety caused by repressed guilt) failed to disappear. The genius of Augustinian Christianity lies in seizing upon the fact of guilt, insisting upon its inescapability, and then elaborating a psychology to explain what has happened. But nothing is possible without the first stage, the interior accusation and punishment. Conscience dominates not merely by judging specific actions to be wrong, but by recognizing a continuous state of culpability. In Freudian terms the superego is overdeveloped and punitive; in Augustinian terms the awakened conscience is aware of God within and quakes with fear of deserved retribution. According to Kierkegaard, "Self-concern forces its way in even deeper after guilt than does any judge, into the heart's most secret chamber, where only God is judge."[17]

The key must be to find God there, at the bottom of the secret heart, and to be able to throw oneself upon his mercy. But this can only be achieved through a remorseless examination of the self, with a commitment to spare and extenuate nothing. To confess in earnest is to adopt a profound suspicion, for as Ricoeur says, "The appearance of acts is called in question; a trial of veracity is begun; the project of a total confession, totally revealing the hidden meaning of one's acts, if not yet of one's intentions, appears at the heart of the humblest 'confession of sins'."[18] Whereas psychoanalysis seeks to relieve the sufferer of guilt, Puritanism actually seeks to intensify it, since without guilt there can be no hope at all. As Haller summarizes the message of Puritan preaching, "We live in danger, our greatest danger being that we should feel no danger, and our safety lying in the very dread of feeling safe."[19]

If the Puritans were outsiders from society, they were also outsiders from the self. Hannah Heaton wrote in her diary in eighteenth-century New England; "Self in myself I hate 'tis matter of my groan."[20] Self-hatred was obligatory and might indeed be deliberately scheduled, as for instance by Cotton Mather, who was expert at it: "This day I set apart for the duties of a secret fast. Inexpressible self-abhorrence, for my abominable sinfulness before the Holy Lord, was the design and the very spirit of my devotions this day."[21] Such a faith presupposed the value and indeed necessity of psychomachia, a presupposition which underlies all Puritan preaching and receives literary expression in Bunyan's allegories. The popular preacher William Perkins declared, for example, "There is a fight between the heart and the heart; that is, between the heart and itself."[22] Richard Sibbes wrote a widely read treatise called *The Soul's Conflict with Itself,* and George Goodwin a poem under the title *Auto-machia:*

> I sing my SELF: my civil wars within,
> The victories I hourly lose and win;
> The daily duel, the continual strife,
> The war that ends not till I end my life.[23]

It would be easy to repudiate outright the false self, treating it as a mere instrument of Satan, and many Puritans did tend to externalize unwanted impulses as if they belonged to somebody else. But in principle such a Manichaean solution was unacceptable; the unwanted self *was* the self just as much as the ideal self was. Thomas Goodwin describes "the workings of my heart," suddenly exposed when he heard a memorable sermon, "as if I had in the heat of summer looked down into the filth of a dungeon, where by a clear light and piercing eye I discerned millions of crawling living things, in the midst of that sink and liquid corruption."[24] Foul though that cesspool is, it is oneself.

   Puritanism in this sense is a state of mind rather than a sociohistori-
cal entity, and may be paralleled by similar temperaments in other
times and places. All versions agree that the inner inquisition is only
possible, as in Kafka, if there is an initial movement of assent: "You
may object that it is not a trial at all; you are quite right, for it is only a
trial if I recognize it as such."[25] But all the same the inner tribunal is
not optional, for it is specifically enjoined by God, as Emily Dickinson
grimly observes:

> Remorse is cureless—the Disease
> Not even God—can heal—
> For 'tis His institution—and
> The Adequate of Hell—[26]

In in such temperaments—by no means confined to Puritanism—the
unmasking of the self's evasions can lead to loathing if not despair. In
Hopkins's words,

> I am gall, I am heartburn. God's most deep decree
> Bitter would have me taste: my taste was me.[27]

   It would be hard to exaggerate the complexity and painfulness of
experience that such a faith entails. As the regular Puritan attention
to "breaking the will" of children indicates, the ideal was a sense of
guilt so comprehensive that there was no need for punishment; a re-
fractory child, once "broken," could grow up into a mild and obedient
adult.[28] Rejecting an integral part of himself, the Puritan had also to
reject the world to which that part owed allegiance, poignant though
the rejection might be. As Bunyan dramatizes the conflict in one of
his doctrinal works,

> Sinner turn (says God); Lord, I cannot tend it, says the sinner.
> Turn or burn (says God); I will venture that, says the sinner.
> Turn and be saved (says God); I cannot leave my pleasures, says
> the sinner: Sweet sins, sweet pleasures, sweet delights, says the
> sinner.[29]

Many Puritans seem to have countered fears of anarchy and disper-
sion by adopting a fierce rigidity, and it is easy to imagine that their
militancy toward others was a reaction to inner humiliation: unacknowledged anger was directed outward.[30] But whatever outward
forms it might take, this psychological mode remained rooted in the
deepest self, where the unsleeping conscience ensured that introspection would remain a necessity as well as a duty. A conviction of divine

mercy was therefore essential if the believer was to have any hope of
relief, for as Thomas Brooks said in *Heaven on Earth* (1654),

> Ah! did not the Lord let in some beams of love upon the soul,
> when it is *Magor-missabib,* a terror to itself; when the heart is a
> hell of horror, the conscience an *Aceldama,* a field of black blood;
> when the soul is neither quiet at home nor abroad, neither at
> bed nor board, neither in company nor out of company, neither
> in the use of ordinances nor in the neglect of ordinances; how
> would the soul faint, sink, and despair for ever!

And he adds in a footnote, "An awakened conscience is like Prometheus's vulture, it lies ever gnawing."[31]

Determinism

The complications of determinism in the Augustinian tradition have
been massively analyzed, especially in the subtle distinctions of Reformation controversy—single and double predestination, semi-Pel-
agianism, infralapsarianism, and the rest. Fascinating though these
doctrines may be as intellectual structures, we cannot and need not
examine them here. Nor is it helpful to examine in isolation the faculty of willing, as in the familiar term "free will." For one thing, the
will is a hopelessly controversial concept—one investigator identifies
eight distinct ways in which it has been understood—and for another,
what is really at issue is the state of freedom or unfreedom that precedes any act of willing.[32] Hobbes brilliantly showed that a strict determinist can easily concede that men are free to do what they will, so
long as he can maintain that they must always will what the chain of
causes obliges them to will; and he concluded, no doubt with some
malice, that his position was identical with that of Reformation theology.[33] So it is the ultimate source of action that we need to consider.
And rather than wondering at the appeal that determinism had for
Puritans, we ought to recognize how desperately they needed it. Like
guilt, determinism was a psychological fact before it was a logical or
theological argument. A thoughtful Puritan knew very well that he or
she was unfree, and longed to exchange a corrupting and destructive
unfreedom for the special form of freedom known as Christian
liberty.

At the heart of Augustine's psychological theory is the prison of
habit, the determinist shackles which Satan puts on his human slaves.
But Satan would have no power if the slaves did not in some sense
welcome him. The divided self harbors an enemy within, collaborat-
ing with the diabolical enemy who invades from without. Thus
Augustine:

> I was [bound] not by another's irons but by my own iron will. The enemy had control of my will, and out of it he fashioned a chain and fettered me with it. For in truth lust is made out of a perverse will, and when lust is served, it becomes habit, and when habit is not resisted, it becomes necessity. By such links, joined one to another, as it were—for this reason I have called it a chain—a harsh bondage held me fast. . . . Thus did my two wills, the one old, the other new, the first carnal, and the second spiritual, contend with one another, and by their conflict they laid waste my soul.[34]

Here is the psychological core of the Puritan world view, and we shall study later some fictional versions of it, Eve's surrender to the tempter in *Paradise Lost* and the divided city of Mansoul in Bunyan's *Holy War*. The crucial point is that freedom, in this context, cannot mean freedom to do whatever one likes, for what one likes is self-destructive. The sinner resembles a drug addict killing himself with his addiction, least free when choosing his habit.

Moreover, when man is enslaved to Satan—as all men and women have been since the primal fall in Eden—the carnal self chooses evil out of sheer perversity. In a memorable episode in the *Confessions* Augustine describes how he and his boyhood companions pillaged a pear orchard even though they were not hungry: "We did this to do what pleased us for the reason that it was forbidden" (II.iv, p. 70). Trapped in this bondage of habit, the sinner lacks all power to fight free, and Augustine therefore bitterly opposed Pelagius, whose name has ironically become attached to relaxed notions of human autonomy. In fact Pelagius was rigidly perfectionist, and as a commentator observes, held that "since perfection is possible for man, it is obligatory."[35] But Augustine knew that perfection was impossible. For him the only hope was a counter-bondage that could free man from dividedness by making him want what God wants. *Eris liber, si fueris servus: liber peccati, servus justitiae:* "You will be free, if you were a slave; if free of sin, a slave of justice."[36] Man can only be free if God overwhelms his sinful resistance.

> Take me to You, imprison me, for I,
> Except You enthrall me, never shall be free,
> Nor ever chaste, except You ravish me.[37]

As with Augustine, so with Luther. When Luther adopted the celebrated principle of *sola fides*—faith as trusting *fiducia*, not as theoretical assent to doctrine—the immense weight of the old Law was lifted from his spirit. And here is the point one must grasp above all else: the surrender of free will is presented as a relief from desperate anxiety.

For my own part, I frankly confess that even if it were possible, I should not wish to have free choice given to me, or to have anything left in my own hands by which I might strive toward salvation. . . . For whatever work might be accomplished, there would always remain an anxious doubt whether it pleased God or whether he required something more, as the experience of all self-justifiers proves, and as I myself learned to my bitter cost through so many years. But now, since God has taken my salvation out of my hands into his, making it depend on his choice and not mine, and has promised to save me, not by my own work or exertion but by his grace and mercy, I am assured and certain both that he is faithful and will not lie to me, and also that he is too great and powerful for any demons or any adversities to be able to break him or to snatch me from him.[38]

As the Anglican preacher Jeremy Taylor described it, this was a determinism which no sane person would resist. "It is a holy and amiable captivity to the Spirit: the will of man is in love with those chains which draw us to God. . . . Christ's yoke is like feathers to a bird, not loads, but helps to motion."[39] And Erik Erikson, in his psychobiography of Luther, urges that such people really do feel free, "while we, being stimulus-slaves, ensnared at all times by a million freely chosen impressions and opportunities, may somehow feel unfree."[40]

If narrative fictions are a combination of plot and character, then what has been said thus far is suggestive of determinism as a function of character, the experience of a personality that feels free when drawn by what it loves and unfree when driven by what it hates. But there is another and harsher side to Augustinian determinism, harsh especially in the form worked out by Calvin: the doctrine of predestination, which rests both on logic and on a number of scriptural texts. Here too we cannot survey the whole complex subject, but its general relevance to narrative plot should be evident.

No Christian theologian can avoid the doctrine of election, but many have argued that all men are potentially elected and that God accepts any who come to him. But Augustine and the Puritans took a hard line on this, maintaining not only that God chooses the elect quite apart from anything they may do, but also that he has chosen or rejected them since before the beginning of time. When Pelagius argued that God foreknew which persons would choose to be holy, and therefore knew that they would deserve to be elected, Augustine retorted that this was to get it exactly backwards: "God chose us in Christ before the foundation of the world, . . . not because we were going to be of ourselves holy and immaculate, but he chose and predestined us that we might be so."[41] In the present life we may have the illusion of acting freely, but it is only an illusion. In Augustine's metapbor in *The City of God* (developing Matthew 13:47–48), men and women are immersed in a sea from which they will later be sorted out: "Many reprobates are mingled in the Church with the good, and both sorts are collected as it were in the dragnet of the gospel; and in this world, as in a sea, both kinds swim without separation, enclosed in nets until the shore is reached. There the evil are to be divided from the good."[42] They swim freely, but only within the net.

This providential (as contrasted with psychological) determinism grew still more rigid in Reformation exposition. Whether or not God's foreknowledge constrains human actions, Luther and Calvin insisted that his foreknowledge was in any case inseparable from his all-controlling will. Luther held in his controversy with Erasmus that the Christian must recognize "that God foreknows nothing contingently, but that he foresees and purposes and does all things by his immutable, eternal, and infallible will. Here is a thunderbolt by which free choice is completely prostrated and shattered."[43] And Calvin declared, "I shall not hestiate to confess plainly with Augustine, therefore, 'that the will of God is the necessity of things, and that what he has willed will necessarily come to pass; as those things are really about to happen which he has foreseen'."[44]

It is important to see that however logical this position may have been—Calvin and Luther certainly thought they had the better of the argument with the Pelagians—its basis is a deep act of faith. On the surface it may look suspiciously similar to the unalterable destiny of the Stoics or the rigid determinism of astrology, comparisons which Augustine and his successors bitterly resented. The difference lies in the fact that astrology is amoral and that Stoicism asserts existential freedom in the face of utter unfreedom. As Hegel said, "It is a freedom which can come on the scene as a general form of the world's spirit only in a time of universal fear and bondage."[45] The Augustinian position is a radically different response to the same cultural anxiety: instead of asserting the freedom of the separate self, it asserts the freedom of the self when merged in the providential scheme of a personal God who is wise and merciful as well as irresistibly powerful.

It was perhaps ultimately a matter of temperament whether one welcomed or hated the doctrine that God mysteriously divides mankind into two groups, rewarding one and dispatching the other to eternal torture. Those who welcomed the doctrine were drawn to it by their conviction of deep sinfulness, which made salvation seem unmerited and indeed impossible unless God should arbitrarily bestow it. Those who hated the doctrine could not reconcile themselves to the paradox of striving when it could do no good to strive. And of course there were those like the eighteenth-century poet Cowper who became convinced of their own damnation, and for whom the faith dreadfully fed neurosis instead of relieving it.

Man disavows, and Deity disowns me:
Hell might afford my miseries a shelter;
Therefore hell keeps her ever hungry mouths all
    Bolted against me. . . .
I, fed with judgment, in a fleshly tomb, am
    Buried above ground.[46]

From a modern point of view, an attitude like Cowper's can be seen as
a last-ditch defiance of Puritanism in an act of rebellion by the ego. It
accepts the weight of guilt but, by choosing punishment, asserts a kind
of autonomy in which it continues to enjoy separate identity instead of
merging itself in the will of God.[47] The Puritans of course knew what
this was: the influence and imitation of Satan. We shall have occasion
again (particularly with respect to Bunyan) to consider the disturbing
attractions of damnation. Cowper himself, on a number of occasions,
explicitly associated himself with Milton's Satan, applying "Evil be
thou my good" to his own condition, and quoting "Me miserable! how
could I escape / Infinite wrath and infinite despair!"[48]

Predestination and eternal damnation eventually declined in authority not because new arguments were urged against them, but because a God who could act like that came to seem morally
unacceptable.[49] Similarly, Puritan guilt waned not because new arguments were advanced, but because people apparently felt less guilty
or found other means to explain and assuage their guilt. But for those
who remained within the Puritan structure it continued to impose
potentially intolerable burdens. Not only must one probe the depths
of one's iniquity, but at the same time one must acknowledge the absolute power of God over every single event that has ever happened in
the history of the universe. Comfortable temperaments that were free
of strong conflict were unlikely to want such a faith. Those that did
want it, as Swift unfairly but shrewdly represented them in his satire
on the "mechanical operation of the spirit," felt themselves to be lived
by forces they could not control. These forces were personified in
Satan, who was understood to possess his victims very literally. According to Thomas Hooker, "The Devil rules in them; he speaks their
tongues, and works by their hands, and thinks and desires by their
minds, and walks by their feet."[50] Servitude to God was the only escape from this horrible bondage. But the danger then was that the
new unfreedom would seem as limiting and dangerous as the old. To
fight free of this trap, everything depended on being able to believe
that the God of justice and predestination is also a God of mercy and
love.

God and Christ

From his years as a Platonist Augustine retained a deep conviction
that love is the basis of man's longing for the divine and for the lost

perfection that could never be attained in this fallen world. *Desiderium sinus cordis:* "It is yearning that makes the heart deep."[51] What the Platonists lacked, he says in the *Confessions* (VII.xxi), was an appreciation of the personal God who loved the world, sent his Son to redeem it, and offers a spousal union with mankind. If sin reflects a ruptured personal relationship, then that relationship can be repaired by love. In developing this theme, Augustine, like many Christian writers after him, uses language that is directly erotic: *Age, domine, fac, excita et revoca nos, accende et rape, fragra, dulcesce: amemus, curramus.* Kenneth Burke calls this passage "breathless, precipitate," and suggests breaking it into short lines:

> Come, Lord,
> Act,
> Rouse and recall us;
> Inflame and seize;
> Be fragrant, be sweet;
> Let us love,
> Let us run.[52]

Eros joins with *agape,* as in the imagery of the Song of Songs.

In addition, Augustine preserved, as Catholicism did after him, a strong feminine element in Mary and in the maternal church, the earthly image of that heavenly Jerusalem we long to see. "There, after the hardships of our anxieties and worries in this mortal state, we shall be comforted like little children carried on the mother's shoulders and nursed in her lap."[53] Protestantism, which hated the veneration of Mary and expelled the feminine element from religion, developed one side of Augustinian thought to reach a position very different from Augustine's: it found itself emphasizing the God of will and wrath while rejecting much that had formerly served as counterbalance. While some writers still drew on spousal imagery, everything now depended on the relationship of sinning child to offended Father, rather than of lover to beloved or of child to mother. So long as the sinner can feel certain that the offended God truly loves him, then feelings of guilt are both appropriate and necessary, for as Kierkegaard says, "If a man in relation to God always suffers a being guilty, then at every moment, whatever happens, he is assured that God is love."[54] It is tempting to recall that Augustine had little use for his father and was drawn to the church by his mother, while Luther and Calvin—not to mention Kierkegaard and Kafka—wrestled spiritually with powerful fathers. In their thinking, the dreadful otherness of God received increasing emphasis.

Rather than a child lovingly gathered into its mother's arms, or even a prodigal son who has run away from his father, man may feel himself a contemptible fragment of being and hopelessly remote from the Unknown God, that *deus absconditus* whose ways are past finding out.[55] The danger is that one's own littleness in the face of God's outraged majesty will come to seem intolerable; the inner accusation will fester and refuse to be healed. Nietzsche powerfully says, *Furchtbar ist das Alleinsein mit dem Richter und Rächer des eignen Gesetzes. Also wird ein Stern hinausgeworfen in den öden Raum und in den eisigen Atem des Alleinseins.* "Terrible is aloneness with the judge and avenger of one's own law. Thus is a star projected into desert space, and into the icy breath of aloneness."[56] The unhappy consciousness projects its accusation outward into a barren void (*öden Raum*), and it does so with an almost physical convulsion—*hinausgeworfen,* "thrown out there." Once "out there" the angry God, as Jonathan Edwards grimly warned, might well permit that punishment to fall which only his inscrutable will was holding in check. "The bow of God's wrath is bent, and the arrow made ready on the string, and justice bends the arrow at your heart, and strains the bow, and it is nothing but the mere pleasure of God, and that of an angry God, without any promise or obligation at all, that keeps the arrow one moment from being made drunk with your blood."[57]

The sole defence against this fearful wrath is God's own freely given mercy, a polarity embodied in the symbolism of the Trinity. "Christ is the only pledge of his love," Calvin says, "without whom the tokens of his hatred and wrath are manifest both above and below."[58] Without this rescue by Christ the wrath of God would indeed be insupportable, so that Luther warns, "If we do not feel the weight of the passion, the cross, and the death, we cannot cope with the problem of providence without either hurt to ourselves or secret anger with God. That is why the Adam in us has to be quite dead before we can bear this doctrine, and drink this strong wine, without harm."[59] Since Christ's intervention is totally undeserved by man, there always remains the possibility that individual men may not receive its benefits. Even Sibbes's *The Bruised Reed and the Smoking Flax,* a consoling treatise (based on Matthew 12:20) that sees suffering as preparatory to salvation, has an undercurrent of grim threat: "Cast thyself into the arms of Christ, and if thou perishest, perish there; if thou dost not, thou art sure to perish. If mercy be to be found anywhere, it is there!"[60] What ominous *ifs* those are!

The Hebrew people lived in closeness with their God even when they disobeyed and offended him. But Puritan faith, despite its affinities with the Old Testament, is deeply un-Hebraic in its radical dualism. As Harold Fisch summarizes the difference, "The stress upon the utterly transcendent nature of God; the purely spiritual character of our relation to him; his distance from the world, which becomes a place of evil under the dominion of Satan; the necessity for some Mediator to overcome this distance by standing between 'our pollution and the spotless purity of God'; these are in essence not Hebraic, but Greek and Gnostic modes of thinking."[61] In tone if not in theological doctrine, Puritan thinking is far more dualist than that of Augustine, who asserts the union of body and soul in terms that Montaigne approvingly quotes at the end of his essay "Of Experience." The common Puritan attitude may fairly be represented by a poem by Baxter entitled "Self-Denial: A Dialogue Between the Flesh and the Spirit," in which the spirit concludes by repudiating the flesh:

> I am resolvèd thou shalt live and die,
> A servant, or a conquered enemy.
> Lord, charge not on me what this rebel says,
> That always was against me and thy ways![62]

Puritan discussions of Christ characteristically stressed his ontological role as mediator rather than his humanness in Bethlehem and Galilee, denouncing Catholic veneration of Christ in his earthly aspect.[63] Of course they did not ignore the incarnation, but they emphasized the otherness of the God who was incarnated rather than the humanness of the condition that he accepted. They also emphasized Christ's dual role as the Logos through whom the universe was created and as the terrible Judge who will preside over the final rejection of the reprobate. Even when proclaiming amorous union with Christ, a Puritan poet like Edward Taylor could dramatize the gulf that Christ has to cross:

> I know not how to speak't, it is so good:
> Shall mortal and immortal marry? nay,
> Man marry God? God be a match for mud?
> The King of Glory wed a worm? mere clay?
> This is the case. The wonder too in bliss.
> Thy maker is thy husband. Hear'st thou this?[64]

It was easy for individual Puritans to suspect that they were indeed too wormlike to deserve this mystic marriage, and to fall into the religious neurosis which Burton, in *The Anatomy of Melancholy,* identifies as a type of love melancholy. And if the love of Christ was withheld, then what followed was an eternity of appalling separation, a gulf across which no gesture of sympathy was permitted even if one should wish it, as Bunyan indicates in his broodings on the parable of Lazarus and Dives:

> One would have thought that this had been a small request, a small courtesy, one drop of water, what is that? Take a pail full of it, if that will do thee any good. But mark, he is not permitted to have so much as one drop, not so much as a man may hold

upon the tip of his finger. This signifies thus much, that they
that fall short of Christ shall be night and day tormented from
year's end to year's end, as I may say, even as long as eternity
lasteth, and shall not have so much as the least ease, no not so
long as while a man may turn himself round, not so much leave
as to swallow his spittle, not a drop of cold water.[65]

Confronting the frightening demands of a complex and dangerous
God, the believer felt a special need to interpret the facts of his personal experience in order to search for signs of grace. From these
tensions the genre of Puritan autobiography was born.

Implications of Autobiography

It has become a commonplace that Puritan autobiography played an
essential role in the development of the novel. This genre is rightly
described as highly conventional and predictable, and two aspects of
its influence are stressed: a new value that was placed on the inner
lives of ordinary people, and a uniform structure of "stages" of conversion and sanctification that furnished a narrative pattern.[66] Without altogether contradicting this interpretation I want to reconsider
and modify it. The attempt to understand private experience and
make it publicly available was far from easy; the more interesting the
writer, the more individual and troubled his gropings toward the
meaning of his life. Conventional patterns existed more as a wished-
for ideal than as a normative principle of explanation. Each person
wrestled in his own way with private experiences that were supposed
to be universal, and tried to detect general patterns even when they
did not reflect what he actually felt.

The essential paradox rested on the obligation to examine closely a
self that ought nonetheless to be despised. In abnegating the self one
strove especially to find symptoms of meekness rather than pride,
since the meek would inherit the earth. To their enemies this preoccupation of the Puritans seemed nothing more than masochism
joined with vanity. In Swift's satire masochism produces an aggressive
demand for persecution: "He would stand in the turning of a street,
and calling to those who passed by, would cry to one, 'Worthy sir, do
me the honour of a good slap in the chaps;' to another, 'Honest
friend, pray, favour me with a handsome kick on the arse.'" And
vanity takes the form of presuming that "the whole universe is interested in his meanest concern," attributing every trivial accident to
supernatural agency. "If he hath got cleanly over a kennel [gutter],
some angel, unseen, descended on purpose to help him by the hand;
if he hath knocked his head against a post, it was the devil, for his sins,

let loose from Hell, on purpose to buffet him." Both aberrations unite in a theology of predestination that explains why the chosen spirit has been singled out for suffering:

> He would shut his eyes as he walked along the streets, and if he happened to bounce his head against a post, or fall into the kennel (as he seldom missed to do one or both) he would tell the gibing prentices, who looked on, that he submitted with entire resignation, as to a trip, or a blow of fate, with whom he found, by long experience, how vain it was either to wrestle or cuff; and whoever durst undertake to do either, would be sure to come off with a swinging fall, or a bloody nose. "It was ordained," said he, "some few days before the Creation, that my nose and this very post should have a rencounter; and therefore Providence thought fit to send us both into the world in the same age, and to make us country-men and fellow-citizens."[67]

Swift's parody imitates what really existed, as may be illustrated from Bunyan's publisher and biographer Charles Doe: "I was travelling to a fair, and about the middle of a field, thirty-five miles off of London, I saw a kind of a bug crawling across my path, and immediately there started into my mind, did God, do you think, from before the foundation of the world, decree and fore-appoint that this little creeping creature and I should meet in this place at this time?"[68]

There must have been a fair number of Puritans who deserved Swiftian satire, but many others were far from complacent in their beliefs, suspecting that their self-scrutiny was indeed motivated by pride and fearing that they were victims rather than beneficiaries of God's predetermining plan. The ultimate imperative for studying one's life was a desperate need to discern signs of election. All Christians agreed that the present life had a bearing on one's eternal fate, a belief that endowed action with crucial importance and gave to earthly existence, as Auerbach says, "a painful, immoderate, and utterly un-classical intensity."[69] For the Puritan, matters were yet more disturbing. His fate was already settled, and his actions contained concealed clues which might disclose that fate to a sufficiently careful examination. One's life thus became a narrative to be interpreted, and Sibbes spoke of being "well read in the story of our own lives."[70] The psychological motive for autobiography was defensive rather than reminiscent, and the universal weight of guilt made the scrupulous study of details all the more anxious. For as Kafka's Joseph K. reflects, "To meet an unknown accusation, not to mention other possible charges arising out of it, the whole of one's life would have to be recalled to mind, down to the smallest actions and accidents, clearly formulated and examined from every angle."[71]

Events are woundingly equivocal. Their meaning has been settled since before the beginning of time, yet it remains obscure to the person to whom it most desperately matters (why did God want Doe to meet that bug, anyway?). Not only that; biographical events are necessarily located in a world of space and time, yet this world is "alienated from the life of God" (Eph. 4:18). Calvinists, for whom the world lacked sacramental value, were particularly drawn to the symbolism of the "stranger in a strange land" (Exod. 2:22). "If heaven is our country," Calvin demanded, "what is the earth but a place of exile?"[72] And in the eloquent words of one of the New England settlers, a group that literally enacted the metaphor of pilgrimage, "Our dwelling is but a wandering, and our abiding but as a fleeting; and in a word, our home is nowhere but in the heavens."[73]

Human life is temporal, and in trying to discern the meaning of events, self-examination inevitably took on narrative form. But it was always a type of narrative intended to identify crucial moments, not a connected tale based on causal sequence. Much of temporal experience is incoherent and not worth recording, as is obvious when an autobiographer like Bunyan ignores what we would consider essential facts. What matters is the involution of time in the inner self, where it can be gathered into what Augustine calls *internum aeternum*, the "internal eternal" light of the Lord.[74] Augustine's profound meditations on time are a demonstration of its psychological status. The past is gone and the future has not yet arrived, so if they exist at all it must be in the perpetual present of the mind. "Perhaps it might properly be said that there are three times, the present of things past, the present of things present, and the present of things future" (XI.xx, p. 293). This theory of time as mental is Augustine's way of reconciling the Platonic eternal with the biblical emphasis on history: just as God holds all time in a simultaneous or eternal present, so do our own minds when illuminated by Jesus, the incarnate God who entered history and is present in us at all times.

These considerations have important consequences for Puritan narrative, and with respect to autobiography they have interesting implications for character. One might imagine that Puritan writers were expert in tracing the subtle evolution of personality, but this is not the case. On the contrary, their fundamental dualism imposed a stark before-and-after contrast between the false self, thrown off at the moment of conversion, and the true self that waited until then to stand revealed. The Catholic saint is an exceptional person whose qualifications for sainthood, confirmed by retrospective canonization, are exhibited during the course of a lifetime. But the Puritan saint is any member of the elect whose status was conferred before the world began, and whose moment of decisive conversion—a feature common to most Puritan lives—is the epiphany or revelation of that status. For all their inwardness the Puritans actually admitted less psychological complexity than classical humanists did; as Nietzsche observes, the idea of sainthood connotes "the immediate *succession of opposites*, of states of the soul regarded as morally antithetical: it was believed here to be self-evident that a 'bad man' was all at once turned into a 'saint,' a good man. The hitherto existing psychology was wrecked at this point."[75] After the road-to-Damascus experience the typical Puritan could well have changed his name just as Paul did; rejection of the former self (the "old Adam") was so vehement as to forbid significant connection between past and present.

This does not mean that the saint is perfect or that vestiges of the repudiated self do not continue to haunt him. The author of the *Confessions,* as his biographer says, is a convalescent rather than a cured man.[76] Since it is impossible to be "already perfected" in this life (Phil. 3:12) the divided self must remain divided in its irreconcilable parts, awaiting a life after death in which the sinful selfhood will at last be purged away. The river of death in *The Pilgrim's Progress* is a perfect symbol of the boundary that divides fallen experience from eternal happiness; in crossing it one leaves the unregenerate self behind. But meanwhile one is bound to act, as Edwards solemnly declares in his *Personal Narrative,* "as one that had no right to himself, in any respect." And this is made possible by welcoming Christ so fervently that one gains oneself by rejecting one's *self.* "I felt an ardency of soul to be, what I know not otherwise how to express, emptied and annihilated; to lie in the dust, and to be full of Christ alone."[77] Mary Rich, Countess of Warwick, who remembered her youthful frivolities with some affection, was nonetheless grateful to God for weaning her from things of the world, "still embittering the stream that I might come to the fountain." After conversion, she says, "I was so much changed to myself that I hardly knew myself, and could say with that converted person, 'I am not I'."[78]

Rejecting the false self in this way, the Puritans were strongly drawn—as satirists like Swift noticed—to a psychology that exteriorized unwanted aspects of behavior. You were responsible for your sin. but in a sense it was not *you* that committed it, but Satan acting in you like an invading infection. (We shall study this conception later in its naive though powerful form in *The Pilgrim's Progress,* and in its sophisticated and powerful form in *Paradise Lost.*) Thus despite their profound interiortiy, writers in this tradition can be seen as mounting a last-ditch defense against modern psychologism, and in important ways seem less complex than many writers and fictional characters in Renaissance secular literature. The sight of past sins, Cotton Mather remarked, would smite a dying sinner "with more horror than if so many rattlesnakes were then horribly crawling about thee."[79] A person in this condition will not be interested in tracing subtle continuities in the experience of a lifetime; rather, the goal must be to reject everything that fails to harmonize with the ideal of salvation.

It is in this context that we can best understand the tendency to cast biography in a conventional sequence of "stages." Calvin called the Psalms "the anatomy of all the parts of the soul, inasmuch as a man shall not find any affection in himself, whereof the image appeareth not in this glass."[80] And autobiographers typically insisted that their experience was typical. "God's dealings," Baxter said, "are much what the same with all his servants in the main, and the points wherein he varieth are usually so small, that I think not such fit to be repeated; nor have I anything extraordinary to glory in, which is not common to the rest of my brethren, who have the same spirit, and are servants of the same Lord."[81] The point of identifying stages of conversion was not really to trace a temporal sequence for its own sake, but rather to be assured of typicality. One wanted, as an Elizabethan diarist said, to understand one's life in a controlling perspective—"That I may so observe mine heart that I may see my life in frame from time to time."[82]

Naturally enough, people tended to understand their lives in terms which they learned from others. Autobiographers were constantly exposed to the conventional scheme in sermons and godly memoirs, and since like Baxter they wanted to see their experience as typical and not exceptional, they looked for evidence of the scheme when they pondered their own lives. But to treat the lives or the fictional works that sprang from them as illustrations of the scheme is to mistake the means for the end. Spiritual counselors like Sibbes and Baxter codified the stages of conversion not because the sequence was obvious but because it was just the reverse. Sinners overwhelmed in a shoreless sea of guilt needed to be told that their condition had a name, was common to most of the elect, and was preparative to a joyful conclusion. And if the goal was invariable, the details of the journey certainly were not; the two parts of *Pilgrim's Progress* show that spiritual experience could take many forms and confront very different temptations. This search for identity in difference was often harrowing, since personal experience might not, even after much effort, conform to the desired structures. With what relief did Rousseau, transforming the Calvinist confessional mode, conclude that an analysis of uniqueness was his true vocation!

We do the masterpieces of Puritan writing a disservice if we reduce them to the level of their run-of-the-mill contemporaries. In the exploration of private experience everything depends on the imagination of the individual writer. It was conventional to search the past for spiritual signs, but exceptional to recognize the psychological complexity of that search. *Da mihi circuire praesenti memoria praeteritos cir-*

cuitus erroris mei: "Grant me to wind round and round in my present memory the spirals of my errors."[83] No Puritan account of conversion which I have read comes close to the subtlety of Augustine's:

> Such words I spoke, and with most bitter contrition I wept within my heart. And lo, I heard from a nearby house, a voice like that of a boy or a girl, I know not which, chanting and repeating over and over, "Take up and read. Take up and read" [*tolle lege, tolle lege*]. Instantly, with altered countenance, I began to think most intently whether children made use of any such chant in some kind of game, but I could not recall hearing it anywhere. I checked the flow of my tears and got up, for I interpreted this solely as a command given to me by God to open the book and read the first chapter I should come upon. . . . I hurried back to the spot where Alypius was sitting, for I had put there the volume of the apostle when I got up and left him. I snatched it up, opened it, and read in silence [i.e., not aloud, as was usual] the chapter on which my eyes first fell. . . . No further wished I to read, nor was there need to do so. Instantly, in truth, at the end of this sentence, as if before a peaceful light streaming into my heart, all the dark shadows of doubt fled away.[84]

The haunting chant of the child is suspended by Augustine's inquisitive intellect while he tries to remember if it is merely an everyday jingle. But no, it is an epiphany, and the light breaks in upon him through the agency of the Word—a passage in Paul which he has certainly read before, but which only now speaks to his heart. Augustine's conversion, Wilhelm Dilthey argued, is exemplary of the moment of interpretation that makes sense of a hitherto confused flux of experience.[85] When he hesitates about the children's game he is expressing the resistance of the mind to the interpretive pattern; clinging to his independence, he is for a last instant reluctant to throw himself upon God. Whereas we today might say that human beings crave structure desperately and invent it where it does not exist, Augustine suggests that we fear structure and try to evade it even when it is inevitable. The act of interpretation lies at the very heart of experience: he is detached and skeptical, yet at the same time weeping and passionately committed.

Insights like these are not often to be found in Puritan memoirs, whose whole purpose is to impose structure and obliterate resistance. Unlike Augustine's astonishingly original *Confessions* they were deliberately derivative, seeking to reduce experience to familiar pattern and meaning, for it was precisely the individuality of experience that these individualists feared. If life was a text to be interpreted, the interpretation had to proceed along highly structured lines; David Levin aptly describes the early New England Puritans as "allegory-bound sinners."[86] In effect these writers are arrested at the first stage of the typology of autobiography which Spengemann deduces from the *Confessions*. In this stage the temporal experience of the past, in all its unpredictability and mystery, is collapsed into a single order, and the breakthrough of conversion enables the narrator to grasp "the eternal form of the life he once lived moment by moment, the true meaning of his false life."[87] From this perspective preconversion motives are despicable when they are not irrelevant. What matters is the use God has made of the subject's behavior, not his own misguided reasons for behaving as he did. But it is also true to say that the rigorously two-part conception of a life cannot stand up under the pressure of detailed and thoughtful narration. To understand one's past is, inevitably, to interweave the past with the present, even in the absence of a Romantic theory of memory and the self, and the pressure of lived experience continually threatens to burst the formal container.

Four Lives

Puritan experience varied greatly according to individual temperament, and Puritan life-writing varied similarly. A look at some individual lives will help, however selectively, to suggest the range of possibilities. Lucy Hutchinson's memoir of her husband illustrates the calm confidence of a militant saint, George Trosse's autobiography the simple two-part schema of old self and new self, and Thomas Shepard's autobiography and journal the more disturbed and uncertain consciousness of an introspective spirit. Finally, Richard Baxter's memoirs throw interesting light on the way in which a famous Puritan could reinterpret his development while moving away from the rigid faith of his youth.

Colonel John Hutchinson (1615–64), as memorialized by his widow, splendidly epitomizes Puritanism as an active faith. Whether defending his town against the Cavaliers, criticizing Cromwell to his face, or preparing for death in a sordid prison after the Restoration, Hutchinson found in Calvinism a perpetual source of strength. He was one of those Christians, Lucy Hutchinson testifies, who reflect "that universal habit of grace which is wrought in a soul by the regenerating spirit of God, whereby the whole creature is resigned up into the divine will and love, and all its actions designed to the obedience of that for the glory of its maker."[88] Hutchinson seems to have been a man who habitually looked outward rather than inward, and although we are told that he wept sincerely for his sins (p. 21), faith was for him a means of channeling the power of the self rather than an obligation to expose its secret faults. Theologically he was "convinced and established much in the way of Mr. Calvin, but not as his way, but the way of God" (p. 6). Calvinism seemed simply true to him, and not difficult to defend in argument: "He was eager in every thing he did, earnest in dispute, but withall very rational" (p. 4).

In Hutchinson, then, inner conviction led easily to outward assurance. "He never did anything without measuring it by the rule of conscience" (p. 6), and this was a conscience that authorized activity, not a conscience that demanded lacerating self-analysis. For such a temperament "liberty" could have the double implication—not always united in other persons—of freedom from external constraint and internal commitment to the divine plan. Thus his father's remarriage, which another man might have found financially and psychologically thwarting, "restrained him from no pleasure, nor needed not, for he was so moderate when he was left at his free liberty that he needed no regulation" (p. 24). Such a man found the doctrine of predestination highly attractive, since it confirmed a feeling of liberty when carrying out the will of God.

Hutchinson's self-restraint and his confidence were both founded on a certainty of election.

> Mr. Hutchinson taking delight in the study of divinity, presently left off all foolish nice points that tended to nothing but vain brangling, and employed his whole study in laying in a foundation of sound and necessary principles, among which he gave the first place to this of God's absolute decrees; which was so far from producing a carelessness of life in him, a thing usually objected against this faith, that on the other side it excited him to a more strict and holy walking in thankfulness to God, who had been pleased to choose him out of the corrupted mass of lost mankind to fix his love upon him, and give him the knowledge of himself by his ever-blessed Son. (pp. 34–35)

In his lofty superiority to "wallowing in the mire of sin and wickedness wherein most of the gentry of those times were miserably plunged" (p. 35) Hutchinson displayed a self-righteousness that undoubtedly made him enemies. Yet on the whole his faith seems to have been generous. Predestination meant freedom.

The civil war was, for such a man, literally a God-given opportunity to express faith in action. There is nothing shallow or conventional about the way in which Lucy Hutchinson interprets historical events; their meaning is guaranteed by Providence, but it is not always a meaning flattering to human aspirations. Describing an abortive seige of Nottingham from which the Cavaliers retreated trailing blood "which froze as it fell upon the snow," she comments on human weakness rather than on inevitable success:

> Indeed, no one can believe but those that saw that day what a strange ebb and flow of courage and cowardice there was in both parties that day. . . .While we are relating wonders of Providence we must record this as such a one as is not to be conceived from a relation [i.e., narrative], in the admirable mercy that it brought forth; but to those who saw it and shared in it, it was a great instruction that even the best and highest courages are but the beams of the Almighty, and when he withholds his influence, the brave turn cowards, fear unnerves the most mighty, makes the most generous base, and great men to do those things they blush to think on. When God again inspires, the fearful and the feeble see no dangers, believe no difficulties, and carry on attempts whose very thoughts would at another time shiver their joints like agues. The events of this day humbled the pride of many of our stout men, and made them after more carefully seek God, as well to inspire as prosper their valour; and the Governor's [Hutchinson's] handsome reproaches of their faults, with showing them the way to repair, retrieved their straggling spirits, and animated them to very wonderful and commendable actions. (pp. 114–15)

While the crisis of war was especially rich in instructive experiences like this one, Puritans in ordinary life—particularly in the vicissitudes of trade—were constantly reminded that their own energies were as nothing unless assisted by Almighty God. Hutchinson is described here as the agent both of rebuke and encouragement, just as the preacher was for many the catalyst of conversion and the source of subsequent confidence.

A kind of fatalism is potentially present in Lucy Hutchinson's reflections, and in fact her husband, when he saw the holy war collapse of its own corruption, seemed to throw himself deliberately upon a martyr's fate in spite of the vigorous negotiations of his friends. When he was dying in prison—his wife darkly suspected poison—he told her, "My blood will be so innocent I shall advance the cause more by my death . . . than I could do by all the actions of my life" (p. 264). This world is not, in the end, the true home of the saint, but only a temporary battlefield where he must play his part until ordered to retreat. As Calvin said, "It is a post at which the Lord has placed us, to be retained by us till he call us away."[89]

Lucy Hutchinson's account of her husband takes on a special flavor from its retrospective thoughtfulness. Gazing back over the years of their intimacy, she can ponder the movement from militant confidence to calm resignation, seeing it as a unified existence embracing both the leadership of the soldier and the piety of the saint. At all points this unity is conferred by Hutchinson's faith that his life has conformed to God's will; his last words were " 'Tis as I would have it. 'Tis where I would have it" (p. 272). More usually, however, the life of a Puritan saint was perceived as breaking into two altogether separate parts, a condition of fearful iniquity before conversion and a regenerated condition afterward. An especially vivid example of this type is the autobiography of George Trosse (1631–1713). Born into a prominent Exeter family, Trosse was brought up to despise Puritans and to favor the ceremonies of the Church of England. Spiritually, however, "I was a very atheist, knowing nothing with a serious affecting knowledge, no not one attribute of God, or any principle of religion."[90] After a brilliant performance in a grammar school he was put into trade, living for a time in Portugal as apprentice to a merchant and giving himself up to sinfulness (chiefly drunkenness and blasphemy) which in classic Pauline terms made him a slave even when he might seem most free. "Mine ears were bored to the Devil's posts for a debasing slavery. His cursed work I loved, and delighted in" (p. 83).

Presently Trosse returned to England and, after some time as an idle and drunken gallant, was abruptly seized by spiritual intimations which he soon recognized as demonic possession. There followed three separate episodes of insanity during which he was committed to a strict regimen in a kind of mental hospital. After apparent cures the old symptoms would always return, characterized by complete helplessness before the power of the enemy within. Vivid hallucinations accompanied a conviction of damnation and provoked attempts at suicide to enact the inevitable punishment; at other times Trosse made futile attempts to evade the avenging deity.

I strongly fancied that God watched opportunities to destroy me; but I also presumed that God must get in by the door, or he would not be able to come at me; and I foolishly conceited, that if I did but tie the door with a particular sort of a knot, he would be effectually shut out. . . . And I fancied I saw upon the wall a great claw, for a long while together; but what the meaning of that was I could not tell. . . .And when they put a glass into my hand to drink of it, methought I saw in the glass a black thing, about the bigness of a great black fly or beetle, and this I supposed to have been the Devil, but yet would drink it; and, methought, the Devil went down my throat with the liquor, and so took possession of me. . . . When I heard the bell ring, I thought it to have been my doom out of heaven, and the sound of every double stroke seemed to me to be, *Lower down; lower down; lower down; (viz.)* into the bottomless pit. . . . When I was off my bed, and my manacles on, I was tempted to break the bones of my arms, and did all that I could to do it, by striking them against the iron; and thus put myself to very great pain: so that, like the

demoniac in the Gospel, I tormented my own flesh, and made
wounds and breaches in it, though I could not break my bones.
(pp. 90–97)

What is remarkable is the completeness of Trosse's recovery from this
psychosis, a recovery which he ascribes to religious conversion. During his long career as an admired Nonconformist preacher, Trosse's
life, like Hutchinson's, exemplified the idea of Christian liberty. Before conversion he was unfree both in theological terms and in psychological ones: his roistering was compulsive and pleasureless
(constantly drunk and, although flirting with women, never proceed-
ing to intercourse), his life shapeless and meaningless. After conversion he was liberated into intellectual pursuits—he went to Oxford
and mastered Latin, Greek, and Hebrew—and into pastoral service.
Trosse's Nonconformity was always moderate, and his difficulties
with the authorities, including an imprisonment, seem due to calm
examination of moral scruples rather than to any powerful desire for
martyrdom. During the time of illusory freedom in his youth "no wise
man would have intrusted me with the keeping of his hogs," so that he
was, as he says in allusion to a parable that was a favorite among Puritans, "a debauched Prodigal" (pp. 132–33). When most devoted to
his lusts he was most manipulated by forces beyond his rational control and understanding. For Trosse the problem of the will was therefore solved in classic Christian terms: he was free only when his will
was merged in God's.

Trosse's autobiography is powerfully imagined and eloquent. Yet it
is striking in its absence of psychological development. No attempt is
made to connect the repudiated sinful self with the regenerated new
self, to understand how the one could turn into the other. Instead the
old self is understood as a passive slave to external powers, personified in Satan. At the time of writing his memoir Trosse did not need
to be told that he was mentally ill when he saw Satan as a black insect.
Indeed there existed (as his modern editor notes) a strong Puritan
tradition of ministering to "hurt imaginations," as Greville called
them:

> Such as in thick depriving darknesses
> Proper reflections of the error be,
> And images of self-confusednesses
> Which hurt imaginations only see;
>   And from this nothing seen, tells news of devils,
>   Which but expressions be of inward evils.[91]

But to recognize the inward source of such visions is only to acknowledge that they are not literally present. It in no way concedes that they
are not, *as imaginations,* prompted by the Devil.

A similar diagnosis, without the cure, is applied by Jonathan Edwards to an unhappy relative:

> My Uncle Hawley, the last Sabbath day morning, laid violent hands on himself, and put an end to his life by cutting his own throat. He had been for a considerable time greatly concerned about the condition of his soul; till, by the ordering of a sovereign Providence, he was suffered to fall into deep melancholy, a distemper that the family are very prone to; he was much overpowered by it; the devil took the advantage and drove him into despairing thoughts: he was kept very much awake a nights, so that he had but very little sleep for two months, till he seemed not to have his faculties in his own power.[92]

Even while this behavior is recognized as neurotic ("melancholy"), it is explained in specifically religious terms as the malice of Satan permitted by the mysterious providence of God. The context is the fervor of the Great Awakening, but instead of attributing Hawley's despair to religious anxieties that fed his neurosis, Edwards attributes the anxieties *and* the neurosis to the machinations of the devil, who has attacked this human victim (no doubt exploiting an existing weakness) in revenge for the successes of others. "Satan seems to be in a great rage at this extraordinary breaking forth of the work of God" (pp. 83–84).

Psychology remains radically dualist. In Trosse's case the false self is exposed for what it is at the decisive moment of conversion, and the true self then emerges to enjoy a lifetime of remarkable harmony. As the example of Edwards's uncle suggests, not all persons, however sincere and dedicated, were so fortunate. The potentiality of Puritanism to encourage ceaseless spiritual disturbance is movingly illustrated in the private writings of Thomas Shepard (1605–49). In his public role Shepard was an altogether attractive and successful figure. One of the many distinguished ministers educated at Emmanuel College, Cambridge, he belonged to the first generation of colonists in Massachusetts and was a pillar of the church, spiritual counselor to the first Harvard students, and a leading exponent of covenant theology. His published writings show a strongly logical intelligence and a stern reliance on orthodox forms of piety, together with uncompromising rejection of the free-spirit Antinomianism with which he had flirted as a young man. This sense of confident mastery made Shepard's pastoral work extremely effective; a writer a few years after his death called him "that gracious, sweet, heavenly-minded and soul-ravishing minister" and declared that "thousands of souls have cause to bless God for him."[93] But Shepard's writings dwell also on the torments of damnation, and on the ubiquity of sin as a continuous state rather than as a series of misdeeds. "Every natural man and woman,"

Shepard declares in *The Sincere Convert* (1655), "is born *full of all sin, Rom. 1:29,* as full as a toad is of poison, as full as ever his skin can hold; mind, will, eyes, mouth, every limb of his body, and every piece of his soul is full of sin; their hearts are bundles of sin" (p. 39). A person may sometimes succeed in avoiding overt sinning, but that is irrelevant, for "Thy heart is a stinking sinkhole of all atheism, sodomy, blasphemy, murder, whoredom, adultery, witchcraft, buggery; so that if thou hast any good thing in thee, it is but as a drop of rosewater in a bowl of poison" (p. 40). Shepard's conclusion, like Donne's in "Batter my Heart," is that salvation is possible only when God overwhelms resistance with seeming brutality. "So long as God's sword is in his scabbard, men have such stout hearts that they will never yield; God must wound, and cut deep, and stab, and thrust to the very heart, else men will never yield, never awaken, till God's fists be about men's ears, and he is dragging them to the stake" (p. 165).

Shepard's *Autobiography,* which reduces to as much order as possible a life that is still being lived, tersely recounts the story of an unhappy childhood, conversion at Cambridge, persecution by the established church during a brief preaching career in England, and emigration to New England in 1635. Like many other Puritans, Shepard seems to have been drawn to his rigorous faith as an avenue of escape from a culture in which he felt isolated and without roots, his mother having died when he was small and his father having married a harsh stepmother. "I have oft thought what a woeful estate I had been left in if the Lord had left me in the profane, ignorant town of Towcester where I was born, that the Lord should pluck me out of that sink and Sodom, who was the least in my father's house, forsaken of father and mother, yet that the Lord should fetch me out from thence by such a sweet hand."[94]

Throughout the narrative God's hand is evident, whether inspiring the celebrated John Preston to preach on a text that would speak to Shepard's needs, or saving a ship he was in when the sailors themselves had abandoned hope. But if God's purposes are clear in the event they are not always so beforehand, and Shepard emphasizes the difficulty of ascertaining the divine will. Thus he learned from a hasty plan to sail for America in winter "never to go about a sad business in the dark, unless God's call within as well as that without be very strong and clear and comfortable" (p. 57). And the difficulty of being sure of the inner call pervades Shepard's *Journal,* a document as circular as the *Autobiography* is linear, recording the welter of conflicting feelings from which a pattern was supposed to be deduced, and like Edwards's diary expressing more anxiety and doubt than the formal *Personal Narrative* that was based on it.

Having overcome a temptation to Antinomianism with its conviction of direct inspiration, Shepard is particularly cautious about the consciousness of grace. As his father-in-law Thomas Hooker said, "The secrecy of God does drive men to much trouble. It is like an unbeaten way to the seamen: they must sound every part of it."[95] In seeking conviction of grace Shepard is determined to regard his sinfulness with horror rather than complacency. But of course the more he manages to achieve the horror, the less he feels confident of grace.

Seeking to placate a remote God of wrath, Shepard constantly throws himself upon the mercy of Christ, the protagonist of "God's deep plot in perfecting the saints' salvation out of themselves in Christ" (p. 141). As with other Puritans, Shepard emphasizes Christ in his ontological role rather than in his human one. "I saw that God takes pleasure in none but in Christ Jesus in whom there is no sin, who stands in the room of all those that have sinned that be elect" (p. 176). And again, "Christ stepped between God and me to save from sin" (p. 208). Augustine's Christ was the loving expression of the One God; Shepard's, whatever his formal theology might be, is an ally against the punitive Father. Only in him can God's dreadful remoteness be overcome: "Faith makes Christ absent present to love, fear, serve him as present and his glory present" (p. 179). The jamming together of the words "absent present" finely expresses the paradox of a Christ who is at once transcendent and immanent. "He had let me desire Christ and taste Christ and roll myself upon Christ" (p. 229).

But what if Christ too should prove difficult of access? That is the worst fear of all: "I saw Christ's frowns would damp all joys" (p. 182). In the end Shepard accepts the idea that God's wrath is essential for salvation, that to evade it would be to admit damnation. "I saw also that sin was a greater evil than wrath because all wrath was for this end, to let the creature feel the evil of that" (p. 178). So a precarious balance is required, courting wrath delierately while never losing sight of the mercy that can allay it. "The greatest part of a Christian's grace lies in mourning for the want of it. . . . The Lord when he shows mercy to any of his, it is in withholding much spiritual life and letting them feel much corruption" (p. 198). Sin becomes a constant companion, almost an obligation, because it is there whether one recognizes it or not, and the recognition can never be sufficiently acute. "I saw that instead of being weary with sin and troubled with it, it was a trouble to watch against it strictly" (p. 209).

The attempt to sound the depths of God's mysterious purpose thus entails a relentless study of the self. "I also saw how apt my heart was to be like the sea, troubled and unquieted with cares, with griefs, with thoughts of future events, with men, with God" (p. 218). Very likely Shepard is thinking of Isaiah 57:20–21, "But the wicked are like the troubled sea, when it cannot rest, whose waters cast up mire and dirt. There is no peace, saith my God, to the wicked." In England Shepard

had felt the solidarity of membership in a militant minority opposing
a corrupt society; in Massachusetts, where Puritan religion influenced
or controlled all aspects of society, he experienced ever more subtle
fears of unworthiness and rejection. Every thought, every mood must
be inspected for spiritual symptoms, but in rejecting the free-will seductions of Arminianism he rejects any hope that improvement in
specific ways can win him merit. "I saw in prayer that my great sin was
continual separation, disunion, distance from God, not so much this
or that particular sin, lying out with a loose spirit from God" (p. 121).
What he seeks is not individual acts of righteousness or relief from
individual sins, but an unattainable sense of unified being. "I felt my
heart in this frame, viz., that though it had some light and affections,
yet they hang together as sand. There was not an inward, ever-flow-
ing, overflowing spring of them, as in winter, which runs with continuity of one part with another" (p. 140).

For Shepard, trapped in the ironies of Calvinist determinism, the
unmerited and gratuitous gift of grace becomes an agonizing problem, not—as it was for Hutchinson and Trosse—a simple fact of experience. "In prayer at night I saw my secret evil was to do God's will
because I will, not because God will, and hence I did what I would and
when I would and so wavered therein" (p. 215). Even righteous actions are wicked if done for the wrong reason, and Shepard is poignantly conscious of a will that can resist God's will or impiously run
parallel with it rather than surrendering utterly to it. In such a perspective, sincerity itself is duplicitous, and only God can judge
whether it is truly present. Thus Increase Mather prays, during a period of agonizing religious doubts, "O my God, if I do not sincerely
desire to glorify thy name then deny my requests, and let me have no
answer of my prayers; but if I do in sincerity desire to serve and
glorify these, then have compassion on me, and deny me not, I pray
thee. Upon these terms let me go either with an answer or a denial."[96]
Introspection is obligatory, but the true nature of the self is just what
one cannot truly know. No wonder that God was seldom prompt, in
such cases, with a decisive "answer or denial."

A related paradox haunts the problem of faith versus works. A
person with faith will necessarily perform good works, but these in
themselves are valueless, even though their absence is strong evidence
of lack of faith. "I saw if I laid the evidence of my salvation upon my
works that it would be various and uncertain as my gracious works
were, and yet on the other side I saw that if I did not walk holily in all
things before God I should not, I could not, have assurance of any
good estate, so that there I was at some stand" (p. 101). From anxieties
like these flow relentless streams of doubts and accusations and
smothered hopes. Shepard has no free will and does what he must do,
but he constantly fears that he is doing what he should *not* do even

though he must. It has been said that under totalitarianism everything that is not forbidden is compulsory. Shepard is subject to an interior totalitarianism that is far more pitiless than the most efficient police state, since it has no need to punish disobedience per se. His problem is as follows: whatever he does carries out God's will, whether his works are good, bad, or indifferent. His bad works, however, are clearly not performed under the influence of God's grace. Is it possible that his good deeds are similarly graceless but compelled, in which case they are thoroughly unreliable indicators of election? The divine total-itarianism is pitiless because it punishes even obedience with damna-tion, if that obedience is not performed in a spirit of grace. Shepard's scrupulous anxiety comes from the fact that he can never discern whether or not his good deeds are impelled by grace, and from the fear that anxious grace-hunting is itself a sign of gracelessness.

Unable either to trust in his own actions or to give way entirely to God's action, Shepard is swept along by the current of his emotions, never sure whether he should let the current carry him or swim man-fully against it.

> I was on my bed praying this morning, and the Lord helped me to pour out my heart before him. And I saw that I could plead nothing in myself in regard of any worthiness or grace or any-thing in regard of God's providence or promise, but only his good pleasure. I saw it was not if I willed but if he will, then I should see and believe and live. And here I hung, pleading how good, how pitiful and tender, how free this will was. I saw it stood immovable till it moved itself toward me. I saw God's will was that I should come, but I was afraid of my own activity and working and hence pleaded, Lord, turn me, draw me, and I shall come. (p. 94)

With what earnest caution—one might even say tact—does Shepard approach God while trying to be certain that the approach is God's doing and not his own! He is happiest when he is able to feel that his action coincides with God's: "I saw also that God's immutable and predetermined purpose doth not hinder prayer" (p. 223). But that conviction is never achieved easily or for long.

It would be impossible to condescend to Shepard, but one can cer-tainly feel pity as well as admiration for his intellectual and moral heroism. No elaborate theory of psychology is needed to show that this is a profoundly troubled personality in which health and sickness are utterly inseparable. One's ultimate impression is of a dreadful loneliness. Shepard's universe is not a sacramental one filled with the good things which God has made, but an echoing expanse where nothing must be permitted to distract him from the sole topic of exis-tence, the glory of God. Even human love at its noblest is a dangerous seduction from that duty: "I began to grow secretly proud and full of sensuality, delighting my soul in my dear wife more than in my God" (p. 55). Such a failure is dreadfully punished. "Then the Lord took my dear wife from me, and this made me resolve to delight no more in creatures but in the Lord and to seek him" (p. 76). This sounds rather like stoicism, in which the self is protected against loss by not loving anything too much, but it is radically different in emphasis because the claim is that loving "creatures" gives positive offence to the deity and must be avoided for his sake rather than one's own. If a child should die, that must be a direct rebuke to the too-doting parent, "which was no small affliction and heartbreaking to me that I should provoke the Lord to strike at my innocent children for my sake. . . . And I saw that if I had profited by former afflictions of this nature I should not have had this scourge" (pp. 69–70).

Many Puritans besides Shepard agonized similarly over what were interpreted as punitive messages from the deity. The very moderate English clergyman Ralph Josselin constantly describes suffering as sent by God, who is often thanked for not sending even more of it; at one point Josselin suggests that because he took too much pleasure in playing chess God punished him by taking away a son. There can be no doubt about the depth of his parental feeling: "Many times I find the memory of my dear babes bitter as death."[97] Perhaps it is the very depth of this feeling that motivates the lacerating self-reproach. Cotton Mather, preaching shortly after the death of his first child (he outlived thirteen of his children in all) recommended submission to God's will, but openly confessed his need to "quiet my own tempestuous rebellious heart."[98]

Most chilling of all, it is easy to project this dire faith upon other people. If a child is spared it must be that he owes a peculiar obligation to the God who could have killed him. When an infant was gravely ill, Shepard in effect negotiated for his survival by urging "the glory the Lord should have by betrusting me with this child: he should be the Lord's forever" (p. 35). The child was in fact spared but the mother was not, and Shepard's admonition to his son is horrifying:

Thy dear mother died in the Lord, departing out of this world to another, who did lose her life by being careful to preserve thine, for in the ship thou wert so feeble and froward both in the day and night that hereby she lost her strength and at last her life. She hath made also many a prayer and shed many a tear in secret for thee, and this hath been oft her request: that if the Lord did not intend to glorify himself by thee, that he would cut thee off by death rather than to live to dishonour him by sin. And therefore know it: if thou shalt turn rebel against God and forsake God and care not for the knowledge of him nor to be-

lieve in his Son, the Lord will make all these mercies *woes* and all
thy mother's prayers, tears, and death to be a swift witness
against thee at the great day. (p. 36)

Small wonder that this son, and Shepard's other sons as well, went on
to become ministers.

Shepard's journal illustrates the type of Puritan experience that
fastens upon a single obsessive theme, and its relation to his *Autobiography* displays a characteristic polarity: endless oscillation in the
private mode, rigid shaping in the public one. On any given day of his
life Shepard seems to have perceived himself as chaotic and helpless;
looking back he detects crucial moments or nodal points from which a
coherent narrative can be deduced. In important ways Shepard's writing thus anticipates the psychological possibilities of the novel, which
seeks to combine the two strands that generally remain separate in
Puritan narrative, the density of lived experience and the pattern
which that experience can be made to yield up. And it embodies a
curiously antithetical conception of the individual, centrally significant to his own story and yet tiny in the ultimate scheme of things,
that likewise has much to do with the emerging novel. As Macaulay
wrote of the Puritans, accurately if sarcastically,

> The very meanest of them was a being to whose fate a myste-
> rious and terrible importance belonged, on whose slightest ac-
> tion the spirits of light and darkness looked with anxious
> interest, who had been destined, before heaven and earth were
> created, to enjoy a felicity which should continue when heaven
> and earth should have passed away. . . . Thus the Puritan was
> made up of two different men, the one all self-abasement, peni-
> tence, gratitude, passion, the other proud, calm, inflexible,
> sagacious. He prostrated himself in the dust before his Maker:
> but he set his foot on the neck of his king.[99]

Writing first as a member of a persecuted minority and then as a
model member of a specialized group of the elect, Shepard experienced unusual tensions in his private and public roles. In the far more
famous Richard Baxter (1615–91), a man ten years his junior who
outlived him by forty years, similar tensions produced very different
results and suggest ways in which the energy that fueled Puritanism
began to find new outlets. Not only in his life and writings but in his
self-perception as well, Baxter reflects the tendency of Puritanism to
relax after the Restoration, its once-intransigent claims giving way to
Whiggism and Dissent. If Shepard provides a striking analogue for
Bunyan, Baxter provides one for Defoe.

An accomplished hypochondriac who lived into his seventies, a
spokesman for humility and peace who was constantly attacked for

controversial excess, a stern critic of rhetorical stratagems who wrote over 160 books, Baxter remained a Puritan in sympathy but defended a broadly tolerant Christianity. Indeed his career very exactly mirrored the general movement of English life, in which Calvinism underwent an unexpected and astonishing collapse, reflecting a reaction both to its angry moralism and to its political behavior.[100] To some extent Baxter's manner remained that of the old warriors, as the friend who edited his memoirs observed: "He had an acrimonious pungent style indeed, contracted by his plain dealing with obstinate sinners, which he told me was much severer than his spirit was."[101] But the substance of his writings lacks the "peculiar ferocity" which Perry Miller attributes in Puritanism to "its absolutism, its refusal to make allowances for circumstances and weakness, from its judging by the highest possible standard, its unremitting measurement of the human by the divine."[102] Baxter in fact was a specialist in making allowances for circumstances and weakness. His gigantic *Christian Directory* was widely used as a compendium of moral adjudications in troublesome cases of ordinary life, and he saw so many sides of so many questions that one opponent (Roger L'Estrange, who is immortalized as Mr. Filth in Bunyan's *Holy War*) published *The Casuist Uncas'd, in a Dialogue betwixt Richard and Baxter*.

Baxter was particularly sensitive to spiritual weakness, writing and preaching comfortingly about religious melancholia in a way that constitutes a direct rebuke to the conventions of Puritan self-scrutiny. His treatise *Cure of Melancholy and Overmuch Sorrow, by Faith and Physic* (1683) describes cases of obsession in terms that could apply very exactly to Bunyan, and is critical of Puritan writers who stimulate fears of damnation: "One of my hearers fell distracted with reading some passages in Mr. Shepard's *Sincere Believer*, which were not justifiable or sound." (Baxter conflates here two Shepard titles, *The Sincere Convert* and *The Sound Believer*.) Baxter concludes that Puritan introspection is self-destructive, seeking evidence for what can never be established without crippling doubt. "Certainty of our faith and [of our] sincerity is not necessary to salvation, but the sincerity of faith itself is necessary. He shall be saved that giveth up himself to Christ, though he know not that he is sincere in doing it." Only by looking outward can a person escape the cruel grinding of self-condemnation: "Pore not all on yourselves, and on your distempered hearts; the best may find there much matter of trouble. As millstones wear themselves if they go when they have no corn, so do the thoughts of such as think not of better things than their own hearts."[103]

Baxter left behind not an autobiography but drafts and fragments of one, collected after his death in a monstrous folio volume aptly entitled *Reliquiae Baxterianae*. It is possible to see in this collection, and indeed in his lifelong compulsive writing, a desperate struggle for unity in a time of disunity. But Joan Webber surely makes too much of the notion that "he does not think of experience as all of a piece."[104] The fact that Baxter never organized his memoirs into a single narrative need not prove that he could not; no one accuses Gibbon, who also left a set of drafts, of disunified experience. It might be more accurate to say that Baxter perceived the *process* of change in his life in a way that earlier Puritans did not, a gradual development rather than a once-and-for-all overturning. In pondering this development he was not inclined to assume, as other autobiographers did, that his private experience directly mirrored the ultimate struggle between the forces of good and evil. On the contrary, he mounted a penetrating critique of such assumptions and the psychology they reflected. In retrospect he saw Puritan spirituality as obsessed with self and with rigid programs of conversion, and in tracing his movement away from that ideal he naturally sought a wider focus, presenting his story as a part of the public events in which he took part rather than as an interior pilgrimage.

Baxter's memoirs are remarkable for their thoughtful, detached, irenic tone. He lived to see the Puritan movement seize power, abuse it, and lose it again, and his own spiritual experience affords a parallel record of development and change. The account begins with the usual catalogue of boyhood sins:

> I was much addicted to the excessive gluttonous eating of apples and pears, which I think laid the foundation of that imbecility and flatulency of my stomach, which caused the bodily calamities of my life.
> To this end, and to concur with naughty boys that glorified in evil, I have oft gone into other men's orchards, and stolen their fruit, when I had enough at home. . . .
> I was extremely bewitched with a love of romances, fables, and old tales, which corrupted my affections and lost my time.[105]

The catalogue is perfectly commonplace and is meant to be—Baxter does not represent himself, as Bunyan does, as the chief of sinners. Robbing orchards was for Augustine a source of insight into man's irresistible impulse to sin. Similarly Bunyan's Mr. Badman as a boy "took great pleasure in robbing of gardens and orchards," an early symptom of reprobation.[106] Baxter treats the matter rather as the sort of thing that boys do, a sin of course but hardly proof of bottomless depravity, and related to subsequent ill health in medical rather than theological terms.

Baxter was brought up in a Puritan family, never strayed from religion, and found his soul awakened by reading a godly book at the age of fifteen, but with no clear intimation of extraordinary change.

"Whether sincere conversion began *now,* or *before,* or *after,* I was never able to this day to know" (p. 3). What is remarkable as he recounts his spiritual life is the perspective from which he criticizes a youthful self-absorption that conformed to the classic Puritan type.

> I was in many years' doubt of my sincerity, and thought I had no spiritual life at all. I wondered at the senseless hardness of my heart, that could think and talk of sin and hell, and Christ and grace, of God and heaven, with no more feeling; I cried out from day to day to God for grace against this senseless deadness; I called myself the *most hard hearted sinner,* that could *feel* nothing of all that I knew and talked of; I was not then sensible of the incomparable excellency of holy love, and delight in God, nor much employed in thanksgiving and praise; but all my groans were for more contrition and a broken heart, and I prayed most for tears and tenderness. (p. 5)

The mature Baxter finely captures the naiveté with which he strove to make his inner life conform to the approved pattern of the religious manuals: he suffered doubts because "I could not distinctly trace the workings of the Spirit upon my heart in that method which Mr. Bolton, Mr. Hooker, Mr. Rogers, and other divines describe; nor knew the time of my conversion, being wrought on by the forementioned degrees" (p. 6).

Pondering the meaning of his life, Baxter puts forward a trenchant criticism of Puritan piety. His new position can be summarized as a dislike of theological controversy, an emphasis on love of God rather than introspection and self-reproach, and an almost ecumenical willingness to believe that truth is widely bestowed upon mankind. Unlike many prolific controversialists Baxter came more and more to feel that controversy was barren. "When I peruse the writings which I wrote in my younger years, I can find the footsteps of my unfurnished mind, and of my emptiness and insufficiency" (p. 125). The events through which he lived impressed Baxter so much with the uselessness of quarreling that he no longer defends abstract principles as strongly as he once did. "Men are so loth to be drenched with the truth, that I am no more for going that way to work; and to confess the truth I am lately much prone to the contrary extreme, to be too indifferent [to] what men hold and to keep my judgment to myself" (p. 126). Bitter experience had taught Baxter, as he said in a letter in 1653 encouraging moderation, that "the devil's last way of undoing is by overdoing, and when it fits his turn he will seem more orthodox and zealous against error than Christ himself."[107] And the *Reliquiae* constantly recurs to the political component in religious controversy, for instance in describing an attempt to soften the Nonconformists' hatred of bishops: "I found that their sufferings from the bishops were the great impediment of my success, and that he that will blow the coals must not wonder if some sparks do fly in his face; and that to persecute men, and then call them to charity, is like whipping children to make them give over crying" (p. 14).

What is wanted, Baxter concludes, is a spiritual rather than a rational knowledge of God. "As the stock of the tree affordeth timber to build houses and cities, when the small though higher multifarious branches are but to make a crow's nest or a blaze: so the knowledge of God and of Jesus Christ, of heaven and holiness, doth build up the soul to endless blessedness, and affordeth it solid peace and comfort; when a multitude of school niceties serve but for vain janglings and hurtful diversions and contentions" (p. 127). More specifically Baxter identifies this essential knowledge of God as a direct apprehension of the Holy Spirit. "Though the folly of fanatics tempted me long to overlook the strength of this testimony of the Spirit, while they placed it in a certain internal assertion or enthusiastic inspiration; yet now I see that the Holy Ghost in another manner is the witness of Christ and his agent in the world" (p. 127).

Applying this idea to his personal experience, Baxter mounts an impressive critique of the Puritan tradition of inner warfare, which he sees as a self-generating source of insecurity and pain. In his own life he came to believe that the way to self-abnegation was an outward-looking contemplation of God, not an inward-looking analysis of self.

> Heretofore I placed much of my religion in tenderness of heart, and grieving for sin, and penitential tears; and less of it in the love of God, and studying his love and goodness, and in his joyful praises, than now I do. Then I was little sensible of the greatness and excellency of love and praise, though I coldly spake the same words in its commendations as now I do. And now I am less troubled for want of grief and tears (though I more value humility, and refuse not needful humiliation): but my conscience now looketh at love and delight in God, and praising him, as the top of all my religious duties, for which it is that I value and use the rest. (p. 129)

Above all Baxter repudiates the inward gaze which the Puritans had cultivated so strenuously. "I was once wont to meditate most on my own heart, and to dwell all at home, and look little higher; I was still poring either on my sins or wants, or examining my sincerity; but now, though I am greatly convinced of the need of heart-acquaintance and employment, yet I see more need of a higher work, and that I should look often upon Christ, and God, and heaven, than upon my own heart" (p. 129). To look outward (or upward) rather than inward is the cure for the gnawing doubts and fears that generate the ceaseless anxiety of Shepard's *Journal* or Bunyan's *Grace*

Abounding. The fundamental assumption is the same as Shepard's or Bunyan's—Christian liberty is achieved through union with Christ, one loses one's life in order to gain it—but the emphasis has shifted with respect to the means of attaining that goal.

Committed to this new mode of piety, Baxter naturally perceives weaknesses in the Puritan's claim of exclusivity and their reliance on the eloquent Word. "I less admire gifts of utterance and bare profession of religion than I once did; and have much more charity for many who, by the want of gifts, do make an obscurer profession than they. I once thought that almost all that could pray movingly and fluently, and talk well of religion, had been saints. But experience hath opened to me what odious crimes may consist with high profession" (p. 130). Not all Puritans were unfair to inarticulate believers— Mr. Feeble-mind is received into heaven at the end of *The Pilgrim's Progress*—but Baxter, like the anti-Puritans, is saying that to insist on fluency of public profession is to invite and even create hypocrisy.

One result of these reflections is a drastic reduction in the importance of theology. "The more I am acquainted with holy men, that are all for heaven and pretend not much to subtleties, the more I value and honour them. And when I have studied hard to understand some abstruse admired book, (as *De Scientia Dei, De Providentia Circa Malum, De Decretis, De Praedeterminatione, De Libertate Creaturae*, etc.) I have but attained the knowledge of human imperfection, and see that the author is but a man as well as I" (p. 129). Every title Baxter mentions embodies a crucial problem in the Puritan analysis of freedom and providence; in his wry conclusion that the authors are only men he writes not like Calvin but like Montaigne. In Baxter Puritanism makes its peace with Renaissance humanism and prepares for life in a more tolerant age.

The element of humanism is important. Baxter's new piety is not that of the left-wing sects, but rests on a rational faith that owes more to natural religion than to direct revelation. While the believer must still feel the spirit in his heart and devote himself to the love of God, his reason is able to ponder and evaluate Christian doctrine with extraordinary detachment. As Baxter says in a remarkable passage,

> My certainty that I am a man is before my certainty that there is a God; for *Quod facit notum est magis notum* [That which makes something known is better known]; my certainty that there is a God is greater than my certainty that he requireth love and holiness of his creature; my certainty of this is greater than my certainty of the life of reward and punishment hereafter; my certainty of that is greater than my certainty of the endless duration of it, and of the immortality of individuate souls; my certainty of the Deity is greater than my certainty of the Christian faith; my certainty of

the Christian faith in its essentials is greater than my certainty of
the perfection and infallibility of all the Holy Scriptures; my certainty of that is greater than my certainty of the meaning of many
particular texts, and so of the truth of many particular doctrines,
or of the canonicalness of some certain Books. So that as you see
by what gradations my understanding doth proceed, so also that
my certainty differeth as the evidences differ. (p. 128)

The essential foundation of Luther's *sola fides* is here shattered. In the
Puritan tradition faith was sustained by the infallible Word, received
directly from the Bible or from its interpreters in the pulpit. For Baxter, however, the Bible is a document whose authenticity needs to be
considered, and he is less certain of its authority than he is of God's
existence, a belief which in turn is less certain than his belief that he
himself exists. In minds like Baxter's theology has moved into the
wider realm of philosophy; his catalogue of graded beliefs would hor-
rify Shepard and Bunyan but would make perfect sense to Descartes
and Locke.

One of Baxter's most popular works was *A Call to the Unconverted*
(1657), which assumes that unbelievers can be brought to belief, and
opens with a reaction to the biblical doctrine of election that falls just
short of incredulity. "It hath been the astonishing wonder of many a
man, as well as me, to read in the holy Scripture how few will be saved,
and that the greatest part even of those that are called will be ever-
lastingly shut out of the kingdom of heaven, and tormented with the
devils in eternal fire."[108] Baxter thus recoils from the doctrine in
which the Puritan saints had rejoiced. And he goes on to argue that
"Nature itself doth teach us all to lay the blame of evil works upon the
doers," implying that the unrepentant sinner is fully responsible for
his fate.

What is significant here is not simply Baxter's assertion that the will
is free, but his passionate conviction that it *must* be free. Rejecting
Calvin's doctrine that God is indeed the author of all that occurs, he
rejects also the many halfway solutions and uneasy compromises with
whose ambiguities the Puritans had wrestled, and pleads with men
simply to turn to a God who waits with open arms. "And is God ready,
the sacrifice of Christ ready, the promise ready, and pardon ready;
are ministers ready, the people of God ready, and heaven itself ready,
and angels ready, and all these but waiting for thy conversion, and yet
art thou not ready?" (p. 398). No longer brooding far away in clouds
of wrath, God is a loving father who welcomes his children. Immer-
sion in English history had taught Baxter that conflict only breeds
conflict, and his presiding metaphor was the heavenly harmony
evoked in his enormously popular work *The Saints' Everlasting Rest*.
"There will not be one for singing, and another against it; but even

those that jarred in discord shall all conjoin in blessed concord, and make up one melodious choir."[109]

Yet it would be wrong to imply that Baxter merely began as a Puritan and ended as something else. On the contrary, his deepest feelings remained Puritan and he never entered the Church of England; it was rather Puritanism itself that changed in Baxter and others like him. To some extent he was made uneasy by the changes, as is apparent in his reflections on his wife Margaret, written within a month of her death. She was a high-strung person, afflicted by agonizing headaches, oppressed by fears of insanity, and so anxious about possible hypocrisy that she was reluctant to pray aloud for fear of falling into conventional insincerity. Although he tried to alleviate such scruples, Baxter admired her abilities profoundly, and paid homage to her inward Puritanism that complemented his outward focus.

> I have these forty years been sensible of the sin of losing time; I could not spare an hour; I thought I could understand the matters in question as well at a few thoughts as in many days. And yet she (that had less work and more leisure, but a far quicker apprehension than mine) was all for staying to consider, and against haste and eagerness in almost everything; and notwithstanding her over-quick and feeling temper was all for mildness, calmness, gentleness, pleasingness and serenity.[110]

The prolific Baxter ruefully admits, "She (and some others) thought I had done better to have written fewer books, and to have done those few better."

By contrast with his wife, Baxter looked outward to the world of practical action, whether pouring forth hasty tracts or striving to reconcile the quarreling saints in their period of political glory. Archbishop Tillotson, writing after Baxter's death, recalled a favorite story that can serve as an emblem of this transitional Puritan temperament:

> Riding with him one day, he told me the fable of an old man and a young boy that rode to market on a poor little ass. As they went, the people cried to this old man and boy, "Are you not ashamed both to ride on the poor ass and kill him?" Then the boy alighted. The next that met them said, "Thou old fool, art thou not ashamed to ride and let the little boy go on foot?" Then the old man alighted and set the boy on his back. The next that met them said, "You young jackanapes, are you not ashamed to ride and let the poor old man go on foot?" Then the boy alighted, and went on foot with the old man and led the ass empty. The next that met them said, "Thou old fool, dost thou and the child both go on foot and have an ass unloaden with you?" Saying he could never do anything to purpose till he got above the censures of people, it being impossible to please all.[111]

Tillotson never forgot the cruel persecution that Baxter had to endure, including a brutal trial (by the notorious Judge Jeffreys) during an anti-Puritan campaign in the Restoration: "Nothing more honourable than when the Rev. Baxter stood at bay, berogued, abused, despised; never more great than then" (p. 294). But his greatness manifested itself in pacifism, not militancy, and his pragmatic good sense looks forward to a world beyond the closed and urgent experience of high Puritanism.

History and Time

Everything that has been said thus far might confirm the impression that the Puritans, who characteristically used the medium of narrative when they surveyed human experience, were keenly interested in temporality. Yet there remain striking ambiguities in their conception of time, and these ought to suggest the distance between their writing and the early novel, even while confirming the line of development between them. For if in one sense they were peculiarly concerned with the possible significance of every moment, in another sense they sought constantly to raise the significant moment *out* of time and to interpret it in the light of eternity.

Modern scholars have been much interested in the system of interpretation known as typology, in which events in the Old Testament are anticipatory "types" of events or doctrines in the New, and by extension historical incidents can be seen as recapitulating eternal patterns. But the implications of typology should not be exaggerated. Puritans believed in an unalterable plan underlying human history. But it is one thing to be sure that a plan exists, and quite another to presume to understand it. The radical millenarians might proclaim immediate enactment of divine prophecy, but most preachers at the Long Parliament were notably reticent in invoking claims of historical fulfillment.[112]

Rather than regarding human experience as a simple message to be decoded, the thoughtful Puritan commonly followed Calvin in emphasizing its mysteriousness, even while affirming that nothing happens by accident in a providential universe.

Let us suppose, for example, that a merchant, having entered a wood in the company of honest men, imprudently wanders from his companions, and, pursuing a wrong course, falls into the hands of robbers and is murdered. His death was not only foreseen by God, but also decreed by him. For it is said, not that he has foreseen to what limits the life of every man would extend, but that he "hath appointed bounds which he cannot pass" [Job 14:5]. Yet as far as our minds are capable of comprehend-

ing, all these circumstances appear fortuitous. What opinion
shall a Christian form on this case? He will consider all the circumstances of such a death as in their nature fortuitous; yet he
will not doubt that the providence of God presided, and directed
fortune to that end. The same reasoning will apply to future
contingencies. All future things being uncertain to us, we hold
them in suspense, as though they might happen either one way
or another. Yet this remains a fixed principle in our hearts, that
there will be no event which God has not ordained.[113]

Providence is a structure of will that determines all things, not a structure of explanation that enables us to interpret specific events. We can
be certain (through faith) that God must have intended everything
that happens, but we can never be sure why, although typological
connections are certainly helpful. As Calvin says, events remain fortuitous *for us* even though they are not so for God.

Confronting the mysteriousness of Providence, and deeply aware
of the crucial importance of each of their actions, Puritans tended to
stress temporal separateness rather than continuity. For the sake of
clarity their attitude may be described in three related ways. First, the
moments of experience are separate and disjunct; second, interest
focuses more on the ongoing present than on past or future; and
third, there is a consistent effort to translate time into eternity, history
into myth.

First of all, experience is fragmented into distinct moments whose
connection is far from obvious. We have already noticed this phenomenon in Puritan autobiography, where as a rule little attempt is
made to trace development of personality, and where everything
hinges on certain crucial moments rather than on a continuum of
experience. Similarly, history is viewed not as process but as discontinuity, in keeping with Calvin's emphasis on the distinctness of each
separate moment and its direct dependence on God's power for its
existence. "The corollary of such a doctrine," G. F. Waller comments,
"is a view of time as consisting in disconnected, unpredictable experiences, their order and overall plan known only to God. Each moment
of time is thus not only radically separate from eternity but also from
any other moment of time. Time becomes experienced primarily as
psychological discontinuity."[114] A traditional Anglo-Catholic philosophy, or for that matter a relaxed latitudinarian one, can afford to see
time (as Fielding does in *Tom Jones*) as a coherent structure with an
Aristotelian beginning, middle, and end. But Puritan thought, in its
quest for the epiphanic moment and its suspicion of human interpretation, is committed to admiring the grace that rescues each
separate instant from the void, rather than tracing the pattern that
connects one instant with another in temporal sequence. One might
well go further and hazard the suggestion that this ahistoricism was

itself historically conditioned, a reaction to the frighteningly chaotic public experience of the sixteenth and seventeenth centuries. It is surely no accident that, as Poulet observes, "The religions of the seventeenth century are all religions of continued grace."[115]

There is another reason to focus so insistently on the present moment. A religion that emphasizes guilt, while committed to analyzing sin and thus predisposed to confessional autobiography, needs to escape the threat of permanent submission to an unalterable past. In Nietzsche's pregnant formulation, "Not backward can the Will will; that it cannot break time and time's desire—that is the Will's lonesomest tribulation."[116] Whether bound or free the will is impotent to will backward, to revise the past. And an Augustinian or Calvinist determinism carries this principle forward as well: the will has no power to influence the future, but can only acquiesce in what God's omnipotent will has already ordained.

Augustine's theology seeks to free man by throwing him wholly upon God, rejecting—as in existentialism—the *Angst* of facticity, imprisonment in a historical process impervious to human influence. But the danger of this theology is that its God will *return* man to that unalterable past by demanding a scrupulous examination of sins. And then the prison closes in, for as Nietzsche says, "No deed can be annihilated: how could it be undone by the penalty! This, this is what is eternal in the 'existence' of penalty, that existence also must be eternally recurring deed and guilt" (p. 154). The ultimate impulse behind Augustinian theology is its attempt to escape the trap of guilt to which Nietzsche refers. Escape is possible only if conviction of sin can bring about conviction of grace through Christ, releasing the believer into the eternal present and bypassing the irresistible stream that carries the predestined future into the past of guilt.

These considerations help to explain why Puritan writers, in one sense so obsessed with the details of life in this world, are in another sense so anxious to translate those details into an artifice of eternity. One has to see that their thinking contains two very different strains that never really get reconciled. On the one hand history does matter. It is filled with specific events which reflect the working out of God's purpose; this world is a place of trial and what we do here is of crucial importance; specific actions must be closely scrutinized to make them yield up their significance. But on the other hand history is understood in universal categories, just as the Bible is interpreted by superimposing the New Testament upon the Old (thereby redefining a book which to the Jews was simply the Bible, not a preliminary story awaiting later fulfillment). If individual actions are versions of eternal truths, then they are best understood typologically or emblematically, and history is raised to the level of myth, its events cross-referenced in a single structure of explanation. In the words of a New England preacher, "Prophecy is history antedated, and history is postdated prophecy; the same thing is told in both."[117] History is a narrative, but the narrative is built up out of timeless symbols.

In Christian thinking in general, as Eliade points out, events are valued not for their own sake but for the revelation they embody, and "historicism as such is a product of the decomposition of Christianity: it could only have come about insofar as we had lost faith in the trans-historical reality of the historical event."[118] Boyd Berry shows in detail that Puritan controversies over observing the Sabbath reflect a deep need to anchor the flux of experience upon eternal and cyclical structures, and he quotes a Puritan writer (Stephen Marshall) using the same Greek terms that Frank Kermode does to distinguish between the *chronos* of mere "duration" and the *kairos* of spiritual significance, "the tempestivity of time, the ripeness of time."[119] These ambiguities in the Puritan conception of time were for a brief period, at the middle of the seventeenth century, acted out in English history. One can easily see this historical activity as reflecting the theology of guilt. Punishing themselves so mercilessly, the Puritans felt free to punish others; as Nietzsche tersely expresses it, *Gewissenbisse erziehn zum Beissen:* "The sting of conscience teacheth one to sting."[120] *Gewissenbisse* is the Joycean "agenbite of inwit," but it is a biting without as well as within. The Puritans were famous as vicious haters of their enemies, as in John Knox's ferocious prophecy: "Their cities shall be burnt, their land shall be laid waste, and their daughters shall be defiled, their children shall fall on the edge of the sword, mercy shall they find none because they have refused the God of all mercy." Walzer comments dryly, "But this was only pious hopefulness."[121]

A hundred years after Knox's diatribe the Puritans got their chance, literalizing the Pauline metaphor of Christian warfare. Predestination was a strong support, as Edward Corbett told Parliament in 1642: "If we have the honor to be God's instruments, we must do the office of instruments and be active. . . . We must go along with Providence."[122] So long as events turned out favorably, men could gladly ride the providential current. "God made them stubble to our swords," Cromwell declared after the victory of Marston Moor.[123] But after the failure of the revolution the very notion of change fell under suspicion, and many Nonconformists shared in the general revulsion against it, while Anglican spokesmen rejoiced in renewed stability. Robert South, preaching against the Puritan abuse of language, declared that *reformation* was "a word which has cost this kingdom above 100, 000 lives, which has pulled down the sovereignty, levelled the nobility, and destroyed the hierarchy, and filling all with blood, rapine and confusion, reformed the best of monarchies into an anarchy, and the happiest of islands into an Aceldama."[124] Even when most confident of their historical role, Puritans had been cautious about interpreting the details of historical experience, and once the holy war had failed they were still less likely to draw conclusions. Living in time, they aspired to a reality beyond time, a disjunction which we will repeatedly consider when we look at literary narratives.

Language and Symbol

All forms of Protestantism were deeply committed to the primacy of God's Word, and Puritanism, with its suspicion of the mediating clergy and their sacraments, had special reason to ponder the ambiguities of interpretation as each believer confronted the invasive Word of which Augustine speaks: "By your Word you have transfixed my heart [*percussisti cor meum verbo tuo*] and I have loved you."[125] As Knott makes clear, this notion of the active power of the Word—"the sword of the spirit," in a favorite scriptural metaphor—pervades Puritan discussions of the Bible, which is not only a text to be construed but also a field of force. The purpose of preaching was above all to communicate its irresistible power. Thus Thomas Hooker:

> Now is there come a great rain, and a mighty wind with it, especially a whirlwind, it carrieth all before it . . . and overturns all things with the violence of it. The doctrine and truth which the ministers deliver, is as the rain; now the holy affection wherewith it is delivered is like the whirlwind. When the truth of God is delivered with a holy violence, and hearty affection of God's servants, evermore it makes way, it beats down, and breaks all before it.[126]

As soon became apparent, however, different people understood this "holy violence" in different ways, and the problem of interpretation returned with a vengeance since Puritans could not rely as Augustine did on the traditional teaching of an authoritative Church. In Augustine's subtle philosophy (which in fact did much to shape that teaching) the Word occupied three different realms: the Word of creation that initiates the realm of time, the distinct words of doctrine that the Bible contains, and the internal Word that construes their meaning.[127] Many Puritan interpreters in effect conflated these three realms. The Word that speaks in the heart is indistinguishable from the Word expressed in the Bible, and that in turn is inseparable from the creative Logos that brought the universe into being. For otherwise the ambiguities of Scripture would require the exegesis of experts, on whose interpretation the ordinary believer would have to rely; so a theorist like William Whitaker could argue that "the scripture is *autopistos,* that is, hath all its authority and credit from itself."[128]

Thus we have the paradox of an inner experience that rests upon a literary document, a phenomenon that could not have existed as a widespread religious movement before the invention of printing made available "the Word of God in the age of mechanical reproduction."[129] When Bunyan was interrogated in prison by justices and clergymen who wanted him to stop preaching, he refused to consider the argument that he knew no Greek and therefore could not interpret the Bible. "I said, that if that was his opinion, that none could understand the Scriptures but those that had the original Greek, &c. then but a very few of the poorest sort should be saved." And later on, when Bunyan declared that the Bible "is infallible and cannot err," the clerk of the court responded reasonably enough, "Who shall be judge between you, for you take the Scriptures one way, and they another?" Again Bunyan refused to be drawn (or, one might almost say, to get the point): "I said, the Scripture should, and that by comparing one Scripture with another; for that will open [i.e., interpret] itself if it be rightly compared."[130] In this naive notion of interpretation, everything depends on the vital presence of the Spirit in the believer's heart, speaking directly to him through a vernacular text whose origin in the dead languages becomes irrelevant. "That person is the best interpreter," one statement ran, "who (besides other helps) hath a comment in his own heart; and he best interprets Paul's Epistles who is himself the Epistle of Christ written by the Spirit of God."[131] Or as Baxter put it in verse,

> Words but the vehicle of matter be,
> God's spirit owns not the translator's words;
> But if, as signs, they with his word agree,
> The sense and matter of them is the Lord's.[132]

In an important sense this kind of assumption led to a renewed emphasis on plain language as the best means of conveying a truth that lay deeper than mere language. The passionate Puritan preacher avoided rhetorical flamboyance and considered himself to be only the instrument through which the Holy Spirit communicated with his hearers.[133] But even if the Bible spoke directly to believers' hearts, it was necessary to admit that it did so parabolically, and many of the more intellectual Puritans became famous for rhetorical complexity and logic-chopping obsessiveness.

> Besides 'tis known he could speak Greek
> As naturally as pigs squeak. . . .
> For rhetoric, he could not ope
> His mouth, but out there flew a trope. . . .
> He could raise scruples dark and nice,
> And after solve 'em in a trice,
> As if Divinity had catch'd
> The itch, of purpose to be scratched.[134]

Whatever their excesses may have looked like to their enemies, the fundamental premise of Puritan divines was that the Word speaks in veiled manner through types and symbols by which one thing stands for another. Adam and Eve were the only human beings who have ever enjoyed unmediated understanding, for as Peter Brown says, one consequence of original sin was "a fall from direct knowledge into indirect knowledge through signs," and Augustine saw the Bible as the system of signs through which fallen man apprehends the divine: "For the meantime, let the Scriptures be the countenance of God."[135] Signs are mysterious and perplexing, and we would certainly be better off if we did not need them, like the angels who behold God's face "without any syllables of time."[136]

For Augustine there was another channel of grace. In addition to the Word as expressed in the Bible, God comes to man directly through the reiterated ritual of the sacraments. But sacraments impute a peculiar significance to material objects, and this the Puritans, who regarded all created things as uniformly "indifferent," were unwilling to allow. Calvin interpreted Christ's saying "This is my body" as merely "metonymical," and urged that since human symbols "are rather emblems of things absent than tokens of things present," God's symbols must be still more disjunct from the truths they symbolize.[137] The Catholic doctrine of transubstantiation was particularly hated because it holds that a symbol turns literally into its referent, bread and wine becoming the body and blood of Christ, even while the *form* of the symbol remains what it was before (the bread and wine unchanged to outward appearance).[138] Protestant attacks tended to focus on the allegedly magical role of the priest whose incantation effected this change, but the deepest opposition was surely at the symbolic level. For it is characteristic of Puritan thought to stress that symbols are *only* symbols; this world is so disastrously warped that it can contain only emblematic reminders of heaven, not direct images of its power. The same people who defaced "images" in churches bitterly opposed any hint of the "real presence" of Christ in the eucharist.

So the Bible occupied an equivocal position. It was at once the vehicle of truth, as guaranteed by the Holy Spirit in each believer, and a complex system of allegory requiring thoughtful interpretation. Puritan theorists insisted on the literal basis of every passage from which allegory was deduced; in Whitaker's words, "When we proceed from the sign to the thing signified, we bring no new sense, but only bring out into light what was before concealed in the sign."[139] And Perkins refused to concede any gap between sign and significance: "There is only one sense, and the same is the literal. An allegory is only a certain manner of uttering the same sense."[140] But the process of getting from the literal to the figurative could be arduous indeed. Our fallen condition not only obliges God to "accommodate" himself to us in earthly symbols, but renders us weak and groping in our attempts to understand them. Calvin says of the first verses of John's Gospel, "If we heard God speaking to us in his majesty, it would be useless to us, for we would understand nothing. Therefore, since we are carnal, he has to stutter, or otherwise he would not be understood by us."[141] But when God's stuttering is matched by man's stuttering, the result threatens to resemble what the priest darkly suggests in Kafka: "The scriptures are unalterable and the comments often enough merely express the commentators' despair."[142]

In themselves words are only words, and what is most dreadful, they may be inefficacious *even if properly understood.* For God's grace is bestowed quite apart from human merit, and even the most accurate understanding may find itself cut off utterly from grace. As Edwards sardonically says,

> The devil is orthodox in his faith; he believes the true scheme of doctrine; he is no Deist, Socinian, Arian, Pelagian, or Antinomian; the articles of his faith are all sound, and in them he is thoroughly established. Therefore, for a person to believe the doctrines of Christianity merely from the force of arguments, as discerned only by speculation, is no evidence of grace.[143]

The most theologically inclined person in *The Pilgrim's Progress* is the spiritually empty Talkative, in debate with whom Christian quotes 1 Corinthians 4:20, "They say and do not: but the Kingdom of God is not in word, but in power;" and Christian adds, "His house is as empty of religion as the white of an egg is of savour."[144] So in the end the words of faith have to rest on the one true incarnate Word, informed and guaranteed by the Logos by whom all things were made.

The literary implications of Puritan ideas about language are thus complicated as well as suggestive. If reality is understood emblematically and if words cry out for exegesis, yet certainty is possible because reality *is* the Word, in the Pauline rather than the Nietzschean sense. It would therefore be wrong to exaggerate Puritan affinities with modern theories of textuality that reduce reality to language; yet it remains true that (potentially at least) Puritans were peculiarly alive to the ambiguities of language and to the ways in which interpretation must labor before it can achieve significance. Luther, the great translator of the Bible, eloquently describes how a scriptural text may yield up the very opposite of its ostensible meaning, if pondered deeply enough under the guidance of the Spirit that informs the Word. When the Canaanite woman asked Jesus to cure her daughter and he replied that it was unfair to take the children's bread and throw it to the dogs, she answered, "Truth, Lord: yet the dogs eat of the crumbs which fall from their masters' table" (Matt. 15:27). Jesus then praised her faith and cured her daughter. Luther comments,

This is written for our comfort and instruction, that we may know how deeply God hides his grace from us, and that we must not think of him according to our ideas and feeling, but only according to his Word. Here we see that though Christ speaks harshly he does not give a final judgment, an absolute "no." All his answers sounded like "no." He did not say that she was a dog. Nevertheless the "no" sounded stronger than the "yes." Yet there was a "yes," deep and secret. This shows the state of our heart when sore pressed. Christ in this story behaves the way the heart feels, for it thinks the answer is "no" when in reality it is not. Therefore the heart must turn away from its feeling and lay hold of the deep secret "yes" under the "no," with firm faith in God's Word.[145]

Despite its insistence on direct apprehension of the Word, this kind of faith is absolutely inseparable from hermeneutics, the task of interpretation. And that means that the Puritans, suspicious of imaginative invention though they were, entertained a conception of reality that made literary imagining attractive if not inevitable.

Fiction

From all that has been said thus far, some conclusions can be drawn about the relationship of Puritan tradition to the early development of prose fiction. Put at its simplest, that development reflects a deep distrust both of microcosm and heterocosm, of Renaissance fabling that claims to shadow forth eternal truths, and of arbitrary fictions that explicitly stand over against reality. For the Puritans there was only one cosmos and only one truth, a conviction reflected in style and structure alike. Bunyan says in introducing *Grace Abounding,* "I could have stepped into a style much higher than this in which I have here discoursed, and could have adorned all things more than here I have seemed to do; but I dare not: God did not play in convincing of me; the Devil did not play in tempting of me; neither did I play when I sunk as into a bottomless pit, when *the pangs of hell caught hold upon me:* wherefore I may not play in my relating of them, but be plain and simple, and lay down the thing as it was" (pp. 3–4).

This emphasis on plainness and literalness is as old as Christianity. In late classical times the Bible was the inspiration for a *sermo humilis* that echoed ordinary speech rather than indulging in rhetorical display.[146] Moreover the Bible is full of stories, and these take the form of cumulative realistic narratives.[147] So in a way certain possibilities of the novel might be said to have been available all along in the Bible. But the situation is more complicated than that, for the Bible asserts a peculiar and unrepeatable authority, and instead of encouraging us to describe our own world freely, it demands that we translate that world into scriptural categories. Auerbach says in his famous analysis of Old Testament narrative, "Far from seeking, like Homer, merely to make us forget our own reality for a few hours, it seeks to overcome our reality: we are to fit our own life into its world, feel ourselves to be elements in its structure of universal history."[148] Again we meet the paradox considered earlier: the meaning of life is embodied in historical events, recounted and understood in temporal narrative sequence, yet the whole purpose of understanding is to break free of temporality and to merge separate events in a universal explanatory pattern.

The ambiguous status of narrative is mirrored in the language that presents it. As Bunyan's comments on "playing" suggest, the plain style was a moral and not just a rhetorical ideal. The complex classical prose style, which might seem to us "objective," struck Puritans as idiosyncratic and therefore subjective in its display of unpredictable connections and decorations.[149] The Puritan ideal (like that of the Royal Society and late seventeenth-century science) is a prose whose simplicity removes all barriers between the reader and the thing described, a transparent window rather than an ostentatiously framed mirror. Defoe recommends "a plain and homely style" in *The Complete English Tradesman* and says that a perfect style would be one in which "a man speaking to five hundred people, of all common and various capacities, idiots or lunatics excepted, should be understood by them all in the same manner with one another, and in the same sense which the speaker intended to be understood."[150] Ambiguity ought ideally to be impossible except for idiots and lunatics.

But simple perspicuity is of all things the hardest to achieve, and the Puritan demand for moral as well as stylistic transparency implied an impossible ideal. David Perkins says of the "sincerity" which Puritanism bequeathed to Romanticism, "In most writers, the ideal of sincerity leads to a suspicion that language is inadequate. We always feel that we mean more and mean it more precisely than we have been able to say, and are troubled with a perpetual restlessness and dissatisfaction, as though we were itching in some internal organ that could not be scratched."[151] What modernism accepts as a familiar paradox was, for Puritan writers, a grave dilemma. They were under a moral obligation to be sincere, to explore and confess the true condition of the inner self, yet language blinded them to what was there and deformed the reports they brought back. Hence their poignant preoccupation with the "Adamic language" before the Fall, when words really did say what they meant.

More generally, the same paradox attaches to their thinking about literary art. On the one hand art is a falsification of unmediated experience, but on the other hand experience itself can only be understood in categories like those employed by art. The truths of the Bible were only truths if they invaded the soul at a far deeper level than that of aesthetic appreciation, and Edwards shows what contempt a Puritan would feel for the modern interest in "the Bible as literature":

> A person by mere nature, for instance, may be liable to be affected with the story of Jesus Christ, and the sufferings he underwent, as well as by any other tragical story. He may be the more affected with it from the interest he conceives mankind to have in it. Yea, he may be affected with it without believing it; as well as a man may be affected with what he reads in a romance, or sees acted in a stage-play.[152]

Still, analogies from art come irresistibly to mind when the mighty events of the inner life are being invoked, and another preacher could easily use literary analogy to excite a horror of eternal damnation:

> When iniquity hath played her part, vengeance leaps upon the stage. The comedy is short, but the tragedy is longer. The blackguard shall attend upon you; you shall eat at the table of sorrow, and the crown of death shall be upon your heads, many glistering faces looking on you.[153]

But if life is a drama, God and not the individual person is the dramatist.

It would be wrong to suppose that Puritans distrusted fictions per se. So long as these could be clearly labelled allegorical, as *The Pilgrim's Progress* is and as Defoe seems to have wanted *Robinson Crusoe* to be, then the incidents they related could be accepted as emblems of spiritual truth. The deeper difficulty arose with the realization, whether fully conscious or not, that a novelist is free to manipulate events exactly as God does. Kierkegaard describes (under the pseudonym Johannes Climacus) his boyhood impression of his father's creative powers: "The father's almighty imagination was capable of shaping everything, of using every childish whim as an ingredient of the drama which was being enacted. To Johannes it seemed as if the world were coming into existence during the conversation, as if the father were our Lord and he were his favorite."[154] For a Puritan artist there can be but one Creation, of which art is at best a faithful mirror, yet as artist he is well aware of his pleasure in creating a heterocosm that stands apart from the true Creation, and indeed competes with it.

Moreover as he manipulates his invented characters the artist is likely to be aware, if only dimly, of the arbitrariness and apparent injustice of the Almighty. God punishes men for inscrutable reasons, but when a novelist punishes his characters, acting as God's deputy in the fictive world, he wants obvious justice to be done. If he thought that he were merely playing at being God, or if he could emphasize the artificiality of his fictions as Fielding did, then there might be no cause for alarm. But the earnest attempt to body forth a faithful image of divine Providence creates the deepest tensions, and accounts for much of the imaginative power, in *Robinson Crusoe* and *Clarissa*. Indeed the mimetic obsession of those works, with their endless circumstantial detail and their pretense of nonfictional veracity, can be seen as a mask to cover up anxiety. If they can be presented *as* true, then one can temporarily forget that they are *not* true. The author knows they are fictional but the reader does not, or, to carry it a step further, is willing to pretend he does not. And in that case he can read them in the same way, and with the same rewards, as he would read "true" stories.

Before pondering the novels, we will need to look closely at the two great masterpieces of Puritan narrative, *Paradise Lost* and *The Pilgrim's Progress*. The relations and differences between them are fascinating, and combine to show the range of literary possibility in the Puritan imagination. Milton is the most learned of our writers, Bunyan one of the least; Milton's sophisticated genius unfolds certain possibilities inherent in Puritan experience, while Bunyan's naive genius unfolds others. The writings of both contain logical cruxes and even contradictions; Milton knows it and strives to reconcile them, while Bunyan seeks above all to express what he feels even if the resulting paradoxes remain unresolved. Milton possessed a highly militant temperament, engaged in tireless propaganda on behalf of revolution, and asserted free will against Calvinist determinism, yet his art teaches patient submission to the will of God. Bunyan's temperament was much more passive; he was tormented by inner doubt and was at ease only when literally in prison, yet his allegory is famous as the supreme expression of Christian militancy fighting the good fight. What both writers most deeply share with the later novel is the conviction that, as Milton's Adam says, "Trial will come unsought."[155] For if the novel was characteristically conceived as a moral test, the Puritan sense of threat and vocation was particularly suited to it.

At the foundation of this inquiry we have to confront the fact of the artist's autonomy. Submit though he may to a system larger than himself, what he writes is his own and no one else's. Strong poets, according to Bloom, have always believed in "an essential purity that constituted their true selves and that could not be touched by mere natural experience," and in consequence "should always be condemned by a humanist morality."[156] Augustinian doctrine asserts the radical fallenness of each person, but fiction, even when committed to this doctrine, is always tempted to dramatize the freedom and purity of the self. The inversion of Augustine in Rousseau's *Confessions* illustrates what happens, in different ways and degrees, in every important nar-

PURITAN EXPERIENCE AND ART 71

rative of the eighteenth century: even as he traces the sources of inexpiable guilt, the writer manages to assert his own autonomy and innocence. Milton and Bunyan will help us to understand the first stages in that process.

Above all we will be tracing the development by which fiction finally broke free from myth, establishing its own reality over against the religious structure which had once provided the sure foundation of all experience. As the unitary truth of the Bible recedes into artistic imagining, the question of guilt and innocence begins to lose its intelligible form; but as Kafka shows, that only makes the relation between art and truth more painful because more equivocal.

"Such acquittals," replied the painter, "are said to have occurred. Only it is very difficult to prove the fact. The final decisions of the Court are never recorded, even the Judges can't get hold of them, consequently we have only legendary accounts of ancient cases. These legends certainly provide instances of acquittal; actually the majority of them are about acquittals, they can be believed, but they cannot be proved. All the same, they shouldn't be entirely left out of account, they must have an element of truth in them, and besides they are very beautiful. I myself have painted several pictures founded on such legends."

"Mere legends cannot alter my opinion," said K., "and I fancy that one cannot appeal to such legends before the Court?" The painter laughed. "No, one can't do that," he said.[157]

3

Art and Truth in
Paradise Lost

Fable, Symbols, Truth

Paradise Lost was written during the Restoration, when the blind and threatened poet felt himself to be "In darkness, and with dangers compassed round, / And solitude."[1] Pondering the failure of human hopes and the mysterious working out of God's will, Milton wrote an astonishingly original epic that exposed the deepest paradoxes in the Christian faith, and with ostentatious daring gave them explicit narrative form. It diminishes his achievement and insults his daring if we read *Paradise Lost* as an illustration of routine orthodoxy. For as Helen Gardner says—and she is hardly a critic hostile to Christianity—"We should salute a moral and intellectual integrity that shirks none of the issues that faith in the God of Israel raises."[2] The entire poem hinges upon its aspiration to "assert eternal providence, / And justify the ways of God to men" (I.25–26). Since Providence is unchanging, its "assertion" should be a simple act of faith, but by the seventeenth century justification must be added. God *is* just and needs no help from man—it is rather man who needs the "justification" conferred by Christ's sacrifice—but somehow this is no longer self-evident. And the project of theodicy is fraught with dangers, for once the idea of justifying God is entertained, God may turn out not to be justifiable.

Considered simply as theology Milton's defense is both simple and traditional: God permitted evil to exist because his creatures would not be free if they could not choose evil, and he is further justified because his providence bends every evil action back into good. Yet it would obviously be absurd to say that evil *is* good; however benign the outcome, it is achieved only at the cost of great suffering. Although God can always wrest good out of evil—the famous *felix culpa* or "fortunate fall"—it would have been far better if evil had never existed at all. What Milton really needs to do, therefore, is to show *how* evil came to be, and to convince his readers of their responsibility for it. The myth of the fall serves this essential function, for as Ricoeur says, "The 'Adamic' myth is the fruit of the prophetic accusation directed against man; the same theology that makes God innocent accuses man."[3] *Paradise Lost* attempts to show that man has no right to accuse the God who rightly accuses man. Our injustice is the counterpart of God's justice.

In pursuing this argument, Milton accepts the right (and responsibility) of each individual to confront the issue in his own heart, and he recognizes that his theology is grounded in a mythic narrative which is mediated through ambiguous symbols. Or to put it the other way round, he does not demand that the believer rest passive in the face of mystery, and he does not claim that abstract dogma is more nearly true than mythic story. On the contrary, he challenges each reader to confront for himself the deep paradoxes of Christianity, and he gives those paradoxes a peculiar vividness by vastly expanding the gnomic tales in which they were originally embedded. In following this course he is well on the way from myth (considered as the primal and authoritative story) to fiction. The myth is now acknowledged to be problematic and is offered to the understanding as a complex narrative, governed by motivation and causation, rather than as a simple tenet of faith.

In primitive cultures, Malinowski says, "Myth is not merely a tale told but a reality lived."[4] If a social *nomos* is sufficiently secure its myth will seem obvious and protective. But Milton was writing when the *nomos* was under tremendous strain, and he insisted on the duty of the individual to stand apart, if necessary, from all of his fellows. Samuel Johnson shrewdly observed, "He had determined rather what to condemn than what to approve. He has not associated himself with any denomination of Protestants; we know rather what he was not, than what he was."[5] In striving to rebuild the fragmenting *nomos* from the ground up, Milton boldly dramatizes what faith had left mysterious, and thereby complicates the conventional distinction that Kermode (for instance) draws between fiction and myth:

> Myth operates within the diagrams of ritual, which presupposes total and adequate explanations of things as they are and were; it is a sequence of radically unchangeable gestures. Fictions are for finding things out, and they change as the needs of sense-making change. . . . Myths call for absolute, fictions for conditional assent.[6]

Milton's myth does demand absolute assent, and its gestures are certainly unchangeable inasmuch as the sacred story is presented as authoritative and permanent. But it is absolutely divorced from ritual, in the Puritan way, and it is radically committed to reconceiving the sacred story in such a way as to "find things out." Milton fictionalizes myth and mythicizes fiction.

In so doing he is as much artist as theologian, for the habit of theology has generally been to discourage narrative expansion. Speaking of the fallen angels Calvin says, "Some persons are displeased that the Scripture does not give us, in various places, a distinct and detailed account of their fall, with its cause, manner, time, and nature. But these things being nothing to us, it was better for them, if not to be passed over in total silence, yet certainly to be touched on but lightly; because it would ill comport with the dignity of the Holy Spirit to feed curiosity with vain and unprofitable histories."[7] Milton takes exactly the opposite course, extrapolating a vast narrative from the terse hints of the Bible. And he does this because ultimately he wants to reconceive the myth psychologically. Just as the Puritan autobiographer understands his life story by a process of introspection, so the Christian story must be framed in terms of intelligible psychic motivation. We may not be able to understand why God made beings who were able to fall, but we can certainly be made to feel what it is like to fall—to be Satan unwilling to repent, or Eve succumbing to Satan's wiles, or Adam succumbing to love for Eve.

Evil in *Paradise Lost* is not the "motiveless malignity" that Coleridge ascribed to Iago, that inscrutable tempter who refuses to reveal his motive even at the end of *Othello,* and it is not the inexplicable fatality by which Coleridge's own Ancient Mariner courts disaster. Shakespeare suggests mysterious depths of evil that are simply impenetrable to psychological explanation; Coleridge presents a symbolic vision in which the unmotivated fact of evil, together with the guilt that flows from it, are taken as simply given. But Milton makes evil and guilt intelligible, so that we are well on the way to a novelistic presentation. It is a truism that Richardson's Lovelace is satanic, but the comparison works both ways: if Lovelace embodies the symbolism of Satan, Satan foreshadows the psychologism of Lovelace. By developing his theodicy in this direction Milton was responsive to the deepest needs of his age, in which doctrine could no longer defend itself without imaginative re-creation. But *Paradise Lost* is not a novel, for it is unequivocally founded upon the biblical narrative and asserts that its artistic stratagems can only grope at ultimate reality. So the psychological and novelistic elements are immensely complicated by their symbolic vehicle, and these are complications which Milton not only faces but deliberately exploits.

The basic facts of the narrative are taken as given, and in one of its aspects *Paradise Lost* is a brilliant elaboration of those facts, a set of imaginative variations on the biblical theme. So long as the Bible was accepted as literally true this was the normal way of thinking about *Paradise Lost*. "Whoever considers the few radical positions which the Scriptures afforded him," Johnson comments, "will wonder by what energetic operations he expanded them to such extent and ramified them to so much variety, restrained as he was by religious reverence from licentiousness of fiction."[8] In this sense there is no "fiction" at all in the poem, only plausible extrapolations from biblical fact. But as Johnson also observes, "the substance of narrative is truth; and as truth allows no choice, it is, like necessity, superior to rule" (p. 174). The constraints imposed by this "necessity" are very great, since Milton is determined to make everything as convincing as he can. In *The Logical Epic* Dennis Burden has admirably shown the many ways in which Milton rationalized or concealed difficulties in his source. To give a single example, the serpent that tempts Eve cannot go on its belly before the Fall, since that is to be its punishment for tempting her, yet it must not go upright either, since only man is erect in stature. Moreover, the Fall is the fault of Satan and not of the animal that served as his unwitting host, yet he chose that animal because it was "more subtle than any beast of the field" (Gen. 3:1) and Milton cannot ignore God's subsequent condemnation of it. So he has to modulate carefully among these various premises, stressing now the guilt of the serpent and now its innocence, now its creeping locomotion and now its partial erectness.[9]

However, the problems run much deeper than details like these, for the Bible is manifestly symbolic, and even if the events it relates are literally true, their interpretation is seldom obvious or easy. Sacred song is imaginatively beautiful as well as doctrinally sound:

> But chief
> Thee Sion and the flowery brooks beneath
> That wash thy hallowed feet, and warbling flow,
> Nightly I visit. . . .
>
> (III.29–32)

But ever since the Fall this beauty has concealed as well as revealed; truth is unified but man is divided. For as Milton says in *Of Reformation*, "The very essence of Truth is plainness and brightness; the darkness and crookedness is our own."[10]

It was a standard position of biblical exegesis that God "accommodates" himself to man's limited understanding by the use of anthropomorphic images. While he does not really get angry or repent or change his mind, by alluding to human experiences like these he can help us to imagine his superhuman nature. But Milton was committed to a Puritan belief that the spirit and letter of the Bible are inseparable, and he was therefore obliged to regard accommodation

literally rather than figuratively. God is not exactly as the Bible describes him, but he is *like* that; the metaphors coincide with truth, and
Milton rejected the Neoplatonist tendency to seek arcane meanings
hidden behind the scriptural text.[11] He says bluntly in *De Doctrina,*
"In short, God either is or is not really like he says he is. If he really is
like this, why should we think otherwise? If he is not really like this, on
what authority do we contradict God?"[12] In its refusal to invoke
cloudy mysteries this statement forces the essential ambiguity into the
open. If God is *not* what the Bible says, then there is no secure basis
for saying anything about him at all (the position taken in all ages by
mystical "negative theology," which stresses God's ineffability). But if
he *is* what the Bible says, then the principle of accommodation cannot
free the interpreter from accepting the literal implications of the text,
disturbing though they may well be. And our fallen condition makes
it impossible for us to see except through a glass darkly; Milton refers
to "the perpetual stumble of conjecture and disturbance in this our
dark voyage,"[13] and the Bible, even though decisively true, can only
be interpreted by stumbling mortals.

According to Milton's theory of symbolism there can thus be no
unmediated contact with truth. Before the Fall God showed himself
to man, but at the moment of the Fall the old immediacy vanished, as
Adam himself says:

> Those heavenly shapes
> Will dazzle now this earthly, with their blaze
> Insufferably bright.
>
> (IX.1082–84)

Henceforth man must grope at knowledge of God through "shadowy
types" (XII.303) that shield him from the now-blinding "unap-
proachèd light" (III.4) in which God dwells. And language is forced
to translate the immediacy of God into a mediate "process of speech":

> Immediate are the acts of God, more swift
> Than time or motion, but to human ears
> Cannot without procéss of speech be told,
> So told as earthly notion can receive.
>
> (VII.176–79)

The Bible is literally true, but its true images are translations. Raphael
says to Adam,

> What surmounts the reach
> Of human sense, I shall delineate so,
> By likening spiritual to corporeal forms,
> As may express them best, though what if earth

> Be but the shadow of heaven, and things therein
> Each to other like, more than on earth is thought?
> (v.571–76)

How closely "like" are the images with which the angel "likens"? The *what if* possibility remains conditional. Raphael never tells us, and we cannot know, whether any particular image does in fact correspond exactly to heavenly reality, though it may. Elsewhere Milton speaks explicitly of the difficulties of interpretation: "I do not know why God's providence should have committed the contents of the New Testament to such wayward and uncertain guardians, unless it was so that this very fact might convince us that the Spirit which is given to us is a more certain guide than scripture, and that we ought to follow it."[14] For Bunyan the spirit and the literal text are inseparable, indeed identical. For Milton the text is a mass of enigmas, owing in part to the limitations of its human authors, and it makes sense only when the Spirit speaks through it.

Images in the fallen world are governed by eternal truths which they shadow forth or are somehow "like," but which can never be directly apprehended by mortal minds. And if this compromises the status of the images and language used to describe that world, it compromises still more the fallen images and words that must try to describe the un-earthly regions where much of *Paradise Lost* takes place. There, paradoxically, the relationship between metaphor and referent gets reversed, and what we normally think of as metaphor takes on unexpectedly literal status, for instance in the famous description of Satan:

> . . . His face
> Deep scars of thunder had intrenched, and care
> Sat on his faded cheek. . . .
> (I.600–602)

In ordinary usage, such a passage would indicate that Satan's features betrayed inner turmoil *as if* their creases had been scarred by lightning. But Satan is a colossal figure who has been hurled headlong from heaven in searing fire, and the lines in his face *were* scarred by lightning. Tenor and vehicle merge in this gigantic realm as they no longer do in our own world.[15]

It cannot be too strongly stressed that what is at stake here is not just a mode of description, but a mode of understanding reality. The subtlety of Milton's images depends on keeping their dual status always in mind: they are drawn from our familiar world (the only source of images available to us) but they point toward, or overlap with, unknowable aspects of an unfamiliar world. This is superbly evident in the allegory of Sin and Death, which Johnson and other critics attacked for confusing abstractions with realities. But the essential point is that sin and death are equivocal, frighteningly real and yet ultimately not real at all. As Anne Ferry remarks, they are products of Satan's disordered imagination, not created by God (Sin is born from his head, and Death from his copulation with Sin). So they can be represented only by abstract allegory, the mode that emphasizes the difference between concrete and abstract meaning, just as Satan at first fails to recognize his own offspring because his divided consciousness cannot connect physical with spiritual reality.[16] Yet Sin and Death are not merely abstract, for if they are unreal in not having been created by God, they are real in embodying a perverted form of a being (Satan the fallen Lucifer) whom God did indeed create. Milton's allegorical images thus reflect the Christian answer to man's ultimate fear. Instead of seeing the absence of life as the norm and living organisms as temporary exceptions to it, Milton's myth allows us to see life as the norm and death as a latecomer that is temporarily real but ultimately unreal. The imagination, Bergson said, is "a defensive reaction of nature against the representation by intelligence of the inevitability of death."[17] Art is thus wish-fulfillment, the *fonction fabulatrice* that denies the reality principle. But Milton claims that only fallen and degraded fables do that. Sacred art points beyond its images to a reality in which the deepest wishes are indeed fulfilled.

Because images are equivocal and because much of the action takes place beyond our world, *Paradise Lost* cannot assume an objective reality against which the reader might measure its veracity, and it cannot be narrated by the anonymous voice of "primary epics" (C. S. Lewis's term) like the *Iliad* or *Beowulf*. On the contrary, the narrator must continually hold the poem together. His voice pervades the entire work, presenting and shaping, commenting and warning and criticizing, and above all directing the reader's response through tone and implication. Milton's poetic voice is notoriously the most individual in our literature. Far from being anonymous as some of the great biblical prophecies are (what is the personality of John of Patmos?) the poem is dominated by an imperial imagination and idiosyncratic style.

Just as *Paradise Lost* psychologizes doctrine, so also it individualizes myth, and Martz is right to see in it the precursor of those works in which "the figure of the poet, representing the individual consciousness of man, will become the only organizing center for the long poem."[18] In this sense *Paradise Lost* falls midway along the line that Lukács traces from epic to novel: it is an epic mediated by consciousness, not (like the older epics) an objectification of the total world that an entire culture shares. It speaks to individual consciousnesses, "fit audience though few" (VII.31), and although it is emphatically not the epic of a world from which God has vanished, it addresses readers who have begun to fear that possibility.

By the very urgency of his narrative self-consciousness, Milton looks forward beyond the relatively naive fictions of Bunyan and Defoe and Richardson, and points the way in which the novel would go in spite of its attempts to be merely mimetic, to deny or conceal the role of the shaping imagination. Bloom says, "Christian liberty, as a doctrine, led to Milton's conception of a sect of one (Abdiel), a church of one (himself). He appealed to the holy light to shine inward, and created English Romanticism by doing so."[19] Milton understood that as epic poet he had to reinvent truth even while striving to be faithful to it ("May I express thee unblamed?" [III.3]), and his immense epic of God and Satan and Man is finally a myth of the inner life. He believed that the myth was true, but he also knew, far more subtly than orthodox critics like Addison and Johnson, that it was myth. This tension—between the need to invent and the danger of invention—pervades the entire poem. For the point of asserting the perspicuity of Scripture, in the face of all apparent evidence to the contrary, is to protect the poet from saying more than God has said. Artistic imagining is a temptation as well as a vocation.

Behind the classical myths lay error; the lovely story of falling Mulciber in Homer is really a distorted echo of the fall of Mammon (I.739–48). But all human art, whether Christian or pagan, shares the burden of fallenness, and Milton's imagination was haunted by the dark implications of the Orphic myth. "The art of Orpheus," Frye comments, "recreated the sympathy between man and nature which existed in Eden, hence Orpheus represents everything that a human being can do to redeem a soul from death. Eurydice was only 'half regained,' but we have the wistful hope that a poet who had been taught a greater song than Orpheus knew, singing 'With other notes than to th' Orphean lyre,' might succeed better with human souls."[20] The reference is to *Paradise Lost* III.17, where Milton implores the aid of a greater muse than the one who failed to save her son Orpheus when, as we are told in *Lycidas*, "His gory visage down the stream was sent." The fear of dismemberment—the ultimate failure of art and destruction of the artist—is invoked in *Paradise Lost* when Milton repudiates the cruel pleasure-seekers of the Restoration:

> Still govern thou my song,
> Urania, and fit audience find, though few.
> But drive far off the barbarous dissonance
> Of Bacchus and his revellers, the race
> Of that wild rout that tore the Thracian bard
> In Rhodope, where woods and rocks had ears
> To rapture, till the savage clamour drowned
> Both harp and voice; nor could the Muse defend
> Her son. So fail not thou, who thee implores:
> For thou art heavenly, she an empty dream.
>
> (VII.30–39)

Orpheus could not bring back his dead wife because art is finally impotent over death, though it achieves some of its noblest effects by temporarily suspending that knowledge, for instance in Euripides' *Alcestis* or Shakespeare's *Winter's Tale*. It is true that Orpheus is a type of Christ, but he is only a type. In actual life, Milton well knows, the dead do not return and the attempt to look at them (in dream as in art) recapitulates the Orphean failure:

> Methought I saw my late espousèd saint
> Brought to me like Alcestis from the grave. . . .
> But, oh! as to embrace me she inclined,
> I waked, she fled, and day brought back my night.[21]

The fallen muse, even of the greatest art, is but an "empty dream," and the heavenly muse must guide us to a conquest of death that takes place beyond this world, not in it. The wonderful achievement of *Paradise Lost* is to confess openly that it is a fallen poem, built up from the materials of a fallen world, that nonetheless aspires to imagine unfallenness. It owes its confidence to a faith in the utter stability of God's universe, but the poem's narrator is not omniscient and omnipotent. Milton is as fallen as his readers are, and the tension between clear doctrine and equivocal myth is at least as painful to him as it is to them.

God and Providence

God is of course an implied presence in all of the fictional works which we shall be considering, but only in *Paradise Lost* does he appear in his own persons. Here above all we are confronted by the difference between doctrine and art. "Anyone who asks what God did before the creation of the world is a fool," Milton declares roundly in his theological treatise, "and anyone who answers him is not much wiser."[22] Apart from doctrinal considerations, it can perhaps be argued that a remote God satisfies a psychological need for an ideal spiritual object who shares none of our human limitations.[23] But Milton clearly believed that God's ways would not seem justified if Satan and Adam were allowed psychological complexity while God was relegated to some far-off realm of ideal perfection. He was therefore prepared to take huge risks in showing something like the humanness of the divine, even if accommodation means in the end that the divine only seems human. Whereas theology (including Milton's in *De Doctrina*) tends to seek abstraction and to stress the inscrutability of God, the imagination wants God to be a father whom it can love, which necessarily means that God must possess qualities that are recognizably human.

If anything, the God of *Paradise Lost* is too abstract rather than too human. Having once decided to show him arguing and explaining, Milton might have gone still further and given him greater emotional appeal. Instead he stresses the cool rationality of the Father, as is perfectly appropriate according to his own theory of accommodation, for if reason is our highest faculty then we understand God best if we conceive him in accordance with reason.[24] But this Father is disappointingly remote in comparison with the anthropomorphic gods of the Greeks, who really do experience anger and even lust. Accommodation is a way of facing the dilemma of having to describe a superhuman deity in human terms, but the dilemma is not thereby resolved, just restated. For we still have to believe that God does not "really" have our passions (at least not the uglier ones), whereas the Greek gods do. Milton's Satan calls God "the thunderer" (II.28); if he were Zeus, whose epithet this is, we could imagine him more confidently. Satan invokes a mythology which, even if mistaken, makes human sense, and what makes human sense is hard to dismiss. As Kermode says, Milton "is constantly disclaiming these heathen fancies, but as constantly putting them in; in poetry all *buts* are partly *ands*."[25]

So I propose the heretical view that far from being too anthropomorphic, Milton's God is not anthropomorphic enough. Once he has descended into a fiction he should descend all the way. In *The City of God* Augustine derides the pagans for their proliferation of gods, one for every trivial action and occurrence; from his point of view (like Milton's when he equates the fallen angels with pagan deities) these are only diabolical parodies of God's unitary goodness. But from an anthropological point of view polytheism is an essential objectification of human experience, whether or not it may eventually lead to monotheism. The god of plowing and the goddess of childbirth are expressions of the significance of human activity.[26] Polytheistic systems tend to regard reality as given, preceding any particular set of deities as the Titans preceded the Olympian gods. But monotheism goes further in asserting a God who symbolizes ultimate power apart from any particular manifestation of it. In this sense Calvin's God is a logical development of Christian thought, an expression of absolute will whose power precedes and underlies any possible context. But to postulate such a God is to risk a terrifying gulf between God and man.

If Milton's God had remained infinitely remote, his purposes could stay hidden in impenetrable mystery. If he were lovingly familiar (as he briefly is in Book VIII) they could be accepted as the wishes of a beloved father. But he is neither; he is emotionally remote but rationally loquacious, constantly defining his behavior in theological language and taking the lead in the project of justifying himself to men.

> So will fall
> He and his faithless progeny: whose fault?
> Whose but his own? Ingrate, he had of me
> All he could have; I made him just and right,
> Sufficient to have stood, though free to fall.
>
> (III.95–99)

In effect this God is committed to theodicy, and such a project is—as the author of the Book of Job saw—extremely risky, for it translates the categories of faith into those of what Blake would call the corporeal understanding, exposing them to analysis and possible rejection on rational grounds. Marvell feared, before reading Milton's poem,

> That he would ruin (for I saw him strong)
> The sacred truths to fable and old song.[27]

There was an equal danger of reducing sacred fable to dogmatic argument. The Book of Genesis is myth that does not attempt to explain itself theologically; *The City of God* is theology that rests on myth but does not attempt to dramatize its argument mythically. *Paradise Lost* risks much by attempting both.

Milton's God is not just cold and rational; in addition he is punitive and wrathful. Augustine's God, let alone Calvin's, has always seemed to many people to resemble what Ricoeur calls the "wicked God" who tempts man.[28] It was a favorite objection to this God to say that his actions were indistinguishable from those of a cruel devil. The Cambridge Platonist Henry More called Calvin's God an idol worse than those of the Aztecs: "To which idol they do not, as the Mexicans, sacrifice the mere bodies of men, but their very souls also; not kicking them down a terrace, but arbitrariously tumbling them down into the pit of Hell, there to be eternally and unexpressibly tormented, for no other reason but because this their dreadful idol will have it so."[29] In *De Doctrina* Milton himself virtually admits that we know God's actions to be good only by the a priori knowledge that God *is* good: "Many visible proofs, the fulfillment of many prophecies and the narration of many marvels have driven every nation to the belief that either God or some supreme evil power of unknown name presides over the affairs of men." Empson comments, "Even Voltaire could hardly have written that icy sentence." Milton's answer is simply this: "But it is intolerable and incredible that evil should be stronger than good and should prove the true supreme power. Therefore God exists."[30] The usual scholarly move is to treat passages like these as sarcastic rejections of stupid errors. But surely they reflect a threat which Milton takes extremely seriously because there is so much in Christian doctrine that seems to support it.

The problem of free will is absolutely central to *Paradise Lost,* central because Milton himself insists upon it. Some thinkers, for example Luther and Calvin, take for granted as an existential fact the unfreedom of the will. Others take freedom as equally indisputable. Milton is unusual in repeatedly asserting freedom while giving full play to the logical and theological arguments that tend to cast doubt upon it. To be sure, he describes the whole problem, early in the poem, as appropriate to the blinded philosophy of the fallen angels:

> Others apart sat on a hill retired,
> In thoughts more elevate, and reasoned high
> Of providence, foreknowledge, will and fate,
> Fixed fate, free will, foreknowledge absolute,
> And found no end, in wandering mazes lost.
> (II.557–62)

The implication is that such questions are both unanswerable and trivial; Leslie Stephen comments that they were "suitable to beings who had an indefinite amount of time on their hands and to whom any distraction would be agreeable."[31] Yet Milton himself will not let them alone, and he makes God repeat them with an obsessive rhythm that is reminiscent of the wandering mazes:

> Happiness in his power left free to will,
> Left to his own free will, his will though free,
> Yet mutable. . . .
> (V.235–37)

We need to take seriously Blake's challenge:

> Say first! what mov'd Milton, who walked about in Eternity
> One hundred years, pond'ring the intricate mazes of
> Providence,
> Unhappy though in heav'n. . . .[32]

Blake sees Milton as "unhappy though in heaven" like his own Satan, and as trapped in intricate mazes of reasoning like his own fallen angels. Imprisoned in his theology, he may seem committed to the logic of predestination even though he wants to deny it.

If nothing ever happens apart from God's will, then it is not easy to see how his will differs from the relentless fate of the pagan philosophers. It is on just such grounds that Belial, the intellectual among the devils, urges acceptance of punishment in Hell:

> Better these than worse
> By my advice; since fate inevitable

> Subdues us, and omnipotent decree,
> The victor's will.
>
> (II.196–99)

And his leader Satan, as many critics have remarked, consistently asserts an ideology of necessity or fate. Now, in a real sense God *is* identified with fate, because his power generates and sustains all of reality.

> Boundless the deep, because I am who fill
> Infinitude, nor vacuous the space.
> Though I uncircumscribed my self retire,
> And put not forth my goodness, which is free
> To act or not, necessity and chance
> Approach not me, and what I will is fate.
>
> (VII.168–73)

The crucial word in that last line is the pronoun "I." It is not in his irresistible power that God differs from the classical fate, but in the personal interest he takes in his creatures. Just so the "I" is operative, as Richard Niebuhr says, in the "I am that I am" which God uttered to Moses, so that "What otherwise, in distrust and suspicion, is regarded as fate or destiny or blind will or chance is now trusted. It is God."[33]

A different but related difficulty has always haunted Christianity: God is not only the source of all power in the universe, but he also foresees everything that will ever take place in it. Many theologians, following Augustine, have thought it an inescapable consequence that everything foreseen by God must necessarily occur. Calvin argued that God's immutable decrees made determinism logically necessary, and Jonathan Edwards argued similarly for God's foreknowledge. But Milton insisted equally strongly that it was not so: "Neither God's decree nor his foreknowledge can shackle free causes with any kind of necessity."[34] These are not abstract issues: they go to the heart of human responsibility, and of the psychology with which Milton must try to explain the disastrous sin that initiated history as we know it. As always, we need to recognize that what may seem palatable enough as doctrine grows far more complicated when its ambiguities are brought into the open in extended narrative.

Before the Fall, God dispatches Raphael to warn Adam:

> This let him know
> Lest wilfully transgressing he pretend
> Surprisal, unadmonished, unforewarned.
>
> (V.243–45)

But God already knows that Adam *will* transgress, so the effect of Raphael's warning can only be to confirm Adam's guilt, thus ratifying the punishment which is going to be meted out. The narrator then declares, "So spake the eternal Father, and fulfilled / All justice" (V.246–47). But the ways of God have been justified at the cost of making it appear that man was set up for an inevitable disaster.

The theological answer, of course, is that it was *not* inevitable. God foreknew what man would do but man was free to have done otherwise. But simply to assert that Milton's theology assumes free will is to overlook the urgency and pain with which he keeps addressing the issue. In explicitly doing so, Milton shows his willingness to test the very limits of his faith; and he does this because he regards the faith as worthless if its assertion of freedom cannot be made convincing in the face of the most serious objections. What is at stake really is not a doctrine considered in itself, but an attitude toward God and the universe he governs. As Danielson has shown, when Milton turned against Calvinism—perhaps during the shock of the failed Puritan revolution—his deepest desire desire was to vindicate the goodness of God. In Arminianism he found a compromise position that seemed to offer the ideal solution:

> Man shall not quite be lost, but saved who will,
> Yet not of will in him, but grace in me.
>
> (III.173–74)

A Calvinist would hold that God's will and grace were irresistible, a Pelagian that human will was efficacious entirely on its own. The Arminian position was that salvation was impossible without grace but that individual men were free to accept or reject that grace. In technical terms Milton was an incompatibilist, rejecting the claim that free will was compatible with God's having decreed or predetermined what men would do.[35] Whatever paradoxes this position entailed, Milton thought them preferable to those of the two extremes he was rejecting: Calvinism that held man responsible for actions he could not help committing, and Pelagianism that imagined man independent of the all-powerful God. Like all compromises this one was uneasy, but it answered a deep temperamental need in Milton, who could not give up either God's omnipotence or man's freedom. From this tension the energies of *Paradise Lost* are born.

In seeking to demonstrate God's goodness Milton seizes on the possibilities in the dynamic relationship between two of the persons of the Trinity. The Father is the embodiment of justice and the Son of mercy; the Son's love counterbalances the Father's wrath. The Son carries out the Father's will in true "filial obedience" (III.269) which is expressed in "unexampled love" (III.410). Indeed love and obedience are inseparable:

> The law of God exact he shall fulfill
> Both by obedience and by love, though love

> Alone fulfill the law; thy punishment
> He shall endure by coming in the flesh
> To a reproachful life and cursèd death. . . .
>   (XII.402–6)

The reference is to Romans 13:10, "Love is the fulfilling of the law."
Since Christ's suffering (unlike that of any other man) is wholly guiltless, his love is able to satisfy the harsh demands of the law and to
placate the divine wrath. As God, Christ embodies the merciful aspect
of the divine; as man, he is the second Adam who saves man from
himself. So the Father tells him,

> Be thou in Adam's room
> The head of all mankind, though Adam's son.
> As in him perish all men, so in thee
> As from a second root shall be restored,
> As many as are restored, without thee none.
>   (III.285–89)

Christ is the indispensable mediator between God and man, a relationship which symbolizes at once an absolute otherness (the gulf
between finite and infinite) and an absolute identity (the literal reality
of the incarnation, defended by Christianity against all the heresies
that opposed it). The descendant (the son) is also the ancestor (the
root).

We saw in the last chapter how crucial the mediation of Christ was
for Puritans in general, and we saw also how they tended to stress
Christ's ontological status rather than his human life. To some extent
an emphasis on Christ can relieve our sense that the Father in *Paradise
Lost* is implacably cold, but this is only to expose the deep difficulties
in dramatizing the persons of the Trinity. It is one thing to treat the
Trinity as a sublime mystery, and quite another to exhibit it in extended conversation with itself. To distribute its attributes among
dramatic characters runs the risk of carrying accommodation too far,
portraying a God who is so human that he is several humans.

Whatever Milton's theological position may have been,[36] there is
something peculiarly disturbing in the picture of one person of the
Godhead inviting another to volunteer for a dangerous mission, and
the divine volunteer doing so in ignorance of its full implications. The
delayed exaltation of Christ, though it provides a plausible motive for
Satan's jealousy and rebellion, arouses other kinds of uneasiness: if
God was going to do it, why did he not do it earlier, or show more
plainly that it was right that it be done? Finally, it is strange that
Milton makes so little of Christ's humanity. Empson notes that the
crucifixion is described abstractly as "shameful and accurst" (XII.413)
rather than evoked in the moving scriptural texts that form the basis

of the Anglican Good Friday services. And Boyd Berry points out that Christ's humiliation and exaltation are presented outside of time in Book III rather than in the temporal narrative of the final books, so that "It is the eternal Son who humiliates himself here, not a Jesus on the cross in time, blood, and sweat."[37] Milton has it both ways and has it disappointingly. Christ exists in time since he was begotten by the Father, rather than being eternal with him; yet he dwells in eternity and has his significance there, rather than in the human world of fallen time which he temporarily entered.

It can certainly be argued, and often has been, that to make God more human than Milton does would be blasphemous. I am suggesting only that in having gone so far in anthropomorphism he might have done well to carry it all the way. His Christ could surely have been more humanly loving, and his Father, even if mysterious and wrathful, more like the Father in the Old Testament who claims man's affection and trust as well as obedience. It may be true that Milton's audience needed to be shown a reasonable God in contrast to the inscrutable God of Calvinism.[38] Still it is important to recognize the drastic weakening of the human side of the paternal image; and this is a theme which will continue to concern us deeply, since the ambiguities of fatherhood will be a fundamental theme throughout this study. Ricoeur, pondering the Freudian analysis of religion, emphasizes the comforting aspect of the symbolism of the father: "The deity becomes a unique person; henceforth man's relationship with him can recapture the intimacy of the child's relationship with his father."[39] But since this intimacy is precisely what Milton's version of the myth denies, *Paradise Lost* is well on the way—despite its commitment to theodicy—to the world abandoned by God which Lukács sees as the seedbed of the novel.

To separate out the divine attributes into paternal wrath and filial mercy is to make all too obvious the objective ferocity of a law which only sacrifice can placate. As Bunyan very grimly says in catechetical style:

> *Quest.* But why did God let [Christ] die?
> *Answ.* He standing in the room of sinners, and that in their names and natures, God's justice must fall upon him; for justice takes vengeance for sin wheresoever it finds it, though it be on his dear Son. Nay, God favoured his Son no more, finding our sins upon him, than he would have favoured any of us: for should we have died? so did he. Should we have been made a curse? so was he. Should we have undergone the pains of hell? so did he.
> *Quest.* But did he indeed suffer the torments of hell?
> *Answ.* Yea, and that in such an horrible way too, that it is unspeakable.[40]

This is a God who is defined by his power to punish, and from here it is but a short step to Edwards's angry God who suspends sinners precariously over the appalling abyss.

Novelists like Defoe and Richardson dramatize the inevitability, and attendant guilt and suffering, of rebellion against one's earthly father. Milton presents such behavior as consequent upon the Fall, which has made fathers tyrannize over their children and children unwilling to obey the ultimate Father who placed Adam and Eve in Paradise "in true filial freedom" (IV.294). But the rebellion of Adam and Eve, as well as being the archetype for all later rebellions, is uniquely dreadful, for they have no human parents and their sole father is *the* Father, an unbearable obligation. Clarissa can turn from her cruel human father to the loving heavenly one, but when Adam and Eve initiate the universal human rebellion it is for them absolute. The Fall would therefore be intolerable if it were not extenuated in some way. For this Milton needs the myth of Satan.

Satan and Evil

Satan and the evil he embodies are absolutely central to *Paradise Lost*. But it was not inevitable that Milton should have psychologized Satan so fully or have given him so elaborate a function in the narrative of the Fall. The myth of Satan is in any case a Christian superimposition on the Genesis story; the Hebrew commentators whom Milton knew do not mention the war in heaven, the fall of the angels, or Satan's entry into the serpent that tempted Eve.[41] And Milton makes Satan central for imaginative reasons as much as for doctrinal ones. Evil must be something that man has freely chosen, but it must also be something inflicted upon man; only this paradoxical doubleness can express its complexity. Sin is what we do and what is done to us, a powerful force and yet utter nothingness. On these polarities the concept of Satan is built.

Before returning to the identification of Satan with evil as privation, we must consider his active role as the fatal tempter, a role that was strongly emphasized in Protestant teaching since it explained the feeling of being embattled in a hostile universe. On a relatively naive level Satan functions simply as antagonist in a familiar story, as for instance in this sixteenth-century Lutheran catechism:

> *Question:* Where does sin come from? *Answer:* Originally from the devil; after that it came down to us from Adam and Eve, our first parents. *Question:* And how did our first parents fall into sin? *Answer:* Having been deceived by the devil, they disobeyed God and ate from the forbidden tree in Paradise.[42]

This explains clearly enough why man fell, but it fails to explain why Satan did or why God allowed him to tempt man.

Milton, like every Christian thinker, had to begin with the fundamental premise that God has deliberately permitted all of Satan's actions. Otherwise Satan would be as powerful as God, the solution adopted by the Manichaean heretics but totally unacceptable to the orthodox. The Manichaean position is simple and coherent, the orthodox one deeply paradoxical, and Milton in *Paradise Lost* sharpens the paradox by giving it full narrative embodiment. As he well knew, orthodoxy itself was in trouble by the middle of the seventeenth century, not least because traditional explanations of the problem of evil were increasingly repugnant to post-Renaissance ethical and logical assumptions. As Hume (an atheist who had been raised a Calvinist) expressed it in the next century, "Epicurus's old questions are yet unanswered. Is [God] willing to prevent evil, but not able? then is he impotent. Is he able, but not willing? then is he malevolent. Is he both able and willing? whence then is evil?"[43] The traditional explanation was based on Augustine's adaptation of the Neoplatonic concept of privation. God created a perfectly good universe in which evil, far from being an entity in itself, is simply the loss of prior good, much as darkness is the absence of light. This explanation has satisfied many Christians in many periods, and ultimately it is the explanation that Milton adopts, but his narrative mode must force him—even if his questioning intellect did not—to confront it imaginatively.

Once Satan and man have been shown electing evil, then it is hard to avoid the feeling that evil is part of the universe God has made and perhaps even an essential element that supplies the darkness out of which light can shine ("The light shineth in darkness," John 1:5). Once it exists God can control and use it, indeed he must do so lest it gain independent power, but that only underscores the fact that it is ultimately *his*, as are the bogs and dens of "A universe of death, which God by curse / Created evil, for evil only good" (II.622–23). For all his rational theology Milton's God, like Calvin's, depends ultimately on power, for two reasons: because his power is the source of everything that exists, and because evil constantly tends toward the chaos from which nothing but power can restrain it. Without that power, the war in heaven could only produce an inconclusive tension between opposed forces:

> War wearied hath performed what war can do,
> And to disordered rage let loose the reins.
> (VI.695–96)

Christ's triumph on the divine chariot is not a gratuitous demonstration of divine tyranny, but rather an intervention by the sole force that can restore harmony to a universe slipping into chaos. No one who had lived through the civil wars of the seventeenth century needed to be told that power is the only answer to power; *Paradise Lost* is a product of its times just as much as Hobbes's *Leviathan* is.

Not only does evil arise out of God's creation, it does so with God's permission, for it is unacceptable to believe that anything ever happens against his will. Satan then is an agent of the will of God, as Calvin forthrightly says: "Since God holds him tied and bound with the bridle of his power, he executes only those things which are divinely permitted; and thus, whether he will or not, he obeys his Creator, being constrained to fulfill any service to which he impels him." This comes dangerously close to making God the author of evil. The usual counter-move was to argue that God permits evil but does not will it, but as Calvin tersely says in another place, this is a distinction without a difference: "They recur to the distinction between will and permission, and insist that God permits the destruction of the impious, but does not will it. But what reason shall we assign for his permitting it, but because it is his will?"[44] Milton certainly appreciates the logic of this, and in several places confronts it directly.

> So stretched out huge in length the arch-fiend lay
> Chained on the burning lake, nor ever thence
> Had risen or heaved his head, but that the will
> And high permission of all-ruling heaven
> Left him at large to his own dark designs,
> That with reiterated crimes he might
> Heap on himself damnation, while he sought
> Evil to others, and enraged might see
> How all his malice served but to bring forth
> Infinite goodness. . . .
>
> (I.209–18)

God cannot be the author of sin, for as Milton says in *Tetrachordon*, "If it be permitted and decreed lawful by divine law, of force then sin must proceed from the infinite Good, which is a dreadful thought."[45] Yet somehow Satan's crimes do execute the will of God. We are faced once again with a paradox which no amount of rationalization can dispel. That Milton clings to it in spite of recognizing its disturbing implications shows how deeply he needs both of these irreconcilable premises, the absolute power of God and the absolute culpability of his creatures. These are both existential facts which he *knows* to be true, whether or not he can reconcile them philosophically, and the dramatized myth exists to show them in action.

Once the philosophical conundrum is seen to be insoluble, it is possible to recognize that Satan (involuntarily, of course) plays the role of executor of God's wrath. Ricoeur reminds us that Satan is the Accuser whom God encourages to test Job, and in Pauline terms he represents the unappeasable Law of the Old Testament from which Christ has released us. "This hell of guilt, engendered by the law and its curse, finds its supreme symbol in the Satanic figure itself. . . . Thus the demon stands not only behind transgression, but behind the law itself, inasmuch as it is a law of death."[46] Rudolf Otto, who stresses the terrifying aspects of the holy *mysterium tremendum,* describes Lucifer as divine wrath cut loose from mercy and intensified into a *mysterium horrendum,* "the negatively numinous."[47] More concretely, King James I called Satan "God's hangman."[48]

In this light it is imaginatively necessary that Satan be personified and shown as active, even though his status as agent of evil fits very uneasily with the philosophical idea of evil as privation and nothingness. For if evil were simply a state of not-good, then God would be wholly responsible for its consequences. It is when evil is mythicized as a being who *rebels against* God that it becomes imaginatively bearable—so long as the basis of God's ultimate responsibility is not too closely examined. Both ideas occur, as if in suspension, in Augustine's *Confessions,* since both are necessary to Christian thought. When he was a Manichee Augustine did not understand "that evil is only the privation of a good, even to the point of complete nonentity." He now understands that it is no entity at all, "not a substance [but] perversity of will, twisted away from the supreme substance, yourself, O God." But at the same time this utter nonentity is personified in a potent agent, the Prince of Darkness who assaults man and seeks to entrap him in endless punishment:

> The adversary of our true happiness keeps after us, and on every side amidst his snares he scatters the words, "Well done! Well done!" . . . In such wise would he possess for himself those who have become like himself, not for a union in charity but for comradeship in punishment. This is he who has decreed to put his throne to the north, so that, darkling and cold, such men may serve him who in a perverse and tortured way imitates you.[49]

The fact of evil exists and cannot be shirked, and the symbolism of Stan is therefore necessary.

Whatever the ambiguities of Satan as principle of evil, his main function in *Paradise Lost* is to act as the primal tempter who incites man to sin. In his first speech in the poem God discusses the Fall (which has not yet occurred) in terms that contrast man's partial guilt with the absolute guilt of the rebel angels. He speaks first of Adam and Eve:

> I formed them free, and free they must remain,
> Till they enthrall themselves: I else must change
> Their nature, and revoke the high decree
> Unchangeable, eternal, which ordained
> Their freedom, they themselves ordained their fall.
> The first sort by their own suggestion fell,
> Self-tempted, self-depraved: man falls deceived
> By the other first: man therefore shall find grace,
> The other none. . . .
>
> (III.124–32)

This speech superbly combines three separate notions that Milton
needs to hold in suspension: first, that God's "decree" made man and
the angels free to act, somehow managing not to determine (as Calvin
claims) *what* they act; second, that man is responsible for his sin, since
Adam and Eve "enthrall themselves," yet not so guilty as the devils
who were "self-tempted" rather than tempted by someone else; and
third, that this extenuation allows man to deserve grace while the fall-
en angels do not.

What Milton cannot afford to dramatize is the actual fall of Satan:
not his physical fall into Hell, but his spiritual fall into sin. We are
taken back behind the fall of man to see the prior fact of a fallen
Satan, but it is impossible to imagine how he got that way, for what
would it really mean to be self-tempted and self-depraved? We can
barely imagine—a point to which we shall return—how unfallen man
could succumb to a fallen tempter. But how did an unfallen angel
succumb to himself? For man sin is both internal and external; for
Satan it had to be wholly internal, as is allegorized in the birth of Sin
from his perverted brain. But in the perfection of heaven how did his
brain grow perverted?

Bunyan ingenuously says, "This Diabolus was made *Son of the morning,* and a brave place he had of it: it brought him much glory, and
gave him much brightness, an income that might have contented his
Luciferian heart, had it not been insatiable, and enlarged as Hell itself."[50] And perhaps this is after all the only answer: Lucifer is Lucifer even in heaven. Theologians had no trouble defining the ways in
which Satan gives in to pride and envy, both of which express a futile
and destructive wish to be separate from God.[51] But this is no explanation, only a tautology: pride and envy are after all what Satan *is,*
not causal factors that seduce him. So Milton is wise to treat the subject allusively rather than trying to dramatize it at length. If we were
to be shown Satan's pride and jealousy, we might well recoil from the
idea that the angel of light could voluntarily choose darkness, just as
we are likely to recoil from Gabriel's claim that Satan was cringingly
hypocritical even before he fell:

> And thou sly hypocrite, who now wouldst seem
> Patron of liberty, who more than thou
> Once fawned, and cringed, and servilely adored
> Heaven's awful monarch?
>
> (IV.957–60)

To ask how a mighty angel could ever behave like this is to risk dangerous questions about what heaven was like, just as we cannot really afford to ask how a third of the angels could choose rebellion, for if we do we are likely to say with Empson, "The passionate loathing for God of this great multitude, their determination to escape from him at all cost, is one of the chief pieces of evidence the poem gives us about his character."[52] More accurately the poem tries to avoid giving us that evidence. The rebellion is a doctrinal premise and is also essential for Milton's dramatization of evil, but he knows he cannot make us understand how it could have happened in the first place. And that is precisely how it seems to Adam and Eve when they hear

> Of things so high and strange, things to their thought
> So unimaginable as hate in heaven,
> And war so near the peace of God in bliss. . . .
>
> (VII.53–55)

Once Satan's fall is taken as given, Milton is free to present him psychologically, which he does with astonishing richness. The old debate about whether or not we find Satan attractive seems largely misconceived: it is really *our* psychology that Satan embodies, in all of his and its complexity. We are attracted to him because we cannot help it, not just because Milton wants to humiliate us by exposing our gullibility in the face of evil. We are attracted to him because he expresses some of the deepest preoccupations of human experience and art, and if these are finally to be rejected, it can only be with immense effort and sorrow.

By beginning *Paradise Lost* in Hell, Milton deliberately gives Satan dramatic prominence. His story introduces the rest of the story. And by stressing his lost glory as an archangel, the majesty and courage that have not yet wholly faded, Milton arouses in us tragic pity and fear rather than the comic contempt that a critic like C. S. Lewis demands. Helen Gardner is right to associate Satan with Faustus and other figures of tragic damnation: he projects an unforgettable image of "enormous pain and eternal loss," and like the heroes and heroines of Renaissance drama he is both terrible and moving. "There would be no difficulty if Satan were simply an Iago; the difficulty arises because he is a Macbeth."[53] Satan has moments in the poem (seeing the earth for the first time, and being moved by the beauty of Eve) when he seems on the point of repenting, but like Faustus he is trapped in the psychology of damnation, and we see that he does not repent because he will not. Paradoxically, then, the principle of absolute evil can temporarily withdraw from its own symbolic nature:

> That space the evil one abstracted stood
> From his own evil, and for the time remained
> Stupidly good, of enmity disarmed,
> Of guile, of hate, of envy, of revenge;
> But the hot hell that always in him burns,
> Though in mid heaven, soon ended his delight.
>   (IX.463–68)

"Here at least / We shall be free" (I.258–59), Satan had proclaimed in Hell, but having given up the free service of God he is trapped in slavery to himself, as Abdiel had already told him (though we hear of it later): "Thy self not free, but to thy self enthralled" (VI.181). Satan continually re-elects damnation, and in that tormented state cannot be happy except in cruelty. "Only in destroying I find ease" (IX.129), he says just before entering the serpent, and again when he rouses himself from the "stupidly good" contemplation of Eve: "Save what is in destroying, other joy / To me is lost" (IX.478–79).

At this point we need to emphasize that Satan plays a dual role in the poem. On the one hand he is the external tempter who provokes, and partly extenuates, the original sin of Adam and Eve. As such he can be quite crudely represented, in the manner of a stage villain who destroys an innocent child (man) to spite its father (God).[54] But on the other hand he embodies the evil and sadism that man recognizes within himself, and if he were merely crude and externalized, Milton's profound analysis of his psychology would be irrelevant as well as impossible. To insist on his nastiness is to ignore, as Werblowsky says in his rich meditation on the cognate myths of Satan and Prometheus, "the most conspicuous and also the most agonizing characteristic of evil, its powerful fascination and attractive beauty."[55] Of course, it is appalling that this should be so. Milton is not "of the devil's party" if by that we mean that he is a covert Satanist. But evil is inseparable from the human condition as we know it, however much we must regret that bitter fact. In this sense we are all Satanists, and Milton is far more imaginative than critics who complacently tell us to despise his Satan on dogmatic grounds.

Seen in this light Satan is the symbolic form of the modern unhappy consciousness, which feels itself alienated from objective reality and must make what order it can out of its own inner experience. It is no accident that the Romantic poets seized on Satan's stoical speech as a kind of manifesto:

> The mind is its own place, and in itself
> Can make a heaven of hell, a hell of heaven.
>   (I.254–55)

But as Hegel argued in his critique of Stoicism, a purely inner freedom is only an illusion; so Satan's position at once embodies modern subjectivism and reveals its anguish. Theologically Satan is of course wrong. Psychologically he is grimly familiar, and in *Clarissa* in particular we shall revisit that psychic abyss of which Joan Webber has said, "Satan's mind is a cave that Satan himself cannot escape, and he is the symbol of human bondage to inner darkness."[56]

Milton, to be sure, places this satanic psychology in a larger context—in *the* larger context—that explains and neutralizes it. But he imagines it profoundly even while he criticizes it, and this is what gives his treatment of Satan such extraordinary power. The narrator constantly reminds us of the objective and permanent reality that lies outside of Satan. Adam and Eve, who lose it, are assured that they will ultimately see it again. Satan refuses to see it. He not only plays a role, he lives it, and this obliges him to draw back into subjective illusion whenever objective reality threatens to break through his defenses:

> Thoughts, whither have ye led me, with what sweet
> Compulsion thus transported to forget
> What hither brought us, hate, not love. . . .
>   (IX.473–75)

Whereas a pious Puritan would externalize evil thoughts and distinguish them from his true or best self, Satan does exactly the reverse, externalizing his good thoughts and rejecting them as seductive temptations. His very soliloquizing is a dire symptom, for as Janet Adelman points out, it is confined in Milton to fallen beings: "Only after the fall is the creature sufficiently self-divided and sufficiently divided from his surroundings to engage in dialogue with himself."[57]

Pleasure and goodness are now intolerable to Satan, as he openly admits.

> The more I see
> Pleasures about me, so much more I feel
> Torment within me, as from the hateful siege
> Of contraries; all good to me becomes
> Bane, and in heaven much worse would be my state.
>   (IX.119–22)

Stein comments that Satan cannot imagine giving up his inner defenses, the Stoic fortress: "He has adjusted so entirely to the 'unchanged' part of his mind, the hell within, that he *needs* hell."[58] Insofar as any human being feels inner division, he or she is feeling Satan within, and since Satan himself is a created being, not just an abstract principle of privation, he too feels that "torment within me." This speech of Satan's is presented, very poignantly, immediately before he tempts Eve and afflicts humanity with his own dividedness. Evil then becomes, *for us*, a force that invades from outside, while *for Satan* it is a psychological condition which he has elected and cannot bring himself to renounce. When Sin and Death undertake to make man "unimmortal" (X.611), the neologism (Milton apparently invented the word) simply means "mortal," but its double negation reflects our inability to imagine immortality except by contrast with mortality.

Only revelation—truth entering the mind, as Milton implores the heavenly muse to make possible, from outside the self—can save man from the cavern of solipsism. But the point cannot be too strongly emphasized that that is where we are. We are all prisoners of Satan's world, even if we owe allegiance to a God who has promised to rescue us, and the errors of the fallen angels are our errors too. In his confrontation with Abdiel Satan impiously asserts that the angels were self-created:

> Remember'st thou
> Thy making, while the maker gave thee being?
> We know no time when we were not as now;
> Know none before us, self-begot, self-raised
> By our own quickening power. . . .
> (V.857–61)

Lewis easily demonstrates the logical fallacy here: the very fact that Satan can't remember his creation proves that he did not accomplish it himself, and makes it at least probable—as Adam rightly reasons— that he was made by someone else.[59] But a logical fallacy is not incompatible with psychological verity. As Freud repeatedly observes, we are literally unable to imagine a world without ourselves, and hence our creation (like our death) remains imaginatively mysterious, whether we attribute our origin to God or evolution or any other agency.

Thus the symbolism of Satan looks in two possible directions. If one is able to believe, as Milton so earnestly does, in the goodness and justice of an all-powerful God, then Satan's condition is dreadful but not inevitable. We can escape it even if he cannot. But as soon as one begins (as Satan himself has done) to doubt God, then providence hardens into fate, and the Christian epic collapses back into a pagan epic that extols heroism in the face of adversity. As Virgil proclaims in the opening lines of the *Aeneid* (in Dryden's translation):

> Arms and the man I sing, who forced by fate,
> And haughty Juno's unrelenting hate. . . .

We know by bitter experience that life is a struggle against obstacles. Satan identifies those obstacles, in the classical-pagan manner, with cruel fate and a hostile deity. Milton brilliantly transforms Satan *himself* into the obstacle; his is the "unrelenting hate," while free will gives us the power to break loose from his bonds and return to the God who loves us.

But individual persons may come to feel that escape is impossible. And for them the symbolism of Satan speaks most deeply of all, responding to the darkest anxieties of the Puritan temperament. Having admitted that he fell through his own free choice Satan exclaims,

> Me miserable! Which way shall I fly
> Infinite wrath, and infinite despair?
> Which way I fly is hell; my self am hell;
> And in the lowest deep a lower deep
> Still threatening to devour me opens wide,
> To which the hell I suffer seems a heaven.
>
> (IV.73–78)

It is the mood of Cowper's lyrics about reprobation and burial alive. Despair is the ultimate fear, and when we come to Bunyan we shall consider it more closely. Satan is both the agent of despair and its greatest victim.

Johnson was struck by Milton's "repugnance to authority" and his apparent hatred of "all whom he was required to obey."[60] More sympathetically one can say that a man who had lived through the Puritan commonwealth, an intimate of Cromwell and close student of politics, had nothing to learn about the complexities of rebellion. Indeed a kind of double negative makes rebellion obligatory: Abdiel rightly rebels against the rebel Satan, just as Milton's contemporaries rebelled against Satan's minion Charles the First.[61] Psychoanalysis suggests that the child learns to define meaning by saying "no." Milton deeply desires a heaven in which meaning is established by saying "yes," but in the fallen world, at any rate, the primal "no" is an inescapable reality. And the Puritans, more than anyone else, were grimly conscious of its implications, as Edwards confirms in a tract called *Men Are Naturally God's Enemies*:

> Men are wont to hate their enemies in proportion to two things, *viz.* their opposition to what they look upon to be their interest, and their power and ability. A great and powerful enemy will be more hated than one who is weak and impotent. But none is so powerful as God. . . . You object against your having a mortal hatred against God that you never felt any desire to dethrone him. But one reason has been that it has always been conceived so impossible by you. But if the throne of God were within your reach, and you knew it, it would not be safe one hour.[62]

C. S. Lewis may cheerily dissociate himself from Satan; Edwards and Milton cannot.

Paradise Lost would not be the great poem it is if Milton merely despised fallen experience. It is a great poem because he dramatizes it so movingly even while insisting that it is mistaken and can be transcended. As with experience, so with the art that describes it: Milton hopes to transcend fallen art but never attempts (as narrower Puritans did) to minimize its appeal.

> Others more mild,
> Retreated in a silent valley, sing
> With notes angelical to many a harp
> Their own heroic deeds and hapless fall
> By doom of battle; and complain that fate
> Free virtue should enthrall to force or chance.
> (II.546–51)

If force were not benign in God, and if chance were not subsumed in providence, then this would be noble art. Milton's Hell, as many critics have noticed, is very different from the stench and filth of Dante's. Pandemonium may be a parody of divine creation, but it *is* a kind of creation, and fallen art likewise retains traces of its unfallen origins. Satan has been described as a type of the modern poet,[63] and if the novel is indeed the epic of a world which God has abandoned, then the symbolism of Satan broods over its birth.

The Fall

The hinge of the action of *Paradise Lost* is the primal sin for which Adam and Eve lose Paradise. If they had resisted temptation then Satan's fall would be irrelevant; he and his supporters would be suffering far away in Hell, while immortal man would enjoy Edenic happiness and would look forward to eventual angelic perfections. The Fall changed all that, and if Milton is to justify the ways of God he must convince us of man's responsibility. But he does not, except incidentally, attempt to do so by theological argument. The emphasis is on narrative, because what is possible is not rational comprehension but imaginative conviction.

Auden suggested that Greek tragedy arouses the feeling "What a pity it had to be this way," and Christian tragedy the feeling "What a pity it was this way when it might have been otherwise."[64] The central premise of Milton's story is that Adam and Eve were free and able to resist temptation. But we know they did not resist and the Fall took place long ago, so that it is in our past even while still in the poem's future. It thus seems avoidable and yet inevitable, and the narrator finely catches this sense of hopefulness without hope when he cries out as Satan approaches Eden:

> O for that warning voice, which he who saw
> The Apocalypse, heard cry in heaven aloud,
> Then when the dragon, put to second rout,
> Came furious down to be revenged on men,
> *Woe to the inhabitants on earth*! that now,
> While time was, our first parents had been warned
> The coming of their secret foe, and scaped
> Haply so scaped his mortal snare. . . .
>
> (IV.1–8)

It is too late, they cannot be warned, and the Fall must occur since we know it did occur. To be sure, it is not as final and dreadful as the ending of a classical tragedy, for a greater power than fate will one day return to defeat Satan the old dragon. Still the fantasy of warning "our first parents" is very powerful, and as Martz says its main effect is "to stress the singer's presence, to tell us of his love and pity, so different from Satan's hate and envy."[65] The note of sympathy is crucial. We are made to feel that the Fall was *almost* inevitable, and consequently that we can understand how it happened even if we will never fully understand why.

The Fall occurs when Eve, followed by Adam, eats the forbidden fruit. The fruit is prohibited not for any intrinsic virtue that it has but simply in order that something should be prohibited, for there can be no free obedience without the possibility of freely disobeying. Milton states this very clearly in *De Doctrina*: "It was necessary that one thing at least should be either forbidden or commanded, and above all something which was in itself neither good nor evil, so that man's obedience might in this way be made evident."[66] The prohibition is several times repeated in *Paradise Lost,* and as Eve tells the serpent at the very moment of temptation, its basis is simply God's word:

> But of this tree we may not taste or touch;
> God so commanded, and left that command
> Sole daughter of his voice; the rest, we live
> Law to our selves, our reason is our law.
>
> (IX.651–54)

In effect the law has separated into two parts: the single "condensed" prohibition which reason cannot understand, and the infinite range of other possibilities which (unfallen) reason can reliably judge.

The Fall of Man is a disaster, but we need to observe how different it is from the huge and irreversible fall of Satan. Satan cannot bear to serve God in any way and asserts his equality, or even superiority, to the Creator. We are told of no specific prohibition that he breaks; he simply rebels. Adam and Eve, on the other hand, are given a simple prohibition, and although they certainly deserve punishment when they break it, they have not rebelled maliciously and comprehensively. What they have done is not so much to choose evil for its own sake as to forget the force of the always-mysterious prohibition.

> For still they knew, and ought to have still remembered
> The high injunction not to taste that fruit,
> Whoever tempted; which they not obeying,
> Incurred, what could they less, the penalty,
> And manifold in sin, deserved to fall.
>
> (X.12–16)

The "not obeying" was as much amnesia as willful disobedience.

Milton explicitly presents the prohibition as at once unmistakable and incomprehensible. And that is logically necessary, for unfallen beings cannot imagine what fallenness would be. They cannot know what sin is when they have never sinned. All they can do (and all they must do) is to remember a single fact, while lacking any psychological context in which the fact could have meaning. Afterwards, of course, the context will be amply clear, but by then it will be too late, as Fulke Greville ruefully says:

> Sin, then we knew thee not, and could not hate,
> And now we know thee, now it is too late.[67]

In the unfallen state the prohibition has to remain external to man, for in order to be fully internalized it would have to be understood, and by definition it cannot be understood, because that would mean possession of the knowledge of good and evil.

This brings us to the ultimate crux. The fruit has no special virtue in itself. The tree is not a magic tree (though Satan pretends it is, and Eve after falling hails it as if it were). Yet its fruit carries the knowledge of good and evil, a doctrine which Milton could not ignore since it is explicitly stated in Genesis. What then is the knowledge which man must not have? Seizing on this point Satan demands,

> Of evil, if what is evil
> Be real, why not known, since easier shunned?
> God therefore cannot hurt ye, and be just;
> Not just, not God; not feared then, nor obeyed.
>
> (IX.698–701)

The Greeks believed that knowledge was always good, so that a god who could withhold knowledge, as in the Prometheus story, must be a tyrant. But in Milton's poem there are different kinds of knowledge, some essential, some neutral—for instance astronomy, which Raphael tells Adam not to worry about—and some destructive. The knowledge of good and evil is of the latter type. Evil cannot be known at all without being lived, and it cannot be lived without entailing death:

> Our death the tree of knowledge grew fast by,
> Knowledge of good bought dear by knowing ill.
> (IV.221–22)

So says the narrator when he describes Eden as the intruder Satan first sees it, and God himself repeats the point when he passes judgment on fallen man:

> Let him boast
> His knowledge of good lost, and evil got,
> Happier, had it sufficed him to have known
> Good by it self, and evil not at all.
> (XI.86–89)

This knowledge is knowledge of sin, which has been gained in the only way possible, by sinning.

Henceforth evil will be the perverted norm and good an exception to it, instead of the other way round, and the specific knowledge of the primal violation becomes general knowledge of endlessly reiterated violations. In our fallen world virtue must be tested by the continual struggle to distinguish evil from good, as Milton says in *Areopagitica*:

> Good and evil we know in the field of this world grow up together almost inseparably; and the knowledge of good is so involved and interwoven with the knowledge of evil, and in so many cunning resemblances hardly to be discerned, that those confused seeds which were imposed on Psyche as an incessant labour to cull out and sort asunder were not more intermixt. It was from out the rind of one apple tasted that the knowledge of good and evil, as two twins cleaving together, leapt forth into the world. And perhaps this is that doom which Adam fell into of knowing good and evil, that is to say of knowing good by evil.[68]

But if we had been spared this arduous form of testing, good would have been known simply in itself rather than by bitter contrast with a world of evil. For us the abnormal has become normal: we know evil all the time, and good only occasionally through the gaps in it. Before the Fall it was just the opposite; innocence "as a veil / Had shadowed them from knowing ill" (IX.1054–55).

For this reason the Greek conception of knowledge is utterly irrelevant. The true word is God's, and it is by a perversion of that word that Satan achieves his goal: "Into the heart of Eve his words made way, / Though at the voice much marvelling" (IX.550–51). The point is of great importance for our study, for it suggests that ultimate limits were placed on language *before* the Fall as well as afterwards. In pondering this theme Luther understands the "word" in a double sense, as the specific commandment not to eat the fruit, and also as the comprehensive Word of creation, the Logos that mediates God's hidden power ("In the beginning was the Word, and the Word was with God, and the Word was God," John 1:1). In Herbert Olsson's interesting exposition,

> The Word of God was above human understanding (*supra intellectum*); man could not penetrate or understand it by means of other words. Thus God in his Word was unsearchable, hidden. The Tempter sought to make use of this fact when he brought man into doubt. . . . The Tempter says, 'Since God is good and has given all of creation to you, he cannot seriously mean that you may not eat of this tree.' Thus he gives a new interpretation to God's Word, speaks it to pieces [*zerredet es*] and puts a new word in its place—and this for Luther is the archetype of all falsification of words.[69]

God's hiddenness is for Luther a fundamental fact even *before* the Fall. In responding to the temptation "Ye shall be as gods, knowing good and evil" (Gen. 3:5), man aspires to uncover what God has veiled: "Thus man wants to attain a higher understanding than the Word, and as it were to raise himself above the Word; he shoves the Word aside, so to speak, and seeks instead to penetrate into God's hidden majesty" (p. 306).

What Luther gives us is not so much an explanation as a myth of God's mystery, like that of Psyche who lost Cupid when she looked upon him—when, that is, she did the one thing that every lover most wants to do. The devil is the first rhetorician, a master of words but not of the Word. But the primary word of prohibition will not brook analysis, will not yield knowledge except at fatal cost; to analyze it at all is to "speak it to pieces."

An important implication of this line of thought is that Satan invades our thoughts as well as our emotions. Not only are our unwanted impulses evidence that he is at work within us, but our minds are always in danger of thinking his thoughts. Hence the peculiar centrality of the Bible: the Word had to be interpreted, but it could not be argued with or superseded by other words. The Puritans, highly intellectual though they were, relied on the Bible as the sole defense against the temptations of reason, and regarded Satan as a master reasoner who could be defeated only if one refused to play his game.

As Thomas Halyburton says, pondering his academic career and interest in metaphysics,

> I hereby learned the danger and vanity of reasoning with Satan. When I began to answer him with my own reasonings, he had still great advantage: he easily evaded all my arguments, and easily repelled my answers and enforced his suggestions; and when his suggestions were not to be maintained in point of argument, he injected them with that impudent violence that I was not able to stand against. Our safest course is to resist, and to hold at a distance, to avoid communing with him.[70]

One's own arguments are not one's own if they contradict faith; in that case they are Satan's arguments and must be repudiated even when they cannot be refuted. To aspire to be as God, to presume to interpret the Word with confidence, is from a Puritan point of view to fall into the Antinomian excesses of people like the Ranters, whose arguments and style Satan tends to echo.[71] However much Milton believes in free will, he does not approve of the extravagant confidence that threatens to turn Eve, as has been well said, into a "prelapsarian Pelagian."[72]

We have seen why God issued his prohibition and why the knowledge of good and evil was properly forbidden. What remains to be explained is why Adam and Eve could ever have "forgotten." In their unfallen state they were perfectly obedient to God, their wills merged with his in perfect liberty. How then was the tempter able to draw them away?

There are really two problems here: God's foreknowledge that man will fall, even if "freely," and man's ability to choose sin at a time when he is still sinless. Calvinism, always rigorous and clear-sighted, had no trouble with either problem. As to the first, Calvin says,

> They maintain that [Adam] was possessed of free choice, that he might be the author of his own fate, but that God decreed nothing more than to treat him according to his desert. If so weak a scheme as this be received, what will become of God's omnipotence, by which he governs all things according to his secret counsel? . . . It is an awful decree, I confess; but no one can deny that God foreknew the future final fate of man before he created him, and that he did foreknow it because it was appointed by his own decree.[73]

As to the second point, which is psychological as well as logical, Edwards sardonically observes,

> Nothing that the Arminians say, about the contingence or self-determining power of man's will, can serve to explain with less

difficulty how the first sinful volition of mankind could take place, and man be justly charged with the blame of it. To say the will was self-determined, or determined by free choice, in that sinful volition—which is to say that the first sinful volition was determined by a foregoing sinful volition—is no solution of the difficulty. It is an odd way of solving difficulties to advance greater in order to it. To say, two and two makes nine, or that a child begat his father, solves no difficulty; no more does it to say the first sinful act of choice was before the first sinful act of choice, and chose and determined it, and brought it to pass.[74]

These are powerful objections to man's freedom before the Fall, and while many Christians have regarded them as irrelevant or misplaced, Milton had formerly been a Calvinist and well knew their force. He rejected them not because he could prove them wrong but because he could not bear to imagine a God like that. Even so—as always—he shirks nothing, but allows these difficulties to disturb the story as he tells it.

The prose Argument to Book V is even more explicit: "God to render man inexcusable sends Raphael to admonish him of his obedience, of his free estate, of his enemy near at hand." Empson makes much of that *inexcusable,* and indeed Milton is treading a fine line, since man's free choice would be compromised if he were told what we can hardly help thinking he deserves to be told. As Empson points out, God tells Raphael that Satan has disturbed Eve in a dream but does not instruct Raphael to tell Adam and Eve that this is so, leaving them to make their own interpretation of the dream.[75] Yet God is willing to give a partial warning which, though inadequate (as he foreknows) to deter the primal sin, will nonetheless make it "inexcusable." This sounds very much like Calvin's explanation of why the Bible is preached to all men even though the reprobate are incapable of responding to it: the reprobate are thereby "rendered more inexcusable at the day of judgment."[76] So grim a position is clearly unacceptable to Milton, but it is hard to see what else he has to fall back on, and for this reason the issue of interpretation arises in all its ambiguity *before the Fall.* Danielson is surely right to propose that even before the Fall there is an "epistemic distance" between God and Man, a relative ignorance that allows man to act freely rather than imposing an irresistible conviction that would oblige him to act in one way only.[77] For if man knew the truth entirely and perfectly, then surely (as Socrates insisted) he would always do what was right. Yet to know it imperfectly is, of course, to bring in yet again the whole nest of problems associated with interpretation: the Word is primary and absolute, yet it cries out to be interpreted.

In Book V of *Paradise Lost* Adam and Even awaken and pray to God. The scene then shifts abruptly to Heaven where God responds to their prayer by dispatching Raphael who descends to earth "like Maia's son" (V.285)—like Hermes, the messenger-god who gives his name to hermeneutics. Raphael duly warns Adam and Eve, but he has to do so in terms that are just ambiguous enough to leave them with the task of interpretation, as he tells Adam in the lines that conclude the first half of the poem:

> But listen not to his temptations, warn
> Thy weaker; let it profit thee to have heard
> By terrible example the reward
> Of disobedience; firm they might have stood,
> Yet fell; remember, and fear to transgress.
>   (VI.908–12)

The powerful Satan might have stood but did not; Adam and Eve may stand but may also fall if they listen to his temptations. So they must stop their ears when Satan speaks the word to pieces, yet the motive for doing so is the deductions they are to draw from a story which, since evil as yet has no meaning for them, they can only understand remotely and incompletely. "Let it profit thee to have heard." And in any case, Eve, Adam's "weaker," is not present and must receive the warning at second hand from Adam, a doubling of interpretation that (once again) helps to make the primal disobedience seem all too possible.

A paradox is not dispelled by calling it a doctrine, as Milton well knew. That is why *Paradise Lost* is a narrative, and why the extended narrative of Book IX, where the Fall at last occurs, is preceded by other narratives that establish the prior possibility and power of evil. By the time we reach Book IX we have been following the story of evil for many thousands of lines, and we are more anxious to know *how* it arrives at the foredoomed temptation than to ask *why* it does. If we ponder the question of God's responsibility we may still find it unanswerable, but the poem no longer invites us to ask that question, even though it frankly admits that the question is important.

What the mythic story of the Fall does is to relate a series of successive stages, translating a moment of caesura into a narrative of transition.[78] This procedure is implicit in the elliptical tale of Genesis 3 and is further supported by Paul: "Adam was not deceived, but the woman being deceived was in the transgression" (1 Tim. 2:14). Rather than being a single inexplicable reversal, the Fall is spread out into stages, each of which can be considered in itself. Adam fell because Eve fell; Eve fell because Satan fell; we no longer ask (though we found no convincing answer when we did) why Satan fell. We *know* he fell, because evil exists and Satan is its embodiment. So there must have been a reason why he fell, and at this point in *Paradise Lost* we are ready to treat Satan's fallenness as a simple narrative fact, not as a problem to be solved.

To spread out the stages of temptation is not necessarily to extenuate them. On the contrary: since Adam, in Paul's words, "was not deceived," his guilt is if anything greater than Eve's. But it replaces simple causal explanation with psychological drama, and allows for the conflict and complexity that pervade each stage of that drama. Man both falls and is pushed; the serpent is, as Ricoeur says, "the *Other* of human evil," and evil thus reflects "a kind of involuntariness at the very heart of the voluntary."[79] We are now invited to attend to the sequence of temptations that Adam afterwards summarizes: "With the serpent meeting / Fooled and beguiled, by him thou, I by thee" (X.879–80).

The problem here is to make it seem plausible—or indeed possible—that an unfallen man and woman could fall, a desire for evil entering minds in which evil had as yet no meaning. This issue has excited a good deal of critical controversy, which has proved inconclusive because the participants have been arguing from different premises. One group holds that the idea of a sinless person falling into sin is *psychologically* inconceivable, so that Milton has had to infect his prelapsarian Adam and Eve with fallen characteristics. The other group holds that the idea, whether conceivable or not, is *theologically* authoritative, and that Adam and Eve—as Milton repeatedly says— were "pure" and "sinless" until they fell.[80] Both sides are right. Milton did want to portray an Adam and Eve who were sinless yet capable of sin, a paradox which after all is central to Christianity. Milton fully appreciated that this was so, and would not have been pleased with defenders who treat it as no problem at all.

Adam is just as puzzled as any modern skeptic could be: "That strange / Desire of wandering this unhappy morn, / I know not whence possessed thee" (IX.1135–37). Thanks to the Genesis story we know whence it possessed her: it was instigated by Satan. And here Milton had the inspiration (literally an inspiration, he would have said) of prefiguring the Fall in the dream which Satan insinuates into the mind of the sleeping Eve. On this the critical controversy, which again is intense, seems merely misguided. The whole point of the episode is its ambiguity. It is entirely true, as one critic asserts, that the dream is instigated by Satan rather than by Eve's unconscious wishes, and that she is therefore blameless. "Satan is not in the poem a metaphor for man's evil impulses. He is the source of them and a real agent in Milton's fable."[81] But we should recall the familiar Puritan idea that our bad impulses are both impelled by Satan and desired by ourselves. Eve is as yet sinless, and her mind is therefore a clean space through which something foul has passed. When she tells Adam how in her dream a beautiful angel (she does not foresee the serpent) offered her the forbidden fruit, he responds with a disquisition on the empty fantasies of imagination and concludes,

> Evil into the mind of god or man
> May come and go, so unapproved, and leave
> No spot or blame behind: which gives me hope
> That what in sleep thou didst abhor to dream,
> Waking thou never wilt consent to do.
>   (V.117–21)

But of course we know that she *will* consent waking to eat the fruit, and even though the evil was "unapproved," still it was evil. How does Adam, in any case, know what "evil" is, not having yet experienced it?

Whatever one thinks of Frye's suggestion that the dream is a Freudian wish-fulfillment,[82] no amount of theological rebuke can evade the fact that Milton, like his readers but unlike the prelapsarian Adam and Eve, can imagine good only in a context of evil. As Ricoeur shows, this is fully implicit in Genesis:

> We no longer know what a *limit* that does not repress, but orients and guards freedom, could be like; we no longer have access to that creative limit. We are acquainted only with the limit that constrains; authority becomes interdiction under the regime of fallen freedom. That is why the naive author of the Biblical story projects into the state of innocence the sort of interdiction that we experience "after" the fall; the God who says Yes—"Let there be light: and there was light"—now says No—"As for the tree of the knowledge of good and evil, thou shalt not eat of it."[83]

In Christian liberty as ideally imagined, the prohibition would be fully accepted, in fact actively desired as good. But in our fallen experience a prohibition always excites the desire to break it, as Augustine grimly saw in his recapitulation of the primal sin, his motiveless boyhood raid on the orchard.

Diane McColley has persuasively suggested that Eve's dream, which is guiltless but fills her with horror, allows her "to experience evil without doing evil."[84] But to experience it in a dream is to do it in the dream, and what our imagination has done has, in a sense, truly happened to us, even if the imagination was manipulated by Satan. Eve is not guilty, but her cheek flushes as if she were—"With tresses discomposed, and glowing cheek" (V.10). However innocent that blush may be, it is hard not to remember it later when sin does indeed call it forth:

> Thus Eve with countenance blithe her story told;
> But in her cheek distemper flushing glowed.
> 　　　　　　　　　　　(IX.886–87)

Innocent possibilities are rendered guilty by Satan's wiles, and Milton was not the only Puritan writer to imagine preparatory stages in Eve's fall. Thus William Whately: "We must not think that there was no sin precedent to the actual eating of the forbidden fruit; yea, her being enticed and drawn away to distrust God's truth, to deny his threats, to affect knowledge against God's allowance, and to be bold to sin when she conceived that no danger would grow from it but much benefit: all these were faults and preparations to the great actual fault."[85] An almost novelistic narrative has been elaborated from the theological myth.

According to commentators (Genesis itself is ambiguous) Eve was alone when the serpent met her, and Milton has to explain why this happened. Other writers on the story of the Fall tended quite carelessly to let Eve be alone by mere chance, but there is no such thing as chance in God's providential universe. Milton has therefore several requirements to meet: Eve must deliberately choose to be alone, Adam must be responsible for letting her go (so that he can share the "original" sin), and she must advance plausible though not irrefutable arguments to persuade him. Thus psychological complexity is forced upon Milton by the very nature of the story as given.[86] But he wants it for its own sake as well. The fall *is* psychological, and justifying the ways of God entails showing the motivation of what happened.

First of all, Eve is given the argument of *Areopagitica*:

> And what is faith, love, virtue unassayed
> Alone, without exterior help sustained?
> 　　　　　　　　　　　(IX.335–36)

We have already seen that this kind of testing belongs to a fallen world in which good is only known through evil. So Eve is wrong, and ought to have stayed with Adam; yet her argument makes sense *to us*. Very reluctantly Adam lets her go, as he must: "Go; for thy stay, not free, absents thee more" (372). He could force her to stay by asserting his authority, but he would then compromise her freedom; he must leave her free to fall, just as God has done.

Eve is behaving willfully at this point, no doubt, but she has not yet fallen, just as the dream was sinless but showed how sin could infect the imagination. The serpent then appears and amazes her with his rational speech, which he ascribes (plausibly enough) to having eaten the fruit of the knowledge of good and evil. In fact he has not eaten it at all, so that his circumstantial narrative is an empty fiction, and Satan becomes the type of the fallen artist who fables falsely. But if the fruit symbolizes knowing good only through evil, then Satan has indeed eaten it, at that prior moment when he rebelled against God.

At the very instant of the Fall Eve invokes what we have seen to be the strongest argument of all.

> What fear I then, rather what know to fear
> Under this ignorance of good and evil,
> Of God or death, of law or penalty?
>
> (IX.773–75)

She cannot *know* what to fear, and the serpent's temptation has succeeded because he has spoken the mysterious Word to pieces and made her want to know. "What hinders then / To reach," she asks, "and feed at once both body and mind?" (778–79). In effect she is asking "What's stopping me?" and the answer of course is "Nothing." The prohibition can only have meaning if it is obeyed by an internal restraint; but that, as Ricoeur says, implies a limit not felt to be inhibiting and limiting. We are unable to imagine it. For us obedience is restraint imposed by a limit. For Adam and Eve it has been free acceptance of an internal limit; but in going off by herself Eve has already defied Adam, and she now disobeys God.

> So saying, her rash hand in evil hour
> Forth reaching to the fruit, she plucked, she ate.
>
> (780–81)

We still cannot know why this failure was possible, but the narrated myth makes us feel we know how it happened.

Once Eve has fallen Adam must fall, and on scriptural authority he must fall "not deceived." Many commentators came to the conclusion that Adam was indeed deceived in some sense, but Milton (following Augustine) treats the text literally and concludes that Adam did fall knowingly, impelled by his love for Eve.[87] This surrender to Eve had long been allegorized as a capitulation of reason to the lower faculties. But by psychologizing both Adam and Eve Milton has introduced troublesome complications: when Eve is treated as a real person the motif has been de-allegorized and no longer works in its old context.[88] Certainly there is something disturbing in Adam's abjectness before the Fall, when Raphael has to rebuke him for excesses such as the claim that "All higher knowledge in her presence falls / Degraded" (VIII.551–52). "Falls" no doubt carries an ironic anticipation of the Fall, and the jump from one line to the next emphasizes the double meaning of "degraded"—lowered in rank or grade, and sunk in moral degradation.

Many readers have felt something tendentious in the claim in the Argument to Book IX that Adam fell "through vehemence of love," where "vehemence" has its Latin force of "mindlessness," and again when Adam expresses his love for Eve and the narrator comments,

> He scrupled not to eat
> Against his better knowledge, not deceived,
> But fondly overcome with female charm.
>   (IX.997–99)

To some extent the story of the Fall does hinge on an ugly denigration of the female, in which the symbolism of "higher" and "lower" faculties is projected on to an actual man and woman. Adam's angry pun, "O Eve, in evil hour thou didst give ear" (IX.1067) carries the implication that woman is the root of all evil, and Mary Douglas tells how appealing this implication was to an African tribe that regarded women both as passive pawns and as active intriguers: "The story of the Garden of Eden touched a deep chord of sympathy in Lele male breasts. Once told by the missionaries, it was told and retold round pagan hearths with smug relish."[89] However, Adam's fall can be seen more sympathetically if we think of it as testing, to the very limit, the Puritan prejudice against "love of creatures." As in Kierkegaard's meditations on the story of Abraham and Isaac, religious meaning supersedes any merely ethical or aesthetic meaning.[90]

Total and unreserved love of another human being, even of Eve the as yet perfect woman, is a disastrous form of self-love, for only God deserves total love. This fatal identification of lover with beloved is foreshadowed when Sin says to Satan, "Thy self in me thy perfect image viewing / Becamest enamoured" (II.764–65).[91] And it is confirmed when Adam would rather preserve this identity than be immortal:

> Our state cannot be severed, we are one,
> One flesh; to lose thee were to lose my self.
>   (IX.958–59)

Various critics have suggested that Adam ought to have divorced Eve and trusted God to make him another mate, but Milton knows how deeply we are bound to sympathize with Adam all the same. This is no simple matter of tempting us into a "fallen" response and then rebuking it. Eve literally is, as Adam calls her, "bone of my bone" (IX.915). To be sure, they are separate persons, and it is quite true that Eve's fall need not entail Adam's. But it seems somehow narrow to argue as Madsen does,

Misinterpreting the metaphor, Adam does not realize that he and Eve are literally two and only metaphorically one so long as they are united in love of God and obedience to Him. When Eve sins, they are no longer metaphorically one. Had Adam realized this, he might have tried to reunite her will to his and to God's instead of justifying his own sin by appealing to their physical union.[92]

For Adam and Eve are not just any two human beings; they are the primal beings, and God himself seems to identify them in the single term *man*: "Man will hearken to his glozing lies" (III.93).

To say that Adam might not have fallen is theologically correct but conceptually intolerable; we simply cannot imagine it. Eve was our primal mother. What would it mean to repudiate her? No doubt Adam does misinterpret the metaphor of "one flesh," but it is easy to see why he does: Eve *was* created from his flesh, and (as with everything else in Eden) the metaphor is more literally true in the unfallen state than any metaphor can be in our fallen world. In the unfallen state experience was unified in a way that is impossible for us. But we can try to imagine it only by extrapolating back from our fallen experience. Husbands and wives *ought* to be one flesh, and if this is only metaphor, that is due to "the mortal sin / Original" (IX.1003–4), the familiar theological term which Milton defamiliarizes by inverting its sequence and splitting it across the line-ending. This was literally *the* original sin, and it was literally mortal with its "mortal taste" (I.2). If it had not been committed man would never have died.

In working backward from fallen images to unfallen ones, Milton subtly complicates the simple structures of his source in Genesis, of which Ricoeur has said,

> The Yahwist would seem to have suppressed all traits of discernment or intelligence connected with the state of innocence, and to have assigned all of man's cultural aptitudes to his fallen state. The creation-man becomes, for him, a sort of child-man, innocent in every sense of the word, who had only to stretch out his hands to gather the fruits of the wonderful garden, and who was awakened sexually only after the fall and in shame. Intelligence, work, and sexuality, then, would be the flowers of evil.[93]

Milton absolutely rejects such an interpretation. His unfallen Adam and Eve are deeply intelligent, are given work to do (like good Puritans, for whom contemplation is never an adequate vocation) and are marvelously gratified sexually. Before the Fall sexuality gives unalloyed pleasure because it participates in God's creative energy.

> Our maker bids increase, who bids abstain
> But our destroyer, foe to God and man?
>
> (IV.748–49)

And the language of love poetry might then be uncontaminated:

> Here Love his golden shafts employs, here lights
> His constant lamp, and waves his purple wings,
> Reigns here and revels. . . .
>
> (763–65)

The shafts of Cupid are not yet random and destructive, and "revels" does not yet have unpleasant connotations.

Forbidden knowledge will include knowledge of fallen sexuality, and the narrator sadly says,

> Sleep on
> Blest pair; and O yet happiest if ye seek
> No happier state, and know to know no more.
>
> (773–75)

When they do know more, the apple acts as an aphrodisiac and passion becomes involuntary, as its etymology (cognate with "passive") suggests.

> That false fruit
> Far other operation first displayed,
> Carnal desire inflaming, he on Eve
> Began to cast lascivious eyes, she him
> As wantonly repaid; in lust they burn.
>
> (IX.1011–15)

Sex is now inseparable from guilt, and fallen lovemaking is "of their mutual guilt the seal" (IX.1043).

The descriptions of unfallen and fallen sex are both imaginatively powerful, and Empson dryly remarks, "Evidently there is some broad human truth here, but it is hard to say what."[94] He mentions Lawrence, and one might well agree: Will and Anna in *The Rainbow* seem most alive sexually at just the points when Lawrence is critical of them. These ambiguities are still more disturbing in Blake, who thought he was correcting Milton's errors about sex. But I believe that Milton is in fact alert to the problem and is deliberately exploiting it. We know good only through evil; we imagine unfallen sexuality only through fallen. Our speech is riddled with obscene double entendres that are intelligible, as Ian Watt says of *Tristram Shandy*, to any "normally contaminated mind."[95] The very conception of normality is thus corrupted from Milton's unfallen world where *nomos* is inherent in the nature of things, "pouring forth more sweet, / Wild above rule or art, enormous bliss" (V.296–97). "Enormous" retains its Latin meaning of "beyond the norm." Nature's fecundity cannot be indulged unchecked; the plants in Eden must be pruned lest they sprawl too far. But that is labor in the service of life, shaping rather than repressing, and the healthy norm has room in it for the enormous. In our fallen world all language is infected, as in the now-corrupted implications in the description of rivers with "serpent error wandering" (VII.302).[96] Most ominously of all, the serpent just before Satan enters it is described in a double negative, "nor nocent yet" (IX.186). "Innocence" contains within itself the idea of harm, *in-no-cence,* just as the German word for innocence, *Unschuld,* is "un-guilt." We know innocence only through guilt.

This is the heart of the imaginative experience of *Paradise Lost,* and will be fundamental to the other texts in the Puritan tradition that we will be considering: every aspect of fallen experience is contaminated, whether in action, in feeling, or in the language that tries to describe them. Even pastoral, the genre that aspires to recreate innocence, can do so only by conscious artifice, for as Anne Ferry says, "For us pastoral is a sophisticated, artificial, conventional recreation of a language which for Adam and the angels was simple, natural, and immediate because it was a true description of the unfallen world."[97] And if fallen and unfallen sex resemble each other, that is in part because we no longer know how to tell them apart. Augustine has been much derided for suggesting in *The City of God* that the unfallen Adam and Eve activated their sexual organs by rational choice. But his idea seems to have been that prelapsarian man enjoyed a condition of "integrity" in which all faculties cooperated together. The sexual organs neither became aroused when arousal was unwanted nor refused when it *was* wanted. Such failures are symptoms of a fallen state in which man is no longer integrated, no longer whole.[98]

In the unfallen world, as many mythologies suggest, desire was perfectly satisfied because it was in perfect harmony with what it needed. But in the fallen world—which is to say in the actual experience of all human beings—desire is defined by lack. Gazing "with jealous leer malign" (IV.503) at Adam and Eve embracing, Satan enviously says,

> Sight hateful, sight tormenting! Thus these two
> Imparadised in one another's arms
> The happier Eden, shall enjoy their fill
> Of bliss on bliss, while I to hell am thrust,
> Where neither joy nor love, but fierce desire,
> Among our other torments not the least,
> Still unfulfilled with pain of longing pines.
>
> (505–11)

Pondering the forbidden fruit, Eve proposes a similar notion, that desire should be defined not by need but by lack:

> . . . His forbidding
> Commends thee more, while it infers the good
> By thee communicated, and our want.
>   (IX.753–54)

Before the Fall sexuality is integrating; afterwards it is goaded by a sense of want that never can be slaked—"agony of love till now / Not felt," as Eve describes it (IX.858–59).

Romantic poets and philosophers transposed the Christian myth by construing it as the fall into consciousness that motivates both civilization and its discontents. And psychoanalysis, that post-Romantic philosophy, seeks to expose consciousness as itself conflicted and meretricious, screening its own deepest impulses from itself. In Freud's system guilt is inseparable from the human condition, an inner voice of accusation that accompanies the repression of inadmissible desires. But in Milton guilt is the result not of repressed desire but of perverted reason. Surely this is why he desexualizes the traditional symbolism of the tree of knowledge, insisting that healthy sexuality was fully indulged before the Fall. It is Satan who perverts knowledge by *making* it sexual in a corrupted form; sexual knowledge in itself imposes no guilt.

In the fallen world the cure for insatiable desire is not to repudiate the love of creatures but to direct it toward the love of God. Just as it was she who precipitated the Fall, so it is Eve who movingly initiates the reconciliation with Adam after bitter quarreling:

> Forsake me not thus, Adam, witness heaven
> What love sincere, and reverence in my heart
> I bear thee, and unweeting have offended. . . .
>   (X.914–16)

"After the Fall," Stein says, "the highest value is love, by which man fell."[99] The highest love is the sacrifice of the God-man Christ, in whom human love is restored, and whose "passion" heals the sickness of passions since the Fall: "As in Adam all die, even so in Christ shall all be made alive" (1 Cor. 15:22). And only in Christ can language rejoin action, words taking shape and meaning from enactment by the Word:

> So spake the almighty, and to what he spake
> His Word, the filial Godhead, gave effect.
>   (VII.174–75)

   Still the Fall remains a disaster, if not an unmitigated one; in accuracy one can speak only of an unfortunate fall.[100] And Michael's famous promise that Adam and Eve will enjoy "a paradise within thee, happier far" (XII.587) does not, as often misconstrued, mean that the inner paradise is happier than the unfallen Eden, but only that it is happier than the wreckage of fallen Eden from which they are now expelled. Fallen experience, and the art that represents it, must henceforward aspire beyond themselves to a realm they cannot see clearly, where vision will be unclouded and self-knowledge will not cut us off from knowledge of otherness. "For now we see through a glass, darkly, but then face to face; now I know in part, but then shall I know even as also I am known" (1 Cor. 13:12). In the deep honesty with which he ponders the fallen state Milton has drawn out essential implications of a comprehensive myth, implications that pervade the works we are now going to examine. And this is so because his concept of evil is rich enough to respond to the universal human experience of the nature of things, even while urging passionately that the Christian solution offers the only hope of release from it. Demanding that she be allowed to go off by herself, Eve asks indignantly whether "this be our condition, thus to dwell / In narrow circuit straitened by a foe" (IX.322–23). It is quite true that Eden had never until then seemed a narrow circuit.[101] But it is also true that Satan, merely by existing, defines it as such. The presence of evil places an obstacle or limit against goodness. The ultimate question, as we have seen, is unanswerable: Why should evil exist at all? But if it exists—and we know it does—then inevitably it threatens and circumscribes good.

   The whole issue of forbidden knowledge and the Word is implicated here, and a contrast with Greek tragedy may be suggestive. The ability to know is central to Oedipus as Sophocles characterizes him: it allows him to solve the riddle of the Sphinx, failure to do which would mean death. However, he must also achieve knowledge about himself, which takes the form of objective knowledge of his status as the son of Laius and Jocasta. When he learns this, he recognizes his guilt in killing Laius and marrying Jocasta, and punishes himself for it. But since it is objective rather than subjective guilt—he never knew who they were until it was too late—he can still become a figure of magical potency in his mysterious old age, and in *Oedipus at Colonus* is taken up strangely into the heavens. Adam's story is utterly different. Man is forbidden to know what God wishes to conceal, and eating the fruit is the first sin. The self is not divided, and it conceals no guilty knowledge, until that moment. After the transgression, punishment is not only inevitable but relentless, for if God were to excuse man his justice would be balked, and providence would be seen to have operated unfairly.[102] So God instructs Michael,

> Haste thee, and from the Paradise of God
> Without remorse drive out the sinful pair.
>   (XI.104–5)

Man's guilt is now bottomless and can be relieved only by the complex action of a God (in the aspect of Christ) who unites with him, suffers for him, and intercedes for him. For the Greek, knowledge, even if terrible, is the path to enlightenment. For the Christian it is the path to death, and can only be repaired by a myth which is "to the Greeks foolishness" (1 Cor. 1:23). Oedipus becomes a god; Christ becomes a man.

At his darkest moment Adam demands,

> Did I request thee, Maker, from my clay
> To mould me man, did I solicit thee
> From darkness to promote me?
>   (X.743–45)

Adam soon arrives at the orthodox answer of radical creaturehood: it is not for him to question God's will. But Mary Shelley quotes his question as epigraph to *Frankenstein,* in which a tragic monster very rightly demands that an incompetent creator justify his ways. As soon as the structural elements of the myth are thrown into flux, the questions which it was supposed to answer return with alarming force, implicated as they are in symbols that retain their imaginative charge even when torn loose from their doctrinal foundations. "Remember that I am thy creature," the monster tells Frankenstein; "I ought to be thy Adam, but I am rather the fallen angel, whom thou drivest from joy for no misdeed. Everywhere I see bliss, from which I alone am irrevocably excluded."[103]

The Fallen World of Time

In the unfallen world change did occur, but in a cyclical harmony that returned always to the same living fullness, so that in MacCaffrey's words it was "an elaborate kind of changelessness, and time only the quiet alternation of night and day."[104] Michael's prophecy to Adam, on the other hand, depicts a world of sequential history where change is irreversible and usually for the worse. The world of fallen language is the world of fallen time in which art, even inspired art like *Paradise Lost,* is obliged to operate within a temporal prison. Without a doubt Milton longs for the realm beyond that prison, but the Fall has left us far removed from the stability of the divine throne "fixed for ever firm and sure" (VII.586), and until the final apocalypse, "till time stand fixed," we are confined to "this transient world, the race of time" (XII.554–55). In the transient world all art is but seeming, just as Eve after falling considers "in what sort" she may best "appear" to Adam (IX.816–18), whereas before the Fall she and Adam "In naked majesty seemed lords of all, / And worthy seemed" (IV.290–91). Seeming was then identical with being; the gulf between appearance and reality, so dear to modern criticism, did not yet exist. But once it has opened, nothing but the Last Judgment can close it. After the Fall has occurred in Book IX the dislocations and flashbacks stop, and Michael gives Adam a single long flashforward in which history is recounted in historical sequence. We are at last leaving—as Adam and Eve must—the world of myth.

We are not yet, however, in the world of fiction, as is confirmed by the narrator's oblique perspective on a story that lies midway between history and fable, historical time and mythic time. At the very outset he speaks allusively of what was "long after known in Palestine" (I.80)—long *after* the time narrated in the poem, long *before* the time in which we read it. When Noah's flood has been shown to Adam the narrator suddenly exclaims,

> How didst thou grieve then, Adam, to behold
> The end of all thy offspring, end so sad. . . .
> (XI.754–55)

Milton's sympathy for our sorrowing ancestor suddenly brings us *forward* to the present moment when Milton is speaking, and pushes Adam *back there* to the long-ago time when he was receiving this prophecy. Shortly afterward Adam laments, "O visions ill foreseen!" (763) and regrets having foreknowledge of events that "must be" (770). These events, as we well know, are all recorded in the Bible, and so they are certainly going to occur. They cannot *not* have occurred. Adam thus experiences a kind of parody of God's foreknowledge.[105] Free will ensures that nothing happens deterministically, yet *for us* these events are irrevocably locked into the pastness of the past. What Adam experiences is stranger still: the pastness of the future.

In these final books the events of biblical history are presented as static tableaux.[106] They are history rather than myth (Hebrew not Greek) but are significant for what they mean rather than as narrative entertainment. Books XI and XII are Adam's introduction, under the guidance of Michael, to the interpretation of the as yet unwritten Bible. So *Paradise Lost* manages to be prior to the text that it is subsequent to, merging our past with the narrative's future. And this has significance for the interpretation of reality. As Lewalski has shown,[107] Michael's prophecy hinges on Hebrews 11:1, "Now faith is

the substance of things hoped for, the evidence of things not seen."
Adam is therefore not able to "see" what can only be apprehended
inwardly. Abraham obeyed God "by faith . . . not knowing whither he
went" (Heb. 11:8), and Michael says,

> I see him, but thou canst not, with what faith
> He leaves his gods, his friends, and native soil.
> (XII.128–29)

This implies a remarkable fact about "reality" as presented in *Paradise
Lost*. The historical events of the Bible have really happened, but we
can "see" them only with the inward eye of faith; so they are shown to
us (and Adam) as visions requiring interpretation, not as dramatized
events. But the mythic events of the war in heaven and the temptation
in Eden are indeed dramatized, very fully so. This means that they
seem more real than the events of history. And so they should, for
Milton regards the myth of Genesis as the ultimate reality, while
earthly life is but a shadow of the myth. We remember that he insisted
on reading the Bible literally, permitting as little allegorical license as
possible. As Fish says, "Reading (or living) history figuratively is not a
repudiation of literalism, but the way to literalism, to the literalism we
enjoyed before the Fall."[108]

What ultimately controls the structure of fallen history is the decisive ending when time will be no more. It is the expectation (by
faith) of that ending that allows Milton to be so confident as he manipulates his levels of temporal sequence. Consider again the exclamation
that opens Book IV,

> O for that warning voice, which he who saw
> The Apocalypse, heard cry in heaven aloud,
> Then when the dragon, put to second rout,
> Came furious down to be revenged on men.

Embedded in this passage are four different chronological stages: (1)
Satan about to tempt Adam and Eve; (2) John of Patmos writing the
Book of Revelation; (3) John Milton writing *Paradise Lost*; (4) the return of Satan (as dragon) and his defeat in the Apocalypse which John
foresees. But the sequence is redistributed in Milton's lines, since the
first stage we hear of is the final one, the Apocalypse which will wind
up temporal sequence and bring the story of Satan to its just conclusion. The fall into time, provoked by Satan's successful temptation of
man, will be "tragic" (IX.6), but the apocalyptic ending will resolve
Satanic tragedy into divine comedy.

So the cyclical scheme does prevail after all, even if, as in Augustine's theory of time in the *Confessions*, temporal history is sus-

pended within it. Noah's rainbow will define a covenant of natural
renewal that will endure until the promised end:

> Day and night,
> Seed time and harvest, heat and hoary frost
> Shall hold their course, till fire purge all things new,
> Both heaven and earth, wherein the just shall dwell.
>   (XI.898–901)

At the end of the poem Michael foretells that after the agony of fallen
history, "To good malignant, to bad men benign" (XII.538), Christ
will return "to dissolve / Satan with his perverted world" (546–47),
and the fatal fruit of Eden will be superseded by the fruit of eternity:
"To bring forth fruits joy and eternal bliss" (551). Without apocalypse, history would be a nightmare from which we could not
awaken. As it is, time is literally temporary, and in Wittreich's words,
"Historical patterns are drawn not for their own sake but to find a
release from them." If epic tends to confirm the order of history,
prophecy exists to overturn it.[109]

So we await the second coming of Jesus, described by Michael in
lines of extreme beauty,

> who shall quell
> The adversary serpent, and bring back
> Through the world's wilderness long wandered man
> Safe to eternal paradise of rest.
>   (XII.311–14)

For Adam and Eve the wandering is just beginning as they "wander
down / Into a lower world" (XI.282–83). *Paradise Lost* is very deeply a
Puritan poem in its commitment, remarked by Max Weber, to active
"deeds" (XII.582) in the fallen world.[110] But Puritans wanted to be in
the world but not of it, as the wonderful closing lines of the poem
suggest:

> Some natural tears they dropped, but wiped them soon;
> The world was all before them, where to choose
> Their place of rest, and providence their guide:
> They hand in hand with wandering steps and slow,
> Through Eden took their solitary way.
>   (XII.645–49)

The allusion is to Psalm 107, "They wandered in the wilderness in a
solitary way. . . . Then they cried unto the Lord in their trouble, and
he delivered them out of their distresses." Adam and Eve are solitary
in Puritan aloneness, yet they are together as companionate spouses

who are sustained by God's providence. And if man can no longer trace God's "footstep" directly in the fallen world (XI.329), God will yet give "many a sign" of his presence (351) and will reveal, however mysteriously, "of his steps the track divine" (354).

If those signs and traces were to become more ambiguous, they would harden into the deliberate artifice of allegory, and we would leave the mythic narrative for the world of *The Pilgrim's Progress*. If they were to lose even that degree of hermeneutic authority, then both myth and allegory would slip into a limbo of tentativeness and hypothesis, and we would find ourselves in the novelistic world of *Robinson Crusoe* and *Clarissa*. As it is, *Paradise Lost* stands poised between myth and novel because of its double focus: Adam and Eve are novelistic while the narrator is prophetic. Or more accurately, Adam and Eve *become* novelistic, and it is precisely that transition—from prelapsarian unity to postlapsarian dividedness—that embodies Milton's imaginative explanation of the origin of evil. There is one last paradox here, for Milton reverses our usual association of freedom with development. Contrasting allegory with the novel, Angus Fletcher comments, "The common criterion for good novels, that they show people growing, may not be capable of articulation into a clear theoretical statement, but it does point to our sense that realism of character is related to freedom of choice in action."[111] Yet it is before the Fall, when Adam and Eve are not as yet complex "characters," that they have perfect freedom of action, while after the Fall their bondage to sin makes them unfree.

Milton is the most imperial of writers, shaping every minute element of his mighty tale, guiding his readers at all points and perhaps even tyrannizing over them. In this sense the myth itself may seem a victim of Milton's gigantic ego, an assertion of will by which "a man's creed widens into a myth yet hardens at the arrogant core."[112] Yet the very potency of Milton's style is surely (as Lewis suggests) an attempt to supply the solitary reader with something like the public magnificence of the epic singer of old.[113] And that is perhaps just another way of saying that the imperial narrator of *Paradise Lost* has to mediate between readers and the lost *nomos,* recreating a culture in which the Christian myth might seem so integrated and self-evident that there would be no need of justifying God's ways to men. Again and again, with humility and dread, Milton prays for God's help lest his work be a satanic substitute for divine reality rather than a shadow or image of it. But he can sustain such a belief only if his symbols point to a transcendent reality that guarantees our fallen and ambiguous symbols. The moment that guarantee is withdrawn, mythic thinking becomes intensely problematic, and the unified Word is spoken to pieces in reality and not just in myth.

4

Experience and Allegory in Bunyan

The Logic of Dividedness

The older scholars, and some modern ones, have seen Bunyan chiefly as a religious thinker, interpreting his work in the light of theological or homiletic tradition. More recent critics treat him as an imaginative writer in the light of current theories about allegory and narrative. I want to do both: to see him as giving imaginative shape to a particular kind of Puritan experience, and also as developing a mode of allegorical narrative that points forward toward the novel even while it resists many of the implications of its form. As always in this study, I shall argue that the relations between form and meaning are both subtle and specific, the logic of a particular work imposing different assumptions from those of other works even by the same author. My goal will be a full consideration of the great *Pilgrim's Progress*, but first I wish to establish the context of Bunyan's autobiography, *Grace Abounding to the Chief of Sinners,* in order to show how the fundamental principles of his allegory spring from essential elements of his inner life.

Like Milton's, Bunyan's career spans the seventeenth century. Born in the year of the Petition of Right, 1628, he died in 1688, the year of the Glorious Revolution (and of the birth of Alexander Pope). An early biographer describes him aptly as "the son of an honest poor labouring man who, like Adam unparadised, had all the world before him to get his bread in."[1] We know very few of the facts that a modern biographer would want to consider, especially at the crucial period in 1644 when his mother and sister died, his father remarried, and at the age of sixteen he joined Cromwell's army. The one fact that Bunyan himself regarded as crucial was his conversion, at some point in the 1650s, to a Calvinist faith. Specifically he became a lay preacher in the sect known as Particular Open-Communion Baptists: "particular" because they affirmed Calvinist predestination and rejected Arminian claims that all men might be saved; "open-communion" because they accepted members who believed in infant baptism as well as those who wanted to confine baptism to adults. Like so many Puritan groups, Bunyan's achieved its sense of integrity by exclusion, forming a tightly knit and mutually sustaining subgroup that asserted its special *nomos* against the larger culture outside. He himself became so energetic a figure in the sect's life that outsiders nicknamed him "Bishop Bunyan," although much of his work had to be carried on from behind bars: unlike Shepard, who fled to the New World, Bunyan endured and indeed courted the punishment of a government that forbade him to preach. He was first arrested in 1660, the year of the Restoration, and was in and out of prison for twelve years, finally freed by Charles II's Declaration of Indulgence in 1672. But political pressure forced Charles to repeal the Declaration, and Bunyan was arrested again in 1675, at which time he began *The Pilgrim's Progress*.

The Particular Open-Communion Baptists, with their oxymoronic declaration of inclusion and exclusion, deliberately shut out the English society by which they themselves were shut out. John Milton, master of the whole of ancient and modern European culture, could at once pose as a spokesman for the British nation and proudly assert himself as a sect of one. John Bunyan was far more isolated and threatened in his Puritan solitude, and badly needed membership in a group that could make sense of his inner experience even while asserting its difference from that of most people. It is no wonder that he was drawn to a type of allegory whose formalized expression of dividedness corresponded closely to his troubled sense of himself.

It is worth emphasizing how much the Puritans felt themselves to be despised and rejected by the larger culture, even while their controversial stance actively invited rejection—reflected in satirical titles like Richard Carpenter's *The Anabaptist Washt and Washt, and Shrunk in the Washing* (1653). As a tinker Bunyan followed a trade that was considered particularly ignoble:

> When tinkers bawled aloud, to settle
> Church-discipline, for patching kettle;
> No sow-gelder did blow his horn
> To geld a cat, but cried Reform.
> The oyster-women locked their fish up
> And trudged away to cry No Bishop.[2]

Many of their enemies regarded Puritanism simply as lower-class hostility to a cultural ethos in which it could not share, whether in learning or in the intellectual "parts" that made learning possible. As a satirical song imagined them proclaiming,

> We'll down with all the Versities
> Where learning is profest,
> Because they practice and maintain
> The language of the Beast;
> We'll drive the Doctors out of doors,
> And parts whate'er they be:
> We'll cry all arts and learning down
> And hey then up go we.[3]

Similar prejudices have survived into recent times. The magisterial Perry Miller, celebrant of the highly intellectual founders of Massachusetts, remarked tartly that in the seventeenth century "Very few Englishmen had yet broached the notion that a lackey was as good as a lord, or that any Tom, Dick, or Harry, simply because he was a good, honest man, could understand the Sermon on the Mount as well as a Master of Arts from Oxford, Cambridge, or Harvard." In a wonderful Harvard touch Miller adds that the Antinomians "came near to wrecking not only the colony but the college as well."[4]

Bunyan made precisely the claim that Miller despises. In an account of his first arrest he records this pregnant exchange with an Anglican vicar sent in to reason with him:

> LINDALE. Indeed I do remember that I have read of one Alexander a coppersmith [2 Tim. 4:14], who did much oppose and disturb the Apostles. (Aiming 'tis like at me, because I was a tinker.)
> BUNYAN. To which I answered, that I also had read of very many priests and pharisees, that had their hands in the blood of our Lord Jesus Christ.
> LINDALE. Aye, saith he, and you are one of those scribes and pharisees, for you, with a pretence, make long prayers to devour widow's houses [Luke 20:47].
> BUNYAN. I answered, that if he had got no more by preaching and praying than I had done, he would not be so rich as now he was.[5]

There was thus a strong class element in Bunyan's faith, a fact that deserves further reflection. In the days of Puritan success an important factor, as Stone says, was "the heady egalitarian wine of the New Testament" that began to reach the lower classes when "literacy and Puritanism went hand in hand."[6] But the failure of the revolution naturally baffled and disheartened Puritans. Many sold out, or to put it more sympathetically, reentered the mainstream of society. Some struggled in other ways to understand what had happened. It was not merely that they had lost their temporary gains, for the Bible was full of examples of God punishing the chosen people for their own good. Beyond that, it was a question of internalizing the faith in a way that made dividedness a condition of existence rather than a prelude to worldly victory. Even Milton, who turned from Calvinism to Arminianism, brooded darkly over fallen history and sang the paradise within; strict Calvinism meanwhile became the refuge of believers like Bunyan, for as Hill observes, "Predestinarian theologies descended the social scale after the English Revolution."[7]

To some extent—as Bunyan's exchange with Lindale suggests— this kind of faith justified the otherwise helpless individual against the social order, and in many places Bunyan bitterly recognizes the hostility of the world that excludes the saint.

> Q. But I am like to be slighted and despised by other little children if I begin already to serve God, am I not?
> A. If children be so rude as to mock the prophets and ministers of God, no marvel if they also mock thee; but it is a poor heaven that is not worth enduring worse things than to be mocked for the seeking and obtaining of, 2 *Kings* 2:23–24.[8]

Bunyan's biblical reference turns out on inspection to be altogether chilling:

> And [Elisha] went up from thence unto Bethel: and as he was going up by the way, there came forth little children out of the city, and mocked him, and said unto him, Go up, thou bald head; go up, thou bald head.
> And he turned back, and looked on them, and cursed them in the name of the Lord. And there came forth two she-bears out of the wood, and tare forty and two children of them.

Many Puritans seem to have sought humiliation which they might well have avoided, glorying in a separateness that to outsiders seemed merely willful. A modern admirer of Bunyan puts it in positive terms: "The Puritan is, amongst other things, a man who refuses to let his beliefs be compromised beyond a certain point, and is thereafter impervious to threats and hostile opinions. It is not so much that he does not see, and rue, the cost of standing out against established opinion or mass opinion, as that he feels he has no choice. Like Luther he 'can do no other'."[9] But *why* can he not? The reasons no doubt differ from person to person, but in Bunyan's case it is above all a question of explaining an otherwise intolerable psychic life, asserting a theology which makes sense of his desperate dividedness and permits its transformation into imaginative form.

The most haunting and disturbing of all Puritan autobiographies is Bunyan's *Grace Abounding to the Chief of Sinners* (1666). In a chapter entitled "The Sick Soul" William James presents Bunyan as "a typical case of the psychopathic temperament, sensitive of conscience to a diseased degree," and *Grace Abounding* furnishes ample evidence for such an opinion. Yet it is also true, as James observes in his chapter "The Divided Self," that Bunyan achieved a remarkable recovery, so that "in spite of his neurotic constitution, and of the twelve years he lay in prison for his non-conformity, his life was turned to active use."[10] It is worth trying to understand how this could be so, and in particular how *Grace Abounding* makes a positive virtue of dividedness and guilt.

From the age of nine or ten, Bunyan tells us, he was haunted by the doctrine of election and reprobation, and in horror of damnation often longed to join the devils and be done with it. "Yea, I was so overcome with despair of life and Heaven, that then I should often wish, either that there had been no Hell, or that I had been a devil . . . that if I indeed went thither, I might rather be a tormentor than tormented myself."[11] Throughout his life a sense of passive helplessness recurred with nightmarish intensity: "I did liken myself . . . unto the case of some child that was fallen into a mill-pit, who though it could make some shift to scrabble and sprawl in the water, yet because it could find neither hold for hand nor foot, therefore at last it must die in that condition" (p. 62). In one sense he might see himself as blameless because incapable of fighting free. "I did compare myself in the case of such a child, whom some gypsy hath by force took up under her apron, and is carrying from friend and country; kick sometimes I did, and also scream and cry, but yet I was bound in the wings of the temptation, and the wind would carry me away" (p. 32). But in another sense Bunyan was all too blameworthy, for his old impulse to join with the devils kept returning as a compulsion to blaspheme, a self-assertion that proceeded from obsessive depths far beyond conscious control.

> In these days, when I have heard others talk of what was the sin against the Holy Ghost, then would the tempter so provoke me to desire to sin that sin, that I was as if I could not, must not, neither should be quiet until I had committed that; now no sin would serve but that: if it were to be committed by speaking of such a word, then I have been as if my mouth would have spoken that word whether I would or no; and in so strong a measure was this temptation upon me, that often I have been ready to clap my hand under my chin, to hold my mouth from opening; and to that end also I have had thoughts at other times to leap with my head downward into some muckhill-hole or other, to keep my mouth from speaking. (p. 33)

Far from rescuing Bunyan from such anxieties, conversion only exacerbated them; this passage describes a period well after the crucial road-to-Damascus experience that arrested him in the middle of a village game. "Just as I was about to strike [the ball] a second time, a voice did suddenly dart from Heaven into my soul which said, 'Wilt thou leave thy sins and go to Heaven? or have thy sins and go to Hell?'" (p. 10). What conversion suggested was damnation, not election, and as so often in his life Bunyan felt defiantly impelled to ratify that condition: "Therefore I resolved in my mind I would go on in sin; for, thought I, if the case be thus, my state is surely miserable; miserable if I leave my sins, and but miserable if I follow them; I can but be damned, and if I must be so, I had as good be damned for many sins as be damned for few" (pp. 10–11).

The remainder of *Grace Abounding* records a harrowing series of oscillations between hope and despair, during which particular biblical texts come unbidden into Bunyan's mind and strike him with the force of unmediated revelation. Sometimes he is hopeful of salvation, sometimes sure that he is damned, and then the old temptation revives to end his suffering by embracing damnation once and for all.

> One morning as I did lie in my bed I was, as at other times, most fiercely assaulted with this temptation, to *sell and part with Christ;* the wicked suggestion still running in my mind, *Sell him, sell him, sell him, sell him,* as fast as a man could speak; against which also in my mind, as at other times, I answered, No, no, not for thousands, thousands, thousands, at least twenty times together; but at last, after much striving, even until I was almost out of breath, I felt this thought pass through my heart, *Let him go if he will!* and I thought also that I felt my heart freely consent thereto. Oh, the diligence of Satan! Oh, the desperateness of man's heart! Now was the battle won, and down I fell, as a bird that is shot from the top of a tree, into great guilt and fearful despair. . . . (p. 43).

Just for one instant Bunyan feels free—"I felt my heart freely consent thereto"—and with that freedom he defiantly chooses eternal unfreedom, falling like a shot bird. But as he finds at once, what he has chosen is worse than what he tried to abandon, a permanent condition of "great guilt and fearful despair."

To sell Christ is to imitate Judas and murder the Lord—"I was convinced that I was the slayer" (p. 68). Just as in childhood, Bunyan's deepest temptation is to assert himself against the God who demands absolute loyalty. In resisting this temptation he encourages himself by pondering the most horrifying of texts, a psalm which he reads typologically as spoken by Christ: "That Scripture also greatly helped it to fasten the more upon me, where Christ prays against Judas that God would disappoint him in all his selfish thoughts which moved him to sell his master. Pray read it soberly, Psalm 109:6, 7, 8, &c." The passage in question reads:

> 6 Set thou a wicked man over him: and let Satan stand at his right hand.
> 7 When he shall be judged, let him be condemned: and let his prayer become sin. . . .
> 10 Let his children be continually vagabonds, and beg: let them seek their bread also out of their desolate places. . . .
> 18 As he clothed himself with cursing like as with his garment, so let it come into his bowels like water, and like oil into his bones.

The temptation to curse always hung powerfully over Bunyan, and whereas other Puritans might read this psalm as a triumphant denunciation of their enemies, Bunyan understood it as an exposure of his true nature. The philosopher Royce, noting that the young Bunyan used joking and swearing as a means of distinguishing himself among his fellows, found it highly explicable that repression of speech should play a central role in the postconversion torments: "This man, a born genius as to his whole range of language-functions, had been from the start a ready speaker, had developed in boyhood an abounding wealth of skilfully bad language, and had then, in terror-stricken repentance, suddenly devoted himself for many months to a merciless inhibition of every doubtful word."[12] Long before he became a writer, Bunyan was a man for whom language was seductive and potentially dangerous. The identification with Judas extended even to physical symptoms: "I felt also such a clogging and heat at my stomach by reason of this my terror that I was, especially at some times, as if my breast-bone would have split in sunder. Then I thought of that concerning Judas, *who by his falling headlong burst asunder, and all his bowels gushed out,* Acts 1" (p. 50).

The exclusion from Eden in *Paradise Lost* is a dire but still intelligible event, and Adam and Eve leave hand in hand to enter a world where Providence will continue to be their guide. Bunyan, however, is obsessed with election (which Milton is not), and the obverse of election is eternal reprobation. "And withal, that Scripture did seize upon my soul, *Or profane person, as Esau, who for one morsel of meat sold his birthright; for you know how that afterwards when he would have inherited the blessing, he was rejected, for he found no place of repentance, though he sought it carefully with tears,* Heb. 12.16–17" (p. 43). This grim text keeps recurring to Bunyan's imagination, explicitly reminding him that the price of eating the fruit of knowledge is an armed sentry that excludes man from the tree of life. "Still that saying about Esau would be set at my heart, even like a flaming sword, to keep the way of the tree of life, lest I should take thereof, and live" (p. 55). Indignantly rejecting this equation of life with forbidden knowledge, Blake proclaims, "The cherub with his flaming sword is hereby commanded to leave his guard at [the] tree of life."[13] Such a rejection is unthinkable for Bunyan, who is therefore committed to the idea that knowledge itself—like language itself—is fatal unless authenticated by God, who is both author and authority.

Bunyan's sense of himself differs from that of simpler Puritans like Trosse in that he continued *after conversion* to fear reprobation, and upwellings of confidence alternated continually with guilt and fear. Even when he was preaching effectively, Bunyan remained painfully aware that the tempter continued to lurk within him, so that only bondage to Christ could counteract Satan's bondage. "Indeed I have been as one sent to them from the dead; I went myself in chains to preach to them in chains, and carried that fire in my own conscience that I persuaded them to beware of" (p. 85). Often, when in the pulpit, Bunyan was assaulted by the old urge to blaspheme, or paralyzed by a dissociation from the sound of his own voice.

> Sometimes again, when I have been preaching, I have been violently assaulted with thoughts of blasphemy, and strongly tempted to speak them with my mouth before the congregation. I have also at some times, even when I have begun to speak the Word with much clearness, evidence, and liberty of speech, yet been before the ending of that opportunity so blinded, and so estranged from the things I have been speaking, and have also been so straitened in my speech, as to utterance before the people, that I have been as if I had not known or remembered what I have been about, or as if my head had been in a bag all the time of the exercise. (p. 90)

Anyone who has ever taught has been in that bag, but for Bunyan this is not just an unsettling psychic quirk; rather, it is a reminder that the Devil is always at hand, ready to invade and poison the unwary victim.

Sin, then, is no abstract privation but something Bunyan wants, loves, and wills to do; so he needs a faith that will not merely promise him election, but will accommodate that promise to the fact of continued sin and guilt. And this is what he gains in a crucial episode when he overhears the conversation of "three or four poor women sitting at a door in the sun."

> They also discoursed of their own wretchedness of heart, of their unbelief, and did contemn, slight, and abhor their own righteousness as filthy and insufficient to do them any good. And methought they spake as if joy did make them speak: they spake with such pleasantness of Scripture language, and with such appearance of grace in all they said, that they were to me as if they had found a new world, as if they were people that dwelt

alone, and were not to be reckoned among their neighbors, Num. 23:9. (pp. 14–15)

The allusion is complicated, for it refers to Balaam blessing the Israelites against the commands of the king of Moab, after God rebuked him by making his ass speak. In Christian commentary Balaam was seen as both prophetic and reprobate, as in Milton's *Paradise Regained,* where Satan tries to persuade Christ to make use of him by saying that God

> vouchsafed his voice
> To Balaam reprobate, a prophet yet
> Inspired; disdain not such access to me.
> (I.490–92)

Bunyan's Puritan women are of the elect, like the Israelites whom Balaam involuntarily blesses, and Bunyan likewise blesses them from the isolation of an outsider, a Moabite. What will make him an insider is a double recognition. First, he must grasp the Pauline message that grace comes unbidden and undeserved, which at first had seemed hostile rather than encouraging: "This Scripture also did seem to me to trample upon all my desires, *It is neither in him that willeth, nor in him that runneth, but in God that showeth mercy,* Rom. 9:16" (pp. 20–21). And second, he has to see that his vehement sinfulness contains in itself the signs of election: all men are sinners, but only the elect are sensitive enough to know it.

Anti-Puritans regarded as megalomaniac the kind of claim that Bunyan makes in calling himself the chief of sinners. "Oh! methoughts, this sin was bigger than the sins of a country, of a kingdom, or of the whole world; no one pardonable, nor all of them together, was able to equal mine, mine out-went them every one" (p. 52). In fact Bunyan's vaunting title is a direct allusion to Paul: "Christ Jesus came into the world to save sinners; of whom I am chief" (1 Tim. 1:15). Scores of writers quoted this text and took Paul as their model; Trosse, for instance, chose it as the text for his own funeral sermon and used it in his epitaph: "Here lies the chief of sinners, the least of saints, the most unworthy of preachers George Trosse."[14] Everyone who truly understands his or her condition is the chief of sinners, for the Fall has left mankind utterly corrupt, and small sins are just as sinful as monstrous ones.

A recognition of guilt is the necessary precondition for salvation, to be actively sought however painful it may be. As Shepard wrote in his diary,

> In morning prayer the Lord let me see (1) that I was the greatest sinner. Because I was a sinner before the Lord in holy duties I

was very vile, and hence I saw my misery would be most great if I perished. (2) I remembered that I deserved nothing but death and hell, and hereupon the Lord abased my soul and made me make this use of it: Why then shall I set out myself? Oh no; let me set out the Lord only: do his will and serve him and myself no more! And this was sweet to me.[15]

To face the utter iniquity of the self is to be freed for service to others, even if this means a radical dualism in thinking about one's own psyche. Many Puritans explicitly compared themselves with Paul, and *Grace Abounding* can well be seen as a Pauline epistle written from prison.[16] From this point of view prison is a setting-free rather than a limitation, for it shuts out the disturbing carnal world and enhances one's sense of apostolic mission. As Bunyan put it in his *Prison Meditations,*

> This gaol to us is as a hill,
>   From whence we plainly see
> Beyond this world, and take our fill
>   Of things that lasting be.[17]

It is notable that in his torments Bunyan never considered atheism, although skeptical doubt was certainly attractive to many of his contemporaries.[18] On the contrary, for him the worst threat of all was the ontological abyss that would open up if there were no God. "Of all the temptations that ever I met with in my life, to question the being of God and the truth of his Gospel is the worst, and worst to be borne; when this temptation comes it takes away my girdle from me, and removeth the foundations from under me" (p. 102). He could not imagine living without Christianity as a structure of explanation, which is why the thinking of Paul was so critical for him (as mediated by Luther's commentary on Galatians): "I began to look into the Bible with new eyes, and read as I never did before; and especially the Epistles of the Apostle St. Paul were sweet and pleasant to me" (p. 17). What Paul offered above all was an explanation of the divided self that could account for the rebellious "not-I" that was yet part of the "I." According to the crucial exposition in the Epistle to the Romans,

14 For we know that the law is spiritual: but I am carnal, sold under sin.

15 For that which I do, I allow not: for what I would, that do I not; but what I hate, that do I.

16 If then I do that which I would not, I consent unto the law that it is good.

17 Now then it is no more I that do it, but sin that dwelleth in me.

18 For I know that in me (that is, in my flesh) dwelleth no good thing: for to will is present with me; but how to perform that which is good I find not.

19 For the good that I would, I do not: but the evil which I would not, that I do.

20 Now if I do that I would not, it is no more I that do it, but sin that dwelleth in me.

Verses 17 and 20 seem to imply that the agent is not the "I" at all, but "sin," an invading force like a disease; as if one should say "It isn't I that do it, but the pneumonia within me." But verses 15 and 19 imply an "I" that is divided (spirit versus flesh) yet remains the same *self*.

Freud had a similar paradox in mind when he developed the terms *ich, es,* and *überich,* misleadingly translated in English by the Latinate abstractions *ego, id,* and *superego.* The *ich* is the "I," the conscious and self-aware agent; the *es* is the "it," the impersonal unconscious that is inseparable from the self but perceived by the "I" as an intrusion of power from some hidden source. According to Freud the superego or "over-I" is allied with the id, and the ego must struggle against the contrary yet obscurely allied forces of conscience on the one hand and libido on the other. Pauline psychology deals with the problem by displacing both of the less-than-conscious elements. The id becomes the flesh which groans in bondage to Satan, and the superego becomes the inexorable Law which fallen man is incapable of obeying unless aided by God's free grace. Yet it is still *oneself* that struggles in bondage to Satan and aspires to satisfy God's demands. Everything must hinge, therefore, on the extent to which the self can feel freed *from* itself, by a divine intervention that restores the unfallen state of wholeness. "O wretched man that I am! Who shall deliver me from the body of this death? . . . For the law of the spirit of life in Christ Jesus hath made me free from the law of sin and death" (Rom. 7:24, 8:2).

Surveying Christian doctrine, Milton sets out to justify the ways of God to men by psychologizing the myth. In Bunyan the process runs in exactly the opposite direction: he wins through to the truth of biblical myth by surviving the anguish of his inner experience, and in seeking to communicate that victory to other men he mythicizes his own psychology. Milton starts with unfallen Man and asks how he fell into guilt; Bunyan starts with a guilty man and asks how he can be healed. As we shall see, this impulse generates an altogether different mode of narrative from Milton's, and one which was destined to be equally influential in the later development of fiction.

The Pauline (and Augustinian) system was powerful just because it held contradictory elements in suspension: a self that was also a not-self, objects that were at once desired and despised. "It was my delight to be taken captive by the Devil *at his will*, 2 Tim. 2:26" (*Grace Abounding*, p. 6). The Law remained fearful even if potentially placable, and from childhood onward Bunyan perceived bondage to Satan as a tempting way to repudiate its intolerable demands. Paul's consolations after all were confined to the elect, a point which Satan (that close student of the Bible) took care to emphasize.

> This Scripture also did seem to me to trample upon all my desires, *It is neither in him that willeth, nor in him that runneth, but in God that showeth mercy*, Rom. 9:16.
> With this Scripture I could not tell what to do; for I evidently saw that unless the great God of his infinite grace and bounty had voluntarily chosen me to be a vessel of mercy, though I should desire and long and labour until my heart did break, no good could come of it. Therefore this would still stick with me, How can you tell you are elected? and what if you should not? how then?
> O Lord, thought I, what if I should not indeed? It may be you are not, said the Tempter; it may be so indeed, thought I. Why then, said Satan, you had as good leave off, and strive no further; for if indeed you should not be elected and chosen of God, there is no talk of your being saved: *For it is neither in him that willeth, nor in him that runneth, but in God that showeth mercy*. (pp. 20–21)

If the dualistic view of reality made it hard for Puritans to connect the preconversion with the postconversion self, what they lost in narrative structure they gained in psychological power, for their special gift was the exploration of inner experience with all of its conflicting impulses.

It is thus important to recognize not only that Bunyan was neurotic but also that he knew it. The scorn of a modern Bunyan specialist is peculiarly insulting:

> At a time when every godly man of the lower orders was potentially a vessel of the Spirit, it was inevitable that the vagaries of the mentally unsound should have taken a religious direction. The tendency of the age to interpret extravagance as a symptom of divine impulse lent itself to the irregularities of those whom we should confine to institutions. . . . England was lighted by the queer radiance of insanity and shaken by the regrettable demonstrations of the inspired.[19]

This is to take the same view of Puritan "excesses" (colored no doubt by the satiric style of Lytton Strachey) that Swift took long ago: But no one would want to argue that Swift himself was not neurotic, and there is something to be said for an imaginative tradition that tries to explore the roots of neurosis instead of jeering at it as mere aberration. As Bunyan saw clearly, it is fundamental to human experience to feel drawn to what it both wants and does not want.

It needs to be emphasized that cases like Bunyan's were far from uncommon, using Calvinist ideas to explain deep feelings of dividedness and guilt. Timothy Rogers, who wrote a treatise on the religious melancholy that tormented him all his life, stressed the bleak isolation of the sufferer, and the difficulty other people usually had in trying to understand and help him. "If you saw a person wounded and torn and mangled on the highway, the sight of so deplorable an object would fill you with compassion; the sight of your friends under this disease which I am now speaking of, ought much more to move you, for it is every moment tearing them to pieces; every moment it preys upon their vitals, and they are continually dying, and yet cannot die." While the immediate damage is done by Satan, this can only happen because God permits it: "[Satan] shoots at us with fiery darts that are extremely painful, and comes to shoot them when we are under a sense of God's displeasure; which is like thrusting a red iron into a wound that is already very sore."[20]

Rogers was writing from a mental imprisonment that he never escaped. Baxter, more objectively, described the compulsive fears of sufferers in terms that can be applied to Bunyan's case with startling exactness:

> Their misery is that what they think, they cannot choose but think. . . . Usually they seem to feel something besides themselves, as it were, speak in them, . . . and they will hardly believe how much of it is the disease of their own imagination. . . . They use to say, this text of Scripture at such a time was set upon my mind; when oft the sense that they took them in was false, or a false application of it made to themselves, and perhaps several texts applied to contrary conclusions, as if one gave them hope and another contradicted it. . . . And most of them are violently haunted with blasphemous injections, at which they tremble, and yet cannot keep them out of their mind, . . . and oftentimes they are strangely urged, as by something in them, to speak some blasphemous word of God, or to renounce him, and they tremble at the suggestion, and yet it still followeth them, and some poor souls yield to it, and say some bad word against God, and then, as soon as it is spoken, somewhat within them saith, "Now thy damnation is sealed, thou hast sinned against the Holy Ghost, there is no hope."[21]

As these testimonies suggest, what is extraordinary in Bunyan is neither the disorder nor the cure, but rather the use his imagination was able to make of inner conflict. It was impossible simply to banish guilt; what was necessary was to find some way to put a positive construction upon it.

For precisely this reason, an attraction that Bunyan particularly feared was the Antinomian assertion that since all men are saved in Christ, they share his total freedom from sin.

> I happened to light into several people's company who, though strict in religion formerly, yet were also swept away by these Ranters. These would also talk with me of their ways, and condemn me as legal and dark, pretending that they only had attained to perfection that could do what they would and not sin. O these temptations were suitable to my flesh, I being but a young man and my nature in its prime. (*Grace Abounding*, p. 17)

The Ranter spokesman Laurence Clarkson said that in his youth he had wept with joy at Puritan sermons on sin.[22] Ranting was an inversion of that self-humiliation, a faith that could explain guilt away. But for Bunyan any faith that denied guilt was a manifest swindle, for even after conversion nothing was more present to him than guilt.

Once the fact of guilt is accepted, one can argue about the best way to allay it. From a psychoanalytic point of view Bunyan resembles those patients Freud mentions who cannot relinquish their neurotic symptoms because their guilt "is finding its satisfaction in the illness and refuses to give up the punishment of suffering."[23] Another analyst speaks of diseases whose careful tending can take the place of religious faith, *la maladie substituée à Dieu*.[24] But since psychoanalysis is itself an explanatory myth, and by no means unchallenged in its claims,[25] one might turn the diagnosis around and conclude that Bunyan substitutes God for a malady. Beginning with the conviction of guilt, he seizes on a theological explanation as soon as he is old enough to understand it, childhood anxieties giving way to a coherent Pauline structure of belief. The disease does not go away, but it becomes intelligible and can be converted to positive ends.

Thus Bunyan reverses the process by which modern psychoanalysis sees neurosis as private religion. "His neurosis allows [the patient] to take control of his destiny—to transform the whole of life's meaning into the simplified meaning emanating from his self-created world."[26] What Bunyan does instead is to transform his private world into a larger and happier one, translating his experience into universal terms and then helping others to do what he has done. The Protestant emphasis on the "calling" is profoundly liberating: "I was made to see that the Holy Ghost never intended that men who have gifts and abilities should bury them in the earth, but rather did command and stir up such to the exercise of their gift" (*Grace Abounding*, p. 84). Take away that structure of explanation, on the other hand, and the symptoms of guilt can be crippling, for as Becker comments, "We see the historical difference between the classical sinner and the modern neurotic: both of them experience the naturalness of human insufficiency, only today the neurotic is stripped of the symbolic world-view, the God-ideology that would make sense out of his unworthiness and would translate it into heroism."[27] That is the heroism of knowing oneself to be the chief of sinners.

Taking the argument a step further, it is not so much that Bunyan needs God as that he also needs Satan. Pretty clearly he felt a strong antagonism to authority, which fueled his childhood desire to join with the devils and is evident in his bitter exchanges with civil and religious officials. Bunyan gladly seized upon a faith that externalized his rebellious impulses as satanic temptations, and he was then able to draw energy from the battle against them, exactly as Luther did from the *Anfechtungen* or "attacks" that he had continually to repel.[28] Like the sufferers Baxter describes, Bunyan especially feared committing the mysterious "sin against the Holy Ghost," which seems to have represented the decisive step of acknowledging his subversive impulses. So there is perhaps some justice in the otherwise appalling opinion that he obtained from an aged believer: "About this time I took an opportunity to break my mind to an ancient Christian, and told him all my case. I told him also that I was afraid that I had sinned the sin against the Holy Ghost; and he told me, *He thought so too*" (p. 55).

Feeling both hostile and helpless, Bunyan achieves peace, as he indicates in a doctrinal work, by ascribing both conditions to man's subtle and implacable enemy.

> For by how much the soul struggleth under these distresses, by so much the more doth Satan put forth himself to resist, still infusing more poison, that if possible it might never struggle more (for strugglings are also as poison to Satan). The fly in the spider's web is an emblem of the soul in such a condition; the fly is entangled in the web, at this the spider shows himself; if the fly stir again, down comes the spider to her, and claps a foot upon her; if yet the fly makes a noise, then with poisoned mouth the spider lays hold upon her; if the fly struggle still, then he poisons her more and more; what shall the fly do now? why she dies, if somebody does not quickly release her. . . . The afflicted conscience understands my words.[29]

Faced with an external enemy and assured of the saving assistance of Christ, Bunyan is able to marshal his resources and fight back until he wins.

If modern theories of the unconscious tell us anything, it is surely that unwanted impulses *are* in a sense external, for the ego has not summoned them and may well find them horrifying. Jung's wise remarks on this point apply very exactly to Bunyan's experience:

> In this precarious situation it would be bad strategy to convince the patient that he is somehow, though in a highly incomprehen-

sible way, at the back of his own symptom, secretly inventing and supporting it. Such a suggestion would instantly paralyze his fighting spirit, and he would get demoralized. It is much better if he understands that his complex is an autonomous power directed against his conscious personality. Moreover, such an explanation fits the actual facts much better than a reduction to personal motives. An apparent personal motivation does exist, but it is not made by intention, it just happens to the patient.[30]

Paradoxically, freedom for Bunyan was a function of control by external forces, for like Augustine he could only escape bondage to Satan by accepting bondage to Christ. And like other militant Puritans he found the oppressions of the Restoration a positive help, for as Macaulay shrewdly observes, "It should seem that Bunyan was finally relieved from the internal sufferings which had embittered his life by sharp persecution from without."[31] In prison Bunyan set himself free.

Words, the Word, and Narrative

As the impulse to blaspheme suggests, Bunyan regarded language as having magical properties, and he often wrestled with the temptation to use it with godlike authority. "One day as I was betwixt Elstow and Bedford, the temptation was hot upon me to try if I had faith by doing of some miracle; which miracle at that time was this, I must say to the puddles that were in the horse pads, *Be dry;* and to the dry places, *Be you the puddles*" (pp. 18–19). It has not been noticed that this passage is specifically blasphemous, alluding to a text in Isaiah in which God "saith to the deep, Be dry" (44:27). But of course the temptation does not proceed from Bunyan alone: he later realizes "that Satan had thus assaulted me" (p. 21). Impulses of conscience are likewise felt to be partly external, as is splendidly expressed by the boy who told Theodor Reik that the voice of his conscience was "a feeling of one's self and the language of somebody else."[32] In Bunyan's case that language is the Word as expressed in the Bible.

Bunyan was very far from sympathizing with enthusiasts who testified to a direct and decisive conviction of grace. Puritans of a Calvinist bent were always suspicious of the duplicities of feeling; thus Shepard, after agonizing about whether to try to approach God, concludes "And then I saw how great a sin it was to make feeling the ground and cause of my faith."[33] Likewise Edwards, though at first inspired by the revivalist excitement of the Great Awakening, had grave doubts about emotionalism and wrote trenchantly about the deceptions that religious ecstasy can mask. Bunyan's first published

works were called forth by controversy with the Quakers, whose celebration of the inner light scandalized him. His own contact with God
tends to come in the form of messages and communications, almost as
in Kafka's *The Castle,* and the text of the Bible is the essential medium.

Hobbes wrote contemptuously, "After the Bible was translated into
English, every man, nay every boy and wench, that could read English
thought they spoke with God Almighty and understood what he
said."[34] The Geneva Bible of 1551 and subsequent editions, by printing the text as a sequence of numbered chapters and verses, encouraged the practice of dwelling on single verses. Each sentence was a
direct oracle from God, and contradictory texts jarred far more painfully than they would have done if organized into narrative or explanatory structures. Again and again Bunyan speaks of a text as "this
word," the direct speech of the divine, and like other Puritans he
imagines human life as so integrated with the Bible that particular
passages have a literal and personal significance. "In the light and
encouragement of this word I went a pretty while, and the comfort
was the more, when I thought that the Lord Jesus should think on me
so long ago, and that he should speak them words on purpose for my
sake" (p. 23).

In keeping with the spirit of Protestantism the Bible is both a collection of texts and a mighty spirit; as has been well said of Luther, "The
Word of God is dynamic, irresistible, mysterious, and uncontained. It
is God's promise; it is God's breath."[35] But in Bunyan's case the two
aspects—texts and spirit—constantly threaten to pull apart, and he
seems to regard himself as a passive theater in which the words are
spoken, rather than as an autonomous person who might consider
and apply them. Naturally he spends much time poring over the Bible, but he still imagines that particular texts fall unbidden upon him
rather than being in any way selected. At times two texts will preoc-
cupy him in manifest opposition, but even then he can only wait for a
resolution to come from outside.

> Lord, thought I, if both these Scriptures would meet in my heart
> at once, I wonder which of them would get the better of me. So
> methought I had a longing mind that they might come both to-
> gether upon me; yea, I desired of God they might. Well, about
> two or three days after, so they did indeed: they bolted both
> upon me at a time, and did work and struggle strangely in me
> for a while; at last, that about Esau's birthright began to wax
> weak and withdraw and vanish; and this about the sufficiency of
> grace prevailed, with peace and joy. (pp. 66–67)

At other times a single text is in question but with two possible interpretations, and Bunyan then seems willing to take an active role
against the diabolical interpreter who speaks the Word to pieces.[36]

> This Scripture also did now most sweetly visit my soul, *And he that cometh to me I will in no wise cast out,* John 6:37. . . . But Satan would greatly labour to pull this promise from me, telling of me that Christ did not mean me and such as I. . . . If ever Satan and I did strive for any word of God in all my life, it was for this good word of Christ, he at one end and I at the other. Oh, what work did we make! It was for this in John, I say, that we did so tug and strive: he pulled and I pulled; but God be praised, I got the better of him, I got some sweetness from it. (pp. 67–68)

But of course Bunyan does not always win the battle, and he darkly declares, "Woe be to him against whom the Scriptures bend themselves" (p. 77). At such times he even wonders whether St. Paul might not have been a cunning impostor (p. 31), and allows himself to imagine the Bible rewritten for his own benefit: "Sometimes again I should think, O if it were not for these three or four words, now how might I be comforted! and I would hardly forbear at some times but to wish them out of the Book" (p. 66).

From a modern vantage point all of these "words" force themselves upon Bunyan because his mind has brought them into consciousness, and his protestations of passiveness are the "disclaiming locutions" noted by psychoanalysts.[37] But from his own point of view the Word is all too clearly external, desired by one part of the self but resisted by another. "In these days I should find my heart to shut itself up against the Lord, and against his holy Word; I have found my unbelief to set as it were the shoulder to the door to keep him out, and that too, even then when I have with many a bitter sigh cried, Good Lord, break it open" (p. 26). The only way out of this impasse is to recognize that Christ *is* the door, as he himself proclaims: "I am the door: by me if any man enter in, he shall be saved" (John 10:9).

Everything now depends on breaking through to the Word that informs the separate words, and this is far from easy. After citing "I am the door" Martin Buber comments on Pauline Christianity, "It is as if . . . a wall had been erected around the Deity, and it is pierced by only one door; he to whom it is opened beholds the God of grace Who has redeemed the world, but he who remains far from it is abandoned to the messengers of Satan, to whom the God of wrath has given over man."[38] In his doctrinal works Bunyan follows Luther in emphasizing the terrors of a God of wrath, and the sacrifice of Christ which alone can save man from that wrath.[39] In *Grace Abounding* he describes "a kind of vision" in which the elect bask in the sunlight of God's love while he himself is compelled to batter against a wall that stands in the way:

> At the last I saw as it were a narrow gap, like a little doorway in the wall, through which I attempted to pass; but the passage being very strait and narrow, I made many offers to get in, but

all in vain, even until I was well-nigh quite beat out by striving to get in. At last, with great striving, methought I at first did get in my head, and after that, by a sideling striving, my shoulders, and my whole body; then I was exceeding glad, and went and sat down in the midst of them, and so was comforted with the light and heat of their sun. . . . The wall I thought was the Word that did make separation between the Christians and the world; and the gap which was in this wall, I thought was Jesus Christ, who is the way to God the Father. (pp. 19–20)

So Christ, the ultimate Logos and Word of God, is the obstacle between the elect and all outsiders but also the gap through which it is possible to break in. Bunyan's imagery here suggests birth, but it is birth *into* rather than *from,* the return to the mother's womb that Christ prescribes for entry into the kingdom of heaven. Only thus can the ambiguities of the Word resolve themselves—"for the Word of the Law and Wrath must give place to the Word of Life and Grace" (p. 67).

Nothing in *Grace Abounding* is ever simple. The Devil's strategy is to suggest that Bunyan has indeed sold Christ and is alone with the wrathful Father. "Now also did the Tempter begin to mock me in my misery, saying that seeing I had thus parted with the Lord Jesus, and provoked him to displeasure who should have stood between my soul and the flame of devouring fire, there was now but one way, and that was to pray that God the Father would be the mediator betwixt his son and me" (pp. 55–56). This of course is a dreadful inversion, for Christ *is* the mediator, and without his help there is no hope of forgiveness. No wonder then that in *Come and Welcome to Jesus Christ* (1678) Bunyan develops all the texts in which Christ invites his children, or that in *Grace Abounding* he recalls the Song of Songs—"The words began thus to kindle in my spirit, *Thou art my love, thou art my love,* twenty times together" (p. 29). As the Puritan saint understands his own psychology, bad dividedness gives way to good dividedness: he has Christ inside him as his best self, and is thereby freed from the prison of this fallen world. "Further, the Lord did also lead me into the mystery of union with this Son of God, that I was joined to him, that I was flesh of his flesh and bone of his bone. . . . Now could I see myself in heaven and earth at once; in heaven by my Christ, by my head, by my righteousness and life, though on earth by my body or person" (p. 73).

Grace Abounding is an autobiographical narrative, but since it is founded on psychic dividedness and ontological dualism, it provides a very equivocal model for later novelistic narratives.

That saying, 2 Cor. 1:9, was of great use to me, *But we had the sentence of death in our selves, that we might not trust in our selves, but in God that raiseth the dead;* by this Scripture I was made to see that if ever I would suffer rightly, I must first pass a sentence of death upon everything that can properly be called a thing of this life, even to reckon my self, my wife, my children, my health, my enjoyments, and all, as dead to me, and my self as dead to them. *He that loveth father or mother, son or daughter, more than me, is not worthy of me,* Matt. 10:37. (p. 97)

Rejecting the love of creatures does not spare Bunyan from bitter grief over the fate of his family when he goes to jail, "especially my poor blind child, who lay nearer my heart than all I had besides; O the thoughts of the hardship I thought my blind one might go under, would break my heart to pieces" (p. 98). But it does permit him to stand apart from the world whose *nomos* he has so flagrantly defied, interpreting his experience in emblematic and typological categories that reject the assumptions of ordinary mimesis. Thus although it is sometimes alleged that *Grace Abounding* presents a coherent novelistic narrative, it is equally possible to complain as Joan Webber does that the work is repetitive and evades the whole problem of authorial control.[40] That is just what Bunyan intended, uninterested as he was in inventing the novel: he perceived his life as a continual oscillation of moods, not as a shapely structure, and oscillation itself becomes his theme.

From another point of view, however, *Grace Abounding* does indeed contribute to the novel, for as Lukács argues the early novel has a strong lyric component, exploring the recesses of individual consciousness.[41] The lyric element in Bunyan is mirrored in the declaration that "I cannot now express with what longings and breakings in my soul I cried to Christ to call me" (p. 24), and again, "Oh! I cannot now express what then I saw and felt of the steadiness of Jesus Christ" (p. 58). From this it is but a short step to Wordsworth in "Tintern Abbey": "I cannot paint / What then I was." For if Wordsworth is profoundly a poet of memory and time, he is also above all the poet of the epiphanic moment that breaks *through* time, when the mind as Bunyan says is "fixed on eternity" (p. 15). Bloom has remarked that Romantic theories of imagination "are all displaced, radical Protestant accounts of the nakedness of the soul before God," and *Grace Abounding,* to borrow another Wordsworthian line, shows human life not in itself but "bare to the eye of heaven."[42]

In return for what he gives up in temporal process, Bunyan gains in the vividness with which he recreates the existential moment, culminating in the wonderful act of risk-taking that concludes his book:

I thought also that God might choose whether he would give me comfort now, or at the hour of death, but I might not therefore

choose whether I would hold my profession [of faith] or no: I
was bound, but he was free; yea, it was my duty to stand to his
Word, whether he would ever look upon me or no, or save me at
the last. Wherefore, thought I, the point being thus, I am for
going on, and venturing my eternal state with Christ, whether I
have comfort here or no. If God doth not come in, thought I, I
will leap off the ladder even blindfold into eternity, sink or
swim, come heaven, come hell; Lord Jesus, if thou wilt catch me,
do; if not, I will venture for thy name. (p. 101)

The ladder of which Bunyan speaks is literal as well as metaphorical:
he had reason to fear tht he might soon have to ascend the gallows.
And this existential leap, this final acceptance of Christ even in the
absence of assurance, is what frees him to operate for the time being
in the fallen realm. As Boyd Berry finely puts it, "Bunyan leaps from
the top of his visionary ladder, and his gesture, carrying him out of
the world, paradoxically permits him to descend into and act within
that world he has left."[43]

The Holy War: Allegory and the Self

It has long been usual to describe *Grace Abounding* as the source or raw
material for *The Pilgrim's Progress,* allegory giving public form to private obsession. Thus the standard modern study of Bunyan concludes, "His originality lies in the power which enabled him to project
his visions and obsessions on to the objective reality of a work of art: to
turn *Grace Abounding* into *The Pilgrim's Progress.*"[44] But such a formulation elides many essential questions. In what sense is the allegory
more "objective," let alone more "real," than the autobiography? Are
the obsessions less obsessive when "projected" in that form? And is
Grace Abounding less "original" than *The Pilgrim's Progress?* It looks as
if scholars have been embarrassed by the rawness and repetitive misery of Bunyan's lived experience, and have been eager to turn to the
safer confines of an allegorical fiction to which "objective reality" can
be ascribed. I shall argue, on the contrary, that the experience of
Grace Abounding is continuous with that of the allegories, rather than
being raw material from which nobler substances are refined. There
are indeed significant differences from work to work, but these are a
function of the choices and possibilities that the works themselves entail, not of a simple development from psychological obsession to aesthetic objectivity.

   The best way to demonstrate this point is to consider the strange
and powerful work that Bunyan wrote in between the two parts of *The
Pilgrim's Progress.* The first part of *The Pilgrim's Progress* appeared in

1678, the second in 1684; meanwhile in 1682 Bunyan brought out *The Holy War,* an altogether different kind of allegory whose implications are far darker than those of the more famous one. Since *The Holy War* is little read today it will be useful to summarize it briefly. Shaddai (God) resides far away from Mansoul in the country of Universe. The town is infiltrated and governed, with its own consent, by Diabolus and his agents through the quisling Willbewill. Shaddai sends his son Prince Emmanuel to eject Diabolus and to live thereafter in the town, but under the influence of Mr. Carnal Security it forgets to honor him, he leaves, and Diabolus returns in greater strength than ever. This time Emmanuel is wrathful and long ignores the pleas of those citizens who realize their folly (although he leaves behind the Lord Secretary, the Holy Ghost, to convey his messages). At length when repentance is complete he returns to secure a second victory.

Throughout the narrative the most visible agent is Diabolus, and the most mysterious figure is the remote deity. In the sources that Bunyan is likely to have consulted, Shaddai is the wrathful God of power and vengeance, "the Mountain One," and Emmanuel is God as manifested in this world, "God with us."[45] As always in Bunyan, words strive against the Word. Diabolus, who is far cruder and nastier than the subtle Satan of *Paradise Lost,* effects his entrance into Mansoul by assaulting the Eargate, and God's forces likewise hurl themselves against that salient: "The King's captains had brought with them several slings and two or three battering-rams; with their slings, therefore, they battered the houses and people of the town, and with their rams they sought to break Eargate open."[46]

The metaphor of spiritual warfare is as old as the epistles of Paul, and is particularly pervasive in Calvin.[47] To some extent it underlies the whole of the Western tradition, for as Trilling rather somberly comments, "In our culture we connect the notion of courage or heroism with the religious life. We conceive of the perpetual enemy within and the perpetual enemy without, which must be 'withstood,' 'overcome,' 'conquered'—the language of religion and the language of fighting are in our culture assimilated to each other."[48] During the seventeenth century this imagery was especially pervasive. John Downame's massive treatise *The Christian Warfare,* based on the imagery of Ephesians 6, stresses the role of the individual believer as a foot soldier in a campaign fought between gigantic antagonists: "No sooner do we receive the Lord's press-money and set foot into his camp, but Satan advanceth against us his flags of defiance, labouring both by secret treachery and outward force to supplant and overcome us." Even the pacific Baxter found this sort of metaphor attractive: "Satan will not be charmed out of his possession; we must lay seige to the souls of sinners which are his garrisons, and find out where his strength lyeth, and lay the battery of God's ordinance against it, and ply it close till a breach be made."[49]

In passages like these the identity between inner and outer often seems blurred: the battles of the interior self are conflated with the battles of saints against sinners and of Roundheads against Cavaliers. Walzer makes the significant point that ideas and action drew close together during this period, as events acted out what had previously been metaphors.[50] But as in the instances studied by Greenblatt in a context of "cultural poetics," to define the self against the alien is to invite mutual destructiveness, so that "any achieved identity always contains within itself the signs of its own subversion or loss."[51] The Puritan triumph was peculiarly unstable, and as soon as it collapsed the war against Satan turned inward again: the enemy was not Charles I or Archbishop Laud but one's own rebellious self. *Unter friedlichen Umständen,* Nietzsche observes, *fällt der kriegerische Mensch über sich selber her*—"Under peaceful conditions the militant man attacks himself."[52] *Herfallen* is peculiarly expressive of externality, a "falling upon oneself" as if from outside; and this dividedness is precisely what Bunyan evokes in *The Holy War.*

The internalization of politics has perplexing implications for the allegory Bunyan wrote. It is easy enough to consider the various aspects of *The Holy War* simply as separate levels, which taken together establish the richness of the work. The history of mankind, of the church, of the British nation, and of the individual soul all enact the same story.[53] But on closer consideration, the relation of the militant saint to external enemies is very different from his strange inner-yet-outer relation to himself. In a study of the vogue for attacking Antichrist, Christopher Hill has shown that it began as a political schema, tracing in English history the dark prophecies of the Book of Revelation, and then moved inward: "Men no longer saw two armies lined up, Christ's elect against the synagogue of Antichrist, 'the anti-christian party': the Holy War is conducted inside each believer."[54] But as Bunyan's allegory suggests, there are still two armies ranged against each other. The real question is what has become of the self that harbors them.

This ambiguity persists throughout *The Holy War,* where Mansoul is sometimes presented as a collection of quarreling individuals, sometimes as a single one. At one point Diabolus refers to the town in the plural as "they" (p. 36), and at the very end Emmanuel addresses it in the singular as "thou" (p. 281). That the ambiguity is deliberate is suggested by the initial description of Mansoul as a "corporation" (p. 8), which in Bunyan's time, according to the *Oxford English Dictionary,* might mean "a number of persons united, or regarded as united, in one body," or in law "a body corporate legally authorized to act as a single individual; an artificial person." In just this way Bunyan's Mansoul both is and is not an individual, a corporation constantly threatening to disincorporate.

The psychomachia Bunyan chose to write clarifies the details of behavior by distributing them among a wide cast of characters (faculties, like Willbewill, and states of mind, like Mr. Carnal Security). But this clarification is obtained at the cost of dissolving any sense of the entire self as a coherent individual, a price which Bunyan is quite prepared to pay since it reflects his own experience. Puritans often spoke of the heart and enjoined believers to dedicate themselves to "heart-work," but in *Grace Abounding* Bunyan writes as if his heart were startlingly externalized: "I found also that whereas before my soul was full of longings after God, now my heart began to hanker after every foolish vanity; yea, my heart would not be moved to mind that that was good, it began to be careless both of my soul and heaven; it would now continually hang back both to, and in, every duty, and was as a clog on the leg of a bird to hinder her from flying" (pp. 25–26). The soul longs to soar away, the heart drags it back to earth, and the self is a hazy and unspecified container for both of them.

In other allegories which Bunyan knew, for example Richard Bernard's *The Isle of Man* (1626), the heart was dramatized in very human terms:

> The place [to find Sin] is a common inn, an harlot's house, called Mistress Heart, a receptacle for all villains, whores, and thieves. . . . But to cover her naughtiness as much as she may, she hath gotten into her house one called Old Man [i.e., the old Adam], corrupted by her deceitful lusts, to become her husband, when indeed she is his own daughter, and so live they in incest together, and keep rout and riot night and day.[55]

In *The Holy War* the heart is a structure, not a person, the interior castle that holds out even when the rest of the town has fallen, and whose doors are opened by faith to Christ: "Then was Captain Credence commanded also to come forth with his power to meet the Prince, the which was, as he had commanded, done; and he conducted him into the castle" (p. 130). In one sense this passage is a simple expansion of the text noted in the margin, "That Christ may dwell in your hearts by faith" (Ephes. 3:17), but in another sense it creates a distance by representing the heart, the deepest self, as something *other*.

To some extent this kind of thing may be a simple function of allegorizing, especially when the writer is unsophisticated. Thus Mr. Mind is wounded in the stomach (p. 225). Since "stomach" connoted courage, this simply means that the mind has become cowardly, yet there is something strange about the mind having a stomach. Other passages are stranger still, if less obviously so: "But oh! how the busy-bodies that were in the town of Mansoul did now concern themselves! They did run here and there through the streets of the town by companies, crying out as they ran in tumultuous wise, one after one manner, and another the quite contrary, to the almost utter distraction of Mansoul" (p. 118). In a marginal gloss Bunyan identifies the busy-bodies as "vain thoughts." So in effect thoughts are described as having thoughts. That this is commonplace in allegory should not blind us to its special appropriateness for Bunyan, whose deepest experience is of the fragmentation of a self that almost ceases to be a self at all. "But, poor hearts! as to themselves, their thoughts would change, and go upon all manner of extremes. Yea, through the working of them backward and forward, Mansoul became as a ball tossed, and as a rolling thing before the whirlwind" (p. 105).

The whole point of Puritan psychomachia, in autobiography as in allegory, is to displace unwanted aspects of the self by identifying them as agents of Satan. When Emmanuel returns to a penitent Mansoul he demands to know if the people in the town are in agreement, and they reply, "All the natives, Lord; but for the Diabolonians that came into our town when the tyrant got possession of us, we can say nothing for them" (p. 120). Bunyan glosses "the natives" as "powers of the soul" and "the Diabolonians" as "corruptions and lusts." In other words lusts are not really expressions of the self at all, but diabolical intruders which it has been seduced into admitting. So also with doubt, which tormented so many Puritans: Satan's final stratagem is to attack the town with an army of Doubters which is described as "outlandish," coming from outside. Mansoul is now pathetically helpless, in vivid imagery drawn from the recent wars in England:

> Now a man might have walked for days together in Mansoul, and scarce have seen one in the town that looked like a religious man. Oh, the fearful state of Mansoul now! Now every corner swarmed with outlandish Doubters; red-coats and black-coats walked the town by clusters, and filled up all the houses with hideous noises, vain songs, lying stories, and blasphemous language against Shaddai and his Son. . . . Nor did they partake or make stroy of any of the necessaries of Mansoul, but that which they seized on against the townsmen's will; what they could they hid from them, and what they could not, they had with an ill will. They, poor hearts, had rather have had their room than their company, but they were at present their captives, and their captives for the present they were forced to be. (p. 233)

In the margin Bunyan significantly cites Romans 7. And the happy ending, even when it comes, suggests how comprehensive were the

Anfechtungen that assaulted a sensitive Puritan: "Thus they buried in the plains about Mansoul the Election-doubters, the Vocation-doubters, the Grace-doubters, the Perseverance-doubters, the Resurrection-doubters, the Salvation-doubters, and the Glory-doubters; whose captains were Captain Rage, Captain Cruel, Captain Damnation, Captain Insatiable, Captain Brimstone, Captain Torment, Captain No-ease, Captain Sepulchre, and Captain Pasthope; and old Incredulity was, under Diabolus, their general" (p. 257).

In psychoanalytic terms these images are all projections of inner anxieties onto the outer world, repudiating the unconscious instead of coming to terms with it. Freud says that in certain neuroses "Impulses appear which seem like those of a stranger, so that the ego disowns them; yet it has to fear them and take precautions against them. The ego says to itself: 'This is an illness, a foreign invasion.' It increases its vigilance, but cannot understand why it feels so strangely paralyzed."[56] But the best that psychoanalysis can offer is a somber picture of the conflicts of the self. One can easily understand the attraction, for a conflicted personality, of a structure of explanation that allows the "true" self to reject the invading army instead of identifying it as the bearer of one's own deepest impulses. Freud's id precedes all morality; Bunyan's Satan is immorality. The id must be accommodated; evil can be demolished.

Here once again is the Christian myth that Milton dramatizes in *Paradise Lost,* according to which evil, though potent, is a latecomer in God's universe. "However *radical* evil may be," Ricoeur says, "it cannot be as *primordial* as goodness. The symbol of defilement already says this about the servile will, and it says it through the symbol of captivity; for when a country falls intact into the hands of the enemy, it continues to work, to produce, to create, to exist, but for the enemy; it is responsible but its work is alienated."[57] Indeed this idea is inseparable from Christianity, as for instance in Donne's memorable rendition:

> I, like an usurped town, to another due,
> Labor to admit You, but O, to no end;
> Reason, Your viceroy in me, me should defend,
> But is captived, and proves weak or untrue.[58]

All the paradoxes of freedom and bondage are embodied in this powerful metaphor. A distinguished editor of *The Holy War* speaks of "the cardinal role given to human free will,"[59] and it is certainly true that Willbewill, if fickle, is active and powerful. But the fundamental premise of Reformation theology is that the will can be *free* to act (because not physically restrained) and yet *obliged* to act in a predetermined way. As Hobbes put it in his controversy with Bishop Bramhall, one can have "freedom to do if he will" and still be altogether lacking in "freedom to will."[60]

In *The Holy War* it is Diabolus, not Emmanuel, who speaks grandly about freedom for mankind: "Your liberty also, as yourselves do very well know, has been greatly widened and enlarged by me; whereas I found you a penned-up people" (p. 23). But he later says less disingenuously to his supporter Lord Incredulity, "Thou shalt lay bands upon them that they may not resist thee, nor shall any of our vassals walk more at liberty but those that shall be content to walk in thy fetters" (pp. 65–66). The only answer, in Mansoul as in Donne's sonnet, is to beseech Christ to batter down the gates of the occupied town and take possession of the interior castle.

> What then shall we say to our Lord? Let him put no trust in his saints; let the Prince dwell in our castle, and make of our town a garrison; let him set his noble captains and his warlike soldiers over us. Yea, let him conquer us with his love and overcome us with his grace, and then surely shall he be but with us and help us, as he was and did that morning that our pardon was read unto us. (p. 128)

The dispersed self is reconstituted by surrendering to Christ, the only agent who can expel the satanic invader who is hated and yet desired.

As the metaphor of the occupied town suggests, this picture of experience is by no means unique to Bunyan, and it has important implications in both sociological and aesthetic terms. Sociologically, Bunyan has rebelled against his culture, and although he willingly endures persecution at the hands of the establishment, this cutting-off is bound to seem disturbing. For as Berger says,

> To go against the order of society is always to risk plunging into anomy. To go against the order of society as religiously legitimated, however, is to make a compact with the primeval forces of darkness. . . . When the socially defined reality has come to be identified with the ultimate reality of the universe, then its denial takes on the quality of evil as well as madness.[61]

Many conservatives, including some like Swift who were far from uncritical of the establishment, did indeed regard Puritans like Bunyan as insane. And Bunyan's temptation to sell Christ and embrace Satan reflects his own recurring suspicion that rebellion must be damnable. *The Holy War* arrives at a solution much like Milton's: just as Abdiel rebels against the rebel Satan, so must Mansoul. This means that Bunyan desperately needs the solidarity afforded by splinter-group sectarianism, which can turn the tables on the larger culture.

Surveying small communities that feel themselves threatened by the society in which they are embedded, Mary Douglas describes their tendency to smell out witchcraft as symptomatic of a need to define evil as an external and invasive force.

> For the social type I have called small group, the universe is divided between warring forces of good and evil. . . . The group boundary is the main definer of rights: people are classed either as members or strangers. Magical danger is associated with the idea of boundary. Evil is a foreign danger introduced by foreign agents in disguise. Group members accuse deviants in their midst of allowing the outside evil to infiltrate.[62]

The Holy War simply internalizes this opposition within the self, whose boundaries are threatened by the infiltration of evil, Satan's agents being represented very literally as foreign agents in disguise. "The typical agent in an allegorical fiction," Fletcher says, "has been seen as a daemon, for whom freedom of active choice hardly exists. This appears to have a major correlate in the theory of compulsive behavior, where it is observed that the mind is suddenly obsessed by an idea over which it has no control, which as it were 'possesses' the mind."[63] It is worth noting that the word "obsession" formerly meant invasion by a diabolical agent like an incubus; in that sense Bunyan would certainly have agreed that he was "obsessed."

Still it would be wrong to pretend that Bunyan's categories can be translated without disturbance into those of psychoanalysis or of literary criticism. Christ remains for Bunyan the Word who makes sense of human words and the master whose service is true freedom, and this implies a radical rejection of the world as we know it. For as Tuve observes, "The large literature of virtues battling with vices, which we are accustomed to think of solely as a great tableau of the psychomachia we call the moral struggle, had running through it another kind of image as well—the spirit's quest for a lost but native noblesse, regainable ultimately but not here."[64] "Yea, I will pull down this town and built it again," Emmanuel declares, "and it shall be as though it had not been, and it shall then be the glory of the whole Universe" (p. 98). Passages like this one undoubtedly imply the total renovation prophesied for the Apocalypse, which each individual may hope to experience in miniature in his inner life.[65] The wonderfully moving conclusion to *The Holy War* is a direct allusion to Revelation (2:24–25) in which Emmanuel declares, "O my Mansoul, how have I set my heart, my love upon thee, watch! Behold, I lay none other burden upon thee than what thou hast already. Hold fast till I come" (p. 285). Meanwhile, however, man must "live upon my Word" (p. 284) while fighting the good fight against the world, the flesh, and the Devil. Christ is God within us, but he is also our mediator with the offended Father, and in bleak times we can only communicate with him from

afar. "The road, I say, was now full of messengers, going and returning and meeting one another, some from the court [of God] and some
from Mansoul; and this was the work of the miserable town of Mansoul all that long, that sharp, that cold and tedious winter" (p. 183).

It is important to recognize that Puritan allegory does not just externalize unwanted aspects of the self; it externalizes *all* aspects of the
self. And in so doing, as Gerd Birkner argues in a penetrating analysis, it helps the individual to come to terms with the demands of an
extremely exigent faith. When the "soul's conflict" (the title of a treatise by Richard Sibbes) is played out at the level of the universal conflict between good and evil, what results is a liberating dialectic
between inner and outer. If self and salvation, as defined by dogma,
are divided in this world by an unbridgeable gulf, then the allegorical
mode offers an imaginative space in which they can be reunited, and a
foretaste of that perfect union with Christ which can never be felt as
more than provisional in this fallen world of doubt and darkness. As
Birkner puts it, the biographical subplot is conflated with the cos-
mographical main plot, and this frees the self from unresolvable anxiety about election. *Heilsweg* is harmonized with *Heilsgeschichte*, the
individual journey of the spirit with the universal history of God's
elect.[66] Then [Emmanuel] gave to each of the three, jewels of gold,
and precious stones, and took away their ropes, and put chains of
gold about their necks, and ear-rings in their ears. Now the prisoners
when they did hear the gracious words of Prince Emmanuel, and had
beheld all that was done unto them, fainted almost quite away; for the
grace, the benefit, the pardon, was sudden, glorious, and so big, that
they were not able without staggering to stand up under it" (p. 121).
Moreover, to dramatize God as Shaddai and Emmanuel is to personify him as a character in a narrative, throwing the emphasis on the
personal aspects of the deity which Puritan thought tended to minimize. As Birkner says (p. 112), the introverted God of Calvinist theology becomes an epic hero, and the interior struggle of the human
soul is made intelligible by translating it into the ultimate contest between good and evil.

The Pilgrim's Progress: *Doctrine and Word*

If one of the archetypal forms of allegory is the battle, the other is the
progress.[67] Bunyan's *The Pilgrim's Progress* stands in a complementary
relation to *The Holy War*, reunifying the divided self and dramatizing
its journey toward salvation in a hostile world. Or to put it differently,
The Pilgrim's Progress projects outward the psychomachia which *The
Holy War* treats internally, and its form imposes very different consequences upon the kind of story that the allegory can tell.

Bunyan's masterpiece is extraordinarily resistant to critical analysis,

partly because its naiveté isolates it—Macaulay remarks that Bunyan
"could not guess what place his allegory would occupy in English literature, for of English literature he knew nothing"[68]—and partly because it combines and confuses the theoretical categories with which
critics try to get a grip on the concept of allegory. It is easy, and not
altogether wrong, to conclude that *The Pilgrim's Progress* is an allegory
straining to become a novel, mimetic realism breaking through the
didactic bonds. Yet to see it so is to miss much that Bunyan cared
passionately about, and we can learn at least as much from the opposite procedure, pondering the allegorical elements in the early
novel. The special interest of *The Pilgrim's Progress*, indeed, lies in the
rich impurity of its combination of literary modes, which helps us to
see affinities between kinds of writing which theory might like to separate. What Bunyan has joined, let no one put asunder.

Modern thinking about allegory has taken two main forms, emphasizing either the ability of its images to denote universal truths, or else
insisting on their arbitrary nature. To some extent the latter position
is radical or postmodern, espoused by theorists like Paul de Man who
stress the paradox that allegory *looks* like vivid representation but concerns precisely those ideas and intuitions that cannot be represented;
the honesty of this arbitrary invention of signs is contrasted with the
grandiose claim of the Romantics (who despised "mere" allegory) to
reproduce ultimate reality in symbolic form.[69] And to some extent
the former position is old-fashioned, reflecting a medieval conviction
that allegories *are* symbolic since what they refer to really does exist:
"Allegory, in its referential aspect, pretends to name not things but
whatever lies under things."[70] But in practice it is impossible simply to
distinguish between an older and a newer way of thinking about allegory, since nearly every critic stresses both aspects—veracity and arbitrariness—depending on the questions being asked at the moment.
Thus C. S. Lewis declares roundly, "The allegorist leaves the given—
his own passions—to talk of that which is confessedly less real, which
is a fiction. The symbolist leaves the given to find that which is more
real."[71] But as A. D. Nuttall comments, our actual mental experience
is so elusive and mysterious that the term "given" is excessively optimistic, and he contrasts the "proto-Lewis" who asserts the artificiality of allegory with the quite different "deutero-Lewis" whose
analysis makes allegorical images seem more "real," because more
fully symbolic, than the data of experience from which they were supposed to start out.[72] What is at issue finally is the status of the reality
being represented, and this has as much to do with the philosophical
premises of the critic as it does with a given literary work.

As De Man's position suggests, the recent interest in semiotics and
hermeneutics has tended to rehabilitate allegory, which instead of
being despised as merely arbitrary is now celebrated as supremely

arbitrary. Maureen Quilligan somewhat chillingly declares, "Other genres appeal to readers as human beings; allegory appeals to readers as readers of a system of signs."[73] (This preoccupation has even invaded the parapraxes of advertising: the Oxford Press recently announced Bunyan's *A Few Sighs from Hell* as *A Few Signs from Hell*.) Such considerations might seem remote from Puritan hermeneutics, which insists on the absolute authority of the Bible as the basis of all symbolism. Yet it is also true that in *The Pilgrim's Progress* doctrine often has an uneasy relation to persons and events. What makes Bunyan peculiarly interesting is the unstable way in which his allegory shifts back and forth between two extremes: on the one hand, this world is the equivocal shadow of a truer world to which his signs point; on the other hand, this world is authoritatively allegorical and therefore the best embodiment of value and meaning. And his very naiveté gives special urgency (as we shall see later on) to the paradoxes of the author as creator.

From the point of view of Puritan theory, any distinction between sign systems and human life is illusory. The two are identical, since all persons, whether they ponder literary narratives or the divinely ordered narrative of their own lives, are compelled to interpret signs. This is why *The Pilgrim's Progress* ignores or abolishes the gap which critics postulate between literal sense and allegorical meaning. Life itself is for Bunyan continuously allegorical, a premise that cuts both ways since allegory is then free to be unembarrassed in its lifelikeness, even while claiming to illustrate abstract and universal truths. An older Catholic view of allegory, deriving from Augustine's technique of protecting the Bible from actually having to mean its more disturbing statements, might denigrate the literal "level" and leap beyond it.[74] But Puritans were deeply suspicious of any interpretation that did not ground meaning in the literal sense, and insisted that words merge with life. Bunyan, whose head was filled with scriptural texts that assaulted him unbidden, perfectly conforms to Quilligan's suggestion that "Language itself must be felt to have a potency as solidly meaningful as physical fact before the allegorist can begin; out of its magic phenomenality—out of language sensed in terms of a nearly physical presence—the allegorist's narrative comes, peopled by words moving about an intricately reechoing landscape of language" (p. 156). But Bunyan wrote at a time when Western culture was abandoning this "suprarealist" idea of language, and (apart from the Romantic episode of "spilt religion") was defining nonmimetic, nonreferential use of language as purely imaginary. The novel comes into being just at this critical moment, and *The Pilgrim's Progress* has much to tell us about the transition.

We shall return to these questions, but it must be by a roundabout route, for it is necessary first to explore the very different terms in

which Bunyan himself conceives of his work, and to show how it constantly strains against its own assumptions. One might be tempted to
proceed at once to the buried implications that he "really" intends,
but that would impose a false (if welcome) clarity on the problems
involved. Bunyan intends several things at once, and these are partly
compatible, partly incompatible. His aim is to dramatize Christian
doctrine by means of an allegorical narrative of the interior self, and
as we have already seen, doctrine and the Puritan idea of the self are
both filled with tensions. *Grace Abounding* and *The Holy War* are content to offer a circumstantial account of what the tensions felt like,
asserting that grace had healed them without really showing how. *The
Pilgrim's Progress* is committed to showing how, and thereby opens
itself to problems that are unresolvable but permanently interesting.

The original title of the work is *The Pilgrim's Progress from This World
to That Which is to Come, Delivered under the Similitude of a DREAM,* and
by far the largest word on the page is DREAM.[75] The analogy of
dreaming is in fact highly significant, suggesting both the imaginative
logic of Bunyan's images and the danger of giving too free a rein to
imagination. In his introductory verses he therefore asks the reader,
"Would'st thou be in a dream, and yet not sleep?" (p. 37). In *The
Pilgrim's Progress* sleep is a seductive alternative to pilgrimage, and
elsewhere Bunyan invokes it as a metaphor for spiritual danger: "If
thou art a little more stirred, [Satan] labours to rock thee sleep again,
by casting thee upon, and keeping thee in evil company, as among
rioters, drunkards, jesters, and other of his instruments, which he
employeth on purpose to keep thee secure, and so to ruin thy soul
and body for ever and ever."[76] The active pleasures of life are thus
imagined as a kind of nightmare somnolence, and Satan adopts the
tender action of rocking the cradle in a dreadful parody of God's
parental watchfulness. Bunyan recurs to the image of passive slumber
in *A Few Sighs from Hell,* where a hardened sinner "will lie like the
smith's dog at the foot of the anvil though the fire-sparks fly in his
face"; and again, "As a man that is fast asleep in an house, and that on
fire about his ears, and he not knowing of it, because he is asleep;
even so, because poor souls are asleep in sin, though the wrath of
God, the curse of his law, and the flames of hell have beset them
round about, yet they do not believe it because they are asleep in
sin."[77]

The Pilgrim's Progress must therefore be a special kind of dream
vision, inspired (as one of Bunyan's marginal glosses makes explicit)
by imprisonment in the jail which he allegorizes as "a den": "As I
walked through the wilderness of this world, I lighted on a certain
place, where was a den; and I laid me down in that place to sleep: and
as I slept I dreamed a dream" (p. 39). As *Grace Abounding* makes abundantly clear, this world did indeed seem a threatening wilderness to

Bunyan; to be locked up by worldly authority was to be liberated into the vision of order that the Bible represents, the explanatory dream that counteracts the nightmare of cradle-rocking Satan. For as Christiana says in the second part of *The Pilgrim's Progress,* "We need not, when a-bed, lie awake to talk with God; he can visit us while we sleep, and cause us then to hear his voice. Our heart oft times wakes when we sleep, and God can speak to that, either by words, by proverbs, by signs, and similitudes, as well as if one was awake" (p. 273).

The invitation "Would'st thou be in a dream, and yet not sleep?" actually suggests not dreaming but daydreaming, in which the imagination can play while remaining under rational control.[78] That dreaming is private and mysterious was obvious long before psychoanalysis; Herrick says in his little poem "Dreams,"

> Here we are all, by day; by night, we're hurled
> By dreams, each one into a several world.

The last thing Bunyan wants is private idiosyncrasy, and for him dreaming is therefore an analogy rather than a model. Fletcher suggests that "The allegorical vision differs crucially from the dream in that it is organized ritualistically, thus conforming rather to the 'waking dreams' of the compulsive or obsessional personality."[79] Since Bunyan, who was just such a personality, desperately feared the symptoms of compulsive daydreaming, he was particularly anxious to find his images confirmed by the infallible Word that makes sense of all reality.

After announcing the dream vision on his title page, Bunyan quotes Hosea 12:10, "I have used similitudes." In the tradition of typology God was imagined as the master allegorist who brings texts to life and permits life to be interpreted as a text. In Donne's often-quoted apostrophe,

> Neither art thou thus a figurative, a metaphorical God in thy word only, but in thy works too. The style of thy works, the phrase of thine actions, is metaphorical. The institutions of thy whole worship in the old law was a continual allegory; types and figures overspread all, and figures flowed into figures, and poured themselves out into farther figures. . . . How often, how much more often, doth thy Son call himself a way, and a light, and a gate, and a vine, and bread, than the Son of God, or of man? How much oftener doth he exhibit a metaphorical Christ, than a real, a literal?[80]

In a sense this sounds very modern (the Bible and life itself are fundamentally metaphorical); but only in a sense. For the metaphors exist to accommodate eternal truth to man's limited powers, and remain a means of communication rather than arrogating to themselves the status of reality. In Tyndale's words,

> When we have once found out Christ and his mysteries, then we may borrow figures, that is to say allegories, similitudes, or examples to open Christ, and the secrets of God hid in Christ, even unto the quick, and to declare them more lively and sensibly with them than with all the words of the world. For similitudes have more virtue and power with them than bare words, and lead a man's wits farther into the pith and marrow and spiritual understanding of the thing than all the words that can be imagined.[81]

Words in themselves are bare, and the similitudes that show forth *through* them are means of opening up the quick, the pith, the marrow. Bunyan makes the same point in the introductory verses to *The Pilgrim's Progress,* where biblical precedent for "dark figures" and "allegories" is asserted, but also their merely instrumental function:

> My dark and cloudy words they do but hold
> The truth, as cabinets enclose the gold.
>   (p. 34)

Every sentence in the Bible has a direct and specific meaning, and the chief goal of *The Pilgrim's Progress* is to exhibit those meanings in narrative guise.

The purpose of *Paradise Lost* was to reimagine biblical truth by dramatizing its myth anew, elaborating what had been elliptical and filling in the puzzling gaps in the story. Bunyan sees the Bible as a collection of one-sentence *texts,* and far from offering a parallel or supplementary myth as Milton does, he moves directly to the allegoresis that aspires to locate the meaning of each separate fragment of the Word. Milton operates in the tradition of midrash that interprets a sacred text (in Kermode's words) "by a process of augmenting the narrative."[82] Bunyan operates in a humbler tradition which, paradoxically, launches him into deep waters that Milton avoids. Since he takes every text to be independently decisive, the texts tend to develop their own unpredictable connections instead of conforming to authorial design, and at many points *The Pilgrim's Progress* wanders away from any strict didactic program.

Bunyan's essential purpose is expressed in the final lines of the introductory poem to the reader:

> Wouldest thou lose thyself, and catch no harm
> And find thyself again without a charm?
> Would'st read thyself, and read thou know'st not what

And yet know whether thou art blest or not,
By reading the same lines? O then come hither,
And lay my book, thy head and heart together.

(p. 37)

The reader loses himself (or herself) by surrender to a convincing
fictive universe, but since it is built up of scriptural texts it is also the
real universe, and so there is no need to suspend disbelief. He finds
himself by learning to read himself, to see how his own life recapitulates the authoritative texts, and he is thereby rescued (as Bunyan in
Grace Abounding struggles to be) from the prison of his own ego.
Above all he is helped to know "whether he is blest or not," whether
his election is sure, and thereby to look forward to the time when his
sinful self will be transformed, crossing the black river of death and
entering the heavenly city. *The Pilgrim's Progress* places the trials of the
self in a context that transcends the self, and takes its life from the
deep paradoxes of dogma. "If any man will come after me, let him
deny himself, and take up his cross, and follow me. For whosoever
will save his life shall lose it, and whosoever will lose his life for my
sake shall find it" (Matt. 16:24–25).

The root metaphors of *The Pilgrim's Progress* are drawn explicitly
from Scripture: the Old Testament patriarchs "were strangers and
pilgrims on the earth" (Heb. 11:13), and Christ declares "I am the
Way" (John 14:6). Bunyan's opening paragraph establishes the method of literalizing biblical metaphor, taking Christian's rags from Isaiah 64:6, his burden from Psalm 38:4, and so on. And as many critics
have noticed, the Bible both supplies Bunyan's images and stands as a
text *within* his text: "The shepherds answered, 'Have you not heard of
them that were made to err by hearkening to Hymeneus and Philetus,
as concerning the faith of the resurrection of the body?'" Individual
verses of Scripture can be used as weapons, literalizing the "sword of
the spirit,"[83] since the God who speaks the Bible can adapt it to every
individual case.

But as God would have it, while Apollyon was fetching of his last
blow thereby to make a full end of this good man, Christian
nimbly reached out his hand for his sword, and caught it, saying
Rejoice not against me, O mine enemy! when I fall I shall arise [Micah
7:8], and with that gave him a deadly thrust, which made him
give back as one that had received his mortal wound; Christian
perceiving that, made at him again, saying, *Nay, in all these things
we are more than conquerors through him that loved us* [Rom. 8:37].
(pp. 93–94)

But it is crucial to remember that no text is fully perspicuous in itself,
for in this life we see through a glass darkly and must struggle to

unravel meanings that are real enough yet maddeningly obscure.[84] "I
have formerly lived by hear-say and faith," Mr. Stand-fast says while
in the midst of the river of death, "but now I go where I shall live by
sight, and shall be with him in whose company I delight myself" (p.
372). The texts from Scripture are the necessary key with which to
unlock Bunyan's allegory, as he says in another place:

> Nor do thou go to work without my key,
> (In mysteries men soon do lose their way;)
> And also turn it right, if thou wouldst know
> My riddle, and wouldst with my heifer plough.
> It lies there in the window. Fare thee well,
> My next may be to ring thy passing-bell.[85]

The narrative is an enclosed place to be entered and then seen *out* of;
Bunyan's gloss identifies the window as "the margent," which is filled
with the scriptural references that explain the events of the story.

Bunyan's practice is in one sense naive, in another profound. It is
naive in that he assumes the mutual consistency of all the texts in that
great miscellany the Bible, and beyond that, their literal application to
his own life so far away from the ancient Middle East. "Remember, I
say, the Word that first laid hold upon you, . . . yea, how you sighed
under every hedge for mercy. Have you never a Hill Mizar [Psalm 42]
to remember? Have you forgot the close, the milk-house, the stable,
the barn, and the like, where God did visit your soul?"[86] But Bunyan's
practice is profound in its recognition that this interrelation of meanings, though decisive, is also problematic. Typology, the art by which
texts are related to each other and to life, is above all an art of interpretation; as has been well said,

> Typology, with its analogical basis, specializes in demonstrating
> or suggesting relationships between things that do not readily
> have resemblances. The typologist . . . does not say "A suggests
> B" or even "A (which is obscure) suggests B." Rather, the user of
> prefigurative imagery says "A (which is obscure) suggests—or
> shadows forth—B (which may also be obscure)." . . . The ty-
> pological relationship is one of the world's oldest literary codes
> and, potentially, one of the most difficult to decipher.[87]

The Word is recalcitrant; one of the functions of Bunyan's narrative
is to force it into action, allegorically, and thereby to force it to explain
itself. The marginal glosses are explanatory in that they refer the episodes to the scriptural "places" which they dramatize, but the episodes
in turn are explanatory in that they expand and clarify the "places."

In the Puritan imagination, interpretation is problematic because
words (as Milton so ruefully shows) are gravely infected by the consequences of the Fall. Knowledge without inner grace is empty, and

preachers constantly proclaimed that the only kind of knowledge worth having was "heart-knowledge"; Bunyan uses the expressive term "heart-work" (p. 122). But as Faithful tells the prattling Talkative, the heart itself is duplicitous: "Not that the heart can be good without knowledge, for without that the heart is naught; there is therefore knowledge, and knowledge: knowledge that resteth in the bare speculation of things, and knowledge that is accompanied with the grace of faith and love" (p. 118). Later on Christian warns Ignorance that "a man's heart may minister comfort to him in the hopes of that thing for which he yet has no ground to hope"; and when Ignorance tries to justify his sense of election by asserting "My heart tells me so, " Christian grimly replies that only the Word of God can bear true witness: "Yes, that is a good heart that hath good thoughts, and that is a good life that is according to God's commandments. But it is one thing indeed to have these, and another thing only to think so" (p. 185). Talk in itself is hollow, and ignorance is no excuse. The Shining Ones bundle Ignorance through trapdoor to Hell in the final lines of Part I, and the narrator comments, "Then I saw that there was a way to Hell, even from the Gates of Heaven, as well as from the City of Destruction. So I awoke, and behold it was a dream" (p. 205). The reader's work, in laying "my book, thy head and heart together" (p. 37), must be to meditate on scriptural truth so deeply that heart and head, life and text merge into unity.

The Pilgrim's Progress: *The Emblematic Self*

Huckleberry Finn's famous remark that *The Pilgrim's Progress* is "about a man that left his family it didn't say why"[88] contains an important insight: the book starts out from the unmotivated and unanalyzable moment of conversion, rejecting one's past self and past life. In a sense it begins like a novel from which the protagonist abruptly breaks away, leaving his familiar town for a mysterious world of mental space:

> So I saw in my dream that the man began to run. Now he had not run far from his own door, but his wife and children perceiving it began to cry after him to return; but the man put his fingers in his ears, and ran on crying, "Life, life, eternal life." So he looked not behind him, but fled towards the middle of the plain. The neighbours also came out to see him run, and as he ran some mocked, others threatened; and some cried after him to return. (p. 41)

Unsympathetic readers have often regarded Christian's flight as selfish, but that would make a travesty of the injunction which Bunyan notes in the margin, and which Evangelist later quotes directly: "If any man come to me, and hate not his father, and mother, and wife, and children, and brethren, and sisters, yea, and his own life also, he cannot be my disciple."[89] The crucial clause is "Yea, and his own life also": the egotist is at the farthest possible extreme from that surrender. But of course in its absoluteness it is appallingly painful, as Kierkegaard observes in quoting the same text from Luke: "This is a hard saying, who can bear to hear it? For this reason it is heard very seldom. This silence, however, is only an evasion which is of no avail." Kierkegaard adds, "To exist as the individual is the most terrible thing of all."[90]

To outsiders, the radical aloneness of the Puritan looks like mental illness, as Worldly-Wiseman indicates in recommending the help of Legality: "He hath skill to cure those that are somewhat crazed in their wits with their burdens" (p. 50). But "legality" is precisely what is wrong with the reprobate world, and the Puritan is therefore committed to rejecting that world utterly, even when it means a permanent break with loved ones. As an ordinary sea captain described his emigration to New England (with a clear reminiscence of the text in Luke), "It was God that did draw me by his Providence out of my father's family, and weaned me from it by degrees. . . . It was God by his Providence that made me willing to leave my dear father, and dear brethren and sisters, my dear friends and country."[91] If even those whom one loves are to be rejected, then it is all the easier to reject everything else. "I leave you far off," Jonathan Edwards sternly told the ungrateful people of Northampton in his farewell sermon, "aliens and strangers, wretched subjects and captives of sin and Satan, and prisoners of vindictive justice; without Christ, and without God in the world."[92] Fish comments that when Christian is remanded back to prison at Vanity Fair, he is condemned to endure "the prison of this life" from which death has set Faithful free.[93]

In *The Pilgrim's Progress* Christian's guilt is represented as a heavy burden, and its relation to the sacred text is deeply thought-provoking. In the opening paragraph he is introduced as a man with "a book in his hand, and a great burden upon his back" (p. 39). Some time later, when Worldly-Wiseman asks "How camest thou by thy burden at first?" Christian replies, "By reading this book in my hand" (p. 49). What has happened, exactly as Paul describes it in Romans, is that the book has *created* the burden by making the sinner aware of the unappeasable Law. "I had not known sin, but by the law; for I had not known lust, except the law had said, Thou shalt not covet. . . . For I was alive without the law once, but when the commandment came, sin revived, and I died" (Rom. 7:7–9). As Paul explains in rather tortuous language, it is not that the law makes sinful what would otherwise have been sinless, but rather that it identifies sin as a necessary prelude to overcoming it. But in itself the Law is merciless, as Christian discovers when he stands trembling below Sinai: "There came words and fire out of the mountain under which poor Christian stood, that made the hair of his flesh stand. The words were thus pronounced, *As many as are of the works of the law, are under the curse; for it is written, Cursed is every one that continueth not in all things which are written in the book of the law to do them*" (p. 55). The text here is from the Epistle to the Galatians (3:10), and it is no accident that it was Luther's commentary on Galatians which, as Bunyan reports in *Grace Abounding*, rescued him from the agonies of "a wounded conscience" (p. 41).

Once again we confront the paradoxes of servitude in which freedom to sin means the most drastic kind of unfreedom. In Luther's thought, sin lies "sleeping" until the law identifies it; in analogies borrowed from Augustine, the law is like the water that makes quicklime begin to boil, or the wind that makes a fire flare up. The more a sinner is aware of the law, the more his or her sinful desires rise up in resentment *against* it and yet in response *to* it. The wages of sin is death, and the law, by disclosing man's radical sinfulness, delivers him over to death. Just as Satan acts as God's involuntary policeman, so the law is the agent of divine wrath (*Amt des Zornes, ministerium irae Dei*). We thus have, as Herbert Olsson observes, "a complex interconnection between the Law on the one hand, and on the other hand sin, God's wrath, death, hell, and the Devil."[94] Luther goes so far as to declare that there is no difference between slavery to the law and to sin. Man is a slave to the law (*servus legis*) because it exacts works which he can never satisfy, and he hates it as an implacable master; simultaneously he is a slave to sin (*servus peccati*), the very condition that makes it impossible to satisfy the Law.[95] In *The Pilgrim's Progress* Moses mercilessly knocks down all who "transgress his law" (p. 106).

Bunyan's doctrinal position is identical with Luther's and is concisely expressed in his didactic writings: "Thus the poor soul is most horribly carried away headlong, and thrown down violently under the curse of the Law, under which it is held all its days, if God of his mere mercy prevent not; and at the end of its life doth fall into the very belly of Hell."[96] What *The Pilgrim's Progress* contributes is not escape from dogma, but allegorical imagery that gives the dogma intelligible shape. Immediately after the episode of Mount Sinai, Christian is admitted at the Wicket Gate ("Knock and it shall be opened unto you") and begins to journey along the one true Way. He is now conscious of election, though like Bunyan still subject to grievous doubts, and is ready for the course in hermeneutics provided by Interpreter's House, where he is shown both pictures and scenes in motion. One of these manifestations so richly conveys the spirit of Bunyan's allegory that it deserves to be considered at length:

Then [Interpreter] took him by the hand, and led him into a very large parlour that was full of dust, because never swept; the which, after he had reviewed a little while, the Interpreter called for a man to sweep: now when he began to sweep, the dust began so abundantly to fly about, that Christian had almost therewith been choked. Then said the Interpreter to a damsel that stood by, "Bring hither water, and sprinkle the room," which when she had done, was swept and cleansed with pleasure.

Then said Christian, "What means this?"

The Interpreter answered: "This parlour is the heart of a man that was never sanctified by the sweet grace of the Gospel; that dust is his original sin, and inward corruptions that have defiled the whole man. He that began to sweep at first is the Law, but she that brought water and did sprinkle it is the Gospel. Now, whereas thou sawest that so soon as the first began to sweep, the dust did so fly about that the room by him could not be cleansed, but that thou wast almost choked therewith, this is to show thee that the Law, instead of cleansing the heart (by its working) from sin, doth revive, put strength into, and increase it in the soul, even as it doth discover and forbid it, for it doth not give power to subdue." (p. 61)

Well-meaning critics sometimes claim that Bunyan's meaning is fully embodied in narrative, as if his narrative were a novel. Even Lewis condemns "the pernicious habit of reading allegory as if it were a cryptogram to be translated" on the grounds that "that method leads you continually out of the book back to the conception you started from and would have had without reading it."[97] But Bunyan, like many other Puritans, regarded life itself as a cryptogram, and it is precisely his aim to lead us out of his book into the permanent truths that it conveys. The emblem of the dusty room requires interpretation:

> I also know, a dark similitude
> Will on the fancy more itself intrude,
> And will stick faster in the heart and head,
> Than things from similes not borrowèd.
> (p. 215)

It is not just that the image makes the point easier to remember, but also that the effort to understand it causes it to "intrude" into the awakened "fancy."

Interpreter's scene brilliantly captures the imaginative basis of the theology of the Law, which in the earlier and simpler images was represented as a threatening landmark (Mount Sinai) and as a brutal assailant (Moses). Here it is a continuous and ever more disagreeable *process*, in which the act of cleaning (the sweeping) produces the opposite of what it intends (the swirling dust). In a sense the scene is static since it performs one action only, but that is exactly how the

Puritans thought of human life: a dreadful repetition of the same disastrous activity over and over again. Dust is a brilliant image for sin because it is so gradual and inevitable; it always accumulates in any room (since the Fall, anyway) and the question is what to do about it. The apparently obvious solution, to ply the broom of the old Law, moves the dust about but also makes it worse, exactly as Paul says in the Epistle to the Romans. So the Law does indeed become punitive, just as Luther holds; in illustrating this scene Blake depicts the broom-wielding Law as a black devil.[98] At the same time, however, sin is fundamentally *external,* a miasma that settles at your feet and then chokes you like a dust storm. And this too is fundamental to Puritan dualism, for if sin is a ubiquitous pollution it is also something alien which God's grace can help us to escape. The mercy of the Gospel has been joined to the justice of the Law, and Christian now understands the difference between himself and the dusty room "that was never sanctified by the sweet grace of the Gospel." As he says some pages further on, "My name is now Christian, but my name at the first was Graceless" (p. 79). Theologically speaking no elected Christian can ever be graceless, but like Bunyan himself he may need years to know his election, and this too is implied in the emblem of the dust, which is still there when the water has settled it, but ceases to dominate one's perception because the Gospel has subdued it.

The extended allegory of *The Pilgrim's Progress* superbly captures the essential Puritan duality of outward militancy and inward passivity. Unlike spiritual autobiographies (including Bunyan's) it begins at the decisive moment of conversion rather than tracing the steps that lead to it, and its purpose is therefore to admonish and encourage the elect in the trials that must continue until death.[99] Once launched on the Way there can be no respite except in appointed places of refreshment like the House Beautiful; at all other times exhausting struggle is obligatory. "I must venture: to go back is nothing but death, to go forward is fear of death, and life everlasting beyond it. I will yet go forward" (p. 75). This is exactly the existential leap that Bunyan makes at the end of *Grace Abounding*—"Lord Jesus, if thou wilt catch me, do; if not, I will venture for thy Name" (p. 101)—but what was there a surrender is now an activity.

So the tone of the book is finely suspended between two attitudes which might seem contradictory but in Puritan experience were both deeply felt: the conviction of election which no power can possibly repeal, and the duty to avoid complacency and engage in unending struggle. By spreading out the myth in extended narrative, Milton, who fervently believes in free will, dramatizes a kind of determinism. Bunyan, whose theology is essentially determinist, atomizes the myth into isolated moments, and this allows him to give a *feeling* of autonomous action within a universe controlled irresistibly by grace. However much he sometimes resembles a character in a novel, Bunyan's protagonist is not so much a man undergoing experiences as a self encountering aspects of itself. To externalize them in this way is to make them less threatening, for it is always easier to face dangers from without than from within. Bunyan, indeed, was one of those Puritans who courted persecution, since the authorities seem to have been genuinely willing to negotiate a compromise by which he could be released from prison. Bunyan *needed* prison, and it is no wonder that he identified with Paul: "Therefore I take pleasure in infirmities, in reproaches, in necessities, in persecutions, in distresses for Christ's sake; for when I am weak, then am I strong" (2 Cor. 12:10). As with Luther, inadmissible aspects of the self are made bearable by externalizing them as *Anfechtungen;* but the procedure is anything but shallow, since the theology of bondage to Satan allows the simultaneous recognition that the hated assailants have been welcomed by the treacherous self.

In *The Holy War,* whose central theme this is, we found it hard to locate the self whose parts behaved in so fragmented a way. *The Pilgrim's Progress* handles the matter more subtly, though not with greater logical consistency: parts of the self are externalized as tempters and assailants, but Christian remains *a* self who strives against them. Discussing *The Pilgrim's Progress* as a prison book, Sharrock comments very suggestively, "The body becomes dehumanized, a thing done to, and in compensation the spirit creates a world of its own."[100] The body is doubly imprisoned, by the flesh as well as by literal jailers, and since the allegorical narrative is cast in terms of body, the "thing done to" is also imaged as a collection of highly aggressive agents. Once again the status of the self grows mysterious, exactly as the Christian paradox requires, for one must lose one's self in order to find it:

> Wouldest thou lose thyself, and catch no harm
> And find thyself again without a charm?
>
> (p. 37)

The loss of self in this special sense can be profoundly consoling, since it implies a successful rejection of whatever is felt to be unacceptable. *Grace Abounding* poignantly records Bunyan's lifelong temptation to blaspheme, and *The Pilgrim's Progress*—in a passage in which the narrating "dreamer" stresses his role as interpreter—explains how this can be:

> One thing I would not let slip, I took notice that now poor Christian was so confounded that he did not know his own voice, and thus I perceived it: just when he was come over against the mouth of the burning pit, one of the wicked ones got behind

him, and stepped up softly to him, and whisperingly suggested many grievous blasphemies to him which he verily thought had proceeded from his own mind. This put Christian more to it than anything that he met with before, even to think that he should now blaspheme him that he loved so much before; yet, could he have helped it, he would not have done it; but he had not the discretion neither to stop his ears, nor to know from whence those blasphemies came. (p. 98)

Christian does not "know his own voice" because it is *not* his own voice, and as Bunyan's gloss makes clear he is deceived by an empty making-believe: "Christian made believe that he spoke blasphemies, when 'twas Satan that suggested them into his mind." Yet it is after all *his* mind into which they have been suggested, and if psychoanalysis would hold that they are indeed Christian's (or Bunyan's) un-acknowledged wishes, Bunyan might well agree. Only the intervention of Christ can heal the self by permanently ejecting its evil aspects. Immediately after this passage we read, "When Christian had travelled in this disconsolate condition some considerable time, he thought he heard the voice of a man, as going before him, saying, *'Though I walk through the Valley of the Shadow of Death, I will fear none ill, for thou art with me'*." The biblical text both generates the allegorical image (the valley of the shadow) and provides the means of escape from it.

Bunyan's most remarkable image of externalized temptation is Doubting Castle with its master the giant Despair. A long theological tradition had established that despair (like everything else) takes opposed forms, the good *tristitia* that provokes repentance and the bad *tristitia* that sins against the Holy Spirit by abandoning hope of salvation.[101] During the Reformation this distinction was further sharpened, Luther for instance insisting that the necessary prelude to salvation was a recognition that one was condemned to death under the old Law: "The commandments . . . are intended to teach man to know himself, that through them he may recognize his inability to do good and may despair of his own ability."[102] This is the spirit of Wesley's paradox, in the challenge that Jacob proclaims to the angel:

> Yield to me now—for I am weak,
> But confident in self-despair.[103]

One way of imagining despair is simply to personify it as Spenser does in a brilliant passage in *The Faerie Queene* (I.ix), where it confronts the Red Cross Knight as an ordinary man in a state *of* despair, with unkempt locks and bewildered gaze. Despair's tactic there is to identify God (just as Milton's Satan does) with "fate" and "strong necessity" and "destiny" (I.ix.42), and in seductive rhythms to lull the knight into accepting an inevitable death.

> Is not his law, Let every sinner die:
> Die shall all flesh? What then must needs be done,
> Is it not better to do willingly,
> Than linger till the glass be all out-run?
> Death is the end of woes: die soon, O faeries' son.
> $\qquad$ (I.ix.47)

Just as Luther suggests, Despair is here a spokesman for the old Law, and its symptom is an acceptance of that Law as fully descriptive of the self.

There is in fact in *The Pilgrim's Progress* an example of this internalized condition, the Man in the Iron Cage who feels irrevocably cut off from Christ:

> I have crucified him to myself afresh. I have despised his person, I have despised his righteousness, I have counted his blood an unholy thing, I have done despite to the spirit of grace: therefore I have shut myself out of all the promises; and there now remains to me nothing but threatenings, dreadful threatenings. . . . God hath denied me repentance; his word gives me no encouragement to believe; yea, himself hath shut me up in this iron cage. (pp. 66–67)

For the reprobate, despair is perfectly appropriate; grace is indeed withheld from him, and he has no part in God's promises. The despair that Christian confronts is very different, a crude giant who throws him and Hopeful into a dungeon, beats them with a club, and invites them to kill themselves. They escape not by fighting or refuting him but simply by recognizing his impotence: "'What a fool,' quoth he, 'am I, thus to lie in a stinking dungeon, when I may as well walk at liberty. I have a key in my bosom, called promise, that will (I am persuaded) open any lock in Doubting-Castle'" (p. 156).

Many of the allegorical details were available in earlier Puritan writers like Perkins and Goodwin: the dungeon, the giant's intermittent "fits after the manner of an ague" (Perkins), the temptation to suicide, and the Gospel as the key that sets Christian and Hopeful free. These details are all drawn from folktale romances, of which Jack the Giant-Killer is a famous variant.[104] From both a theological and an imaginative point of view, this robust externalization is wholly appropriate, for by definition the elect cannot despair, even if they temporarily think they do when they forget the promise. As Una asks Red Cross after helping him to break free, "Why shouldst thou then despair, that chosen art?" (I.ix.53). Bunyan represents Despair in familiar images of oppression from without: not just the ogre of romance, but also the heartless landowner who has caught a couple of poor men trespassing on his property.[105] Sin is a burden that Christian carries on his back, but it is a burden that can be detached, and guilt—that tormentor of every Puritan soul—is likewise an external agent that assails those whose faith is weak. "With that, Guilt with a great club that was in his hand struck Little-faith on the head, and with that blow felled him flat to the ground where he lay bleeding as one that would bleed to death" (p. 164).

To a modern taste all of this externalizing may seem to miss the point. We are likely to be attracted to psychologized myths like that of Blake, who alludes to Bunyan's Despair in his account of the dire Spectre of Urthona that symbolizes the self-tormenting imagination,[106] and who depicts Christian's burden pictorially as a dreadful polypus that grows organically out of his back (see p. 166). But the romance convention also has its psychological appropriateness, as Frye indicates:

> Because of the frequency [in romance] of the convention of escape, we may sometimes feel that there is something illusory about the dungeon or whatever: however dark and thick-walled, it seems bound to turn into a womb of rebirth sooner or later. This theme is clearest when the romance has allegorical overtones, as in the prison of Orgoglio in *The Faerie Queene* or of Giant Despair in *The Pilgrim's Progress*. There is also in this case some connection with the atmosphere of a nightmare, from which one can always escape by waking up.[107]

Release from despair is indeed felt as an unexpected shift of mood, a sudden recovery of one's better self rather than a gradual process of introspection, and for that reason it can well be represented as escape from a grotesque giant who suddenly loses his power to harm.

As Bunyan understands it, the ultimate reason for this escape is theological, not psychological: the mental distress of *Grace Abounding* would be endless but for the unmerited intervention of Christ the Savior. Annotating the passage about the fiend that whispers blasphemies, Coleridge comments,

> [This] distemper of the imagination . . . can scarcely not happen under any weakness and consequent irritability of the nerves to persons continually occupied with spiritual self-examination. . . . Luther is the great model; ever reminding the individual that not he, but Christ, is to redeem him; and that the way to be redeemed is to think with will, mind, and affections on Christ, and not on himself. I am a sin-laden being, and Christ has promised to loose the whole burden if I but entirely trust in him. To

William Blake, "Christian Reading in His Book," watercolor. Copyright the Frick Collection, New York.

torment myself with the detail of the noisome contents of the fardel will but make it stick the closer first to my imagination and then to my unwilling will.[108]

Imprisoned within his obsessive mind, the Bunyan of *Grace Abounding* is always in danger of falling back into this tormented state. The reader who loses himself in *The Pilgrim's Progress,* with its promise of grace that both generates action and rewards it, is thereby encouraged to break free of the "unwilling will" that interprets Satan's promptings not as threats from without but as initiatives from within.

Since this liberation is only possible through Christ, the Cross must be the central symbol of *The Pilgrim's Progress,* and the way in which it is presented is a fascinating example of narrative expounding emblem. Evangelist warns Christian, first of all, that Worldly-Wiseman likes morality because "it saveth him from the Cross," and urges him to keep journeying toward it (p. 53). Next comes the instructional interlude of Interpreter's House, and after that the crucial epiphany:

> He ran thus till he came at a place somewhat ascending; and upon that place stood a Cross, and a little below in the bottom, a sepulchre. So I saw in my dream that just as Christian came up with the Cross, his burden loosed from off his shoulders, and fell from off his back; and began to tumble, and so continued to do till it came to the mouth of the sepulchre, where it fell in, and I saw it no more.
>
> Then was Christian glad and lightsome, and said with a merry heart, "He hath given me rest, by his sorrow, and life, by his death." Then he stood still a while, to look and wonder; for it was very surprising to him that the sight of the Cross should thus ease him of his burden. He looked therefore, and looked again, even till the springs that were in his head sent the waters down his cheeks. (pp. 69–70)

This is indeed surprising, and is explained by the inner process by which a bare sign or emblem is transformed into a living symbol. In itself it is a blank and unremarkable object, like the market cross to be seen in many English towns. What it *means* is very different: the whole story of Christ's life as a man, and the mysterious sacrifice by which the death of that man is an act of saving love by God.

In *Some Gospel-Truths Opened* Bunyan proclaims, against the Quaker notion of a purely symbolic Christ, that "the man Christ rose again out of the grave with the same body which was crucified and laid in the grave, and was taken up above the clouds into heaven with the same real body."[109] And in another doctrinal work he meditates movingly on the human suffering that Christ endured (with italics that are worth preserving for their expressiveness):

My God, my God, saith he, *why hast thou forsaken me?* now in my *greatest* extremity; now *sin* is laid upon me, the *curse* takes hold on me, the *pains* of *hell* are clasped about me, and thou hast *forsaken* me. O sad! Sinner, this was not done in *pretence,* but in reality; not in *show,* but in very *deed;* otherwise Christ had *dissembled,* and had not spoken the *truth;* but the truth of it, his *bloody* sweat declares, his mighty *cries* declares, the things what, and for what he suffered declares. Nay, I must say this much, that all the *damned* souls in *hell,* with all their *damnations,* did never yet *feel* that torment and *pain,* that did this blessed Jesus in a *little* time.[110]

But however vividly Bunyan imagines Christ's sufferings, he knows that they can only be imagined, and he fully shares the Puritan iconoclasm that is expressed (for instance) by William Perkins:

Behold him often, not in the wooden crucifix after the Popish manner, but in the preaching of the word, and in the sacraments, in which thou shalt see *him crucified* before thine eyes, Gal. 3:1. Desire not here upon earth to behold him with the bodily eye, but look upon him with the eye of truth and lively faith, applying him and his merits to thy self as thine own, and that with broken and bruised heart, as the poor Israelites stung with fiery serpents even to death, beheld the brasen serpent.[111]

Just as the crucifixion was typologically anticipated by an emblem (the brazen serpent) so it is to be remembered by an emblem (the Cross), but not by a lifelike representation of the tortured body of Christ, for that would turn the emblem into an image whose specific potency would get in the way. Christ did suffer on the cross, but as always in Puritan thinking what is crucial is the death of the immortal and unchanging God, which is literally unimaginable and should be kept free of physically limiting imagery.

So Bunyan's Christian is confronted with the Cross, is astonished to feel his burden fall away, and then stands in meditation to try to understand what this means—"He looked therefore, and looked again." Only later on, when Christian recounts the event to Piety, does the reader learn what was happening: "I went but a little further, and I saw one, as I thought in my mind, hang bleeding upon the tree; and the very sight of him made my burden fall off my back" (pp. 81–82). *As I thought in my mind* perfectly captures Bunyan's sense of an allegory that bodies forth interior states but never forgets their interiority. We only understand in retrospect how an emotional response transformed the Cross as emblem into the Cross as symbol. Christian comes to *a* cross, and in meditating on its amazing power he perceives it to be *the* Cross.

Once again, Bunyan's apparently naive mode of allegory permits him to express the deepest paradoxes of Christian faith, in which the unimaginable becomes human. Auden's reflections on Christian art are profoundly relevant here:

> The Incarnation, the coming of Christ in the form of a servant who cannot be recognized by the eye of flesh and blood, but only by the eye of faith, puts an end to all claims of the imagination to be the faculty which decides what is truly sacred and what is profane. A pagan god can appear on earth in disguise but, so long as he wears his disguise, no man is expected to recognize him nor can. But Christ appears looking just like any other man, yet claims that He is the Way, the Truth and the Life, and that no man can come to God the Father except through Him. The contradiction between the profane appearance and the sacred assertion is impassible to the imagination.[112]

Auden has in mind the difficulty, endemic to Christian painting, of representing the God-Man without making him a man and not a god. In classical myth apparent humanness is due either to deliberate deception by the god, or else to an ironic failure of comprehension, as when Pentheus in *The Bacchae* refuses to recognize Dionysus in the mysteriously smiling stranger. In the Christian myth the incomprehensible is made visible, but that only sharpens the paradox.

By paring icons down to minimal form—just as they smashed the faces of statues in English churches—the Puritans insisted on the conceptual rather than literal significance of what they imagined, even while affirming that Christ had literally lived on earth and yet was literally God. Only after crossing the river of death might they hope to see directly what they had had to peer at through the glass of emblems, as the Shining Ones tell Christian: "In that place you must wear crowns of gold, and enjoy the perpetual sight and visions of the Holy One, *for there you shall see him as he is*" (p. 201; 1 John 3:2). Until that time God speaks to man, just as in *Paradise Lost* after the Fall, through types and symbols and enigmatic traces. But he does speak, and what makes communication possible is that he lives *within* us, where we bear his image as an earnest of eventual union. "We all, with open face beholding as in a glass the glory of the Lord, are changed into the same image from glory to glory, even as by the Spirit of the Lord" (2 Cor. 3:18).

In Part II of *The Pilgrim's Progress* Mercy asks for and receives a looking glass, glossed in the margin as "the Word of God," which merges the image of the crucified Christ with that of the individual person who bears it.

> Now the glass was one of a thousand. It would present a man, one way, with his own feature exactly, and turn it but another way, and it would show one the very face and similitude of the

Prince of pilgrims himself. Yea I have talked with them that can
tell, and they have said, that they have seen the very crown of
thorns upon his head, by looking in that glass, they have therein
also seen the holes in his hands, in his feet, and his sides. (pp.
345–46)

Richard Mather had written similarly, some years earlier, "By much
beholding the glory of the Lord in the glass of the Gospel, we are
changed into the same image."[113] In reading the Bible, as in reading
the allegory which Bunyan intends as a sustained dramatization of its
images, the believer sees himself and Christ in himself; but he sees
both in the medium of the glass, a figure that superbly expresses identity and otherness at once. The mirror, which traditionally symbolizes
both art and narcissism, is here subsumed by a divine personality that
authenticates art and liberates the self from the prison of selfhood.[114]
The mirror of mimesis is transformed into the glass of allegory.

The Pilgrim's Progress: *Allegory and Novel*

Critics have long regarded *The Pilgrim's Progress* as a kind of proto-
novel, sometimes on the relatively trivial grounds that it has "realistic"
language and characters, sometimes on subtler grounds such as Iser's
claim that Calvinist predestination could only be borne by giving a
new significance to subjective experience.

> Christian's story is one of an increasing self-awareness, and in
> this respect it is indisputably a novel, or at least a novel in the
> making. Self-awareness requires experience, and this is what
> Christian gains in his confrontation with the world. In the novel,
> experience is the keynote of the action, whereas in the epic and
> allegory everything was subsidiary to the idea.[115]

Attractive though it is, this kind of explanation perhaps raises more
questions than it answers. Self-awareness and experience are surely
fundamental in earlier writers whom nobody would call novelists, and
Iser does not inspire confidence with his breezy claim that "Mere allegory is surpassed through the sheer aliveness of the characters" (p. 3),
or that "It is through this inner self that the character outstrips the
allegory" (p. 16). For the characters seem at many points program-
matic rather than sheerly alive (surely Chaucer's are more so) and the
interiority of the work applies to the experience of all men and wom-
en, not of novelistic individuals. Still less can one endorse the initial
premise of Iser's book that "The history of the novel as a 'genre' began in the eighteenth century, at a time when people had become
preoccupied with their own everyday lives" (p. xi)—as if the contemporaries of Langland or Shakespeare were not.

Yet *The Pilgrim's Progress* does, after all, have deep affinities with the novel, even if these are complex and hard to define. The discussion just completed should suggest a real duality in the idea of the self implied in this work, on the one hand living in an experiential world as Iser suggests, but on the other hand dispersed into externalized entities and arrested in separate moments of emblematic stasis. Above all we have to remember that Bunyan is not testing biblical doctrine by the standard of lived experience, but on the contrary is seeking to interpret experience in the light of doctrine. It might be said that the eighteenth-century novel emerges not from the simple transformation of allegory into circumstantial narrative, but rather from the jolting that occurs when the two modes run uneasily in harness together.

Just because spiritual truth is so hard to imagine and to integrate with living, Bunyan is drawn irresistibly to the novelistic devices that critics have always noticed in his work. But he regards them with profound suspicion, and seeks at every point to detach them from corporeal reality—a hard thing to do, since in his allegory spirit is expressed by body—by recalling them to the nonspatial and nontemporal world toward which man's earthly journey leads. Hill reminds us that it is Milton rather than Bunyan who is this-worldly: "Bunyan's *Pilgrim's Progress* is about getting to heaven, where we seek our reward; all Milton's great poems are about living on earth."[116] In Bunyan's view the world we live in is totally inverted, as the people of Mansoul unwittingly testify when they have sold out to Satan and fear God's agents: "Help, help! The men that turn the world upside down are come hither."[117] The Royalists did indeed accuse the Puritans of turning the world upside down,[118] and Bunyan here reverses the accusation, implying that the world was upside down to begin with and could only be set upright again by Puritan other-worldliness.

Not even our inmost selves are to be trusted (remember the duplicity of the "heart") unless we break free from self and live as if in the other world. So Evangelist tells Christian,

> You are not yet out of the gun-shot of the Devil: you have not resisted unto blood, striving against sin: let the Kingdom be always before you, and believe steadfastly concerning things that are invisible. Let nothing that is on this side [of] the other world get within you; and above all, look well to your own hearts, and to the lusts thereof; for they are deceitful above all things, and desperately wicked: set your faces like a flint, you have all power in heaven and earth on your side. (p. 123)

A flinty countenance can repel the Devil's gunshots, and the eye of faith can penetrate the disguises of the heart, but only if the seductions of the fallen world are repudiated. When Christian says that he is journeying to Mount Sion, Atheist laughs uproariously and replies, "There is no such place as you dream of in all this world." That is of course true in a literal sense, since the allegory describes a spiritual world for which our physical one is but a metaphor, but in a deeper sense it is untrue, since *The Pilgrim's Progress* is a dream whose allegorical world *is* the real world. To Atheist's forceful monosyllables Christian replies with equal force, "But there is in the world to come" (p. 174). As Fish observes, Atheist is an empiricist who "refuses to consider the existence of anything that cannot be confined within the structures of time, space, and reason."[119] He is a comfortable inhabitant of the world of Hobbes and Locke, and his preferred literary form would doubtless be the mimetic novel. Bunyan, on the other hand, transposes even landscape details into a mental world where ordinary space-time values do not apply, and where what one sees is a function of one's spiritual condition rather than of the objective environment.[120] Likewise time is the *kairos* of a perpetual "Gospel-day," not the developing *chronos* of ordinary experience.[121] And these emphases are quite simply those of Christianity itself, whose sacred narratives are filled with circumstantial detail and yet insist on a scheme of interpretation that transcends the world of the familiar. *Figura* is a means of understanding existence, not just a literary device; Auerbach contrasts the sensory realism of Tacitus and Petronius, who obey the conventions of specific aesthetic traditions, with the conflict in the Gospels "between sensory appearance and meaning, an antagonism which permeates the early, and indeed the whole, Christian view of reality."[122]

What seems to have worried Bunyan most, though it also gave him great pride, was a sense that *The Pilgrim's Progress* had emerged unexpectedly from a deep source of inspiration that he did not wholly understand. In the prefatory "Apology" he says that he "fell suddenly into an allegory" with no idea of what would come of it:

> I only thought to make
> I knew not what, nor did I undertake
> Thereby to please my neighbour; no, not I,
> I did it mine own self to gratify.

But once started he found he could not stop, and "still as I pulled it came" (p. 31). The metaphor seems to be taken from flax-working, but it may not be fanciful to imagine a sexual component, as again in the verses that conclude *The Holy War:*

> It came from mine own heart, so to my head,
> And thence into my fingers tricklèd;
> Then to my pen, from whence immediately
> On paper I did dribble it daintly.
>
> (p. 286)

Against the imputation that these are mere self-indulgent fictions Bunyan opposes the tradition of dark similitudes, but clearly the question "Is it feigned?" (*Pilgrim's Progress*, p. 33) causes deep anxiety. For in Puritan thought, feigning is but little removed from lying, and lying has also a (punningly) revolting sexual aspect. Mr. Wiseman says in *Mr. Badman*, "A lie then is the brat of hell, and it cannot be in the heart before the person has committed a kind of spiritual adultery with the devil. That soul therefore that telleth a known lie, has lien with, and conceived it by lying with the devil, the only father of lies."[123]

"Romance they count it, " Bunyan says bitterly of critics of *The Pilgrim's Progress* (p. 215), and it is easy to see why they might, especially if we recognize its sources in popular chapbooks rather than in "high" literary romance.[124] It happens indeed that Bunyan's grandfather was a travelling "chapman" who sold them.[125] But like other Puritans Bunyan repudiated these seductive tales as enemies of truth, not least because they reduced the Word to just another book: "The Scriptures, thought I [before conversion], what are they? a dead letter, a little ink and paper, of three or four shillings price. Alas, what is the Scripture, give me a ballad, a newsbook, George on horseback, or Bevis of Southampton, give me some book that teaches curious arts, that tells of old fables; but for the Holy Scriptures I cared not."[126]

So it was crucial for allegory to base itself securely on the "literal sense" of the Bible, as Tyndale declared in attacking the fictions of Catholicism: "If I could not prove with an open text that which the allegory doth express, then were the allegory a thing to be jested at, and of no greater value than a tale of Robin Hood." The Catholics, Tyndale says, forbid their people to read the Bible in their own language but encourage "Robin Hood, and Bevis of Hampton, Hercules, Hector, and Troilus, with a thousand histories and fables of love and wantonness, and of ribaldry, as filthy as heart can think."[127] Romances were wicked both because they were untrue and because they stimulated sexual thoughts, which is why Mr. Badman "would get all the bad and abominable books that he could, as beastly romances, and books full of ribaldry, even such as immediately tended to set all fleshy lusts on fire" (p. 175). The ulterior purpose of romances, in Bunyan's opinion, was to stimulate action, as is made clear in *The Holy War:* "Wherefore [Diabolus] caused, by the hand of one Mr. Filth, an odious, nasty, lascivious piece of beastliness to be drawn up in writing, and to be set upon the castle gates, whereby he granted, and gave licence to all his true and lusty sons in Mansoul, to do whatsoever their lustful appetites prompted them to do." The gloss explicitly identifies this as "odious atheistical pamphlets and filthy ballads and romances full of baldry" (p. 35).

Bunyan's intention in *The Pilgrim's Progress* is not just to clarify Christian doctrine by reenacting it in familiar narrative forms. Rather it must be to rehabilitate the fiction-reading impulse by gathering it into a higher mode of religious interpretation, much as Milton gathers the pagan myths into the one true myth which they in part resemble. So long as both Bible and romance remained familiar to his readers he seems to have succeeded remarkably well, as Walter Scott testifies: "We remember with interest the passages where, in our childhood, we stumbled betwixt the literal story and metaphorical explanation; and can even recall to mind a more simple and early period when Grim and Slaygood, and even he 'Whose castle's Doubting, and whose name's Despair," were to us as literal Anakim as those destroyed by Giant-killing Jack."[128] Three different kinds of writing are here conflated: the gigantic sons of Anak in the Old Testament, the giant Despair in Bunyan's psychological allegory, and the folktale victims of Jack the Giant-Killer. All are felt as equally metaphorical, or alternatively as equally literal.

In contrast with traditional romancers Bunyan secures the integrity of his narrative in two ways, by insisting on its symbolic universality, and by asserting that heavenly images can transform earthly ones. At Interpreter's House Christian is shown a picture of a man looking up to heaven with "the best of books" in his hand, and he is told, "The man whose picture this is is one of a thousand; he can beget children, travail in birth with children, and nurse them himself when they are born" (p. 60). Whereas the Devil "lies" with men to beget lies, Evangelist is androgynously able to beget, give birth to, and nurse his children, as the marginal references make clear:

> For though ye have ten thousand instructors in Christ, yet have ye not many fathers: for in Christ Jesus I have begotten you through the gospel. (1 Cor. 4:15)

> My little children, of whom I travail in birth again until Christ be formed in you. (Gal. 4:19)

> But we were gentle among you, even as a nurse cherisheth her children. (1 Thess. 2:7)

Through the direct interpolation of biblical images, the world of experience is compelled to express the paradoxes of a truer world, as Interpreter explains a little later: "*For the things that are seen are temporal, but the things that are not seen are eternal* [2 Cor. 4:18]. But though this be so, yet since things present and our fleshly appetite are such near neighbours one to another, and again, because things to come and carnal sense are such strangers one to another, therefore it is that the first of these so suddenly fall into amity, and that distance is so continued between the second" (p. 63).

Milton, with his appreciation of the ambiguities of all interpretation, makes Raphael say that spiritual forms can be likened to corporeal ones and may even properly reflect them—

> . . . though what if earth
> Be but the shadow of heaven, and things therein
> Each to other like, more than on earth is thought?
>   (V.574–76)

Bunyan in effect rejects that subtle conditional. One interprets correctly only by recognizing that all images are meretricious and are most reliable when least mimetic. Christian sees a crucified man, but he sees him in his mind, not on the cross. If romance can be decontaminated in this way, then Bunyan welcomes it as an instrument for spiritual education. So long as it is not taken as a guide to conduct (as the depraved Badman takes it) then its dislocations of time and space are highly appropriate for the story he wants to tell.

Romance is often accused of being wish-fulfilling, but so is Christianity. Frye's various treatments of romance are all of them deeply suggestive for Bunyan's work, above all in recognizing its un-novelistic causation:

> In realism the attempt is normally to keep the action horizontal, using a technique of causality in which the characters are prior to the plot, in which the problem is normally: "given these characters, what will happen?" Romance is more usually "sensational," that is, it moves from one discontinuous episode to another, describing things that happen to characters, for the most part, externally. We may speak of these two types of narrative as the "hence" narrative and the "and then" narrative.[129]

In this paratactic mode, the things that happen are externalized and incidents are not causally linked. And our reflections on the ambiguities of the self in Bunyan are supported by Frye's remarks elsewhere about romance characterization:

> The romancer does not attempt to create "real people" so much as stylized figures which expand into psychological archetypes. . . . That is why the romance so often radiates a glow of subjective intensity that the novel lacks, and why a suggestion of allegory is constantly creeping in around its fringes. . . . The novelist deals with personality, with characters wearing their *personae* or social masks. He needs the framework of a stable society, and many of our best novelists have been conventional to

the point of fussiness. The romancer deals with individuality, with characters *in vacuo* idealized by revery, and, however conservative he may be, something nihilistic and untamable is likely to keep breaking out of his pages.[130]

One might almost guess that it is in order to tame his anarchic impulses—to get a familiar mask back on the isolated self conceived in reverie—that Bunyan is pulled toward novelistic detail. For however corrupt and dangerous this fallen world may be, it is less alarming than the dizzying abysses of the inner life, as *Grace Abounding* abundantly makes clear.

Moreover, Bunyan was writing at just the time when interpretation of the Bible was breaking away from figural and typological schemes, reflecting a new realism or literalism that treated scriptural narrative like other narratives instead of allowing it a privileged status. Whereas formerly the world we live in was interpreted through biblical categories, the procedure was now reversed and the stories in the Bible were required to conform to normal criteria of verisimilitude.[131] And just as biblical stories were now appreciated specifically as *stories*, so allegory also was susceptible to this kind of emphasis, for as many theorists have observed, no allegory can be unremittingly emblematic, and the literal "level" is always important.[132] Rosemond Tuve goes further and declares—like Coleridge denying that a long poem can be uniformly poetical—that a successful allegory must have elements that are nonallegorical. "It seems to me to have been grasped early as a principle that narratives would necessarily be *intermittently* capable of allegorical reading. This is best exemplified in the romances; current readers of allegory are often much more unwilling than earlier writers of it to allow some characters or some portions to serve simply and only the story-or-historical reading."[133] One should therefore be dubious about modern theories that postulate allegory as seamless and then identify as "novelistic" any exceptions to this artificial rule. The same thing is true of style and imagery, which in Bunyan's case do often seem prophetic of the novel, as indeed Puritan preaching in general has been alleged to be.[134] For as Lewis remarks with his usual sweeping range of allusion, "Bunyan stands with Malory and Trollope as a master of perfect naturalness in the mimesis of ordinary conversation."[135] Trollope and Malory are both masters of "natural" dialogue, but they are not both novelists. A "natural" style may serve to raise the familiar to the symbolic rather than the other way round.

What draws *The Pilgrim's Progress* most toward the novel is not so much the presence of "novelistic" details that might equally be found in Chaucer or Malory, but the way in which its characters are allowed to *be* characters when one might have expected them to symbolize interior states. In part this is simply due to the procedure of symboliz-

ing inner experience by physical phenomena. It has been well said of
Grace Abounding that "Bunyan's silences constitute a formal principle.
Everything is excluded but what touches on his inner life."[136] This is
exactly reversed in the externalized allegory of *The Pilgrim's Progress,*
where Doubting Castle is more vividly present to us than Bedford
Gaol was in *Grace Abounding.* If spiritual suffering is described in
powerful physical images, it will certainly develop a kind of mimetic
immediacy, as in the torture of Faithful: "First they scourged him,
then they buffeted him, then they lanced his flesh with knives; after
that they stoned him with stones, then pricked him with their swords;
and last of all they burned him to ashes at the stake" (p. 134). One
might compare Magwitch's first apparition to Pip in *Great Expectations:*
"A man who had been soaked in water, and smothered in mud, and
lamed by stones, and cut by flints, and stung by nettles, and torn by
briars."[137] For after all body and mind (or spirit) both belong to
human beings, and just as Bunyan's descriptions have a Dickensian
mimetic dimension, so Dickens's have a Bunyan-like symbolic
dimension.

Beyond details of presentation like these, what makes *The Pilgrim's
Progress* look forward to the novel is the way in which it displays characters in action. That Bunyan was capable of a much more schematic
kind of allegory, we know from *The Holy War,* where a highly fragmented self is dramatized in a tightly organized narrative. In *The Pilgrim's Progress* the opposite tendency appears: an eddying and
unpredictable narrative displays the experience of highly coherent
selves. Fish has emphasized the double meaning of the "way" as the
scene of every Christian's salvation—Christ's "I am the Way"—and as
a spiritual state which is valid only if realized within the individual
believer. Formalist and Hypocrisy, who climb over the wall instead of
entering at the Wicket Gate, are not really "in" the way at all.[138] As is
repeatedly made clear, the way is reserved for those who belong in it:

> *Christian.* Is this the way to the Celestial City?
> *Shepherds.* You are just in your way.
> *Christian.* How far is it thither?
> *Shepherds.* Too far for any but those that shall get thither
> indeed.
> *Christian.* Is the way safe or dangerous?
> *Shepherds.* Safe for those for whom it is to be safe, *but trans-
> gressors shall fall therein.* (p. 158)

There is no absolute distance, only the interiorized distance of the
individual pilgrim, yet it is indeed absolute in the sense that you either
get there or you don't. For the Calvinist there are no partial successes.

What Christian learns from the shepherds is that *the* way has to
become *his* way, and it is the ceaseless, exhausting labor of achieving

this that accounts for the much-noted unprogressiveness of *The Pilgrim's Progress.*[139] Form thus embodies meaning: the emblematic dream is a permanent world of the spirit which can be repeatedly reentered—on p. 162 the dreamer actually wakes up, and then goes back to sleep and resumes his dream—rather than a causally consecutive narrative that must be experienced from beginning to end.[140] The drama of man's rebellion against God and his recapture by grace calls naturally for a formal shape, as in *The Holy War.* The drama of the individual soul in its efforts to remain in the "way" is necessarily repetitive, as Faithful's song affirms:

> The trials that those men do meet withal
> That are obedient to the heavenly call,
> Are manifold and suited to the flesh,
> And come, and come, and come again afresh.
> (p. 109).

Brian Nellist proposes a suggestive contrast with Spenser, whose several heroes are shadowy because they look outward at a reality beyond themselves, while the characters whom Christian meets are all aspects of himself, so that what matters is the quality of his self-discovery. In *The Faerie Queene* the forces of evil "gradually coalesce into a secret hierarchy" organized against mankind, whereas the various tempters and opponents in Bunyan have no communication with each other, being separate projections of Christian's inner state.[141] But in fact both allegories presuppose confrontation with a reality beyond the subjective self, whether it is generalized or localized. For as Tuve wisely says,

> It is an error to bend and cripple an allegorical fiction into the shape that would be taken by a psychological biography, whether of Everyman or another. This is true even of a pilgrimage allegory, because it includes what the protagonist learns as well as what happens; it has many eddies and pools of this kind, where what we think of as the action stands still while something is examined, clarified, elucidated. . . . Allegory is supremely fitted to examine closely the nature of great abstractions as they touch men's lives.[142]

The Holy War is in the most limiting sense a psychomachia, while *The Pilgrim's Progress* is a more open and adventurous exploration of what it means to confront experience and learn from it. The great doctrines of the Bible preside over the narrative, but Bunyan's tendency is always to ground them in the individual rather than to assert the universal. If Renaissance humanist writers tended to assume a symbolic unity among all parts of the universe, macrocosm mirrored in microcosm, the Puritans preferred to look for analogies and examples rather than identities. Or if all of the elect do share a common pattern, then their endeavors to discern that pattern may still be richly various; as has been said of Bunyan in *Grace Abounding*, "He seems to suspect that he remains the vehicle of a metaphor: a man *like* a saint."[143] In *The Pilgrim's Progress* events and images change as the experiencing self changes: moving through his allegorical landscape Christian comes to understand what he had formerly seen but not understood. Vanity Fair is identical with the City of Destruction from which he started out, but it seems different because he is different, no longer a guilty and frightened refugee but a saint who can patiently endure abuse and for whom the seductions of the Fair no longer hold any attraction.[144]

This brings us to the most significant affinity between *The Pilgrim's Progress* and later novels: its recognition of the differentness of different persons. To have remained a consistent allegory it ought perhaps to have confined itself to symbolic versions of events inside Christian's head, who is presumably still living at home (mending pots or whatever) while undergoing an interior "progress" up hills and through sloughs. But as soon as other characters appear who are distinct from Christian—Obstinate and Pliable who refuse the journey, Faithful who joins him—we are invited to imagine a series of separate though correlative spiritual journeys. And the subjectivity of Part I of *The Pilgrim's Progress* gives way in Part II to a much more social emphasis: the former examines the believer as a private self, the latter as a member of a sect or community.

Faithful and Hopeful can never be anything but what their names imply—"You have been Hopeful ever since I knew you" (p. 199)—and most of the other characters in Part I are dealt with summarily: "And thus much concerning Pliable" (p. 47). But if the characters in Part I are projections of the interior self, those in Part II reflect Bunyan's post-prison experience when he became "Bishop Bunyan," a figure like his own Great-heart who busied himself in helping others. The judges kept asking Bunyan whether he called the people together (that is, acted as an unauthorized preacher), and he answered equivocally. In fact it might be argued that it was the people who called *him* together, giving him a positive identity and healthful work, and freeing him from the obsessive need to reconcile his inner conflicts. Talon usefully suggests that Great-heart is "Christian under another name and at another stage in his growth,"[145] and certainly he is invulnerable to many of the tribulations that Christian had to endure. He is clad in the allegorical armor of Ephesians (Christian had no armor), and unlike Spenser's Red Cross he never misuses it or gets caught without it. He is not a struggling sinner as Christian was, but a hardy guide who beheads every giant that crosses his path, and is prepared even to lead a successful foray into Doubting Castle to dispatch the giant Despair. Obviously this cannot mean that despair has vanished from the world, but rather that those who allow Great-heart to guide them may never have to face it.

Like Baxter's development, Bunyan's seems to illustrate a gradual escape from Puritan inwardness, the prison of the sole self. I see no evidence that (as is sometimes asserted) the focus on women and children in Part II suggests that they are weaker and less heroic than men, or more in need of help from an organized church. It is rather that Christian continually goes astray through his own folly, while his wife in following him—in answer, as she says, to his prayers (p. 232)—is more willing than he was to know her own weakness and to accept advice. (In *Grace Abounding* Bunyan repeatedly rues his own tendency to give in to pride and to rely on his good works.)

The symbolism of Part II thus reflects the Christian ideal of trusting surrender which has moved so many strenuous temperaments, that of Edwards for instance: "I very often think with sweetness, and longings, and pantings of soul, of being a little child, taking hold of Christ, to be led by him through the wilderness of this world."[146] Part I was predicated on the doctrine of election but left its nature mysterious; Part II proposes a series of analogies that go impressively far toward making one feel what election must be like. As Interpreter explains to Christiana—using emblems which her husband had not been shown—invincible activity is the fruit of obedient passivity. First she is told how a hen has a "special call" for her chicks (p. 249), which is later identified as "a special grace" (p. 262), and then she is given a literal version of a central New Testament metaphor:

> "And sir," said Christiana, "pray let us see some more." So he had them into the slaughter-house, where was a butcher a-killing of a sheep; and behold the sheep was quiet, and took her death patiently. Then said the Interpreter: "You must learn of this sheep to suffer, and to put up wrongs without murmurings and complaints. Behold how quietly she takes her death, and without objecting she suffereth her skin to be pulled over her ears. Your King doth call you his sheep." (p. 250)

Puritans took seriously the metaphors by which to fight the good fight was also to be led into green pastures, or as one translator rendered the text in the Twenty-third Psalm, "He *drives* me to the streams / Which run most pleasantly."[147]

Whatever its loss in adventurous excitement, the great ambition of Part II is to dramatize the full internalizing of God's will, with a sense of freedom that is embodied in moral effort rather than merely received from above. The elect may not always feel a decisive "call." Mercy fears to enter the Wicket Gate because she is only accompanying her friend Christiana, whose invitation "was from the King, and mine was but from her, wherefore I fear I presume" (p. 236). But the keeper of the gate raises her up, leads her in, and says "I pray for all them that believe on me, by what means soever they come unto me;" in the margin Bunyan adds "Mark this" (p. 237). In effect she learns what in Part I had been localized (very movingly) in the personification of Hopeful:

> But I replied, "Lord, I am a great, a very great sinner;" and he answered, *"My grace is sufficient for thee."* Then I said "But Lord, what is believing?" And then I saw from that saying *He that com-eth to me shall never hunger, and he that believeth on me shall never thirst* that believing and coming was all one, and that he that came, that is, run out in his heart and affections after salvation by Christ, he indeed believed in Christ. Then the water stood in mine eyes. . . . (182)

As in Augustine's *Confessions,* one comes to belief and believes in order to come.

Just as allegory contains both emblem and story, so the characters in it can be at once symbolic and individual. Coleridge's much-quoted remark should really be taken as identifying a commonplace, not as exposing a special weakness in Bunyan: "Narrative allegory is distinguished from mythology as reality from symbol; it is, in short, the proper intermedium between person and personification. Where it is too strongly individualized, it ceases to be allegory; this is often felt in the Pilgrim's Progress where the characters are real persons with nick names."[148] It is quite true that Bunyan's characters tend to describe themselves adjectivally rather than to embody noun-concepts. "The old gentleman blushed and said, 'Not Honesty in the abstract, but Honest is my name, and I wish that my nature shall agree to what I am called" (p. 300). But this simple distinction probably cannot bear the explanatory weight that critics have given it, for depending on context the same character can be both person *and* personification, and theoretical inconsistencies may give no offence in practice. No reader minds, and most probably do not even notice, that Mercy is a timid recipient of mercy as well as its embodiment.[149]

In Prudentius's *Psychomachia* Modesty fiercely stabs Sodomita Libido instead of confining herself to blushing, and Nuttall wearily concludes that "If the mind of man is conceived as a battlefield of warring *homunculi,* it is not surprising—just tedious—to discover that the *homunculi* themselves are composed of even tinier *homunculi.*"[150] On the contrary, tedium is far likelier in a narrative confined to wholly consistent abstractions, while inconsistency allows a writer like Bunyan to present an analytical allegory *and also* a human drama. His Mr. Fearing represents the kind of thing that Nuttall criticizes, since he has "a

Slough of Despond in his mind." Strictly speaking this makes non-sense of the allegory, for where *is* the Slough if not in the mind? But there is no reason to speak strictly, and the context makes perfect sense of the apparent inconsistency:

> The Celestial City, he said he should die if he came not to it, and yet was dejected at every difficulty, and stumbled at every straw that anybody cast in his way. Well, after he had lain at the Slough of Despond a great while, as I have told you, one sunshine morning, I do not know how, he ventured, and so got over. But when he was over, he would scarce believe it. He had, I think, a Slough of Despond in his mind, a slough that he carried every-where with him, or else he could never have been as he was. (p. 303)

Great-heart goes on to talk about doubts of election, and there is a sense in which every believer is capable of "fearing" in this way. But there are also certain believers whose fear is rooted and crippling, and these both deserve and receive special assistance: the Valley of the Shadow of Death "was as quiet while he went through it, as ever I knew it before or since. I suppose those enemies here had now a spe-cial check from our Lord, and a command not to meddle until Mr. Fearing was passed over it" (p. 306). Mr. Fearing's interior Slough of Despond is not a fumbling with allegorical counters but a recognition that the symbol can operate in either of two ways. As an expression of the universal human condition, it is a region that all men must enter; as an emblem of the psychology of a specific kind of individual, it is carried "within," even though in the first sense Mr. Fearing himself is already within. What is occasional for other people is continuous for him.

All of the symbols of *The Pilgrim's Progress* are alterable in this way. As Macaulay remarked, Faithful dies at Vanity Fair, "not in shadow, but in reality," though logically speaking he should wait for the River of Death.[151] But what reader would object to that? As a character in the story he dies before Christian does; as a character in his own story he would no doubt die after crossing the river; as an aspect of the believer's mind he cannot die at all (the point is that faith transcends death and attains heaven, not that it dies and leaves Christian without faith). And Christian's own complexity is made far richer by the fact that Faithful does have this partial existence as a character. Van Ghent points out that Faithful carries no burden and struggles through no slough: "Beside the bright firm surface of Faithful, Chris-tian is thrown into relief as a man who has suffered and been afraid and wallowed in mud, a man of complex and difficult temperament, vainglorious at times in his strength, at other times doubtful or despairing."[152]

Christian's experience is typical for many persons but it is by no means universal, as is very clearly stated at the Valley of Humiliation:

> Then said Mr. Great-heart, "We need not be so afraid of this Valley; for here is nothing to hurt us, unless we procure it to ourselves. 'Tis true, Christian did here meet with Apollyon, with whom he also had a sore combat; but that fray was the fruit of those slips that he got in his going down the Hill. For they that get slips there, must look for combats here. And hence it is that this Valley has got so hard a name. For the common people when they hear that some frightful thing has befallen such an one in such a place, are of an opinion that that place is haunted with some foul fiend or evil spirit; when alas it is for the fruit of their doing that such things do befall them there." (p. 288).

In passages like this, personification gives way to characterization in a way that reflects the larger movement of Puritanism from dogmatic clarity to ethical complexity, a change which we have seen in Baxter and will shortly consider in Defoe. The world of *Grace Abounding* is indeed haunted by foul fiends and oppressed by a determinist sense of behavior. *The Holy War* shows that theologically Bunyan never relinquished this ethos, but the second part of *The Pilgrim's Progress* shows how differently he came to regard its implications for practical living.

There is no reason to conclude that in aesthetic terms this was a good thing, or to adopt a literary teleology by which anything that leads toward the novel is to be praised. Bunyan's *The Life and Death of Mr. Badman* is sometimes hailed as a precursor of the novel, yet it is one of the most relentlessly tedious of didactic works, a dialogue between Mr. Wiseman and Mr. Attentive made up of instructive "true stories, that are neither lie nor romance," and that issue always in heavy moralizing:

> *Attentive.* But what was that other villain addicted to? I mean young Badman's third companion.
> *Wiseman.* Uncleanness; I told you before, but it seems you forgot.
> *Attentive.* Right, it was uncleanness. Uncleanness is also a filthy sin.
> *Wiseman.* It is so; and yet it is one of the most reigning sins in our day.[153]

If *Mr. Badman* is a novel it is a very crude one, and no attempt whatever is made to show how this appalling brute can be (as is alleged) the son of pious, loving parents, apprentice of a pious, tender master, and husband of a pious, faithful wife. Instead he illustrates the grimness of the Calvinist doctrine of reprobation: "God gave him up now to a reprobate mind, to hardness and stupidity of spirit; and so was that scripture fulfilled upon him, 'He hath blinded their eyes,' and that, 'Let their eyes be darkened that they may not see'" (p. 284). The tragedy of damnation holds no interest for Bunyan. And in fact the dire exempla in *Mr. Badman* are taken directly from printed collections, in which notorious sinners are swallowed up by the earth or snatched through barred windows in a flurry of blood; the book is offered as a sort of propaganda anthology rather than as fictional narrative.[154]

In tending toward the novel, Part II of *The Pilgrim's Progress* sacrifices much of what makes the first part immortal, its psychological intensity. When Bunyan stresses the social environment of the pilgrims in Part II, he loses the strangeness and terror of inner experience which had been the special province of the Puritan imagination. Revisiting and commenting on the scenes of Christian's journey, the characters in Part II in effect read rather than relive Part I, but at his greatest Bunyan is able to show how "reading" one's life is inseparable from the existential burden of living it—"by reading his work upon me," he says of God in *Grace Abounding* (p. 2). Great-heart "had in his pocket a map of all ways leading to or from the Celestial City; wherefore he strook a light (for he never goes also without his tinder-box) and takes a view of his book or map, which bids him be careful in that place to turn to the right-hand-way" (p./ 357). But the great point of Part I was that the Bible is mediated through symbols that have to be lived before they can be understood, and cannot furnish a map to be infallibly followed at every specific turning-point. As in the buried (and perhaps unacceptable) lesson of the Fall in *Paradise Lost,* knowledge is not knowledge until we have experienced it, and hence we can only know good through evil. In Part II experience is depressingly vicarious; Great-Heart is a veteran Sherpa who has made this climb often.

To prefer Part I of *The Pilgrim's Progress* in this way is not in the least to claim that it detaches itself from familiar reality. Rather it is to insist that Puritan art at its best sees reality as pervaded with symbols and shaped by them. So long as the Bible remained central in the culture, Bunyan's allegory continued to have this power. Fussell has shown how working-class soldiers during the First World War cherished it as the one text that could make sense of their appalling condition, providing a model for endurance in suffering which they found to be literally indescribable.[155] At all times humble people have been drawn to its vision of ultimate worth, learning as Christian does to resist Shame who "objected the base and low estate and condition of those that were chiefly the pilgrims; also their ignorance of the times in which they lived, and want of understanding in all natural science"

(p. 107). Christ "stripped himself of his glory" for the sake of the poor, and made many pilgrims into princes "though by nature they were beggars born, and their original had been the dunghill" (p. 86). No doubt there is some taint of Nietzschean *ressentiment* in the punitive conclusion to the final vision of glory: "When he shall sit upon the Throne of Judgement, you shall sit by him; yea, and when he shall pass sentence upon all the workers of iniquity, let them be angels or men, you also shall have a voice in that judgement, because they were his and your enemies" (p. 201). But just as the black slaves in America sought to bear their sufferings by invoking the rich imagery of the Bible, Bunyan, by his awareness of suffering in this life, gives special poignancy to his account (in the language of the Book of Revelation) of ultimate release:

> *Christian.* There is an endless Kingdom to be inhabited, and everlasting life to be given us; that we may inhabit that Kingdom for ever.
> *Pliable.* Well said, and what else?
> *Christian.* There are crowns of glory to be given us, and garments that will make us shine like the sun in the firmament of heaven.
> *Pliable.* This is excellent; and what else?
> *Christian.* There shall be no more crying, nor sorrow; for he that is owner of the place will wipe all tears from our eyes. (p. 44)

But Pliable goes home and never gets there.

Above all *The Pilgrim's Progress* is powerful because it compels the reader to share in the pilgrimage. Fish has shown how a series of increasingly distanced endings, as the dreamer awakes and challenges the reader to interpret what he has read, returns us to "our reading of the world we will re-enter when the book is closed."[156] In so doing Bunyan faces an issue that will occupy us increasngly in the remainder of our study, the difference between the coherence of art and the uncertainty of life. Typology may in theory propose a reliable means of interpreting events, but in actual practice, as one of its most distinguished expositors observes, that can never be so. "The existence 'given' by God is still existence in a history which is always in detail unrepetitive, unprecedented, and demanding, an existence from which . . . terror of the future may still tempt us to draw back."[157]

Bunyan's special genius is expressed in a union of emblem with mimesis that has as many affinities with lyric intensity as with novelistic breadth. Compare Herbert's lines:

> At length I got unto the gladsome hill
> Where lay my hope,

> Where lay my heart; and, climbing still,
> When I had gained the brow and top,
> A lake of brackish waters on the ground
> Was all I found.[158]

The lake of tears is a fully realized experience, for tears *are* frustration and disappointment, not just their symptom or consequence. And *The Pilgrim's Progress* is potent above all in bringing to life the images of inner precariousness that fill *Grace Abounding:* "O how gingerly did I then go, in all I did or said! I found myself as on a miry bog, that shook if I did but stir" (p. 27). It is never quite clear whether Bunyan's emblems exist only to be interpreted by the one authoritative Word—this of course would have been his own account—or whether they are a troubling foreground behind which no merely human author can confidently penetrate. Seeking to unriddle the riddle of his own life, Bunyan found himself almost involuntarily creating dark similitudes. "Still as I pulled it came."

5

Myth and Fiction in Robinson Crusoe

Mimesis, Allegory, and the Autonomous Self

In 1719, at the age of fifty-nine, the businessman, pamphleteer, and sometime secret agent Daniel Defoe unexpectedly wrote the first English novel. The affinities of *Robinson Crusoe* with the Puritan tradition are unmistakable: it draws on the genres of spiritual autobiography and allegory, and Crusoe's religious conversion is presented as the central event. But this primal novel, in the end, stands as a remarkable instance of a work that gets away from its author, and gives expression to attitudes that seem to lie far from his conscious intention. Defoe sets out to dramatize the conversion of the Puritan self, and he ends by celebrating a solitude that exalts autonomy instead of submission. He undertakes to show the dividedness of a sinner, and ends by projecting a hero so massively self-enclosed that almost nothing of his inner life is revealed. He proposes a naturalistic account of real life in a real world, and ends by creating an immortal triumph of wish-fulfillment. To some extent, of course, Defoe must have been aware of these ambiguities, which are summed up when Crusoe calls the island "my reign, or my captivity, which you please."[1] But it is unlikely that he saw how deep the gulf was that divided the two poles of his story, the Augustinian theme of alienation and the romance theme of gratification.

Recommending *Robinson Crusoe* to his readers as a didactic work, Defoe compared it to *The Pilgrim's Progress* and called it "an allusive allegoric history" designed to promote moral ends, in terms which explicitly distinguish this kind of writing from immoral fictions that are no better than lies:

> The selling [sic] or writing a parable, or an allusive allegoric history, is quite a different case [from lying], and is always distinguished from this other jesting with truth, that it is designed and effectually turned for instructive and upright ends, and has its moral justly applied. Such are the historical parables in the Holy Scriptures, such "The Pilgrim's Progress," and such, in a word, the adventures of your fugitive friend, "Robinson Crusoe."[2]

Crusoe's "original sin," like Adam's, is disobedience to his father. After going to sea against express warnings, he is punished by shipwreck and isolation, converted by God (who communicates through a monitory dream during sickness, an earthquake, and the words of the Bible), and rewarded in the end beyond his fondest hopes. More than once Crusoe likens himself to the Prodigal Son, a favorite emblem for fallen man in Puritan homiletics, and a shipwrecked sea captain indignantly calls him a Jonah. In the providential scheme his sojourn on the island is both punishment and deliverance: punishment, because his wandering disposition must be rebuked; deliverance, because he (alone of the crew) is saved from drowning and then converted by grace that overcomes the earlier "hardening" of his heart (pp. 11, 14). As Ben Gunn summarizes a similar lesson in *Treasure Island*, "It were Providence that put me here. I've thought it all out in this here lonely island, and I'm back on piety."

Yet Defoe's story curiously fails to sustain the motif of the prodigal. His father is long dead when Crusoe finally returns—there is no tearful reunion, no fatted calf, not even a sad visit to the father's grave— and by then he has come into a fortune so splendid that he exclaims, "I might well say, now indeed, that the latter end of Job was better than the beginning" (p. 284). Far from punishing the prodigal Crusoe for disobedience, the novel seems to reward him for enduring a mysterious test. Crusoe's father had wanted him to stay at home and, two elder sons having vanished without a trace, to establish his lineage in a strange land (he was "a foreigner of Bremen" named Kreutznaer, p. 3). But "a secret over-ruling decree" (p. 14) pushes Crusoe on toward his wayfaring fate, and it is hard not to feel that he does well to submit to it, like the third son in the fairy tales whom magical success awaits.

Robinson Crusoe is the first of a series of novels by Defoe that present the first-person reminiscences of social outsiders, adventurers and criminals. Since the Puritans were nothing if not outsiders, the "masterless men" of the seventeenth century can appear (as Walzer observes) either as religious pilgrims or as picaresque wayfarers.[3] Whether as saints or as rogues they illustrate the equivocal status of the individual who no longer perceives himself fixed in society. And by Defoe's time the attempt to create a counter-*nomos* in the Puritan small group—Bunyan's separated church—was increasingly a thing of the past. Puritanism was subsiding into bourgeois Nonconformity, no longer an ideology committed to reshaping the world, but rather a social class seeking religious "toleration" and economic advantage. The old Puritans, glorying in their differentness, would have regarded the Nonconformists as all too eager to conform.

Defoe was both beneficiary and victim of the new ethic, and two facts are particularly relevant to the allegorical implications of *Crusoe:* he was twice disastrously bankrupt during a rocky career as capitalist and speculator, and he regretted an unexplained failure to enter the Presbyterian ministry—"It was my disaster," he says mysteriously in his one reference to the subject, "first to be set apart for, and then to be set apart from, the honour of that sacred employ."[4] John Richetti, in the subtlest interpretation of *Crusoe* that we have, sees Defoe as celebrating a mastery of self and environment which implicitly contradicts his religious premises: "The narrative problem . . . is to allow Crusoe to achieve and enjoy freedom and power without violating the restrictions of a moral and religious ideology which defines the individual as less than autonomous."[5] But the tension was always present in the ideology itself; it grows directly from the implications of a faith like Bunyan's, in which temptations are projected outside the self and determinism is a force with which one learns to cooperate. What is new is the effective withdrawal of God from a structure which survives without him, though its inhabitants continue in all sincerity to pay him homage.

At the level of conscious intention Defoe undoubtedly wanted *Robinson Crusoe* to convey a conventional doctrinal message. The island probably suggests the debtors' prison in which he was humiliatingly confined, and it certainly allegorizes the solitude of soul needed for repentance and conversion. "I was a prisoner," Crusoe exclaims, "locked up with the eternal bars and bolts of the ocean. . . . This would break out upon me like a storm, and make me wring my hands and weep like a child" (p. 113). Very much in the Puritan tradition Crusoe learns to recognize the "particular providences" (p. 132) with which God controls his life. When he discovers turtles on the other side of the island he thinks himself unlucky to have come ashore on the barren side, and only afterwards realizes, on finding the ghastly remains of a cannibal feast, "that it was a special providence that I was cast upon the side of the island where the savages never came" (p. 164). Once aware of the cannibals he must find a cave in which to conceal his fire, and Providence, having permitted him years of conspicuous fires without harm, now provides the very thing he needs. "The mouth of this hollow was at the bottom of a great rock, where by mere accident (I would say, if I did not see abundant reason to ascribe all such things now to providence) I was cutting down some thick branches of trees to make charcoal . . ." (p. 176). Most notably of all, Crusoe is rescued from hunger when some spilled chicken-feed sprouts apparently by chance; eventually he understands that although it was natural for the seeds to grow, it was miraculous that they did so in a way that was advantageous to him (pp. 78–79).

In a Puritan view the normal course of nature is simply the sum total of an ongoing chain of special providences, for as a modern expositor of Calvin puts it, "Bread is not the natural product of the earth. In order that the earth may provide the wheat from which it is made, God must intervene, ceaselessly and ever anew, in the 'order of nature,' must send the rain and dew, must cause the sun to rise every morning."[6] In the eighteenth century, however, there was an increasing tendency to define providence as the general order of things rather than as a series of specific interventions. Wesley bitterly remarked that "The doctrine of a particular providence is absolutely out of fashion in England—and any but a particular providence is no providence at all."[7] One purpose of *Robinson Crusoe* is to vindicate God's omnipotence by showing the folly of making such a distinction. And Crusoe's isolation (like Ben Gunn's) encourages him to think the matter through. When Moll Flanders, in Defoe's next major novel, is finally arrested and thrown into Newgate, she suddenly perceives her clever career as the condign punishment of "an inevitable and unseen fate." But she admits that she is a poor moralist and unable to retain the lesson for long: "I had no sense of my condition, no thought of heaven or hell at least, that went any farther than a bare flying touch, like the stitch or pain that gives a hint and goes off."[8] Moll sees only at moments of crisis what Crusoe learns to see consistently.

In keeping with this message the narrative contains many scriptural allusions, which are often left tacit for the reader to detect and ponder. The sprouting wheat, for instance, recalls a central doctrine of the Gospels: "Verily, verily I say unto you, Except a corn of wheat fall into the ground and die, it abideth alone; but if it die, it bringeth forth much fruit. He that loveth his life shall lose it, and he that hateth his life in this world shall keep it unto life eternal" (John 12:24–25). Crusoe's life recapitulates that of everyman, a fictional equivalent of what Samuel Clarke recommended in the study of history: "By setting before us what hath been, it premonisheth us of what will be again; sith the self-same fable is acted over again in the world, the persons only are changed that act it."[9] Like other Puritans Crusoe has to grope toward the meaning of the types embodied in his own biography. Defoe often likened himself to persecuted figures in the Bible, but wrote to his political master Harley that his life "has been and yet remains a mystery of providence unexpounded."[10] Translating his experience into the quasi-allegory of *Crusoe* permits him to define typological connections more confidently, from the coincidence of calendar dates to the overarching theme of deliverance (typified in individuals like Jonah, and in the children of Israel released from Egypt).[11] Thus the temporal world, however circumstantially described, can be seen in the Puritan manner as gathered up into eternity. Crusoe's fever is not only a direct warning from God but also, as Alkon shows, a rupture in his careful recording of chronology by which he is "wrenched outside time," an intimation that the various incidents in the story must be subsumed in a single structure.[12] As in other Puritan narratives, separate moments are valued for their significance in revealing God's will, and become elements in an emblematic pattern rather than constituents of a causal sequence.

Nearly all of the essential issues cluster around the crucial theme of solitude. Defoe clearly gives it a positive valuation, and suggests more than once that Crusoe could have lived happily by himself forever if no other human beings had intruded. "I was now in my twenty-third year of residence in this island, and was so naturalized to the place, and to the manner of living, that could I have but enjoyed the certainty that no savages would come to the place to disturb me, I could have been content to have capitulated for spending the rest of my time there, even to the last moment, till I had laid me down and died like the old goat in the cave" (p. 180). However obliquely Defoe's *Serious Reflections of Robinson Crusoe* (published in the following year) relates to the novel, it must be significant that it begins with an essay "Of Solitude" which moves at once to the claim that we are solitary even in the midst of society:

> Everything revolves in our minds by innumerable circular motions, all centering in ourselves. . . . All reflection is carried home, and our dear self is, in one respect, the end of living. Hence man may be properly said to be alone in the midst of the crowds and hurry of men and business. . . . Our meditations are all solitude in perfection; our passions are all exercised in retirement; we love, we hate, we covet, we enjoy, all in privacy and solitude. All that we communicate of those things to any other is but for their assistance in the pursuit of our desires; the end is at home; the enjoyment, the contemplation, is all solitude and retirement; it is for ourselves we enjoy, and for ourselves we suffer.[13]

Critics have unfairly quoted this disturbing and memorable passage as symptomatic of a peculiar egotism in Defoe. In fact it reflects the logical consequence of Puritan inwardness, also susceptible of course to the charge of egotism—the descent into the interior self that impels Bunyan's Christian to reject his family in order to win eternal life. And it is compatible, as Defoe goes on to make clear, with the traditional view that "Man is a creature so formed for society, that it may not only be said that it is not good for him to be alone, but 'tis really impossible he should be alone" (pp. 11–12). The good man or woman ought to associate with others but seek in meditation that solitude which can be attained anywhere, symbolized in *Robinson Crusoe* by "the life of a man in an island" (p. 2).

In effect Defoe literalizes the metaphor that Descartes (for example) uses: "Among the crowds of a large and active people . . . I have been able to live as solitary and retired as in the remotest desert."[14] But to literalize the metaphor creates profound complications, for it is one thing to live *as if* on a desert island and another to do it in earnest. Jonathan Edwards writes that in his meditations on the Song of Songs, "an inward sweetness . . . would carry me away in my contemplations, . . . and sometimes a kind of vision, or fixed ideas and imaginations, of being alone in the mountains, or some solitary wilderness, far from all mankind, sweetly conversing with Christ, and wrapt and swallowed up in God."[15] This rapture of self-abnegation is very far from Crusoe's experience. The difference is partly explained by the bluff common sense of Crusoe, not to mention of Defoe; Dickens comments, "I have no doubt he was a precious dry disagreeable article himself."[16] But beyond that it is due to the way in which Defoe takes a *topos* of allegory and literalizes it in mimetic narrative. Even though he may believe that the result is still allegorical, he has transformed—to borrow a useful pair of terms from German—*Jenseitigkeit* into *Diesseitigkeit*, collapsing the "other side" of religion into the "this side" of familiar experience. In *The Pilgrim's Progress* everyday images serve as visualizable emblems of an interior experience that belongs to another world. In *Robinson Crusoe* there is no other world.

Another way of saying this is that *Crusoe* reflects the progressive desacralizing of the world that was implicit in Protestantism, and that ended (in Weber's phrase) by disenchanting it altogether. Defoe's God may work through nature, but he does so by "natural" cause and effect (the seeds that sprout), and nature itself is not viewed as sacramental. Rather it is the workplace where man is expected to labor until it is time to go to a heaven too remote and hypothetical to ask questions about. "I come from the City of Destruction," Bunyan's Christian says, "but am going to Mount Sion."[17] In *Crusoe*, as is confirmed by the feeble sequel *The Farther Adventures of Robinson Crusoe*, there is no goal at all, at least not in this world. But the world of *The Pilgrim's Progress* was *not* this world: after conversion the believer knew himself to be a stranger in a strange land. Defoe keeps the shape of the allegorical scheme but radically revalues its content.

Defoe is no metaphysician, and his dislocation of the religious schema may seem naive, but in practice if not in theory it subtly images the ambiguity of man's relation to his world, at once a "natural" home and a resistant object to be manipulated. Milton's Adam and Eve fall from the world in which they had been at home, and Bunyan's characters march through the fallen world like soldiers passing through enemy territory. Defoe has it both ways, defining man over against nature and at the same time inventing a fantasy of perfect union with it. As technologist and (halting) thinker Crusoe finds himself in opposition to nature, as when he builds a "periagua" so grotesquely huge that he is unable to drag it to the water, or when he does make a successful canoe but is nearly swept out to sea by unexpected currents. And his concepts function to define his human status in contrast with nature, in keeping with the moral tradition that saw man in a "state of nature" as living in continual fear of death.[18] But as a concord fiction *Robinson Crusoe* still more strongly suggests that man can indeed return to union with nature, so long as other men are not present to disturb him. In important respects the island is an Eden.

This equivocation between punitive doctrine and liberating romance has remarkable consequences in Defoe's treatment of psychology. In effect he carries to its logical conclusion the externalizing of unwanted impulses which we have seen in Bunyan and other Puritan writers. With God generalized into an abstract Providence, Crusoe's universe is peopled by inferior beings, angelic spirits who guide him with mysterious hints and diabolical spirits who seek his ruin. Of these the latter are the more interesting, and Crusoe is scandalized to find that Friday is unaware of any Satan, merely saying "O" to a pleasant but ineffectual deity called Benamuckee who seems not to know how to punish men. Defoe needs the Devil—and this must be his never-articulated answer to Friday's trenchant question, "Why God no kill the Devil?" (p. 218)—because man's unacknowledged impulses have to be explained. Like the older Puritans Defoe externalizes such impulses by calling them tricks of Satan, but he altogether lacks the subtle dialectic by which the Puritans acknowledged man's continued complicity with the hated enslaver.

Defoe's late work *The Political History of the Devil* (1726), once one gets behind its frequent facetiousness, expresses deep anxiety about the power of a being who "is with us, and sometimes in us, sees when he is not seen, hears when he is not heard, comes in without leave, and goes out without noise; is neither to be shut in or shut out" (II.iii, p. 221). Yet in a sense this ominous figure is welcome, for he furnishes a comforting explanation of feelings which must otherwise be located in one's self. After discussing the case of virtuous persons whom the Devil causes to behave lasciviously in their dreams, Defoe tells the haunting story of a tradesman, "in great distress for money in his business," who dreamt that he was walking "all alone in a great wood" where he met a little child with a bag of gold and a diamond necklace, and was prompted by the Devil to rob and kill the child.

He need do no more but twist the neck of it a little, or crush it
with his knee; he told me he stood debating with himself,
whether he should do so or not; but that in that instant his heart
struck him with the word Murther, and he entertained an horror of it, refused to do it, and immediately waked. He told me
that when he waked he found himself in so violent a sweat as he
had never known the like; that his pulse beat with that heat and
rage, that it was like a palpitation of the heart to him; and that
the agitation of his spirits was such that he was not fully composed in some hours; though the satisfaction and joy that attended him, when he found it was but a dream, assisted much to
return his spirits to their due temperament. (II.x, pp. 361–62)

One may well suspect that this desperate and guilty tradesman was
Defoe himself, and perhaps it is not fanciful to think that the famous
episode in *Moll Flanders,* in which Moll robs a child of its watch but
resists the temptation to kill it, is a kind of revision and expiation of
the dream. Guilty impulses like these are doubly repudiated on
Crusoe's island: first, because they are projected on to Satan and the
cannibals whom Satan prompts, and second, because so long as
Crusoe is alone he could not act upon them even if he wanted to. The
return of human beings means the return of the possibility of sin, as
indeed he realizes when he longs to gun down the cannibals in cold
blood.

In *Robinson Crusoe,* therefore, we see the idea of solitude undergoing a drastic revaluation. Instead of representing a descent into the
self for the purpose of repentance, it becomes the normal condition
of all selves as they confront the world in which they have to survive.
Puritans of Bunyan's generation sometimes welcomed imprisonment
because it freed them from external pressures and made self-scrutiny
easier. Baxter for example says, "If you be banished, imprisoned, or
left alone, it is but a relaxation from your greatest labours; which
though you may not cast off yourselves, you may lawfully be sensible
of your ease, if God take off your burden. It is but a cessation from
your sharpest conflicts, and removal from a multitude of great temptations."[19] This liberation from outer attacks, however, was supposed
to encourage a deeper attention to inner conflict, as in the widespread
custom of keeping diaries. But that is precisely what Crusoe does not
do. He keeps his diary *before* conversion, and stops with the flimsy
excuse (on the part of the novelist) that he ran out of ink and could
not figure out how to make any. At the very moment when the Puritan's continuous self-analysis begins, Crusoe's ends.

The function of Crusoe's diary, it seems, is not to anatomize the
self, but rather to keep track of it in the modern fashion that Riesman
describes: "The diary-keeping that is so significant a symptom of the
new type of character may be viewed as a kind of inner time-and-

motion study by which the individual records and judges his output
day by day. It is evidence of the separation between the behaving and
the scrutinizing self."[20] This new way of presenting psychology goes
far toward explaining what critics of every persuasion have recognized, the peculiar opacity and passivity of character in Defoe's fiction. Novak observes that "frequently a passion appears to be grafted
on to the characters, an appendage rather than an organic part of
them," and Price says that "conflicts are settled in Crusoe or for him,
not by him."[21] And it also helps to explain why, as Fletcher notices in
his survey of allegory, much in Crusoe is dispersed into externalized
daemonic agents.[22] A similar procedure made Bunyan's Christian
seem more complex and human by analyzing his psyche into complex
elements; it makes Crusoe seem, if not less human, at least less intelligible, because we are encouraged to look outward rather than inward. So long as we imagine ourselves looking outward *with* Crusoe,
we see what he sees and feel what he feels, but what we perceive is
always external. Starr shows in a brilliant essay that Defoe's prose constantly projects feelings on to the outer world, and that the reality
thus presented is subjective rather than interior, a defense of the ego
"by animating, humanizing, and Anglicizing the alien thing he en-
counters."[23] If we try to look *into* any of Defoe's characters we find
ourselves baffled; when Crusoe, on seeing the footprint, speaks of
being "confused and out of my self" (p. 154), we have no clear idea of
what kind of self he has when he is in it.

In Defoe's behaviorist psychology, as in that of Hobbes, people live
by reacting to external stimuli, and while we may get a strong sense of
individuality, there is little sense of the psyche. His frightened behavior after seeing the footprint, Crusoe says, "would have made any one
have thought I was haunted with an evil conscience" (p. 158). If beasts
and savages are allegorical symbols of inner impulses, then of course
he does have an evil conscience; but in the mimetic fiction they are
simply beasts and savages, and conscience becomes irrelevant. Moreover Crusoe describes how he *would have looked* to an observer if one
had been there, even though the total absence of other people was
precisely what made him comfortable, and the advent of other people
is what filled him with horrible fears. Riesman's point about the split
between the behaving and the observing self is thus confirmed.

In contrast with the self the Puritans believed in, utterly open to
God and potentially open to careful introspection, the self in Defoe
participates in the general cultural revaluation epitomized by Locke:
"Man, though he have great variety of thoughts, and such from which
others as well as himself might receive profit and delight; yet they are
all within his own breast, invisible and hidden from others, nor can of
themselves be made to appear." Locke goes on to describe the role of
language in bridging (but not abolishing) this gap by means of con-

ventional signs. Hume characteristically goes further and argues that the self is invisible *to itself* as well as to others: "Ourself, independent of the perception of every other object, is in reality nothing; for which reason we must turn our view to external objects."[24] This psychology is quite directly a rejection of Puritan introspection, which is not surprising since Locke championed toleration against fanaticism—he wrote a book entitled *The Reasonableness of Christianity*—and Hume turned atheist after a Calvinist upbringing. If God can see every hidden corner of the self, the believer is obliged to try to see it too; but if God withdraws or vanishes, then the anguish of self-examination is no longer necessary.

These considerations suggest a way of reconciling two very different interpretations of Crusoe's psychology. One holds that the self is fragmented in a state of turbulent flux, [25]the other that the self precedes and resists alteration: "We always feel as we read that personality is radically primary, that it existed before events and continues to exist in spite of circumstances that seek to change or even to obliterate it."[26] In effect this is the distinction, already noted, between solitude as self-abnegating introspection and solitude as self-assertive independence. Whenever Defoe allows his narrators to try to look within, they do indeed find a chaos of unfocused sensations, but most of the time they simply avoid introspection and assert themselves tenaciously against a series of manageable challenges. The notoriously extraneous ending of *Robinson Crusoe,* in which the hero successfully organizes his traveling party to fight off wolves in the Pyrenees, may symbolize the mastery that Crusoe has attained on the island, but if so it is a mastery of external objects rather than a richer organization of the psyche. No wonder all of Defoe's characters, like their creator, habitually resort to alias and disguise.

This assertion of the autonomy of the self is mirrored in the disappearance of Crusoe's father, with his oracular warning, "That boy might be happy if he would stay at home, but if he goes abroad he will be the miserablest wretch that was ever born" (p. 7). What the miserable wretch gets is an idyllic, self-sufficient existence that for generations has made *Robinson Crusoe* a special favorite of children. And Crusoe thereby achieves what Milton's Satan so heretically desired, a condition of self-creation. Despite its mimetic surface, *Robinson Crusoe* closely anticipates the Romantic pattern discussed by Bloom: "All quest-romances of the post-Enlightenment, meaning all Romanticisms whatsoever, are quests to re-beget one's own self, to become one's own Great Original."[27]

The Romantic poets and philosophers interpreted the Fall as the birth of consciousness of one's finite self, and Blake explicitly identified it with the onset of puberty. *Robinson Crusoe* is a resolutely sexless novel, with only the most covert prurience: "I could not perceive by my nicest observation but that they were stark naked, and had not the least covering upon them; but whether they were men or women, that I could not distinguish" (p. 183). In fact *Crusoe* is a fantasy of retreat into an innocence before puberty, with a vision of solitude among vegetable riches that literalizes the metaphors of Marvell's "Garden":

> Such was that happy garden-state,
> While man there walked without a mate:
> After a place so pure and sweet,
> What other help could yet be meet!
> But 'twas beyond a mortal's share
> To wander solitary there:
> Two paradises 'twere in one
> To live in paradise alone.

Milton's sober Puritanism leads him to elaborate the ways in which the original helpmeets drag each other down, while implying the unacceptability of Marvell's playful fantasy of life without a mate. But Marvell was after all a Puritan, and wrote somberly elsewhere that every man must be "his own expositor, his own both minister and people, bishop and diocese, his own council; and his conscience excusing or condemning him, accordingly he escapes or incurs his own internal anathema."[28] Defoe evades the internal anathema, invents a world without sexuality, and gives a positive valuation to the shelter behind a wall of trees which in *Paradise Lost* was a guilty escape from God's eye:

> O might I here
> In solitude live savage, in some glade
> Obscured, where highest woods impenetrable
> To star or sunlight, spread their umbrage broad. . . .
> (IX.1084–87)

Adam and Eve are expelled from Eden and sent out into the world of history; Crusoe retreats from history into an Eden innocent of sexuality and of guilt. To be sure, Defoe makes him now and then refer to his "load of guilt" (p. 97) or bewail "the wicked, cursed, abominable life I led all the past part of my days" (p. 112), but no details are ever given, and on the island the absence of other people makes guilt irrelevant.

Solitude is power. "There were no rivals. I had no competitor, none to dispute sovereignty or command with me" (p. 128). And again: "It would have made a Stoic smile to have seen me and my little family sit down to dinner; there was my majesty the prince and lord of the whole island; I had the lives of all my subjects at my absolute command. I could hang, draw, give liberty, and take it away, and no rebels among all my subjects" (p. 148). The subjects are a parrot, a dog, and two cats; the cruelties that might tempt a despot among men would be absurd among pets. Christianity always dealt uneasily with Stoicism, which recommended an indifference to the world that seemed appealing, but also a preoccupation with self that seemed un-Christian. Regal in solitude, Crusoe would indeed make a Stoic smile. Absolute power is a function of freedom from social power; only when the cannibals arrive does the Hobbesian state of nature resume, as Defoe describes it in his poem *Jure Divino* (1706):

> Nature has left this tincture in the blood,
> That all men would be tyrants if they could.
> If they forbear their neighbours to devour,
> 'Tis not for want of will, but want of power.[29]

So long as he is by himself Crusoe escapes Hobbes's war of all against all and rejoices in the war of nobody against nobody.

Defoe makes it absolutely explicit that Crusoe's Eden is an escape from guilt. "I was removed from all the wickedness of the world here. I had neither the *lust of the flesh, the lust of the eye, or the pride of life*" (p. 128; the reference is to a favorite Puritan text, John 2:16). To be alone with God is to be alone with oneself and to find it good:

> Thus I lived mighty comfortably, my mind being entirely composed by resigning to the will of God, and throwing myself wholly upon the disposal of his Providence. This made my life better than sociable, for when I began to regret the want of conversation, I would ask my self whether thus conversing mutually with my own thoughts, and, as I hope I may say, with even God himself by ejaculations, was not better than the utmost enjoyment of human society in the world. (pp. 135–36)

Crusoe has nothing to hide. Whereas Bunyan trembled in the knowledge that God sees "the most secret thoughts of the heart,"[30] Crusoe often applies the word "secret" to emotions of self-satisfaction: "I descended a little on the side of that delicious vale, surveying it with a secret kind of pleasure" (p. 100). This is not the Puritan use of the term, but an ethical and aesthetic ideal that Defoe may have picked up from Addison: "A man of a polite imagination . . . meets with a secret refreshment in a description, and often feels a greater satisfaction in the prospect of fields and meadows than another does in the possession."[31] The solitary Crusoe has no one to keep secrets from; the word "secret" defines his privacy, individuality, possessiveness, and sole claim to pleasure.

Self-congratulation merges with the frequently mentioned "secret hints" of Providence until Crusoe learns to identify Providence with his own desires. When after a time he reflects on his role in saving Friday from paganism, "A secret joy run through every part of my soul" (p. 220). For the older Puritans determinism was a crucial issue, whether one concluded like Milton that man was free to cooperate with God's will in his own way, or like Bunyan that man must learn to make his will conform to the irresistible force of predestination. In strictly theological terms Defoe seems to have followed Baxter in stressing God's desire to welcome all of his children, rather than his power of predestination.[32] But imaginatively Defoe shares with the Puritans a feeling of unfreedom, of being compelled to act by some power beyond himself. In the imaginary world of fiction he can embrace that power instead of resisting it. In its simplest terms this amounts to asserting that Crusoe is an agent of Providence as well as its beneficiary, as he himself indicates after masterminding the defeat of the mutineers:

> "Gentlemen," said I, "do not be surprised at me; perhaps you may have a friend near you when you did not expect it." "He must be sent directly from heaven, then," said one of them very gravely to me, and pulling off his hat at the same time to me, "for our condition is past the help of man." "All help is from heaven, sir," said I. (p. 254)

But beyond this, Defoe's determinism becomes a defense of his own impulses, whereas for Puritans it would have been a confirmation of their sinfulness. Providence is seen as responsible not only for what happens but also for what does not, for what Crusoe is not as well as what he is. "Had Providence . . . blessed me with confined desires" (p. 194) none of the misfortunes—and none of the rewards—would have come about. But Providence did not. Where then does responsibility lie?

The more one ponders this question, the more equivocal the role of Providence becomes, as is vividly apparent when Crusoe reflects on his very first shipwreck.

> Had I now had the sense to have gone back to Hull and have gone home, I had been happy, and my father, an emblem of our blessed Saviour's parable, had even killed the fatted calf for me; for hearing the ship I went away in was cast away in Yarmouth Road, it was a great while before he had any assurance that I was not drowned.
>
> But my ill fate pushed me on now with an obstinacy that nothing could resist; and though I had several times loud calls from my reason and my more composed judgment to go home, yet I had no power to do it. I know not what to call this, nor will I urge that it is a secret overruling decree that hurries us on to be the

instruments of our own destruction, even though it be before us, and that we rush upon it with our eyes open. Certainly nothing but some such decreed unavoidable misery attending, and which it was impossible for me to escape, could have pushed me forward against the calm reasonings and persuasions of my most retired thoughts, and against two such visible instructions as I had met with in my first attempt. (p. 14)

The passage is filled with interesting negatives: (1) Crusoe would have been like the prodigal if he had gone home, but he did *not;* (2) he will *not* say that his fate was compelled by "a secret overruling decree"; (3) yet *nothing but* such a decree can account for it.

One can try to explain these complications in orthodox Christian fashion, as Coleridge does:

> When once the mind, in despite of the remonstrating conscience, has abandoned its free power to a haunting impulse or idea, then whatever tends to give depth and vividness to this idea or indefinite imagination increases its despotism, and in the same proportion renders the reason and free will ineffectual. . . . This is the moral of Shakespeare's *Macbeth,* and the true solution of this paragraph—not any overruling decree of divine wrath, but the tyranny of the sinner's own evil imagination, which he has voluntarily chosen as his master.[33]

Coleridge adds, "Rebelling against his conscience he becomes the slave of his own furious will" (p. 316). But Crusoe does not go so far as this toward accepting the orthodox solution. He shows that he is aware of it, and hence hesitates to ascribe misfortunes to fate or God, but nevertheless the sense of involuntary behavior is so strong that he can only attribute it to "some such decreed unavoidable misery."

An emphasis on God's "decrees," comforting for the elect and dreadful for the reprobate, was fundamental to Calvinism. But Crusoe uses Calvinist language here to suggest that he cannot be morally responsible for actions in which he is moved about like a chess piece. In many places Defoe discusses the kinds of necessity in ordinary life (finding food, self-defense) that may not extenuate crime but impel it so irresistibly that the criminal is simply not free to behave otherwise.[34] A character in *Colonel Jack* says, "I believe my case was what I find is the case of most of the wicked part of the world, *viz.* that to be reduced to necessity is to be wicked; for necessity is not only the temptation, but is such a temptation as human nature is not empowered to resist. How good then is that God which takes from you, sir, the temptation, by taking away the necessity?"[35] Surely the corollary must also hold: the sinner can hardly be blamed if God does *not* remove the temptation by removing the necessity.

Obeying necessity, Crusoe allows himself to ride the current of his secret destiny and is magnificently rewarded. A Puritan reading of *Robinson Crusoe*—such as Defoe himself might have endorsed—would hold that by seeking self-fulfillment and creating a private *nomos,* Crusoe is an abject sinner. But the logic of the story denies this. Starr has shown that Defoe was fascinated with the science of casuistry,[36] which treats necessity as an ethical excuse for behavior instead of—as in Calvinism—a moral condemnation of it. The inverted egotism of Bunyan's "chief of sinners" is turned right-side-up again, as Crusoe's island refuses to remain a metaphor for captivity and quickly develops positive qualities. Since Crusoe is a fictional character and not a real person, what is really involved is Defoe's imaginative conception of the island. And this at bottom is a powerful fantasy of punishment that can be willingly accepted because it ceases to punish. The autonomy of solitude is the happy culmination of those mysterious impulses that first sent Crusoe to sea, and in achieving it he makes his destiny his choice.

The much-discussed economic aspects of *Robinson Crusoe* are suggestive of ambiguities very like the religious ones. On this topic the *locus classicus* is Ian Watt's chapter on *Crusoe* as a myth of capitalism. It is not really relevant to argue, as critics of Watt have done, that Crusoe has little of the rational calculation of the capitalist. For Watt's point is that the book is a myth and not a literal picture, reflecting the dynamic spirit of capitalism rather than its practical application. "Crusoe's 'original sin' is really the dynamic tendency of capitalism itself, whose aim is never merely to maintain the *status quo,* but to transform it incessantly. Leaving home, improving on the lot one was born to, is a vital feature of the individualist pattern of life."[37] The island permits Crusoe (and Defoe) to evade the contradictions in capitalist individualism, and to imagine a Puritan Eden in which work yields gratification instead of vexation and defeat.

The special status of the island makes possible Crusoe's reaction, in a famous passage, when he finds a quantity of coins on board the wrecked ship.

> I smiled to myself at the sight of this money; "O drug!" said I aloud, "What art thou good for? Thou art not worth to me, no not the taking off of the ground, one of those knives is worth all this heap, I have no manner of use for thee, e'en remain where thou art, and go to the bottom as a creature whose life is not worth saving." However, upon second thoughts, I took it away. . . . (p. 57)

Ever since Coleridge, readers have perceived irony in those second thoughts, but the irony is at society's expense rather than Crusoe's. If ever he returns to the world whose lifeblood is money, then this money will be useful if not indispensable. With his usual good sense he therefore saves it. But on the island, as if by enchantment, money is truly valueless, and Crusoe is free of the whole remorseless system whose lubricant it is. His personification of the coins as a "creature" carries its traditional Puritan meaning: all earthly things are "creatures" which the saint is to restrain himself from loving too much. Only on Crusoe's island is it possible to despise money as a useless and indeed harmful drug.

Crusoe is no anchorite. Things retain their value, and in pillaging the ship he never repents the urge to accumulate. "I had the biggest magazine of all kinds now that ever were laid up, I believe, for one man, but I was not satisfied still" (p. 55). What matters now is use, exactly as Crusoe indicates in the "O drug" passage, and as he confirms in a later reference to the saved-up coins: "If I had had the drawer full of diamonds it had been the same case; and they had been of no manner of value to me, because of no use" (p. 129). Crusoe notes about his early voyages that since he was a gentleman, a person with money but no skills (p. 16), he was a mere passenger and could do nothing useful. On the island he has to work with his hands, something no gentlemen would do, and recovers the dignity of labor which his father's "middle station" might have insulated him from. Just as money becomes meaningless, labor becomes meaningful. "A man's labour," Hobbes says, "is a commodity exchangeable for benefit, as well as any other thing."[38] Marx was hardly the first to notice the joylessness of work performed solely for what it can buy. On the island Crusoe has no market in which to sell his labor, and bestows it either on making things he really wants or as an end in itself. It may take him forever to make a pot, but Franklin's maxim has no meaning here: time is not money. Defoe was a speculator and middleman; Crusoe literalizes the labor theory of value in a miniature world where speculation is impossible and the middleman does not exist.

Relating *Robinson Crusoe* to the myth of Mammon, Starr surveys writers who tried to reconcile Christ's injunction "Take no thought for the morrow" with the duty of labor by emphasizing that the labor must be performed in cooperation with Providence.[39] On the island Crusoe need no longer attempt this difficult reconciliation, whereas capitalism, being rational, must always take thought for the morrow. Thus in sociological terms Crusoe escapes the prison of alienated labor, just as in religious terms he escapes the prison of guilt. He inhabits a little world where his tools and products fully embody his desires (or would if he could make ink) and where necessity authenticates his desires instead of punishing them. "The liberty of the individual," Freud says, "is no gift of civilization."[40] It is Defoe's gift to Crusoe.

Yet even in the imagination, this dream of wholeness is at best provisional. The economic system, according to Weber, "is an immense cosmos into which the individual is born, and which presents itself to him, at least as an individual, as an unalterable order of things in which he must live."[41] On the island Crusoe breaks free from that order, but in a deeper sense he has already internalized it, along with the religious order that undergirds it. What is possible finally is only a fantasy of escape, from desire as well as from civilization, that anticipates the poor man's reward in the New Testament.

> I looked now upon the world as a thing remote, which I had nothing to do with, no expectation from, and indeed no desires about: in a word, I had nothing indeed to do with it, nor was ever like to have; so I thought it looked as we may perhaps look upon it hereafter, *viz.* as a place I had lived in, but was come out of it; and well might I say, as Father Abraham to Dives, *Between me and thee is a great gulf fixed.* (p. 128)

In a wonderful poem called "Crusoe's Journal," to which this passage is given as epigraph, Derek Walcott sees Crusoe through Friday's eyes as an invader rather than a hermit, using the Word to colonize Friday's mind as well as his body.

> . . . even the bare necessities
>   of style are turned to use,
> like those plain iron tools he salvages
>   from shipwreck, hewing a prose
> as odorous as raw wood to the adze;
>   out of such timbers
> came our first book, our profane Genesis. . .
>   in a green world, one without metaphors;
>   like Christofer he bears
> in speech mnemonic as a missionary's
>   the Word to savages,
> its shape an earthen, water-bearing vessel's
>   whose sprinkling alters us
> into good Fridays who recite His praise,
>   parroting our master's
> style and voice, we make his language ours,
>   converted cannibals
> we learn with him to eat the flesh of Christ.[42]

The Augustan satirists mocked man's lust for money—Swift's Yahoos with their bright stones, Pope's India millionaires—but Defoe cannot step outside the system, can only transport it to an imaginary island where he no longer recognizes it. And the naiveté of the "natural" speech that Walcott exposes, so full of hidden assumptions and hidden metaphors, brings us back to the Puritan anxiety about fiction and truth which takes on special urgency in the early novel.

Realism, Invention, Fantasy

In a sense Defoe's realism is perfectly obvious. His characters have names and experiences like those of ordinary English people, and even in exotic circumstances they remain prosaically familiar. "Realism" in this minimal sense is simply a representation of experience and (especially) of material details that confirms a culture's sense of the way things are. It also implies a rejection of the more ostentatious devices of art, either because the writer cunningly wants to give an illusion of unmediated fact, or because he naively believes that facts can actually be unmediated. Haller says that "artless realism" characterizes Puritan autobiography, and Ortega provides a social context by remarking that "In epochs with two different types of art, one for minorities and one for the majority, the latter has always been realistic."[43] Augustan satire, written very much for the cultivated minority, constantly made fun of the artless realism affected by the new novels. *Gulliver's Travels* is in part a parody of *Robinson Crusoe,* and Swift delighted in a bishop's solemn pronouncement that he "hardly believed a word of it."

Some of the critical ambiguities in Defoe's realism may be inevitable in any fiction that masquerades as nonfiction. Ralph Rader says of *Moll Flanders,* "Knowing it to be a fiction in *fact,* critics try to understand it as if it were a fiction in *form.*"[44] Still, to turn from autobiography to the novel is to turn away from the Puritan tradition with its genuinely artless realism. A committed Puritan had no use for fiction, despising it as a form of lying and as an inexcusable preoccupation with worldly things. This distrust of fiction was no temporary phase, but persisted long in the evangelical tradition. In her youth George Eliot wrote that novels were "pernicious," declaring that she would carry to her grave "the mental diseases with which they have contaminated me." It was not only a question of possible immorality in fiction, but also of the status of fictionality itself: "Have I . . . any time to spend on things that never existed?"[45]

Defoe was well aware of such objections, and by stressing his allegorical intentions he did his best to counter them.[46] But more deeply, I believe, he opposed them not only because he thought Puritan faith compatible with fiction, but also because he was moved to test Puritan faith *through* fiction. To write novels, with however didactic an intention, was a subversive innovation. Insofar as Puritanism does indeed contribute to the rise of the novel, it is a case of the storytelling impulse asserting itself against the strongest possible inhibitions. So the mimetic realism that Watt stresses can be seen as a kind of mask to cover up what is actually happening: if the story can be presented *as* true, then it is less dreadful that it is *not* true. The author knows that it is fiction but the reader pretends not to, and so is not hurt by it—one is encouraged to read it in the same way, and with the same rewards, as one would read a true story.

Conversely, criticism's passion for detecting and analyzing the stratagems of art is a direct violation of the demands that such a novel makes, as Macaulay remarks in contrasting adult and childhood reading of *Robinson Crusoe:*

> He perceives the hand of a master in ten thousand touches which formerly he passed by without notice. But, though he understands the merits of the narrative better than formerly, he is far less interested by it. Xury and Friday, and pretty Poll, the boat with the shoulder-of-mutton sail, and the canoe which could not be brought down to the water edge, the tent with its hedge and ladders, the preserve of kids, and the den where the goat died, can never again be to him the realities which they were. . . . We cannot sit at once in the front of the stage and behind the scenes. We cannot be under the illusion of the spectacle while we are watching the movements of the ropes and pulleys which dispose it.[47]

To some extent we must simply accept the fact that criticism is an anesthetic (and often a contraceptive). But beyond this, Defoe's kind of realism repels criticism because the pretense of *not* inventing reflects an emotional need, not just a novelistic program, which he does his best to protect by concealing it from view. Fielding ostentatiously shows us the ropes and pulleys, but Defoe pretends they do not exist.

What complicates matters profoundly is the commitment of Puritan autobiography to faithfully reporting the "dealings" of God with his creatures. By making up Crusoe and his adventures Defoe unavoidably becomes the shaping deity of the narrative, and as Homer Brown says,

> The "real" self of Defoe's various "memoirs" is a fictive self. Defoe's confessions are not *his* confessions at all. The pattern of Christian truth has become the design of a lie masked as actuality, the plot of a novel. . . . While Defoe is impersonating Robinson Crusoe, he is also impersonating on another level Providence itself.[48]

Hesitating in retrospect between incompatible ways of presenting his work, Defoe claims that "the story, though allegorical, is also historical." At one moment he will imply that the island is an extended metaphor: "It is as reasonable to represent one kind of imprisonment by another, as it is to represent anything that really exists by that which exists not." But at another moment he will claim that it is all literally true: "It is most real that I had a parrot and taught it to call me by my name; such a servant a savage, and afterwards a Christian, and that his name was called Friday."[49] In the preface to the novel itself Defoe says with superb equivocation, "The editor believes the thing to be a just history of fact; neither is there any appearance of fiction in it" (p. 1).

The issue is not, as it was for Sidney, the philosophical legitimacy of fiction, but rather the dilemma incurred by a narrative that claims to confirm religious faith by showing what really occurs rather than what an author might wish. This was not a serious problem for Bunyan, who could meet the charge of fictiveness by reminding the reader that *The Pilgrim's Progress* is only a dream and that it demands interpretation. Defoe is not prepared to make such an admission, which would explode the evidentiary claims of his tale. It was usual in Puritan biographies to marvel at a recurrence of significant dates that proved God's secret management of a person's life. Much is made of this in *Robinson Crusoe* (p. 133). But the coincidence can only seem compelling if we are able to forget that Defoe, not God, has planted them in story.

Consider the early episode in which Crusoe escapes from slavery in North Africa. First of all Defoe gets him out to sea in a boat built by an English carpenter in a land without Englishmen. On page 19 Crusoe says he had no fellow Englishman to talk with; on page 20 the carpenter "also was an English slave"; and on page 24 we learn that the boy Xury picked up his English "by conversing among us slaves," which makes it appear that there were several Englishmen. Presumably the carpenter occurred to Defoe for purely practical reasons—a native boat might go belly up whereas a stout English craft would not—but this indifference to consistency suggests that his freewheeling imagination is not tied down to narrow verisimilitude.

Once Crusoe is at sea Defoe still faces a minor annoyance. He can let Xury accompany Crusoe, but he must find some way to get rid of an adult Moor who is bound to cause trouble if he stays.

> Giving the boy the helm, I stepped forward to where the Moor was, and making as if I stooped for something behind him, I took him by surprise with my arm under his twist [crotch], and tossed him clear overboard into the sea; he rose immediately, for

he swam like a cork, and called to me, begged to be taken in, told me he would go all over the world with me; he swam so strong after the boat that he would have reached me very quickly, there being but little wind; upon which I stepped into the cabin, and fetching one of the fowling-pieces I presented it at him, and told him I had done him no hurt, and if he would be quiet I would do him none; "But," said I, "you swim well enough to reach the shore, and the sea is calm, make the best of your way to shore and I will do you no harm, but if you come near the boat I'll shoot you through the head, for I am resolved to have my liberty;" so he turned himself about and swam for the shore, and I make no doubt but he reached it with ease, for he was an excellent swimmer. (pp. 22–23)

In its leisurely unfolding this long sentence conceals important questions. Why was there a Moorish slave at all? Because it is implausible that Crusoe would be allowed to go fishing with no companion but a boy. Why does the man swim like a fish? Because Defoe wants no blood on Crusoe's hands. The whole incident seems contrived to give Crusoe a chance not to be guilty, allowing us as usual to focus on his cleverness as a problem-solver rather than on his alleged iniquity as a sinner.

Defoe's contemporary Charles Gildon makes a penetrating remark: "Though he afterwards proves so scrupulous about falling upon the cannibals or men-eaters, yet he neither then nor afterwards found any check of conscience in that infamous trade of buying and selling of men for slaves; else one would have expected him to have attributed his shipwreck to this very cause."[50] If this criticism had seemed relevant to Defoe he would have dealt with it not by making Crusoe feel guilty but by revising the story to leave out the slaves. In point of fact Defoe supported the slave trade without reservation and regarded the exploitation of slaves as a sign of business ability.[51] When Xury in his turn ceases to be useful Crusoe cheerfully sells him into new slavery, an action that has scandalized many readers. But Defoe seems not to worry about it; Xury is willing, and we hear of him no more.

If Crusoe's island were really a scene of deserved punishment, it would have been easy to have burdened him with punishable crimes. He might have shot the cannibals, or at the very least the Moor might have drowned. But Defoe as creator is never able to work for long in harness with Defoe as homilist, not because his faith is hypocritical but because he cannot resist exploiting its inner tensions and forcing both guilt and determinism to gratify desire instead of opposing it. The autobiographical genre, far from encouraging confessional introspection, liberates Defoe to share in what Richetti calls "Crusoe's serene omnicompetence,"[52] giving embodied form to whatever he likes to imagine. Looking for a creek to land his raft in, Crusoe duly finds a creek, and comments splendidly, "As I imagined, so it was" (p. 51).

Ricoeur summarizes Freud's theory of art in terms that have suggestive affinities with Defoe's fantasy of kingship and freedom:

> The artist, like the neurotic, is a man who turns away from reality because he cannot come to terms with the renunciation of instinctual satisfaction that reality demands, and who transposes his erotic and ambitious desires to the plane of fantasy and play. By means of his special gifts, however, he finds a way back to reality from this world of fantasy: he creates a new reality, the work of art, in which he himself becomes the hero, the king, the creator he desired to be, without having to follow the roundabout path of making real alterations in the external world.[53]

Moreover, the apparently artless naiveté of first-person narration permits Defoe to bypass the external world even while appearing to confirm its details with unblinking accuracy. The mimetic texture works to conceal the existence of fantasy, while the intermittent presence of pattern is explained by attributing it to God rather than to the novelist.

The fantasy, incidentally, is comprehensive enough to shift from a solitary to a political form, and not just in the obvious sense that Crusoe colonizes Friday. The twenty-eight years of Crusoe's exile coincide with the period from the fall of Puritan rule in 1660 to the overthrow of the Catholic James II in 1688—and by a happy coincidence these were the first twenty-eight years of Defoe's life.[54] So Crusoe enjoys an exile that is also an assertion of hidden authority, commensurate with the underground status of Puritanism during those years. And then suddenly he becomes absolute sovereign over a mixed polity consisting of cannibals, Spaniards, and Englishmen; the childhood fantasy of mastery over an unpeopled world is succeeded by an adolescent fantasy of mastery over other men (women do not appear on the island until the *Farther Adventures*). Perhaps this is a last expression of Puritan wish-fulfillment in the political realm, a fantasy revenge for the disappointments of the Glorious Revolution of 1688 as well as for the bitterness of the Restoration of 1660.

There are further paradoxes in a desert-island realism. The book is realistic in lovingly presenting a wealth of miscellaneous details, but is remote from any evocation of a social reality. J. P. Stern's treatment of this kind of exceptional case is helpful:

> May not a special plea on behalf of a single man's experience be true? It *is* true, so long as it remains special: so long as it is offered as a single man's experience. Its characteristic form of ex-

pression is lyrical poetry. It becomes available to realism only at the point where the experience is worsted in the disillusioning conflict with the world of other people.[55]

This is why I argued at the outset of this study that Lukács is right: a strong lyric impulse underlies the earliest novels.[56] Crusoe redefines (or perhaps escapes) the disillusioning world of other people, and elaborates a seemingly realistic world out of the private experience of one man. Among the many possible reasons why Defoe's later novels are inferior to *Robinson Crusoe,* an essential one is their failure to recapture this dream in the midst of society.

Yet *Robinson Crusoe* is no lyric poem, and it is equally important to remember how consistently it refuses to let us see *into* Crusoe, defining his experience instead as a series of reactions to outward objects. "I carried two hatchets to try if I could not cut a piece off of the roll of lead, by placing the edge of one hatchet and driving it with the other; but as it lay about a foot and a half in the water, I could not make any blow to drive the hatchet" (p. 85). Anyone who has tried to strike a blow under water must feel the rightness of this, and it thus achieves its purpose of making one feel that it must be true: if it had not happened, who would think to make it up? But Defoe did make it up, and the outwardness of *Crusoe* is an invented mask for the inwardness of Defoe.

Allegory and mimesis are both, in the end, cover stories for the unacknowledged fantasy. But critics interested in Defoe's religious and economic ideas have tended to take his "realism" at face value, giving insufficient attention to the extraordinary extent of narcissistic wish-fulfillment in *Robinson Crusoe.* In this light Marthe Robert's analysis is deeply interesting, whether or not one wants to adopt the psychoanalytic explanation that she uses to organize her insights. As the title of her book makes clear—*Roman des Origines et Origine du Roman*—she identifies the origin of the novel/romance with the Freudian "family romance" in which the child imagines its own origin. *Robinson Crusoe* is for Robert the prime example of the foundling fantasy in which the child repudiates its parents, dreams of nobler and more powerful ones to whom it actually belongs, and elaborates a dream of omnipotence in a paradisal world undisturbed by other people and (especially) by sexuality. "Having wished to be nobody's son [Crusoe] becomes in fact completely orphaned, completely alone, the innocent self-begetter in a kingdom of complete solitude."[57] Reborn from the sea after the shipwreck—many critics have noticed the birth imagery as he struggles ashore—Crusoe enters an ambiguous Eden that expresses, but cannot reconcile, both the guilt that landed him there and the innocence that fantasy seeks to recreate. "He is unsure whether he is chosen or damned, miraculously taken to the heart of unsullied nature, or condemned to a hell of silence and oblivion" (p. 85).

In the extended "apprenticeship to reality" (p. 93) that follows this rebirth, Crusoe recapitulates civilization's growth to maturity, reinventing its arts and ideas (including a naive version of theology) and reaching the point where he can become a surrogate father to Friday, guardian of other castaways, and emperor of his little kingdom. But of course this is still very much a dream of omnipotence, however disguised as realism, and Robert sees the realistic novel's repudiation of mere "art" as reflecting its achievement in accommodating fantasy to the world of experience. "Unlike all other representational genres the novel is never content to *represent* but aims rather at giving a 'complete and genuine' account of everything, as if, owing to some special dispensation or magic power, it had an unmediated contact with reality" (p. 32). A fantasy of innocent gratification is put forward as being perfectly consistent with the reality principle. And Defoe's dogged defense of the new realism, naive though it may seem to later critical theory, exactly captures that sense of magically unmediated truth that Robert describes. Puritan writers in earlier generations had aspired to unmediated contact with God, but had recognized that all human expression is necessarily mediated through emblem and type (which is what makes them in a certain sense seem "modern" today). In Defoe's world the divine recedes ever farther away into the remote heavens, ceasing to be the essential guarantor of understanding, and the symbols he inherits from Puritanism are now free to assert their independent reality.

If the Puritans believed that they had to study the clues in their lives with fierce attention, they also believed that the ultimate interpretation was reserved for God, not themselves. "In theistic religions," Frye says, "God speaks and man listens."[58] But in *Robinson Crusoe* God himself becomes a kind of fiction, even if an indispensable one, and Crusoe has to do his own interpreting because if he does not, no one else will. *Paradise Lost* and *The Pilgrim's Progress* were texts that depended upon a superior text, the Word of God. *Robinson Crusoe* contains plenty of scriptural allusions, but now they are only allusions. The narrative offers itself as autonomous and freestanding, and in a profound sense it is secular. Here is where the "realism" of Crusoe telling his own story conflicts with the impulse to interpret, and the story tends to roll onward with a momentum of its own rather than successfully embodying the pattern to which it aspires. Crusoe is moved by his father's advice "but alas! a few days wore it all off" (p. 6), and this sets the tone for everything that follows. In a way Defoe participates in the state of continuous starting-over that is characteristic of modern writing, "something whose *beginning* condition, irreducibly, is that *it must always be produced, constantly.*"[59] So in a curious way

Defoe's problems lead logically to the solutions of Sterne, who perfectly fulfills Barthes's definition, "Le texte scriptible, c'est *nous en train* d'écrire."[60] But one must not claim too much; *Robinson Crusoe* resists any theoretical explanation that sees its meanderings as planned. A recent writer proposes, modestly enough, that "there is a deliberate avoidance of rhetorical or dramatic closure in Defoe's method."[61] The impersonal and passive construction is all too apt: the method itself (not Defoe) does not want to end, and the avoidance of ending is somehow "in" the method.

If Crusoe watches himself writing, Defoe pretends to watch neither Crusoe nor himself, affecting an utterly unsubordinated prose whose heaped up clauses suggest the mind-numbing inconsequentiality of experience. Here is the first half of a typical sentence, with the connective words italicized for emphasis:

> A little after noon I found the sea very calm, *and* the tide ebbed so far out, *that* I could come within a quarter of a mile of the ship; *and* here I found a fresh renewing of my grief, *for* I saw evidently, *that* if we had kept on board, we had all been safe, *that is to say*, we had all got safe on shore, *and* I had not been so miserable *as* to be left entirely destitute of all comfort and company, *as* I now was; *this* forced tears from my eyes again, *but* as there was little relief in that, I resolved, *if* possible, to get to the ship, *so* I pulled off my clothes, *for* the weather was hot to extremity, *and* took the water, *but* when I came to the ship, my difficulty was still greater to know how to get on board, *for* as she lay aground. . . . (p. 48)

In Bunyan the paratactic style suggested the welter of experience that God pulls together into a single shape. In Defoe it just suggests the welter of experience, and the prose keeps toppling forward of its own weight.

Christian faith is well on the way to providing a nostalgic schema rather than an informing principle, even if as Lukács says it has left permanent scars on the landscape: "The river beds, now dry beyond all hope, have marked forever the face of the earth."[62] Defoe's later novels are exceptionally episodic, not only failing to make their inner logic conform to providential plan, but failing to develop an inner logic at all. And the *anomie* that *Robinson Crusoe* held at bay returns with a vengeance. The later characters live under aliases while struggling, usually as criminals, to survive in a society that offers no *nomos*, no status that confirms the essential order of things. And guilt is no longer managed by assimilating it to a coherent determinism generated from within. Moll Flanders's rationalizations may be partly shared by the author, but he certainly appreciates the dreadful emptiness (and Pauline urgency) in Roxana's bitter confession: "With my eyes open, and with my conscience, as I may say, awake, I sinned, knowing it to be a sin, but having no power to resist."[63] We cannot know exactly what Defoe thought he was doing in this enigmatic novel, but we do know that it was his last. As one critic puts it, "Defoe stopped when he reached the end."[64]

Meanwhile *Robinson Crusoe* survives in all its richness, the starting point of a new genre and yet strangely unfruitful for imitation; it spawned no tradition of its own as *Don Quixote* and *Pamela* did. Later fictions continued to draw upon Christian ideas and to pursue the dream of confirming them, but never again in the naive and direct way that Defoe at first believed possible. *Robinson Crusoe* is a remarkable and unrepeatable reconciliation of myth with novel, whose fantasy of isolation without misery and labor without alienation retains all of its remarkable imaginative power. "I am away from home," Kafka wrote to his closest friend, "and must always write home, even if any home of mine has long since floated away into eternity. All this writing is nothing but Robinson Crusoe's flag hoisted at the highest point of the island."[65]

6

Clarissa *and the Waning of Puritanism*

Society and the Heart

In important respects *Robinson Crusoe* is a post-Puritan novel, despite its didactic program, and the later novels of the eighteenth century reflect the further fragmentation of the Puritan narrative tradition, whether they seek to adapt it or openly reject it. In this regard Samuel Richardson's *Clarissa* is particularly interesting, that once neglected masterpiece which has lately been overwhelmed with scholarly attention (three books on it in 1982 alone). In these proliferating studies the religious theme that Richardson emphasized has tended to become marginal, or at least to be translated into some other preferred realm of explanation: economic relations, sexual politics, and above all the duplicities of language and signs. These approaches are illuminating and have deeply influenced my own interpretation, but I believe there is still much to be gained by bringing Richardson's theme back to the foreground, for the tensions and ambiguities of *Clarissa* are precisely those that pervade the religious tradition. Indeed, it looks as if Richardson and his culture, just because they were no longer preoccupied with the old doctrinal framework, were able to liberate implications in Augustinian symbolics which doctrine had tended to repress.

The essential story is simple. Nineteen-year-old Clarissa Harlowe rebels against her family's demand that she accept a rich but horrible suitor, suffers house arrest and persecution in consequence, and then is tricked by the rakish Robert Lovelace into escaping with him. Though she soon perceives his wickedness and resists him as best she can, he takes advantage of her inexperience and her family's cruelty to keep her in his power. Eventually, having failed to break her will, he drugs her into unconsciousness and rapes her. She then rejects the world utterly, falls into a decline, and dies a saintly death that arouses the belated grief of all who knew her. The story is not narrated, either by the heroine herself (as in Defoe's novels) or by an omniscient narrator (as in Fielding's), but rather is presented in a long series of letters written by Clarissa, Lovelace, their confidants Anna Howe and Jack Belford, and other characters from time to time.

In the Everyman edition which is the only one currently in print,[1] this not very complicated tale requires four volumes and rather more than two thousand pages. Clarissa speaks of death as "the winding-up of our short story" (IV, 324) and it might seem that Richardson's job is to make a short story long. Yet the available abridgements are disastrously selective, both in unevenness of emphasis and in speeding up the slow, groping, struggling confrontation with experience that Richardson superbly presents. *Clarissa* stands as a permanent refutation of the old saw that art is long and life short: this novel inaugurates the effective concern of literature with *durée*, the sheer psychological fullness of time as we live it. Johnson said memorably, "If you were to read Richardson for the story, your impatience would be so much fretted that you would hang yourself,"[2] a remark that is perfectly consistent with his admiration for *Clarissa*. The book's power lies in its density and inexorability; it is like a glacier that moves slowly but crushes everything in its path. By imprisoning the reader—along with the characters—in a succession of suspended moments, it develops an atmosphere of gathering nightmare, of increasing horror and desperation, that any Puritan would recognize as suggestive of fallen life.

The term "Puritan," however, though often associated with Richardson, needs some explanation, since he was a very conventional Anglican, committed to a broadly orthodox Christianity and hostile to Methodist "enthusiasm" as well as to deism and skepticism.[3] *Clarissa* was published, moreover, in 1747–48, a full century after the high tide of Puritan success. The Puritans of the seventeenth century sought power eagerly, wielded it with relish, and relinquished it reluctantly; their brief triumph and long humiliation provoked in Milton and Bunyan a profound reinterpretation of the communal myth, abandoning political militancy for the warfare within. In Defoe we find the paradoxes of an inwardness that becomes an assertion of self rather than a criticism of it, and a relation to the social world so tenuous that it can be symbolized by solitude on a tropical island. Writing thirty years after Defoe, Richardson takes the structure of society far more for granted as the locus of human activity, and his first novel, *Pamela, Or Virtue Rewarded*, celebrates a happy union of piety with money. But for whatever reason—Fielding's shrewd satire in *Shamela* and *Joseph Andrews* no doubt had something to do with it—Richardson went on to achieve in *Clarissa* an unforeseeable masterpiece, a study of the soul's relation to the world in which the old Puritan themes come alive once more, with their intrinsic tensions more provocative than ever. Above all Richardson is true to the spirit of Puritanism by exploring the plight of the inner self when it cannot withdraw from social reality, like Bunyan's Christian with his fingers in his ears or like Crusoe on his island, but must acknowledge the endlessly tangled web of relationships that human beings have to live with. In particular this means—as it has continued to mean in most of the great novels since *Clarissa*—an exploration of private experience within the constraints of that prime agent of socialization, the family.

None of Defoe's characters after Crusoe has the luxury of perfect autonomy, but all of them go to great lengths to remain mysterious to their fellows, and all enjoy the freedom of the picaresque in which relationships can be disposed of by a simple change of name and place. Clarissa on the other hand never forgets that she is Clarissa Harlowe, and her tragedy grows directly from the persistence with which she seeks reconciliation with her implacable family. The root of the trouble is economic. The nouveau-riche Harlowes want to consolidate their position by arranging advantageous marriages for the three children of John Harlowe, whose brothers have undertaken to remain unmarried lest the fortune be divided into too many channels. Most of the planning revolves around Clarissa's brother James, for as she reminds him in a devastating letter written to be opened after her death, a son is "more worth in the family account than several daughters" (IV, 362). Whether or not she intends the phrase "the family account" ironically, Clarissa perfectly echoes here the financial metaphors that fill her family's imagination. When her uncle Antony does begin to think of marriage he tells his intended (Anna Howe's mother) that they will be happy in sharing "but one interest betwixt us: to reckon up our comings-in together; and what this day and this week has produced—O how this will increase love! Most mightily will it increase it!" (II, 351).

In a period when rich (often Nonconformist) merchants were criticized for avoiding taxation that was based on landed property,[4] the Harlowes are anxious to consolidate their "real estate," as distinguished from "unreal" paper wealth, and to use it to achieve noble status. In their own minds they are selflessly committed to the mutual good while Clarissa threatens to upset their planning, encouraged by her grandfather's mistake of bequeathing an estate to her (the youngest grandchild) in gratitude for her special love toward him. As she herself reports,

> Nobody indeed was pleased; for although every one loved me, yet being the youngest child, father, uncles, brother, sister, all

thought themselves postponed, as to matter of right and power (who loves not power?); and my father himself could not bear that I should be made sole, as I may call it, and independent, for such the will, as to that estate and the powers it gave (unaccountably as they all said), made me. (I, 54)

Clarissa has the further misfortune to be extremely attractive sexually, which incites the dangerous Robert Lovelace after he has paid insultingly brief attentions to her sister Arabella. Their brother James had fought a duel with Lovelace, whom he continues to hate and fear, and James and Arabella are thus eager to prevent the match. But beyond that they want to make sure that Clarissa does not decide to accept the grandfather's estate as her own, as they suspect she will shortly be advised to do: "Her Cousin Morden will soon be here: so all must be over before that time, or she'll be made independent of us all" (I, 266). Indeed she is so captivating that the uncles themselves may forget the family contract: "This little siren is in a fair way to *out-uncle*, as she has already *out-grandfathered* us both" (I, 58).

To forestall this disaster the family determines to marry Clarissa to a despicable person known generally as "Rich Solmes" (I, 25), whose chief qualification is that he will forgo the customary dowry in return for the honor of allying himself with so distinguished a family. Money being everything, even Clarissa's fond but ineffectual mother takes Solmes's financial offer as evidence of "spirit" (I, 207), but Clarissa sees him very differently: "He is said to be an insinuating, creeping mortal to anybody he hopes to be a gainer by; an insolent, overbearing one where he has no such views; and is not this the genuine spirit of meanness?" (I, 126). When Clarissa later refers to his "diabolical parsimony" (I, 158) one may well think of Milton's Mammon, "the least erected spirit that fell / From heaven" because he gazed always at the pavements of gold.[5]

Unfortunately Solmes is not only morally groveling but also physically repellent, as Clarissa testifies in a famous passage:

> He took the removed chair and drew it so near mine, squatting in it with his ugly weight, that he pressed upon my hoop. I was so offended (all I had heard, as I said, in my head) that I removed to another chair. I own I had too little command of myself. It gave my brother and sister too much advantage. I dare say they took it. But I did it involuntarily, I think. I could not help it. I knew not what I did. (I,68)

In eighteenth-century comedy and satire, the function of clothing is to allure rather than defend, and the goal of courtship is a fruition that ratifies the social order.

To fifty chosen sylphs, of special note,
We trust th' important charge, the petticoat:
Oft have we known that sev'nfold fence to fail,
Though stiff with hoops, and arm'd with ribs of whale.[6]

In Richardson, courtship and seduction move far from the world of comedy, and as Clarissa desperately exclaims, union with Solmes would be a kind of suicide: "I had rather be buried alive, indeed I had, than have that man!" (I, 87). The eventual rape by Lovelace is prefigured by a dream that does indeed involve burial alive, and Solmes too is a kind of rapist: "He even snatched my trembling, my struggling hand; and ravished it to his odious mouth" (I, 400). Life with Solmes would be a hellish "duration of woe" (I, 287), and his ultimate offence is "endeavouring to force a free mind" (I, 406).

In dramatizing the conflict between individual integrity and psychosocial oppression, *Clarissa* draws its special power from the frightening tyranny of old Harlowe and the pious submissiveness with which Clarissa seeks to placate him. Calvin, Walzer says, "radically deemphasized the natural and affective aspects of fatherhood, and dramatically stressed its authoritarian features."[7] In later thinkers, non-Calvinist as well as Calvinist, a pervasive concern with power tended to politicize the family by assimilating it to an authoritarian model. "If a man has some estate," Harrington wrote, "he may have some servants or a family, and consequently some government or something to govern; if he has no estate he can have no government."[8] But since many of the same people urged an ideal of marriage as voluntary union between equal individuals, there was an obvious conflict between two different codes of value, and Walzer adds that "Pamela and Clarissa, as yet unknown, were the true subjects of the tedious treatises on family government" (pp. 193–94).

At their best, "Puritan" social attitudes, centering on the patriarchal family, were in fact traditional English ones that were held with special urgency by Puritans at a time when all value seemed to be breaking down.[9] But if old Harlowe is eager to invoke the patriarchal tradition, he neglects the concomitant idea of interdependence among families as the basis of social organization (exhibited in institutionalized form in Puritan New England, but deriving from traditional English patterns). The Harlowe family is self-contained, extending no further than the unmarried uncles, as if Harlowe Place were an ark, and one of Solmes's chief recommendations is his willingness to marry Clarissa without abridging that autonomy.[10] Only Cousin Morden in far-off Italy offers hope of intervention, and he is detained abroad until too late, as if to emphasize the Harlowes' isolation from effectual influence. Those within the house, by a combination of argument, cajolery, and force, are organized into a united front, and marriage is regarded simply as commerce carried on by other means, aggrandizing the buccaneer family at the expense of its competitors. It is the aristocratic Lovelace whose class still represents social pattern, albeit a hierarchical pattern in which the upstart Harlowes are demoted, while Clarissa's family is nakedly on the make and demands that she be sold to the bidder whom the family firm approves. Yet it is Clarissa who feels moral duty intensely, and who does her best to satisfy her family's expectations. In so doing she experiences (much to Anna Howe's irritation) the lacerations of the Puritan temperament: cut off from the solidarity of the group, she must depend for a sense of integrity on an inner conviction of divine support. "If you are determined," her mother sternly declares, "to stand in defiance of us all—then indeed may you go up to your chamber (as you are ready to do)—and God help you!" (I, 108). That is exactly what it finally comes to.

That Clarissa learns to seek the paradise within, awaiting salvation in a better place, is of course the great theme of Richardson's novel, but whatever emblematic devices he may sometimes employ, he treats the events of fallen life as inescapably real. The fundamental experience in *Clarissa*—and this is altogether new in narrative literature, though not in the drama—is of being painfully constrained by the pressure of other people. Life is seen not only as a series of significant events, but also as an ongoing *condition*; or to put it differently, power is felt as pervasive even when it is not overtly exercised.

Brooding on the resemblance between political and familial abuses of power, Richardson's friend Johnson wrote with magisterial bitterness that parental authority "may wanton in cruelty without control, and trample the bounds of right with innumerable transgressions, before duty and piety will dare to seek redress, or think themselves at liberty to recur to any other means of deliverance than supplications by which insolence is elated, and tears by which cruelty is gratified." In another essay Johnson writes of "innumerable modes of insult and tokens of contempt, for which it is not easy to find a name, which vanish to nothing in an attempt to describe them, and yet may, by continual repetition, make day pass after day in sorrow and in terror."[11] For hundreds of pages Clarissa endures just this kind of incessant, minutely varied cruelty, and she begins to talk helplessly about rejecting life well before Lovelace tricks her into leaving home:

> I wish—but I don't known what to wish, without a sin! Yet I wish it would please God to take me to his mercy! I can meet with none here. What a world is this! What is there in it desirable? The good we hope for, so strangely mixed, that one knows not what to wish for? And one half of mankind tormenting the other, and being tormented themselves in tormenting! (I, 265)

With their "arm-in-arm lover-like behavior to each other" (I, 374) James and Arabella cooperate in sadism until at last Clarissa is goaded to exclaim to her aunt, "I see, I see, madam, that I am considered as an animal to be baited, to make sport for my brother and sister, and Mr. Solmes. They are all, all of them, wanton in their cruelty" (I, 404).

Thus far we have been considering Clarissa as an innocent victim, both of social circumstances and of her position in a selfish family. What makes this novel a profoundly Puritan fiction is the way in which victimization is shown to proceed from within the sufferer as well as from without. Pleading to know whether Clarissa harbors an unacknowledged attraction to Lovelace, Anna Howe writes, "Nothing less than the knowledge of the inmost recesses of your heart can satisfy my love and my friendship" (I, 188). From Johnson onward Richardson's genius has been identified with "the recesses of the heart," with the implication, as in Diederot's celebrated image of the hideous Moor in the cavern, that what the recesses conceal is dishonorable if not horrible.[12] In a sense this is simply a return to the old Puritan suspicion of the self, in reaction against an age infatuated with sentiment and benevolism. Diderot's formulation can in fact be paralleled in Calvin: "I grant indeed that all these crimes are not exhibited in every individual, yet it cannot be denied that this monster lurks in the hearts of all."[13] As has often been remarked, Clarissa's letters have much in common with the Puritan diary, providing—as an eloquent misprint in *The Rise of the Novel* confirms—"an opportunity for a much fouler and more unreserved expression of the writer's own private feelings than oral converse usually affords."[14]

If Puritanism enjoined knowledge of the heart, it also emphasized the obstacles that lie in the way. Johnson's remark that "there is always something which she prefers to truth" is not, as Kinkead-Weekes comments, entirely fair, since Clarissa strives almost superhumanly to lay bare the truth.[15] Still it must be admitted that she is at first ingenuous in her ideas about self-examination. We can only pity her when she tells her mother, "I declare to you that I know not my own heart, if it be not absolutely free" (I, 72), and she later confesses to Anna a discovery of "more *secret* pride and vanity than I could have thought had lain in my unexamined heart" (I, 420). What Puritan psychology offers finally is a confession of mystery, a recognition of inadmissible impulses that inhabit every person and not just exceptional villains. Classically trained writers like Dryden constantly celebrated the new scientific psychology that could lay bare the deepest "springs of action"; the Puritan tradition of mimetic veracity permitted a deeper descent which ultimately (as Scholes and Kellogg argue) leads onward beyond mimesis: "Mimetic characterization, if pushed far enough, leads to its own destruction. When the narrative artist finally penetrates the labyrinth of the psyche, he finds there not a mechanical marvel but a world of myth and monsters."[16] The empiricist psychology that writers like Dryden admired is really an epistemology, explaining mental experience as a reaction to external stimuli and a mechanical reshuffling of sensory materials. Richardson anticipates Romanticism in seeking, however haltingly, to expose the structures in the mind that *shape* experience.

Beneath this openness to experience lies Richardson's commitment to didactic message, which many critics have seen either as an unavoidable nuisance or as a screen that lets him hide his real motives from himself. It would be more accurate to say that character and motive are measured against, and in part formed by, a rigid structure of didacticism. The constant pressure of this measuring and forming is a fundamental source of the novel's power. Current criticism is much interested in the process of *Clarissa*'s composition, which was shown to friends when first drafted, published in installments that permitted further redirection, and extensively modified in subsequent editions. In particular Richardson sought to influence readers by inserting "editorial" footnotes commenting on the implications of the action. Most of the time this involves nothing more than reemphasis of details that are already in the text, and does not really differ in principle from the elbow-nudging comments of omniscient narrators in Fielding or Thackeray. But at times, notably when suggesting that Clarissa is not strictly a realistic character because "she is proposed as an *example*" (II, 314), Richardson seems unexpectedly to jeopardize the mimetic pose with which his story is presented. William Warner is quite right to say that at these moments "Clarissa is not just a character with the nature of a 'real' person, but a trope—an element in the rhetorical functioning of a work of art."[17] Still she is not a trope in the sense that Bunyan's Christian and Hopeful are. If they are allegorical characters seeking to become novelistic, Clarissa is emphatically a novelistic character looking back at allegory from a perspective that remains outside it. If she becomes a trope it is because she *sees herself* as one. Instead of criticizing Richardson, therefore, for imposing a didactic interpretation on his story, one might well admire the subtlety with which the struggle between self-assertion and ethical convention is embodied in the imaginations of the characters themselves.

In the first letter of the entire collection Anna says "You see what you draw upon yourself by excelling all your sex" (I, 2); the whole enormous unwinding of the story is an elaboration of that truth. In part, this means seeking to live out the traditional Puritan ideals of self-examiner, virtuous example, and saint.[18] But more largely it involves a profound exploration of the meaning of "character," which from the Renaissance onward had become a disturbing problem. Clarissa strives to *have* a character in the moral sense, to earn or deserve it, while Lovelace is content to *be* a character in the dramatic sense.[19] In defining character in absolute terms, setting "the heart" over against the demands of society, Clarissa and her creator respond to the Puritan conviction that life is a test in which character is both shaped and valued. For as her mother sternly warns, "You have had no trials till now; and I hope that now you are called to one you will not fail in it" (I, 78–79). And again, "You have never been put to a test till now, that deserved to be called a test" (p. 98). At times, undoubtedly, Richardson's didacticism is heavy and tiresome, but it informs everything that makes *Clarissa* a great novel, and can endow even the cautionary-tale obviousness of Belton's death with a Shakespearean poignancy: "Now his voice is not to be heard; all inward, lost; not so much as speaking by his eyes: yet, strange! how can it be? the bed rocking under him like a cradle" (IV, 169–70). Edward Young, a much narrower kind of moralist, wrote that in purifying the novel Richardson "has cast out evil spirits; has made a convert to virtue of a species of composition once most its foe, as the first Christian emperors expelled daemons, and dedicated their temples to the living God."[20] But it would be more accurate to say that before he could cast out demons (or daemons, for that matter) he had first to raise them.

Will, Desire, Sainthood, Death

Bunyan's Christian can put his fingers in his ears and leave his pleading family behind because the outward action is only an allegorical equivalent of inner experience. In the literal reality of Bedfordshire such a person would presumably continue to live among his family while withdrawing from them spiritually. Defoe seems to have intended something similar in *Robinson Crusoe,* although the allegory of spiritual solitude keeps mutating into a fantasy of total freedom from other people. The footprint on the beach is shocking not only because it belongs to a cannibal, but also because in a deep sense Crusoe does not *want* other human beings, however much he may protest that he does. "Zuleika, on a desert island, would have spent most of her time in looking for a man's footprint";[21] it is the last thing Crusoe wants to see. In *Clarissa* Richardson succeeds in dramatizing, as no previous writer of narrative had done, the anguish and deformation of spirit that attend any serious exclusion from other people. *Pamela* had its origin in conduct books, including Richardson's own *Familiar Letters,* which were designed to help people integrate themselves into society. *Clarissa* stands utterly outside of such a structure. Its heroine is painfully inimitable, and finds herself ensnared in a dilemma that no code of conduct can extricate her from. Clarissa must learn with wrenching pain that, as Anna says, she is "alien" to her family (I, 282); beyond that she must learn what eighteenth-century Christianity tended to minimize, that every Christian soul is alien to this fallen world and must seek its true *nomos* elsewhere.

At the beginning Clarissa wholeheartedly accepts the traditional ideal of female subservience, so that she proposes "obedience" as likely to reform Lovelace. "A great deal of the treatment a wife may expect from him will possibly depend upon herself. Perhaps she must *practise* as well as *promise* obedience, to a man so little used to control; and must be careful to oblige" (I, 199). But Clarissa's own mother pathetically exemplifies the hopelessness of such a plan, for despite her "prudence and fine understanding" (p. 206) she has "no will of her own" (II, 1), or as she herself puts it, she is tormented by having "a will without a power" (II, 291). What Clarissa eventually learns is to combine her mother's goodness with her father's strength of will, a point that is not lost on the frustrated Lovelace:

> How came the dear soul (clothed as it is with such a silken vesture) by all its steadiness? Was it necessary that the active gloom of such a tyrant of a *father* should commix with such a passive sweetness of a will-less *mother,* to produce a constancy, an equanimity, a steadiness, in the *daughter,* which never woman before could boast of? (III, 151)

Anna Howe is far more "modern" than Clarissa in advocating feminist independence, speaking witheringly of marriage as "a state of bondage or vile subordination: to be courted as princesses for a few weeks, in order to be treated as slaves for the rest of our lives" (I, 131). Anna would certainly appreciate De Beauvoir's thesis that society forces women to take on the status of "the Other," thwarting the ego's desires by encouraging a woman to regard her own self as external and inessential.[22] But whereas Anna is prepared to accept a tepid marriage in order to secure a reasonable measure of independence in the world, Clarissa returns to an old-fashioned Christianity that renounces both world *and* self. She chooses sainthood, with all the social and psychological complications that that entails.

The problem of the will echoes throughout *Clarissa,* and Richardson exposes its paradoxes with masterly skill. In a profound sense, as we shall see later on, this novel is a tragedy of forced actions and fated consequences. But in an equally profound sense it is a celebration of freedom of choice, and ultimately confirms Clarissa's naive assertion at the outset, "We have nothing to do but to choose what is right" (I, 94). In a letter to her father pleading to be released from the attentions of Solmes, she begs him "to dispense with a command, which, if insisted upon, will deprive me of my free-will, and make me miserable for my whole life" (I, 152). Lovelace, recognizing this impulse in Clarissa, bends all his energies to subduing it by trapping her in a position in which—as in a forced move in chess—her only possible action will be the one he dictates. "You are to consider, madam, you have not now an option; and to whom it is owing that you have not; and that you are in the power of those (parents why should I call them?) who are determined that you shall *not* have an option. All I propose is, that you will embrace such a protection [i.e., his own]; but not till you have tried every way to avoid the necessity for it" (I, 182–83).

By the time of the flight from Harlowe Place, Clarissa's will is battered but increasingly strong, and she has learned to distinguish between the constraints of physical circumstance and the inner freedom that cannot be constrained. "If you go back," Lovelace says insinuatingly at the last instant when she might still return, "it must be from the impulses of a yielding (which you'll call a dutiful) heart, tired and teased out of your own will." But Clarissa has learned that there is a third principle besides duty to parents and egotistical self-assertion, and she replies angrily, "I have no patience, sir, to be thus constrained. Must I never be at liberty to follow my own judgment? Be the consequence what it may, I will not be thus constrained" (I, 483). In the short run she is tragically wrong, for a moment later an accomplice raises a prearranged alarm and she is deceived into fleeing with Lovelace, but in the long run she is exactly right, and he learns that in controlling her body he loses all hope of influencing her spirit. In the end she will indeed secure "my own liberty and freedom of choice" (I, 443).

Critics unfriendly to Clarissa have noted that saintly passivity can itself be a form of power, an insight which would not have been news to Socrates or St. Francis or Gandhi, and have detected something insidious in her tendency to deny it. "Clarissa's apparent passivity helps to protect her dominance, by making her position seem 'natural' and inevitable, rather than political."[23] But such "power" as this only exists if other people are willing to recognize it—Clarissa's relatives do recognize it in the end, but they wait until it has cost her her life—and far from representing cunning passivity, it involves a mode of action that is all the more heroic for abaondoning the normal stratagems of politics.

For a long time Clarissa attempts to assert her freedom in negative terms by promoting delay, continuing to hope that her "friends," as she calls them, will relent at last. This strategy requires much thought and a continual exertion of will, since both Lovelace and the Harlowes are working so ruthlessly to compel her surrender, but it is futile and only makes the crisis worse when it comes. Only then does she realize that she can assert a different kind of existential freedom *after* the irrevocable choice has been made. Her family and Lovelace agree in regarding the choice as being between two suitors, refusing to countenance the *tertium quid* of the "single life" that she and Anna long for. In the end Clarissa too understands that the choice was a binary one, but also that its alternatives were nothing less than good and evil, with both Lovelace *and* the Harlowes on the evil side.

In hoping that she might fit into a social *nomos* and at the same time remain autonomous (*auto-nomos*), Clarissa had tried to live out a central Puritan dream. It has been accurately said that "Clarissa needs to be both Adam and Crusoe, paradisal within and independent without, self-contained, dutiful, and free."[24] Since this is impossible, she has been slowly crushed between two millstones; but her suffering, which is real and agonizing, teaches her to seek an altogether different freedom. Power now means self-mastery, not mastery of others, though Richardson is aware that the saint possesses a kind of power over others. In the words of an ode "By a Lady" that Clarissa sends to Anna, she must pray "For power, its amplest, best extent, / An empire o'er my mind" (I, 275).

In achieving this religious resolution Clarissa is almost intolerably alone, more so indeed than earlier Puritans who believed they could detect the ubiquitous guidance of Providence. Warner says eloquently that "Clarissa stands like a figure in a Vermeer painting—bathed in the holy light that streams through the window on the left, but imprisoned in the mundane actuality of an ordinary room and prosaic activity."[25] The holy light comes from *outside*, and however much it may illuminate her path, Clarissa still has to act as best she can in a claustrophobically indoor world. For her, determinism might be a blessing, since as Augustine and Luther knew, a Pelagian commitment to salvation by one's own efforts is appallingly hard, and although Clarissa's faith never wavers her God is as remote as Bunyan's was immanent. From afar God consigns her to a moral struggle to the death, literally to the death, and while she never doubts that his grace sustains her, the decisions throughout must be entirely her own.

In the spiritual dialectic that Clarissa traces, her first move and her ultimate goal must be the rejection of the world; but this is not so easy as might first appear, for she is imprisoned in a fallen selfhood as well as in destructive relationships with other people. Clarissa's preparations for dying dominate the second half of the novel, and Watt, with his sociological interest, represents this as Richardson's prudential defense of a religion in trouble: "The reason for this emphasis on death seems to have been the belief that the growing secularisation of thought could best be combated by showing how only faith in the future state could provide a secure shelter from the terrors of mortality."[26] The thought might be translated into terms closer to Richardson's by saying that a desacralized world is not worth living in. If the novel is the epic of the world abandoned by God, then a true Christian—just as Bunyan believed—should abandon the world and go to join him. In New England, when Puritanism felt itself to be in retreat it sought more ritual rather than less, and placed particular emphasis on funeral ceremonies that signified the welcoming of death.[27]

There is a sense, perhaps, in which Clarissa's death is elected and therefore a covert suicide, but Richardson does his best to make clear that she dies because it is time for her to die. "The world is unworthy of her!" Belford exclaims after Clarissa's merits have converted him from profligacy (IV, 248), alluding to the saints "of whom the world was not worthy" extolled in the Epistle to the Hebrews (11:38). Repeatedly Clarissa aspires to die as the appointed fulfillment of a pilgrimage like Bunyan's. "Death will be welcomer to me than rest to the most wearied traveller that ever reached his journey's end" (III, 507); and again,

> What then, my dear and only friend, can I wish for but death? And what, after all, *is* death? 'Tis but a cessation from mortal life: 'tis but the finishing of an appointed course: the refreshing inn after a fatiguing journey: the end of a life of cares and troubles; and, if happy, the beginning of a life of immortal happiness. (III, 521)

In his postscript to *Clarissa* Richardson issues a challenge: "Who that are in earnest in their profession of Christianity, but will rather envy than regret the triumphant death of Clarissa?" (IV, 558). And in a letter to his favorite correspondent, Lady Bradshaigh, he asserts that mimesis itself requires such a conclusion, since reality would be falsified if the world were described as adequate for the saint. "A writer who follows nature and pretends to keep the Christian system in his eye, cannot make a heaven in this world for his favourites, or represent this life otherwise than as a state of probation. Clarissa I once more aver could not be rewarded in this world." Richardson then quotes an ad hominem argument of his friend's, and replies with a Sternean gesture:

> "How can any one," say you, "think with pleasure of parting with what they love, supposing their end ever so glorious?— Could *you*, sir?—Have you ever made it your own case?"
> Ah; madam!—And do you thus call upon me?—Forgive an interrupting sigh; and allow me a short silence.[28]

Richardson sighs because even an admirable person like Lady Bradshaigh cannot face the plain substance of her avowed faith. As Swift showed with satiric irony, there was no longer any question of embracing "real Christianity, such as used in primitive times (if we may believe the authors of those ages) to have an influence upon men's beliefs and actions," and what is left is only "nominal Christianity, the other having been for some time wholly laid aside by general consent, as utterly inconsistent with our present schemes of wealth and power."[29]

Meanwhile it is necessary to confront those inner demons which haunt even the most saintly. In Richardson's imagination this means above all a confrontation with one's passionate nature, of which sexuality is the chief but far from the only expression. Clarissa is accustomed to being told that she has a feeling heart, and she wears her sensibility with a confidence that her family may possibly be forgiven for resenting.

> "Dear Bella," said I, hand and eyes lifted up, "why all this? Dear, dear Bella, why—"
> "None of your dear, dear Bella's to me. I tell you I see through your *witchcrafts*" (that was her strange word). And away she flung, adding as she went, "And so will everybody else very quickly, I dare say."
> Bless me, said I to myself, what a sister have I! How have I deserved this? (I, 35)

On a later occasion, when Clarissa goads Arabella to strike her, "A tear would stray down my cheek. . . . Bella has not a *feeling heart*. The highest joy in this life she is not capable of: but then she saves herself many griefs by her impenetrableness" (I, 218). The kindly uncle John is surely right when he complains that Clarissa's vehement nature has exacerbated the crisis: "If you will trust to your sharp-pointed wit, you may wound: yet a club will beat down a sword: and how can you expect that they who are hurt by you will not hurt you again? . . . If you *were* envied, why should you sharpen envy, and file up its teeth to an edge?" (I, 304).

The impenetrableness of which Clarissa speaks is indeed a central issue in her world, [30]and she has to learn very painfully that her cherished sensibility is no guarantor of happiness or even of rectitude. She is not hypocritical in scenes like these, just lacking in self-knowledge, and later on she will bitterly recognize it. Meanwhile she persists in believing that other people, even Lovelace, must surely conform to the sentimental ideal. "We have heard that the man's head is better than his heart; but do you really think Mr. Lovelace can have a *very* bad heart?" (I, 181). He certainly can, and so in her own way can Clarissa herself. She primly tells her brother that "the principal end of a young man's education at the university is to learn him to reason justly, and to subdue the violence of his passions" (I, 138); while James richly deserves the rebuke, Clarissa herself must learn how hard it is for reason to govern passion.

Above all she has to recognize, as the Puritans did, the duplicity of the language of the heart, which uses sincerity as a mask for unacknowledged desire. Assuring an anxious Anna that she does not care for Lovelace—"Indeed, my dear, THIS man is not THE man"—Clarissa earnestly adds, "If ever I should have the misfortune to think it love, I promise you, *upon my word*, which is the same as *upon my honour*, that I will acquaint you with it" (I, 47–48). She imagines that language is truth, and that her "word" possesses a kind of sanctity in sustaining an "honor" that is both sexual purity and ethical good faith. Meanwhile she blindly advances in attraction to Lovelace, insisting all the way that it cannot be so, as is illustrated by her smokescreen of passive constructions and syntactic evasions:

> I should be very blameable to endeavour to hide any the least bias upon my mind, from you: and I cannot but say that this man—this Lovelace—is a man that might be liked well enough, if he bore such a character as Mr. Hickman [Anna's pallid suitor] bears; and even if there were hopes of reclaiming him. And further still, I will acknowledge that I believe it possible that one might be driven, by violent measures, step by step as it were, into something that might be called—I don't know what to call it—a *conditional kind of liking*, or so. But as to the word LOVE, justifiable and charming as it is in some cases (that is to say, in all the *relative*, in all the *social*, and, what is still beyond *both*, in all our *superior* duties, in which it may be properly called *divine*); it has, methinks, in the narrow, circumscribed, selfish, peculiar sense in which you apply it to me (the man, too, so little to be approved of for his morals, if all that report says of him be true) no pretty sound with it. (I, 134–35)

Emerging from these impacted clauses, one sees why Richardson's contemporaries praised him for knowledge of the heart. Among earlier Puritan writers only Milton suggests so well the confused, earnest good intentions that mask the darker intentions beneath; and Milton's epic control imposes a final shape upon a kind of experience which Richardson, like no one before him, is able to present in all of its unfinished complication. "I declare to you," Clarissa tells her mother, "that I know not my own heart, if it be not absolutely free" (I, 72). It turns out that she does not, and although her mother is weak she is not stupid: "Ah, girl, never say your *heart is free*! You deceive yourself if you think it is" (p. 103).

It is of course true that Clarissa does desire Lovelace, "a man I had not absolutely intended to encourage" (I, 123), even though she admits to Anna that he too is finally "impenetrable" (p. 201). But this is no extraordinary insight: everyone in the novel shares it, from misogynistic Uncle Antony who thinks that women want whatever is for-

bidden (p. 161), to Anna's mother—whom Antony later courts!—
who cynically dismisses love as a simple tension needing release: "It is
a *fervour* that, like all other *fervours,* lasts but a little while; a bow over-
strained, that soon returns to its natural bent" (p. 294).

In the comic tradition of the eighteenth century, the purpose of
exposing the recesses of the heart is to reveal what a woman really
wants, and thereby to encourage her to get it.

> Just in that instant, anxious Ariel sought
> The close recesses of the virgin's thought. . . .
> Sudden he viewed, in spite of all her art,
> An earthly lover lurking at her heart.[31]

The difference between Pope's account of the "recesses" and Richardson's is not just that the poet is elliptical, omniscient, satiric, and
mock heroic, but, far more deeply, that to detect an earthly lover in
Clarissa's heart is to identify the question rather than the answer.
What does it mean to have unacknowledged desires, and what would
it mean to act upon them? What Clarissa learns is not that she ought
to accept Lovelace, as Pope's Belinda should the Baron, but rather
that passion is always ready to subvert even the steadiest virtue. "But,
O my dearest friend, am I not guilty of a punishable fault, were I to
love this man of errors? And has not my own heart deceived me,
when I thought I did not?" (II, 438).

Without question Clarissa harbors unacknowledged sexual feelings
for Lovelace, but it is also true—as the description of Solmes pressing
against her hoop shows—that she is in part pushed *toward* Lovelace by
revulsion *from* Solmes, a feeling made all the stronger by James's sadistic identification with the appalling suitor: "My brother pretends to
court me as his proxy, truly" (I, 33). Clarissa is never very explicit on
the subject of sex, but much later she does bring herself to tell Anna
that what most horrified her in Solmes was the prospect of "the marriage intimacies" (II, 167). And Lovelace never understands, at least
not until far too late, that he stands no chance of fanning Clarissa into
wanton desire, and that she too is forever "impenetrable" to his wiles
if not his person.

> All my fear arises from the little hold I have in the heart of this
> charming frost-piece: such a constant glow upon her lovely fea-
> tures: eyes so sparkling: limbs so divinely turned: health so flor-
> id: youth so blooming: air so animated—to have an heart so
> impenetrable: and *I,* the hitherto successful Lovelace, the ad-
> dresser—how can it be? . . . How then can she be so impenetra-
> ble? (I, 148)

Clarissa the frost-piece is not playing hard to get, she *is* hard to get,
because whatever her unadmitted interest in Lovelace may be, she will

never allow it to dictate her behavior. Lovelace then alludes to *Othello*: "Perdition catch my soul, but I *do* love her" (p. 149). He never learns how she can be so impenetrable, and perdition does catch his soul.

The rape of Clarissa, when at last it occurs, is morally blameless with respect to her, since she is unconscious at the time. From Lovelace's point of view it is an admission of failure, since only thus can he accomplish what she will never willingly permit. But for Clarissa it is still literally the fate worse than death, and she writes immediately afterwards that the murder of her person would be "a much lighter crime than that of my honour, which the greatest villain on earth has robbed me of" (III, 213). In a mysterious way the rape—which Richardson has the art to leave undescribed and unknowable—is endowed with permanent symbolic form by the absoluteness with which Clarissa regards it. Mary Douglas observes that virginity is often a special ideal of minority groups that feel themselves threatened, expressing beliefs "which symbolize the body as an imperfect container which will only be perfect if it can be made impermeable."[32] Or, in Richardson's language, if it can survive physical penetration by substituting spiritual impenetrability.

Clarissa closely resembles the old Puritans in espousing a radical dualism of body and soul—the former defiled, the latter inviolate—but she differs from them in her freedom from obsessive guilt. She abandons the life of the body because it has proved abhorrent, not because she acknowledges any permanent attraction to it. No true Puritan would say, as Clarissa at the end repeatedly does, "I have never been faulty in my will" (IV, 359); "My fault was not that of a culpable will" (IV, 365). In Ricoeur's phenomenology of evil her attitude corresponds to the category of "scrupulousness," admitting defilement but surmounting or transcending guilt.[33] The next step, therefore, is to relinquish the body, which is seen not as the self but as a hindrance to the self. After becoming upset by a confrontation with the insolent maid Betty, Clarissa writes to Anna, "O, my dear, what a poor, passive machine is the body when the mind is disordered!" (I, 377). Long afterward, when she is about to die, she exclaims "Yet how this *body* clings! How it encumbers!" (IV, 201). And this is as much as to declare that she is indeed, in Pauline terms, an alien in the fallen world. "Let me repeat that I am quite sick of life; and of an earth in which *innocent* and *benevolent* spirits are sure to be considered as *aliens*, and to be made sufferers by the *genuine sons* and *daughters* of *that earth*" (III, 383).

For this reason Clarissa's famous symbolic dreams have a specific and limited significance in Richardson's eyes (though the fact that Richardson imagined them may have other kinds of significance in modern eyes). Contemporary psychological theory held that dreams were strictly meaningless, being nothing more than confused recombinations of sense-perceptions. "It is true, we have sometimes in-

stances of perception whilst we are asleep, and retain the memory of
those thoughts: but how extravagant and incoherent for the most part
they are, how little conformable to the perfection and order of a rational being, those who are acquainted with dreams need not be
told."[34] Richardson follows the older belief that dreams do convey
meaning, often transmitting messages from the spiritual world (not
necessarily wholesome ones). But the very notion that they can be
introduced into the mind suggests that the dreamer, like Milton's Eve,
is not fully responsible for them, and at most they express only the
lower passions. Modern readers may assume that the recesses of the
heart conceal the real self that expresses itself when the censor is
asleep, but Richardson sees there the most chaotic and animal element in man, that which is least part of the real self.

Many readers have been struck by the conflation of sex and death
in Clarissa's lurid nightmare:

> Methought my brother, my Uncle Antony, and Mr. Solmes had
> formed a plot to destroy Mr. Lovelace; who discovering it, and
> believing I had a hand in it, turned all his rage against me. I
> thought he made them all fly into foreign parts upon it; and
> afterwards seizing upon me, carried me into a churchyard; and
> there, notwithstanding all my prayers and tears, and protesta-
> tions of innocence, stabbed me to the heart, and then tumbled
> me into a deep grave ready dug, among two or three half-dis-
> solved carcasses; throwing in the dirt and earth upon me with
> his hands, and trampling it down with his feet. (I, 433)

Whatever import these images may have carried in Richardson's unconscious mind, in Clarissa's they mean simply that she foresees death
as a punishment for her covert attraction to Lovelace and destruction
of her family's tranquillity. The dream is a way of accepting a punishment which she feels she deserves for her pride and disobedience.
Rather than marry Solmes, she has twice declared to her mother, she
would prefer to be buried alive (I, 87, 143); in the dream Solmes helps
to carry out that fate. What is ultimately involved is not (as some have
suggested) a recognition that she wants Lovelace to rape her—which
she certainly does not—but rather a loathing of the world of perverted desire, and a weaning from the body until its dissolution no
longer fills her with horror, and she can cheerfully order her coffin
and live with it as a continual *memento mori*.

We have seen how paradoxical the Puritan hope was of being in the
world but not of it, and (one might add) in the body but not of it. In
gladly choosing death Clarissa only does what numerous devotional
manuals recommended, whether or not many people actually fulfilled the ideal.[35] And her aspiration to sainthood reflects the intro-

spective element in Anglicanism, for example in William Law's *Serious Call to a Devout and Holy Life,* that stressed the imitation of Christ. By sharing in his atonement the believer could aspire to a "perfection" (a frequent term in *Clarissa*) for which earthly sufferings are the necessary preparation.[36] Quite similarly, Emerson's intelligent and strong-willed aunt, whose life was "a fruit of Calvinism and New England, ' had her bed made to resemble a coffin and wore her grave-shroud both indoors and out. "Destitution is the Muse of her genius," Emerson comments, "—Destitution and Death. I used to propose that her epitaph should be: 'Here lies the angel of Death.' " But from Emerson's own perspective, this protracted mortality is irresistibly droll. "Her friends used to say to her, 'I wish you joy of the worm.' And when at last her release arrived, the event of her death had really such a comic tinge in the eyes of every one who knew her, that her friends feared they might, at her funeral, not dare to look at each other, lest they should forget the serious proprieties of the hour."[37] In presenting Clarissa's death Richardson cannot permit the slightest hint that her preparations are disturbingly obsessive, and neither Clarissa nor anyone else perceives the least trace of the comic.

In this life, of course, literal perfection is impossible, and Clarissa ruthlessly exposes the pride with which she formerly enjoyed her exemplary role. "What a pride did I take in the applause of every one! What a pride even in supposing I had *not* that pride!" (II, 378). Exemplary though she continues to be, Clarissa is thus a far subtler character than Pamela, who like the snow (as Aaron Hill wrote unctuously to Richardson) "covers every other image, with her own unbounded whiteness."[38] Up to the very end Clarissa uses biblical texts to confess this primal sin: "How much reason have I to say, 'If I justify myself, mine own heart shall condemn me; if I say I am perfect, it shall also prove me perverse'?" (IV, 60; see Job 9:20). But she treats with deserved contempt James's gift of *Francis Spira* (II, 256), the book about damnation that brought both Trosse and Bunyan close to despair. The biblical texts that she transcribes as "Meditations" expose her sinful pride, but they also assure her—as Richardson comments in republishing them separately—that "the Almighty expects not perfection even in his saints. His chastisements she looks upon as a mark of his approbation; and declares her affiance in Him."[39] The term "affiance" persisted into the nineteenth century with twin meanings: faith in God, and the plighting of troth between fiancés. On her deathbed Clarissa is dressed as a bride, and her last words are "Come—O come—blessed Lord—JESUS!" (IV, 347).

Clarissa's death is not without a strong element of revenge. She leaves a set of posthumous letters for each of her offending relatives, exerting an unanswerable power from beyond the grave, and Colonel Morden alarmingly observes,

> How wounding a thing, Mr. Belford, is a generous and well-distinguished forgiveness! What revenge can be more effectual, and more noble, were revenge intended, and were it wished to strike remorse into a guilty or ungrateful heart! But my dear cousin's motives were all duty and love. (IV, 430).

Very likely Richardson does not perceive the extent of the irony here—his self-identification with the dying Clarissa must have been profound—but he probably does perceive some of it. For even if Clarissa does not mean to glory in her triumph, it remains a triumph all the same, and there is truth in what she writes to her spiritual adviser Dr. Lewen (himself about to die):

> The man whom once I could have loved, I have been enabled to despise: and shall not *charity* complete my triumph? And shall I not *enjoy* it? And where would be my triumph if he *deserved* my forgiveness? Poor man! He has had a loss in losing me! I have the pride to think so, because I think I know my own heart. (IV, 186)

Whether successfully or not, Richardson is trying to distinguish here between sinful pride *in* oneself and allowable pride in what God has made possible *through* oneself. And of course he believed that Clarissa's triumph over her survivors was the necessary incentive to their conversion, a continuation of the lifelong vocation by which, as even the venal servant Joseph Leman testifies, "She goes nowhere, but saves a soul or two, more or less" (I, 492).

But whether Clarissa's death is interpreted as divine agency or as personal revenge, it remains an existential crisis which she confronts with extraordinary directness. Ortega writes that anyone who really looks at reality will feel himself lost:

> Instinctively, as do the shipwrecked, he will look round for something to which to cling, and that tragic, ruthless glance, absolutely sincere, because it is a question of his salvation, will cause him to bring order into the chaos of his life. These are the only genuine ideas; the ideas of the shipwrecked. All the rest is rhetoric, posturing, farce. He who does not really feel himself lost, is without remission; that is to say, he never finds himself, never comes up against his own reality.[40]

Rhetoric, posturing, and farce are precisely the characteristics of Lovelace, who refuses to lose himself and therefore cannot be saved. Shipwreck is what happens to Crusoe, but we are never really made to believe that it happens psychologically as well as literally, and if this traditional religious symbol is *not* psychological it becomes weirdly displaced and incoherent, since to depsychologize it is to end up with a symbol without a referent. The New Testament metaphor of dying in order to live is not just a metaphor: it demands a stripping away of the false self, a profound reconciliation of ego with superego at what Erikson calls "the unconquered frontier of tragic conscience."[41] Early in the narrative Clarissa sees herself as the helpless helmsman driven out of control by a storm (I, 345–46); by the end she has accepted shipwreck as the path to renewal. *Robinson Crusoe* is an immortal fantasy of triumphant narcissism; Clarissa too has her narcissistic aspect (who does not?) but her story is an attempt to redirect it and make it healthy.

In sociological terms Clarissa's highly public death forces those who know her to confront the ultimate threat to their *nomos*; for as Berger says, "Death radically challenges *all* socially objectivated definitions of reality."[42] From Eagleton's Marxist point of view Clarissa's death exposes the contradictions in her society but resists the theoretical implications—"Nobody could be more submissive to patriarchal order, more eloquent an ideologue of bourgeois pieties, than Clarissa Harlowe."[43] But this is not really fair: like all Puritanisms that genuinely reject the world, Clarissa's position is radical in the ultimate sense. Richardson knows very well that the *nomos* is sick. Patriarchy and piety may be his ideals as well as Clarissa's, but they are ideals only after they have been purged—just as in *Paradise Lost*—from the revolting perversions of those who use them to consolidate power. A "good death," Berger goes on to say, can repair the ruptured social *nomos* by integrating it with "an all-encompassing sacred reality" (p. 44), and this is exactly what Richardson hopes that Clarissa—and *Clarissa*—can achieve.

God and Satan

In order to free the patriarchal ideal from false imaginative forms, Clarissa has to learn to disobey her dreadful father, and Richardson has to distinguish between the punitive God whom that father resembles and the loving God who desires and rewards Clarissa's assertion of her own integrity. In theological terms old Harlowe is like the voluntarist God of the Reformation, resting his irresistible authority on will rather than reason. "I will be obeyed!" he roars at Clarissa when Solmes is first proposed; "I have no child, I *will* have no child, but an obedient one" (I, 36). When she timidly interrupts "I hope, sir—" he replies ominously, "Hope nothing." Again and again the primacy of the paternal will is affirmed, for example by Clarissa's mother: "Well you know, that were Mr. Lovelace an angel, and your father made it a point that you should not have him, it would be in vain to dispute his will" (p. 82). After she is imprisoned in her room Clarissa writes to beseech that he not "reprobate his child," and his rejoinder, signed "A JUSTLY-INCENSED FATHER," is that she must "continue banished from my presence, undutiful as you are, till you know how to conform to my will" (pp. 120–21). When her mother calls him "a jealous father" (p. 80) one may surely think of the jealous God of the Old Testament.

Old Harlowe's agents, like those of Calvin's God, use the language of predestination while continuing to demand obedience as if his subjects were free to choose. "It is absolutely determined," Mrs. Harlowe says (p. 71). Uncle John writes "You know your destiny; and have nothing to do but to yield to it" (p. 154). We do what we must, but we are expected to welcome it, for as Harlowe himself says, "She had better make a merit of her obedience" (p. 192). If Clarissa does surrender she will receive "grace": "This is the last time that grace will be offered you" (p. 207). Harlowe is of course only a man, and a badly misguided one at that, but his appropriation of divine attributes is no casual matter, reflecting a favorite theme of moralists. As William Ames said in his popular work *Conscience* (1643), "Parents in regard to their children do bear a singular image of God, as he is the creator, sustainer, and governor."[44] In Clarissa's case the identification is all the more powerful because it exploits her deep wish to satisfy her father's demands, however irrational they may appear. "Is it not sought to ensnare, to entangle me in my own desire of obeying?" (I, 103).

After many days of communication through messengers, the turning point comes when Clarissa obtains a promise that she can see her father face to face, and in a brilliantly realized scene is thwarted once again, as she implores him to open his door and let her in.

> This sentence I heard thundered from the mouth of one who had a right to all my reverence: "Son James, let the rebel be this moment carried away to my brother's [to marry Solmes]—this very moment—she shall not stay one hour more under my roof!"
>
> I trembled; I was ready to sink. Yet, not knowing what I did or said, I flew to the door, and would have opened it: but my brother pulled it to, and held it close by the key. "O my papa!—my dear papa," said I, falling upon my knees at the door—"admit your child to your presence! Let me but plead my cause at your feet! Oh, reprobate not thus your distressed daughter!"
>
> My uncle put his handkerchief to his eyes; Mr. Solmes made a still more grievous face than he had before. But my brother's marble heart was untouched.
>
> "I will not stir from my knees," continued I, "without admission. At this door I beg it! O let it be the door of mercy! and

open it to me, honoured sir, I beseech you! But this once, this once! although you were afterwards to shut it against me for ever!"

The door was endeavoured to be opened on the inside, which made my brother let go the key on a sudden; and I pressing against it (all the time remaining on my knees) fell flat on my face into the other parlour; however without hurting myself. But everybody was gone, except Betty. . . . (p. 390)

It is impossible not to think of Christ's promise in the Sermon on the Mount, "Ask, and it shall be given you; seek, and ye shall find; knock, and it shall be opened unto you" (Matt. 7:7). In Matthew this text follows shortly after a retributive warning which the Harlowes would do well to remember—"Judge not, that ye be not judged"—and in Luke it comes just after Christ teaches his disciples the Lord's Prayer. But it is superbly appropriate here that when the door passively opens ("was endeavoured to be opened") the father has vanished, the *deus absconditus* of Clarissa's world.

If Harlowe is a dreadful parody of the Augustinian God, the parody comes uncomfortably close to the original. Augustine very movingly ends the *Confessions* by quoting "Knock, and it shall be opened" as a loving invitation. *A te petatur, in te quaeratur, ad te pulsetur*: *sic, sic accipietur, sic invenietur, sic aperietur*: "From you let it be asked. In you let it be sought. At your door let us knock for it. Thus, thus is it received, thus is it found, thus is it opened to us."[45] But earlier in the book Augustine observes that the Scriptures, though speaking in humble language and the most open words (*verbis apertissimis*), nevertheless preserve "the dignity of their hidden truth within a deeper meaning" (VI.v, p. 140). In many Puritan temperaments, as we have seen, the simultaneous openness and hiddenness of the Bible could seem almost intolerable, and Clarissa's unapproachable father is like a figure out of their worst nightmares.

The Gnosticism which Augustine had once espoused solved this difficulty by fragmenting God into two parts, a wicked (or at least incompetent) demiurge, who made the fallen world, and a true God of light far away. As E. R. Dodds comments, such a procedure is psychologically attractive because it reflects "a splitting of the individual father-image into its corresponding emotional components: the conflict of love and hate in the unconscious mind is thus symbolically resolved, and the gnawing sense of guilt is appeased."[46] But in this solution the good God is unacceptably remote, for what Augustine wants is a God who is deeper than his inmost self as well as higher than any height he can attain: *Tu autem eras interior intimo meo et superior summo meo.*[47] Clarissa, too, attains an intimate conviction of divine support, but God sends her none of the overt messages that Crusoe receives, and she is sustained entirely by faith in things unseen. Meanwhile she must endure the oppression of a punitive father who has much in common with the Gnostic demiurge—not because the unscholarly Richardson had ever heard of Gnosticism, but because similar psychological impulses dictate his splitting of the symbolism of God. And gradually she fights free of the emotional trap that her father had set with his language of "grace" and "reprobation," transferring her allegiance to the true Father on high and replacing the Old Law with the New.

It may not be fanciful to suggest that Clarissa is aided in doing this by the memory of her grandfather, whose "will" (as Arabella punningly notes) is now a document requiring interpretation, even while their father continues to enforce his own "will" directly: "Let me tell you, my pretty little flighty one, that your father's *living* will shall control your grandfather's *dead* one" (I, 230). In one sense it is as if the biblical sequence had been inverted: first the loving God of forgiveness, then the jealous God of punishment. But in another sense the grandfather too is a version of Calvin's God, for what strikes the family as "unaccountable" (p. 54) is the arbitrary election which the will pronounces. "Because my dearest and beloved granddaughter Clarissa has been from her infancy a matchless young creature in her duty to me, and admired by all who knew her, as a very extraordinary child; I must therefore take the pleasure of considering her as my own peculiar child" (p. 21). Just as Clarissa's father is not an adequate image of the wrathful God and must finally be disobeyed, so the grandfather is not an adequate image of the smiling God, and his arbitrary behavior has thrown the domestic kingdom into disarray.

Fighting against her father's remorseless demands, Clarissa asserts an obedience which is nonetheless self-assertive, as her analogies and exaggerations often make clear: "Do I either seek or wish to be independent? Were I to be queen of the universe, that dignity should not absolve me from my duty to you [her mother] and to my father" (I, 79). What she needs is something like Christian liberty, obedience not because God is all-powerful but because what he asks is right, the obedience merged with love that Christ offers in *Paradise Lost* (III.266–71). Such a God would not bar the door because—in the image that Bunyan developed so fully—he *is* the door. "Then said Jesus unto them again, Verily, verily, I say unto you, I am the door of the sheep" (John 10:7).

At a critical point in the story when she needs to hold Lovelace at bay, Clarissa writes to him as follows:

> I am setting out with all diligence for my father's house. I am bid to hope that he will receive his poor penitent with a goodness peculiar to himself; for I am overjoyed with the assurance of a

thorough reconciliation, through the interposition of a dear, blessed friend whom I always loved and honoured. (IV, 157)

Lovelace of course believes that she means her earthly father, but she is speaking of reconciliation with her heavenly Father through the intercession of Christ. Simply as casuistry her stratagem would have had the approval of that expert casuist Richard Baxter: "If I find a man in an ignorance or error which I am not bound to cure . . . I may either be silent, or speak darkly, or speak words which he understandeth not (through his own imperfection) or which I know his weakness will misunderstand: but I must speak no falsehood to him."[48] It is not falsehood, even though Clarissa knows Lovelace will misconstrue it, because it is his own fault that he is blind to truth. He is one of those "outsiders" in the Gospels of whom Kermode writes, condemned to be excluded from the hermeneutic system that brings salvation.[49] Belford later tells Lovelace that Clarissa intended the letter as "an innocent allegory" (IV, 246), and Lovelace is shocked, as Warner comments, because "he had lulled himself into thinking he had an artist's control over all the sign systems of his fiction, that all that lay before him was an intelligible text of his own devising."[50] Clarissa invokes a signifying universe where human texts imitate divine ones, and where God is good even if his purposes are "at present impenetrable" (III, 232).

In the theological family romance, Clarissa's brother James describes her repeatedly as a "fallen angel" (I, 169) who stands in need of being "redeemed" (p. 381), but as Anna says it is the family themselves who are "devilish" (p. 414). James plays a role like that of Satan the Accuser in the Book of Job, inciting the Old Testament God to punitive measures, and he is also a kind of parodic Christ who creates conflict instead of mediating, and who is eager to judge (like Christ on the Last Day) but unwilling to forgive. But the real Satan in this novel, of course, is Robert Lovelace, as scores of allusions continually remind us. The theme is ironically announced when Anna Howe uses a casual expression that will later prove all too literal: "Talk *of the devil* is an old saying. The lively wretch has made me a visit and is but just gone away" (I, 52). The time is not far off when Anna will say more darkly, "I believe indeed he is a devil in everything but his foot" (II, 107), when Clarissa will liken him to a snake (II, 53), and when a servant will artlessly write, "Squire Luveless is a devil" (III, 334).

As with old Harlowe, so also with Lovelace, the symbolism gives significance to human actions by lending them the resonance of the Christian myth. Lovelace is like Satan in many ways, above all in pride and in the "damned fondness for intrigue" which he eventually recognizes as his "curse" (IV, 456). He can bear no master of any kind, and for this reason, despite his violent attraction to Clarissa, is incapable of that true love which is traditionally celebrated as the ascent to God: he proposes to write "upon LOVE, which I hate, *heartily* hate, because 'tis my master" (I, 152). Like Satan the shape-shifter, he is a "master of metamorphoses" (II, 13); Clarissa calls him "a perfect Proteus" (II, 82), and learns that his mode of operation is to hide wickedness under a mask of goodness. "He can put on the appearance of an angel of light; but has a black, a very black heart" (III, 66). Lovelace has "providences" of his own (II, 115) which allow him to manipulate other people's actions, and although Clarissa calls him a "cruel implement of my brother's causeless vengeance" (III, 267), from his own perspective it is the Harlowes who enact his script:

> I knew that the whole stupid family were in a combination to do my business for me. I told thee that they were all working for me like so many underground moles; and still more blind than the moles are said to be, unknowing that they did so. I myself, the director of their principal motions; which falling in with the malice of their little hearts they took to be all their own. (I, 493–94)

In a way the Harlowes are as evil as Lovelace—"I only guide the effects; the cause is in their malignant hearts" (II, 100)—but one might rather say that James is a sort of Moloch to Lovelace's Satan, a crude and stupid agent of his schemes.

The appropriateness of the satanic analogy is gradually brought home to Lovelace himself. At first he is merely flippant, as when he reports that Clarissa's beauty startled him into dropping his disguise "like the devil in Milton (an odd comparison though!)" and that the maid "could not keep her eye from my foot; expecting, no doubt, every minute to see it discover itself to be cloven" (III, 41–42). But later on he has a complicated, turbulent dream in which Clarissa is raised up angelically into heaven while he himself plunges into a hellish chasm,[51] and by the end he likens himself to the damned: "Nothing but the excruciating pangs the condemned soul feels, at its entrance into the eternity of the torments we are taught to fear, can exceed what I *now* feel, and *have* felt for almost this week past" (IV, 305). "Have I not earned her dearly?" he demands while awaiting news of her death. "Is not damnation likely to be the purchase to me, though a happy eternity will be hers?" (IV, 342). Lovelace is a human being, just as old Harlowe is, but as Clarissa suggests in her disturbed jottings after the rape, he is closely identified with the devil:

> O Lovelace, you are Satan himself; or he helps you out in everything; and that's as bad!
> But have you really and truly sold yourself to him? And for how long? What duration is your reign to have?
> Poor man! The contract *will* be out; and then what will be your fate! (III, 210)

By doing Satan's bidding Lovelace is unquestionably satanic, which raises in Clarissa's mind the old question, "Oh, why was the great fiend of all unchained, and permitted to assume so specious a form, and yet allowed to conceal his feet and his talons, till with the one he was ready to trample upon my honour, and to strike the other into my heart!" (III, 18). The answer must be, as always, that the devil involuntarily carries out God's will. Love is the focus of those passions which Clarissa must learn to recognize and control, and if Uncle Antony is merely vulgar in saying that "The devil is love, and love is the devil" (I, 164), Clarissa might still have heeded Anna's warning at the outset, "A beginning love is acted by a subtle spirit, and often-times discovers itself to a bystander, when the person possessed (why should I not call it *possessed*?) knows not it has such a demon" (I, 45). We have seen that Clarissa must be tested. Lovelace, cynically but accurately, casts himself as the Accuser who is licensed to carry out the test.

> Has her virtue ever been *proved*? Who has dared to try her virtue?
> . . . Thou, Lovelace, the tempter (thou wilt again break out and say), to be the accuser!
> But I am *not* the accuser. I am an arguer only, and in my heart all the time acquit and worship the divine creature. (II, 36–37)

Accusation is possible precisely because of this disorted "worship," which encourages a responsive feeling in the reluctant Clarissa and allows Lovelace to exclaim, "Let LOVE, then, be the motive:—Love of *whom*? A *Lovelace,* is the answer" (p. 37).

To the extent that Lovelace's identification with Satan is represented psychologically, it mirrors the prison of self-bondage that Milton exposes in *Paradise Lost,* and far from simplifying the character, the emblematic schema makes it deeper and stranger. But before we go on to consider Lovelace as a person, we need to recognize what the satanic symbolism implies for Clarissa. In this context what matters is not what she sees *in him* but what he elicits *in her*. In Ricoeur's terms Solmes would represent stain and Lovelace guilt, for while stain is external and unwanted, guilt is the price of wanting what we must not want. Exactly as in *Paradise Lost,* therefore, the serpent Lovelace represents "the psychological projection of desire."[52] As Ricoeur expounds this idea, with allusions to Paul on the flesh and James on man's temptation by "his own lust" (1:14), this symbol allows evil to be at once within and without, desired and yet rejected. And this is the ultimate lesson of an exploration of the "heart":

> The serpent, then, would be a part of ourselves which we do not recognize. . . . Arguing from the fact that our freedom is beset by desire, we seek to exculpate ourselves and make ourselves

appear innocent by accusing an Other. Thus we allege the irre-
sistibility of our passions in order to justify ourselves. That is
what the woman does when she is asked by God, after the fatal
deed: "Why have you done this?" She answers: "The serpent
beguiled me." Bad faith, then, seizes upon the quasi-externality
of desire in order to make it an alibi for freedom. (p. 256)

Just as critics who jeer at Milton's Satan fail to appreciate that he is
inevitably attractive because he is already in us, so critics who despise
Lovelace miss the painful lesson that Clarissa is wise enough to draw.
Lovelace is despicable, certainly. But desire had to be in Clarissa before Lovelace could exploit it, and it is a measure of her understanding that she does not make her desire "an alibi for freedom," but fully
acknowledges guilt while striving to achieve freedom of an altogether
different kind.

Contrasting the pure Clarissa with the heroine of Rowe's *The Fair
Pentitent,* Belford says disapprovingly of Calista that "her devil is as
much *within* her as *without* her" (IV, 118). Clarissa, wiser than Belford,
knows that for her it is both. Richardson himself was shocked that
readers found Lovelace attractive, and went to considerable lengths to
discourage them, but that only proves that he was a more timid critic
than artist. In a way the contemporary writer was right who accused
him of acting "the part of the serpent" in dramatizing the progress of
lust: "You tempt [readers] to swallow the forbidden fruit of the tree
which they were commanded not to eat."[53]

If Lovelace is Satan, then Clarissa is Eve, an analogy which she
herself notes after the elopement when she speaks of being "driven
out of my paradise" (I, 502). Lovelace describes her "wavy ringlets" as
"wantoning" (p. 511), a clear reminiscence of Eve whose "wanton
ringlets waved" at a time when wantonness was as yet unfallen.[54] And
at several points he resembles Satan in pausing "overawed, checked,
restrained" (III, 275) by the force of Clarissa's virtue and beauty.
Gillian Beer observes that Milton moves from myth down to human
psychology while Richardson works in the opposite direction, starting
with human figures and surrounding them with mythic implications.[55] Thanks to Christ's sacrifice Clarissa is enabled to reverse the
Fall, an Eve who acknowledges evil within but resists the tempter
without. "Compulsion shall do nothing with me," she heroically tells
Lovelace. "Though a slave, a prisoner in circumstance, I am no slave
in my will!" (III, 260). Margaret Doody suggests surprisingly but persuasively that Clarissa "demands the same kind of attention as
Milton's Satan; she manifests a strength of will and desire which resists all obstacles and humiliations, and, fiercely asserting her integrity, refuses to be a mere victim."[56] This is possible because she fully
recognizes the force of desire within herself, while imploring God to
give her the strength to redirect it.

Whatever awkwardness and unevenness may sometimes impede Richardson's great conception, his novel thus carries forward Milton's psychological theme while surrounding it with mimetic realism. Some measure of his achievement may be indicated by a comparison with *Robinson Crusoe*, which asserts a similar religious theme but in fact displaces it radically. Crusoe's sin amounts to ignorance and rejection of God, rather than specific desires or crimes, and once an act of grace has produced forgiveness little further attention is paid to it. Clarissa, although she had far greater provocation than Crusoe for disobeying her father, never gets over the revelation of her disobedience, recognizing that she remains the person who was capable of it. Her sin lay not in giving way in a moment of confusion to Lovelace's scheme, but in possessing impulses that made it possible for him to lure her into his power. She repents the sin but is still the potential sinner, a subtlety far beyond anything in Crusoe's rough-and-ready world. In *Clarissa* imprisonment is not a metaphor for autonomy, as in Crusoe's island, but a vision of human cruelty—at Harlowe Place and then in Mrs. Sinclair's brothel—in a world which Clarissa is glad to leave behind. And the diabolical is fully internalized, as the satanic element in Lovelace but also as the Lovelace element in Clarissa.

Rather than invoking a populous world of spirits and miracles as Bunyan and Defoe do, Richardson presents a strangely quiet and opaque universe governed by a God who is trusted but never seen or heard. Weary of guilt, Bunyan can make us feel what the real presence of Satan might seem like; weary of guilt, Defoe displaces sin on to a Satan who bears it away like a scapegoat. Richardson's achievement is a more difficult but also more remarkable one, looking forward to Dostoevski as much as back to Bunyan. He shows what the *idea* of Satan might mean to men and women in general, even to those who do not believe in him and never think of him.

The World According to Lovelace

It should be apparent by now that "knowledge of the heart" implies much more than a plausible representation of human behavior. At times, indeed, the behavior may be implausible, since Richardson is working with extreme types under extreme pressure. It is no wonder that many readers then and now have identified with Anna Howe, for as Anna herself says,

> One observation I will add, that were *your* character and *my* character to be truly drawn, mine would be allowed to be the most natural. Shades and lights are equally necessary in a fine picture. Yours would be surrounded with such a flood of brightness,

with such a glory, that it would indeed dazzle; but leave one
heartless to imitate it. (II, 131)

What makes the exploration of the heart so profound is a double
movement in the narrative: a dramatization of the radically different
ways in which individual characters perceive reality, and an elaboration of all of these separate realities within a larger symbolic structure.
The two movements are related, since if Richardson seeks to contain
Lovelace within a traditional Christian pattern—the Satan myth
which we have just been considering—his imagination develops a
Lovelace who has a highly coherent counter-pattern of his own, and
the novel is always threatening to escape from its author's control and
to say more than he wants it to say.

If the Harlowes and their allies are obsessed with money, Lovelace
and his friends are obsessed with sexual adventure. "My predominant
passion," he says smugly, "is *girl*, not *gold*" (II, 20). But this vocation is
attended by a dreadful emptiness, for even while asserting that wom-
en "like an uncontrollable passion" and want to be "eaten and drunk
quite up by a voracious lover" (II, 209), Lovelace confesses that sexual
gratification is disappointing—"*Preparation* and *expectation* are in a
manner everything: *reflection* indeed may be something, if the mind
be hardened above feeling the guilt of a past *trespass*: but the *fruition*,
what is there in that? And yet that being the end, nature will not be
satisfied without it" (I, 172–73). It has been well said that for him a
seduction "is, like climbing Mount Everest, a matter of planning and
stamina," but it is not quite right to add that "there is no pleasure in it:
the pleasure lies in the satisfaction of having done it."[57] Of course
there is pleasure, but it is never adequate to the fantasies of desire;
Lovelace would agree with Shakespeare's Troilus, "This is the mon-
struosity in love, lady, that the will is infinite, and the execution confined; that the desire is boundless, and the act a slave to limit."[58]

Love for "Love-less" (Richardson undoubtedly intends the pun) is
above all an assertion of will, and will is best gratified in overcoming
obstacles, the more the better. This is why even his fellow rakes shake
their heads at the complexities he insists on creating, and why he
chaffingly tells Belford,

> Thou knowest nothing, Jack, of the delicacies of intrigue; noth-
> ing of the glory of outwitting the witty and the watchful; of the
> joys that fill the mind of the inventive or contriving genius,
> ruminating which to use of the different webs that offer to him
> for the entanglement of a haughty charmer, who in her day has
> given him unnumbered torments. Thou, Jack, who, like a dog at
> his ease, contentest thyself to growl over a bone thrown out to
> thee, dost not know the joys of the chase, and in pursuing a
> winding game. (II, 30)

In Lovelace's opinion it is Belford who is the animal, content with mere gratification, while he himself represents lust spiritualized and made intelligent.

Richardson's opinion is of course not Lovelace's. To spiritualize lust only makes it worse, as the body points out to the soul in Marvell's poem:

> What but a soul could have the wit
> To build me up for sin so fit?[59]

But the bitter irony is that since Lovelace prefers women who are both innocent and proud—no callous deflowerer, he enjoys sparing a humble innocent whom he nicknames Rosebud (I, 171)—Clarissa is inadvertently the ideal object for his assault. By resisting him imperiously she enacts the classic role of the Petrarchan lady, and this inflames Lovelace. Her behavior can easily be translated into the categories he is familiar with from his fantasy life, and she is therefore assimilable, although with grotesque inappropriateness, to his mental world. Moreover she is highly intelligent, which makes her a fit opponent in the game he insists on setting up, as she herself begins to realize with increasing terror. After calling him a Proteus she exclaims, "Would to Heaven I were not to play! For I think, after all, I am held to a desperate game" (II, 82).

For Lovelace, who despises marriage as "the life of shackles" (II, 36), the ever-renewed pursuit is a sustained assertion of freedom, and as Traugott says, "A queen mated is the signal for the game to begin anew."[60] Though in desperation he finally rapes Clarissa this is an admission of defeat, for as he had declared earlier, "There is no triumph in *force*. No conquest over the will" (II, 398). Yet he has reason for thinking the gamble worth taking, for according to his notions Clarissa will never admit she has physical desires until he has compelled her to acknowledge them. The strength of Clarissa's will is precisely what attracts him, and his goal is to make her openly *want* him, stealing her not only from her family but also "from herself" (II, 34). There is indeed a grim parallelism between her will and his, and their antagonism draws its energy from a kind of symmetrical tension. Other men may want simply to "rifle" women's bodies (to borrow a term that Fielding applies to the ignoble Blifil); Lovelace wants to insinuate himself into their minds.

I was *originally* a bashful mortal. Indeed I am bashful still with regard to this lady—bashful, yet know the sex so well! But that indeed is the *reason* that I know it so well. For, Jack, I have had abundant cause, when I have looked into *myself*, by way of comparison with the *other* sex, to conclude that a bashful man has a

good deal of the soul of a woman; and so, like Tiresias, can tell
what they think, and what they drive at, as well as themselves.
(II, 55).

The significance of this passage is noted by Rachel Brownstein, who
explores the ways in which both Lovelace and Clarissa are committed
to an assertion of power: she wants to reform him, he to conquer her,
and each implies a denial of the other person's essential being.[61] This
is not to suggest that both are equally guilty or even equally responsible. Clarissa's hopes are virtuous and soon abandoned, while Lovelace's are vicious and prosecuted to the bitter end. But it does go far
toward explaining the fatality with which each reacts to the other in
ways that entangle them further. "Ever since I knew you," Clarissa
says, "I have been in a wilderness of doubt and error" (III, 47–48);
Lovelace for his part complains that he has been journeying "through
infinite mazes, and as infinite remorses" (III, 200).

Literary and cultural models tend to shape the way in which people
regard themselves, and of course they shape the ways in which novelists
regard their inventions. As many critics have noticed, Clarissa enacts
the role of the heroine in a Restoration "she-tragedy," while Lovelace
likes to see himself as a combination of the clever rake of Restoration
comedy and the swaggering despot of heroic drama.[62] At times these
allusions allow Lovelace to suggest a kind of pathos in the limited
scope for action that his culture affords:

> Hannibal was called *the father of warlike stratagems*. Had Hannibal
> been a private man, and turned his plotting head against the
> *other sex*; or had I been a general, and turned mine against such
> of my fellow-creatures of *my own*, as I thought myself entitled to
> consider as my enemies, because they were born and lived in a
> different climate; Hannibal would have done less mischief,
> Lovelace more. That would have been the difference. . . . I have
> three passions that sway me by turns; all imperial ones. Love,
> revenge, ambition, or a desire of conquest. (II, 494–95)

We know that Richardson despised the martial epic,[63] and he probably wanted this sort of bluster to suggest something like the reductive
irony of Swift: "The very same principle that influences a bully to
break the windows of a whore who has jilted him, naturally stirs up a
great prince to raise mighty armies, and dream of nothing but sieges,
battles, and victories."[64] But many sensitive people in the eighteenth
century—most notably Pope—looked back with real nostalgia to the
unified ethos that the classical epics present, and it makes sense to say
as Anthony Winner does that Lovelace is a victim of the transition from
epic to novel. "Preying upon the society of the other sex, forced to
battle in its settings and often on its terms, the heroic code is threat-

ened with dishonor, led into the mediated and compromised stratagems that constitute novelistic, as opposed to epic, reality."[65] Ironic
detachment and comic exaggeration allow *The Rape of the Lock* to avoid
(if only barely) calling compromise and dishonor by their right names,
ending up with the rather complacent suggestion that mating is the
universal human goal. In *Clarissa* nothing is shirked, and Clarissa's
resistance, unlike Belinda's, is all the more impressive because Lovelace is exploiting assumptions that are deeply rooted in the culture. As
Traugott says, "Her will to dignity in a society which, as Lovelace
knows, often makes women sublime in order to gain the pleasure of
humiliating them by sexual aggression, is a moving spectacle."[66]

Lovelace's passion for improvisation has come in for a good deal of
attention lately, amounting at times to whitewash. To some extent he
does prefigure the heroes of Gothic romance who turn play into
crime as a challenge to the ultimate order of things. Auden's reflections could well be an analysis of Lovelace:

> Man desires to be free and he desires to feel important. This
> places him in a dilemma, for the more he emancipates himself
> from necessity the less important he feels.
> That is why so many *actes gratuites* are criminal: a man asserts
> his freedom by disobeying a law and retains a sense of self-im-
> portance because the law he has disobeyed is an important one.
> Much crime is magic, an attempt to make free with necessity.
> An alternative to criminal magic is the innocent game. Games
> are *actes gratuites* in which the players obey rules chosen by them-
> selves. Games are freer than crimes because the rules of a game
> are arbitrary and moral laws are not; but they are less
> important.[67]

Like Auden, Richardson does not believe that moral laws are arbitrary, and it makes sense for him to insist that Lovelace's moral "principles" are sound. The power of this characterization, like that of
Satan, depends on continual recognition of the counter-ideal which it
attacks but cannot overcome. Lovelace likes to see life as a jest, but he
well knows that it is a grim one and has irrevocable consequences. "A
jest, I call all that has passed between her and me; a mere jest to die
for—for has not her triumph over me, from first to last, been infinitely greater than her sufferings from me?" (IV, 261).

The ultimate point of Lovelace's literary allusions is that they are
only allusions, even when they involve the book that was supposed to
control interpretation of all other books.

> The subject of the discourse [at church] was particular
> enough; it was about a prophet's story or parable of an ewe lamb
> taken by a rich man from a poor one, who dearly loved it, and

whose only comfort it was: designed to strike remorse into
David, on his adultery with Uriah's wife Bathsheba, and his
murder of the husband. . . . Nathan, which was the prophet's
name, and a good ingenious fellow, cried out (which were the
words of the text) *Thou art the man!* By my soul I thought the
parson looked directly at me: and at that moment I cast my eye
full on my ewe lamb. . . .

When we came home, we talked upon the subject; and I
showed my charmer my attention to the discourse, by letting her
know where the doctor made the most of his subject, and where
it might have been touched to greater advantage: for it is really a
very affecting story, and has as pretty a contrivance in it as ever I
read. And this I did in such a grave way, that she seemed more
and more pleased with me. . . . (II, 221)

The story of David was a traditional resource for excusing sexual license, as Dryden does with Charles II at the beginning of *Absalom and
Achitophel,* but Lovelace shows that he partly understands the relation
of the story to himself. He cannot stand altogether outside the value-
system of his culture (and of Richardson's novel), and his uneasiness is
therefore real enough, but he deflects it with a time-honored stratagem for evading moral issues: he performs an act of literary criticism. Moreover, his interpretation is defective, for Clarissa surely
corresponds to the poor man being robbed of his honor, not to the
ewe lamb. To Nathan, the real sin is against Uriah, and Bathsheba is
only property; and that is exactly what Clarissa seems to everyone
except herself and Anna Howe.

What shocks Lovelace most, even as he partly longs for it, is the
possibility that Clarissa can make him redefine himself and his
"heart" in her own terms.

Cannot I *indeed* reform? I have but *one* vice; have I, Jack? Thou
knowest my heart, if any man living does. As far as I know it
myself, thou knowest it. But 'tis a cursed deceiver; for it has
many and many a time imposed upon its master—*master,* did I
say? That am I not now; nor have I been from the moment I
beheld this angel of a woman. (I,145)

Like Satan pulling himself together after being stunned by Eve's
goodness, Lovelace keeps forcing himself into the old track, and as
Winner splendidly says, "plays Iago to his own Othello."[68]

Behind everything that Lovelace does is a deeply disillusioned view
of human behavior that closely resembles that of Hobbes. Crusoe de-
serted from the war of all against all; Lovelace enthusiastically enlists
in it. According to Hobbes the ultimate human motive is not the pur-

suit of pleasure, which is bound to be unsatisfying since the passions are in constant agitation from outside stimuli, but rather "a perpetual and restless desire of power after power, that ceaseth only in death."[69] In a famous analogy he compares life to a race in which men have "no other goal, nor other garland, but being foremost," and he furnishes a list which fits Lovelace exactly:

> To endeavour, is *appetite*. . . .
> To see another fall, is disposition to *laugh*. . . .
> Continually to be out-gone, is *misery*.
> Continually to out-go the next before, is *felicity*.
> And to forsake the course, is to *die*.[70]

Lovelace's virtues tend to resolve on inspection into Hobbesian motives. He is well known as a good manager of his estate, but at one point he discloses that this is to ensure that no "bumpkin with his hat on" (i.e., not doffing it) can take advantage of his master's slackness to intimate "that he had it in his power to oblige you, and if you behave civilly may oblige you again." Lovelace adds sarcastically, "I, who think I have a right to break every man's head I pass by, if I like not his looks, to bear this!" (II, 67). He forgoes little Rosebud because his power can be affirmed just as much by abstention as by conquest, so long as it *is* affirmed. "Many and many a pretty rogue had I spared, whom I did *not* spare, had my power been acknowledged, and my mercy in time implored" (I, 170). His laughter is Hobbesian in its glorying over others, often overtly joined with class privilege as when he savagely humiliates Clarissa's landlord and manhandles a journeyman who says "'Twas well I was a gentleman, or he would not have taken such an affront" (IV, 131). And his mental life is at all times devoted to stratagems that promote gratification, in the spirit of Hobbes's maxim, "The thoughts are to the desires, as scouts, and spies, to range abroad, and find the way to the things desired."[71]

Like everyone else in Richardson's world, Lovelace prides himself on knowing the "most secret recesses" of human nature—"more particularly female nature," he adds conceitedly (III, 139)—but this amounts in the end to a grossly mechanistic theory of behavior, as in the letter in which he denounces Clarissa's doctor for not restoring her to health.

> Let me tell thee, Belford, that already he deserves the *utmost* contempt, for suffering this charming clock to run down so low. What must be his art if it could not wind it up in a quarter of the time he has attended her, when, at his first visits, the springs and wheels of life and motion were so good that they seemed only to want common care and oiling! (IV, 322)

Hobbesian psychology is both reductive and predictive. It claims that one can always explain a person's behavior if furnished with enough data, and manipulate it confidently if the right stimuli are applied. Much of what Lovelace sees in human behavior does seem to confirm this view, which is supported by his neoclassical typecasting of people and by the consistent (and manipulable) cruelty that the Harlowes display. Even Anna Howe, idly tormenting the lackluster Hickman, is capable of views that are disturbingly similar to Lovelace's (and reveal that the behaviorist model of the "pecking order" is no recent discovery):

> *Men,* no more than *women,* know how to make a moderate use of power. Is not that seen every day, from the prince to the peasant? If I do not make Hickman quake now and then, he will endeavour to make me fear. All the animals in the creation are more or less in a state of hostility with each other. . . . I remember that I was once so enraged at a game-chicken that was continually pecking at another (a poor humble one, as I thought him), that I had the offender caught, and without more ado, in a *pet of humanity,* wrung his neck off. What followed this execution? Why, that other grew insolent as soon as *his* insulter was gone, and was continually pecking at one or two under *him.* Peck and be hanged, said I—I might as well have preserved the first, for I see it is the *nature of the beast.* (II, 134)

So much for "humanity"; such a pronouncement by Clarissa's best friend shows how profound her moral isolation really is.

The one clear contradiction of Lovelace's bleak philosophy is the manifest goodness of Clarissa, to whom he is irresistibly drawn. What he really wants is not to rape her, least of all when she is unconscious, but to show her his true colors *and still* induce her to admit his mastery. Nietzsche has a powerful analysis in "The Natural History of Morals" that distinguishes this type of motivation from that of simpler seducers:

> As regards a woman, for instance, the control over her body and her sexual gratification serves as an amply sufficient sign of ownership and possession to the more modest man; another with a more suspicious and ambitious thirst for possession sees the "questionableness," the mere apparentness of such ownership, and wishes to have finer tests in order to know especially whether the woman not only gives herself to him, but also gives up for his sake what she has or would like to have—only *then* does he look upon her as "possessed." A third, however, has not even here got to the limit of his distrust and his desire for possession: he asks himself whether the woman, when she gives up everything for him, does not perhaps do so for a phantom of him; he wishes first

to be thoroughly, indeed profoundly well known; in order to be loved at all he ventures to let himself be found out. Only then does he feel the beloved one fully in his possession, when she no longer deceives herself about him, when she loves him just as much for the sake of his devilry and concealed insatiability, as for his goodness, patience, and spirituality.[72]

Clarissa of course recoils from Lovelace the more she understands his devilry, but he certainly exhibits the compulsion to reveal himself that Nietzsche describes. In this he is, one may say, a Satan psychologized beyond the one in *Paradise Lost,* a Satan fully humanized even while he remains diabolically inhuman (even today people shrink from psychologies like Augustine's or Hobbes's or Nietzsche's that identify cruelty as human).

Whatever her attraction to Lovelace, Clarissa's anguish derives from her realization that he may call her an angel or goddess but simply does not know who she is. He desires her as a collection of attributes, physical of course but also mental and even spiritual. What he does not desire and cannot even imagine is Clarissa herself: the integrated self that holds all the attributes together. Hence he tries to pick away at her defenses, never grasping that the more he does so, the more he must outrage her essential being. What Defoe naively dramatizes in the solipsism of Crusoe is subjected to grim analysis in Clarissa's struggle to achieve a genuine openness between minds. The pathos of her relation with Anna Howe—who writes "You are me" (I, 43)—is that Anna's brisk common sense belongs to the Lovelace world, however much she may abhor Lovelace himself. So the one person to whom Clarissa's soul was open is, in the end, closed to her too.

Ill-read though he may have been, Richardson clearly knew a good deal about the way his culture was adopting empiricist psychology, which increasingly defined man as a sum total of sense-impressions that need not share any common denominator.[73] Such a position might seem to resemble that of Pascal in the meditation "Qu'est-ce que le *moi?*" by doubting the possibility of knowing a self that is not just the sum of its parts: "One never loves a person, but only qualities."[74] But Pascal is writing from within the heart of the Augustinian tradition, and would see in the position of Hobbes and Lovelace an accurate account of fallen nature but also a fearful blindness to the need for grace.

> In a word, the *moi* has two qualities: it is unjust in itself, in making itself the center of everything; it is disagreeable to others, in wanting to enslave them: for each *moi* is the enemy and would like to be the tyrant of all the others. (141/455)

The true and only virtue is then to hate oneself (since one is hateful for one's concupiscence), and to seek a truly lovable being to love. But since we are unable to love what is outside ourselves, it is necessary to love a being who is within us and yet is not ourselves, and this is true of every single man. Now, there is only the universal Being who is like this. The kingdom of God is within us: the universal good is in us, is ourselves, and is not ourselves. (699/485).

In its ultimate tendency *Clarissa* is a comprehensive restatement of this Pauline and Augustinian position, and offers the entwined experience of Lovelace and Clarissa as its authentication in the world of familiar experience.

To put it simply, Lovelace's view of reality defines him as a damned soul, like Bunyan's Mr. Lustings who boasts at his trial that his will cannot be curbed and that he glories in doing what "not only I, but almost all men do either secretly or openly countenance, love, and approve of."[75] And the ultimate message of *Clarissa,* as of more openly didactic Puritan texts, is that reprobate behavior is its own punishment: "My self am hell."[76] "The retribution for disobedience," Augustine says somberly, "is simply disobedience itself. For man's wretchedness is nothing but his own disobedience to himself, so that because he would not do what he could, he now wills to do what he cannot."[77] If Lovelace is continually frustrated by the gap between desire and fulfillment, that is because he acts out—to borrow Ricoeur's words—the vision of evil as "the danger of not being able to love any more, the danger of being a dead man in the realm of ends."[78]

Tragedy and Novel, Structure and Deconstruction

Writing to a friend that he intended "more than a novel or romance by this piece," Richardson explicitly defined *Clarissa* as an example of "the tragic kind."[79] Scholars have found no difficulty in showing that the characters, language, and incidents all have antecedents in the drama. In the book itself Belford serves as a chorus to remind us that "this affair will end tragically" (II, 483) and will furnish "a fine subject for tragedy" (IV, 117). But there is nothing simple in such an identification, for tragedy is the strangest and most complicated of literary forms. By invoking it Richardson expresses his nostalgia for a genre that finds structure in (or imposes it upon) otherwise intolerable experience, and at the same time his imagination is liberated, through the subversive element that all good tragedy harbors, to hint at fears and uncertainties that resist form. In experimenting with the countless possibilities of the novel—from one point of view radically mim-

etic, from another radically symbolic—he raises more questions than
he himself is aware of, and inaugurates the era of modern fiction in
which we still live. The imaginative richness of *Clarissa* opens out in
many directions, and there can be no single "right" exposition of its
tragic implications; we must be prepared to circle round through a
series of different yet interrelated points of view.

At the heart of *Clarissa* lies the ancient truth embodied in Her-
aclitus's maxim that character is destiny. "Your merit is your crime,"
Anna tells Clarissa. "You can no more change *your* nature than your
persecutors can *theirs*" (I, 282) Anna's interpretation of character
tends to be openly fatalistic, as she recognizes when she contrasts her
own temperament with Clarissa's. "What is this but praising, on both
sides, what neither of us can help, nor perhaps *wish* to help? . . . What
then is it in either's approving of her own natural bias but making a
virtue of necessity?" (II, 131). Just as Horatio or Laertes would not
suffer Hamlet's anguish, so Anna (like Fielding's Sophia Western)
could easily have escaped from the dilemma that imprisons Clarissa.
As so often in tragedy it is the subsidiary figure, Anna or Belford,
who is free to be flexible, while the great protagonists are locked by
their absoluteness in a structure of disaster. Belford begins as a rake
and is converted to goodness, but Lovelace like Satan is unwilling and
even afraid to change. Clarissa is similarly locked into a role, in her
case an exemplary one that leads to martyrdom.[80]

From Anna's point of view this role-playing entails an unncessary
and disastrous delicacy. "Twice already have you, my dear, if not of-
tener, *modestied* away such opportunities as you ought not to have
slipped" (II, 295). It is quite true that Clarissa's modesty makes it impossible for her to learn everything about Lovelace that she needs to
know, the "multitude of other evils" which her cousin Morden calls
"too gross, too shocking, to be mentioned to a person of your delicacy" (II, 260). It is also true that if things had gone differently Clarissa might well have married Lovelace, as so many of Richardson's
friends and readers hoped she would. At the very beginning her aunt
declares that "we should make the finest couple in England," her
mother protests weakly "that *her* only dislike of his alliance with either
daughter was on account of his reputed faulty morals," both uncles
approve strongly, Arabella petulantly gives up any claim to him, and
only old Harlowe holds out on the strength of an angry letter from
James (I, 9–10). James himself says later, "Your friends are as weary
of confining you as you are of being confined" (I, 263), and in a way
Clarissa resembles Hamlet as Wilson Knight sees him, the brooding
figure in black who disturbs an otherwise comfortable world.[81] But in
the subtlety of Richardson's conception the "bad" destiny is actually a
good one, since to marry either Solmes or the diabolical Lovelace
would be spiritual death, and Clarissa is absolutely right to resist.

"*After what I have suffered by thee,* it would be *criminal* in me to wish to bind my soul in covenant to a man so nearly allied to perdition" (III, 223).

In the protracted struggle between Lovelace and Clarissa, two modes of being are destructively entwined. It has been said that Lovelace is transitive, Clarissa intransitive,[82] and certainly she builds her resistance on a kind of indomitable passivity. But if she often feels as helpless as "a feather in the wind" (I, 413), her antagonists see her very differently, for example when she tears herself away from James: "I struggled so vehemently to get from him, that he was forced to quit my hand; which he did with these words: 'Begone then, Fury! How strong is will! There is no holding her!'" (I, 406). Yet in an ultimate sense Clarissa *is* passive, for however energetically she struggles when provoked by immediate insults, and however doggedly she persists in her refusal to accept Solmes, any hope of success is fatally compromised by her unceasing wish to find a way to please her persecutors. In answer to Anna's objections Clarissa rather primly replies, "There are other duties, you say, besides the filial duty; but that, my dear, must be a duty prior to all other duties; a duty anterior, as I may say, to your very birth; and what duty ought not to give way to that when they come in competition?" (II, 123). In this Clarissa resembles Sophocles' Antigone, noble in the urgency with which she defends a "duty" which is right and yet destroys her—a dilemma which Hegel defined as central to the tragic situation.

There is, however, no single central tragic situation, and an equally suggestive analogue is available in Euripides' *Hippolytus* and its adaptation in Racine's *Phèdre,* the tragedy of passion that destroys even while it is resisted. Or one might say that *Clarissa* is a kind of inverted *Romeo and Juliet:* the lovers are star-crossed because the obstacles are internal as well as external, and the tragedy would be far worse than it is if they succeeded in getting married. By unconsciously inclining to Lovelace, Clarissa is seduced away from what she consciously wants, and as Anna says, "You are drawn in by a perverse fate against inclination. . . . It is my humble opinion, I tell you frankly, that on inquiry it will come out to be LOVE" (I, 46).

Lovelace, meanwhile, says that the god of love "brought to me my adorable *Nemesis*" (II, 494). Instead of roistering onward as a carefree sexual athlete, he finds himself obsessed by a woman whose spiritual integrity both fascinates him and provokes his self-destructive plotting. Much to his surprise and even horror, this passion lures him into moments of near surrender from which he is barely able to retreat—"Didst thou ever before hear of a man uttering solemn things by an involuntary impulse, in defiance of premeditation, and of all his own proud schemes?" (II, 142). As the story continues Lovelace increasingly sees himself as "a machine at last, and no free agent" (III,

146), but this is rationalization, as we realize immediately afterward when he quiets his conscience by pretending to strangle the pen that gives it language. "Didst thou not see that I had gone too far to recede? Welter on, once more I bid thee! Gasp on! *That* thy last gasp, surely! How hard diest thou!" (p. 147). The Lovelace who has gone too far to recede is a prisoner, like Macbeth, of the tragedy of damnation, and he dies railing against "a cursed fate" (IV, 529).

We know, of course, or Richardson wants us to know, that what looks like fate is actually the Providence which (in Belford's words) has "taken the punishment of these unhappy wretches into its own hands" (IV, 467). And by definition Providence will always produce the best possible results, whether or not mere humans can understand it. Anna, rebuking her own pride as well as Clarissa's, declares that "it is better, and safer, and juster, to arraign ourselves, or our dearest friends, than Providence; which must always have wise ends to answer in its dispensations" (II, 280). As against theories of "poetic justice" that demanded a happy ending, Richardson like Addison insisted on the compatibility of earthly suffering with eternal rewards.

Clarissa states this position emphatically when Anna worries about the possible fulfillment of old Harlowe's curse.

> Be comforted; be not dejected; do not despond, my dearest and best beloved friend. God Almighty is just and gracious [i.e., filled with grace], and gives not His assent to rash and inhuman curses. Can you think that Heaven will seal to the black passions of its depraved creatures? If it did, malice, envy and revenge would triumph; and the best of the human race, blasted by the malignity of the worst, would be miserable in both worlds. (II, 171)

The hypothetical or conditional note is interesting, though: the universe would be malignant *if* what we normally experience were in fact normal, and not an appalling lapse from the transcendental norm. Johnson, very similarly, finds an argument for eternal happiness in the unhappiness of our present condition:

> It is scarcely to be imagined that Infinite Benevolence would create a being capable of enjoying so much more than is here to be enjoyed, and qualified by nature to prolong pain by remembrance and anticipate it by terror, if he was not designed for something nobler and better than a state in which many of his faculties can serve only for his torment, in which he is to be importuned by desires that never can be satisfied, to feel many evils which he had no power to avoid, and to fear many which he shall never feel: there will surely come a time, when every capacity of happiness shall be filled, and none shall be wretched but by his own fault.[83]

In confronting the sufferings of this life Christianity is a tragic religion, however happy its ending may be. Johnson goes on to say (citing the same text from Hebrews that Belford applies to Clarissa), "All the distresses of persecution have been suffered by those 'of whom the world was not worthy'; and the Redeemer of mankind himself was 'a man of sorrows and acquainted with grief.'"

Christian tragedy at its best paradoxically combines inexorable fate with ethical responsibility. Faith in ultimate justice is entirely compatible with a feeling, at any given moment, of helpless misery, as Clarissa indicates by quoting the Dryden-Lee adaptation of *Oedipus*:

> It were an impiety to adopt the following lines, because it would be throwing upon the decrees of Providence a fault too much my own. But often do I revolve them, for the sake of the general similitude which they bear to my unhappy, yet undesigned error.

> > To you, great gods! I make my last appeal:
> > Or clear my virtues, or my crimes reveal.
> > If wand'ring in the maze of life I run,
> > And backward tread the steps I sought to shun,
> > Impute my error to your own decree:
> > My FEET are guilty; but my HEART is free.
> >   (II, 266)

Clarissa capitalizes "feet" because she has altered the original "hands."[84] Oedipus did commit crimes, however unwittingly; Clarissa only ran away from home when a cunning trickster had frightened her into doing so. Yet she is right to see this as an "error," the *hamartia* which—whatever it may have meant to the Greeks—has always carried a double meaning in modern consciousness. It is at once the mistake that might have been avoided (getting into the garden where Lovelace could have his chance) and the flaw of character that produces the tragedy (the unacknowledged attraction to Lovelace that made it possible for Clarissa to be in the garden with him). And rather than allude to Oedipus, she might well identify with the plight of Racine's Phèdre:

> Grâces au ciel, mes mains ne sont point criminelles.
> Plût aux dieux que mon coeur fût innocent comme elles!
>   (I.iii)

("Thanks be to heaven, my hands are not criminal. Would to the gods my heart were as innocent!")

Lovelace prefers the shallower metaphor of the helpless chess piece.

Leave this sweet excellence and me to our fate: that will determine *for* us, as it shall please itself: for, as Cowley says,

> An unseen hand makes all our moves:
> And some are great, and some are small;
> Some climb to good, some from good fortune fall:
> Some wise men, and some fools we call:
> Figures, alas! of speech—For destiny plays us all.
>
> (II, 397)

No Augustinian would deny that man is determined, but determinism
is part of the paradoxical system of Christianity that asserts at the
same time the presence of personal responsibility. Following his own
inclination compulsively, Lovelace would like to see himself in Cowley's terms, but Richardson does his best to make us see him in terms
like those of Boethius. What gives *Clarissa* its unique power is the way
in which it combines two different tragedies, the irresistible plunge
toward destruction of Lovelace as a kind of Lucifer, and the conflict,
misery, and ultimate restoration of Clarissa as a kind of Eve.

Lovelace is constantly referred to as a "man of violence" (for instance by Clarissa after the rape, III, 239) with perhaps an echo of the
psalm, "Evil shall hunt the violent man to overthrow him" (140:11).
As Lovelace himself involuntarily testifies, the wages of sin is death.
" 'By my soul,' said he, and grasped my hand with an eagerness that hurt
it, 'we *were* born for one another: you *must* be mine—you *shall* be mine
(and put his other arm round me), although my damnation were to be
the purchase!' " (II, 302). Clarissa's tragedy is more complicated, and
from an aesthetic point of view triumphantly so: *Clarissa* is one of the
few works of literature that seriously challenge Simone Weil's disturbing observation, "Imaginary evil is romantic and varied; real evil is
gloomy, monotonous, barren, boring. Imaginary good is boring, real
good is always new, marvellous, intoxicating."[85] It is absolutely the
case that Lovelace, for all his shape-shifting and inventiveness, is hor-
rifyingly monotonous in his monomania. And Clarissa, for all her
conventional sanctity—one might say in spite of it, since Richardson is
an uneven writer—exhibits a goodness that is hard-won and ever
renewed.

Clarissa learns to assert an existential freedom that defies earthly
determinism. Whether her choice of death seems arbitrary or inevitable must surely depend in part on the values held by the individual
reader. As Richardson's revisions and footnotes show all too clearly, it
is impossible for the story to be told in a way that will totally control
interpretation. Someone standing far outside Richardson's ethos
might well agree with Berger that one may rebel against the "bad
faith" of a society and yet succumb to a different kind of bad faith,

ascribing inevitability not to the social order but to universal law.[86] In this sense tragedy can be seen as ratifying *nomos,* as in Bradley's Hegelian interpretation of Shakespeare in which suffering results from the agonized but successful effort of good to expel evil.[87] Yet this does nothing to allay the pathos of isolation, whatever may be the fortunate consequences for the survivors, and Clarissa's plight is exactly that described by Lukács, "the torment of a creature condemned to solitude and devoured by a longing for community."[88] Like Antigone, Clarissa leaves the world because it cannot accommodate her, not because she does not want it.

By contrast with the drama, the novel is usually thought of as peculiarly committed to a given cultural milieu. A recent sociological critic states as self-evident that "The characters of a novel are bound to a specific society and a distinctive web of social relationships. The novelist cannot create tragedy out of myth but must find it within reality itself."[89] *Clarissa* does both, deriving its deepest energies from the tensions in Christian doctrine even while affirming the characters' imprisonment in the demands and attitudes of their culture. Yet it is also true that the novel, written to be read silently by a private reader rather than enacted by human beings on a stage, is capable of making all social issues external to the deep drama of the self. And in fact the treatment of the isolated individual in Puritan narrative, searching though it is, achieves its depth in part from what it is prepared to leave out.

Hamlet does not have the luxury of voluntary withdrawal from the world. His problem rests like Clarissa's on who he is, but also—unlike Clarissa's—on what he must *do.* Although society is rotten and he himself is temperamentally unfitted for the role that has been forced upon him, yet his obligation, as announced by an authoritative voice from the dead, is to heal the sick society by the shocking commission of murder.

> The time is out of joint. O cursèd spite,
> That ever I was born to set it right!
>   (I.v.188–89)

Hamlet is paralyzed by the inability to act; Clarissa has no need to act except in the inner battleground of the mind, and no obligation is required of her that would correspond to murdering Claudius. It is enough that she accept her isolation from the social world and preserve her integrity until death, a task which is heroic enough but very different from Hamlet's, and one indeed which he might have performed with little difficulty.

As has already been hinted, Richardson's closest affinities are not with Shakespeare but with a dramatist whom he may well have known little about, the bleak Jansenist Racine. The *deus absconditus* of Jansenism (Pascal uses the term) is, according to Goldmann's thesis, cut off from communication with man because his image no longer shapes either the physical universe or the human community.[90] This is true even when, as was certainly usual in the eighteenth century, people continued to insist that God's image was essential. As Goldmann puts it, Descartes was a believer but Cartesianism is atheistic (p. 17). For those who were naturalized in the disenchanted world, the new mechanistic model appeared wholly adequate, and Goldmann's account is exactly applicable to *Robinson Crusoe*: the new model gave intellectuals an intelligible universe and artisans a subjected one (*un univers soumis*) in which "Men and things became simple instruments, objects of the thought or action of the rational and reasonable individual" (p. 41).

Goldmann sees the tragic spirit of this period as an acceptance of the values of the new individualism, together with a radical rejection of the reality that individualism claims to affirm. Since God is far away, the self has no recourse but to work out its destiny within the world that it rejects, and this yearning for the absolute in the midst of contingency generates the morally charged ethos of mimetic realism. It is also closely related to the traditional Augustinian ideal of being *in* the world but not *of* it: "The insurmountable distance that separates from the world the being who *lives* there exclusively but *without taking part* in it, liberates its consciousness from current illusions and customary impediments, and turns tragic thought and art into one of the most advanced forms of realism" (p. 66). Even as human actions are endowed with mythic significance, the world in which they take place is radically desacralized. Whereas myth in its "high" form normally distinguishes between sacred and profane, everything in the world of creatures is now profane, and the self owes its allegiance to a higher world from which it is withheld by tragically painful obstacles. It is easy to see how the myth itself could be contaminated by contact with the inimical world, and might find itself *of* the world as well as *in* it.

From Richardson's point of view, tragedy offered a reliable model for explaining and justifying human suffering. While it is true that different characters in *Clarissa* see life in terms of different genres—Lovelace is always trying to impose a comedy upon Clarissa's tragedy—it is tragedy which occupies the privileged place in Richardson's imagination, and Lovelace is made to say ominously (under color of commenting on Otway's *Venice Preserved*), "The devil's in it, if a confided-in rake does not give a girl enough of tragedy in his comedy" (II, 340). But the deepest affinity between *Clarissa* and the drama is not formal at all: it lies in the mode of experience that this remarkable novel evokes. For it totally lacks the normal basis of narrative, the presence of a teller and a tale. On the title page Richardson calls it

"The History of a Young Lady," but this is a history without a historian, and in a letter he refers tellingly to "my No-Plan, as I may call it" as enabling an omnivorous account of his characters' experience.[91] Richardson is a *narrator absconditus* miming the hidden God who presides over the sublunary world but never shows his hand directly, the Pascalian deity who *est toujours et ne paraît jamais*.[92] The putative "editor" is no violation of this principle, for he never gets inside the story and exists simply to help us interpret it from outside. In its density and prolixity *Clarissa* has epic size but totally rejects the epic mode.

The tragic model, as Goldmann's thesis suggests, was particularly attractive in a historical period when Christian dogma and culture were under unprecedented strain. Like many of his contemporaries, Richardson exploits the implications of tragedy while doing his best to look the other way.[93] Clarissa invokes the Oedipus story and then shies away from it because it implies a pagan, or existential, relation to fate; very similarly, the God of Pascal and Racine is so hidden that he threatens to vanish altogether. Even the tragedy of damnation, potentially impending over every sinner according to the Augustinian tradition, is carefully limited. Richardson locates it entirely in Lovelace, and he does his best—in a way that the older Puritans would have despised—to protect Clarissa from it.

Within the novel, each character strives in his or her own way to impose a structure. Lovelace manipulates events like a dramatist, but proves in the end to be an involuntary actor in God's drama. Clarissa's crucial letter about her Father's house is a return to Puritan allegory, seeing religious pattern in what Lovelace had been determined to see as secular play ("play" as both game and drama). No doubt Richardson himself wanted to endorse this emergence of allegory from within the mimetic medium. But his method commits him to an astonishing medley of forms and styles,[94] and Clarissa's scrupulous analysis is a recollection, though not in tranquility, that cannot overcome the fragmentary quality of immediate experience. "Were I rapidly to pursue my narration, without thinking, without reflecting, I believe I should hardly be able to keep in my right mind: since vehemence and passion would then be always uppermost; but while I *think* as I write, I cool, and my hurry of spirits is allayed" (I, 387). Whereas Lovelace enjoys narrating, and complains when Belford fails to do so (II, 490), Clarissa resembles the old Puritans in constantly transposing narration into detached reflection, which in turn becomes a kind of allegorical interpretation for which death is the only appropriate ending. And by his very obsession with Clarissa, Lovelace constantly permits his actions, free and arbitrary though he intends them, to be captured by the allegorical mode which Clarissa both employs and represents.[95]

In the imaginative world of *Clarissa* there are more than enough genres to go around, and while the book as a whole participates in the mode of tragedy that Goldmann describes, Clarissa herself—with

Richardson's collusion, of course—seeks to turn it into something like a romance. For does not Frye's account of romance correspond closely to the ethos of Clarissa, if not of *Clarissa?*

> At the lowest point of such a heroine's career . . . she gives the impression of someone living in a world below the one that she ought to be living in. . . . With the rise of the romantic ethos, heroism comes increasingly to be thought of in terms of suffering, endurance, and patience. . . . This is also the ethos of the Christian myth, where the heroism of Christ takes the form of enduring the Passion. Such a change in the conception of heroism largely accounts for the prominence of female figures in romance.[96]

But whereas the logic of romance, as exemplified in the late plays of Shakespeare, is to deflect tragedy into the longed-for harmony, the logic of *Clarissa* runs in the other direction. *Tom Jones* is a wonderfully wish-fulfilling fiction that merges romance into comedy; *Clarissa* is a wish-denying fiction that collapses romance into tragedy.

Against the impulse to find or impose structure, the book with its "No-Plan" strenuously resists structure, and the two most crucial events—the elopement and the rape—are postponed so maddeningly that the reader experiences the first out of sequence and the other only by remote indirection.[97] To some extent this produces a story in accordance with the assumptions of Lockean empiricism, in which the reader has to pick out significant details from the flux of circumstance.[98] But the method also has antecedents in Puritan narrative, where the details can be left unshaped because only God knows how to shape them, and with both God and Richardson now *absconditi,* it is never clear that a comprehensive structure is possible.

Similar ambiguities attend the status of time in this relentlessly temporal novel. Clarissa's desire is certainly to transform *chronos* into *kairos,* as her coffin emblem of the serpent of eternity suggests.[99] But if hers is the last word, it is hardly the only word, and there is much to be said for Lovelace's vision of the persistence of the transitory moment, "my momentary ecstasy . . . which has brought upon me such *durable* and such *heavy* remorse" (IV, 263). This is the notion of tragedy as a condition (rather than an Aristotelian action) that underlies Wordsworth's lines which Coleridge applied to *Hamlet:*

> Action is transitory—a step, a blow . . .
> Suffering is permanent, obscure and dark,
> And shares the nature of infinity.[100]

What gives *Clarissa* its peculiar power is its extraordinary slowness, the slowness of life itself, a mimesis of the exasperatingly heavy movement of inner experience as it confronts external reality. (Sterne, al though more famous than Richardson for mimicking states of consciousness, achieves his liveliness by abolishing external reality and allowing experience to have a purely psychological structure.) At the same time *Clarissa* is dramatic in the profound sense that its events are represented, in Richardson's own phrase, when they are as yet "generally dubious" (I, xiv). Each letter points forward, as Preston says, to an undetonated future, and moreover awaits reenactment in the temporal present of the reader's imagination. We are confronted therefore not with *kairos* but with a heightened sense of the urgency of *chronos*.[101] This commitment to the as yet unknown future, though it has deep roots in the Puritan way of interpreting experience, finds its closest literary analogue in the drama rather than in conventional narrative.

C. S. Lewis's Screwtape very strikingly remarks, "Nearly all vices are rooted in the future. Gratitude looks to the past and love to the present; fear, avarice, lust, and ambition look ahead."[102] By refusing to be a retrospective narrative, *Clarissa* forces the reader to participate in the always-about-to-happen tension of Lovelace's lust and Clarissa's fear. Clarissa herself breaks free of this pattern well before the end of the novel, rejecting the world of time and initiating herself into the world of eternity, but the reader continues to hope and fear long after she has ceased to do so. Only at the very end, when Belford and the others ponder the meaning of Clarissa's short life, does dramatic urgency give way to retrospection.

It is of course true that if Richardson did not write *Clarissa*, nobody did, but I want to insist finally on the autonomy which the work acquires as the reader reads. It is not life—it is purely and simply an invention—but one reads it *as if it were* life, which is the essential premise of realism and nowhere more splendidly achieved than here. Recently a number of deconstructionist readings have been proposed, all of them revealing much of interest in the play of texts and countertexts within the body of *Clarissa*. A fascination with textuality is encouraged by Richardson himself, who preferred to address his friends on paper rather than in person, and who sometimes rose to such astonishing meditations as this:

> Who then shall decline the converse of the pen? The pen that makes distance, presence; and brings back to sweet remembrance all the delights of presence; which makes even presence but body, while absence becomes the soul.[103]

But Richardson is protomodern, not postmodern, and the passage ends bathetically, "and leaves no room for the intrusion of breakfast-calls, or dinner or supper direction, which often broke in upon us." Whereas a postmodern theorist would be particularly interested in the *absence* that presence conceals, Richardson is concerned with the *presence* that is possible even in absence. And in this he is supported by his view of the veracity of language, which in the Puritan tradition is open to suspicion and yet in Shepard's words can make the "absent present."[104]

Since *Clarissa* strives above all else to seem a collection of real letters by real people, its closest contemporary analogue is a nonfictional work of mingled kinds like Boswell's *Life of Johnson*. Outrageously but suggestively opposing the *auteur* theory of biography, William Dowling describes Boswell's enormous book in terms that can easily be extended to Richardson's:

> To view Boswell's narration in the *Life* not as a containing but as a distributed embodiment of his consciousness, much as we view Hamlet's or Lear's speeches in those plays, is to expose the network of antithetical relations that remains obscure when we assume him, even when wholly silent, to be hovering attentively somewhere above the biographical story. The biographical narrator who hovers thus invisibly, mysteriously implying speech even in his silence, is an illusion created not by the *Life* but by an inadequate model of narrative structure.[105]

Freed by his method to identify totally with Lovelace as well as with Clarissa, Richardson is able to confess that when writing "I am all the while absorbed in the character. It is not fair to say—I, identically I, am anywhere, while I keep within the character."[106] And however much he wants his readers to derive an authoritative pattern from the data in *Clarissa,* what actually results is more like what Dowling describes in Boswell: "It is not a matter of competing versions of an identical reality, as one might hear, say, in courtroom testimony, but of realities competing with one another."[107]

The Richardson who invents Clarissa is also the Richardson who invents Lovelace, and no arcane psychological theory is required to see that he could not do that without some measure of imaginative identification. Whatever interest this fact may have in the context of Richardson's biography, it is surely of preeminent interest as a feature of cultural history. In the terms of Blake's myth in *Visions of the Daughters of Albion,* the rapist Bromion, the guilt-ridden lover Theotormon, and the raped and innocent Oothoon are all aspects of human consciousness. Richardson, like Lovelace, is a Tiresias who vicariously experiences the life of both sexes (II, 55), or to put it less kindly, he is like the eunuch in *Antony and Cleopatra* who loves to think what Venus did with Mars. To some extent *Clarissa* remains imprisoned within its enabling fictions; to some extent it transforms them into art and confirms Girard's definition of the novel as springing from "an obsession that has been transcended."[108] But above all *Clarissa*

remains an extraordinary masterpiece because its peculiar characteristics—some intended, some accidental—allow traditional Puritan
themes to flower in an atmosphere of unparalleled freedom, where
fantasy can develop without inhibition before conscience returns to lay
down the law.

To put it another way, Richardson's historical moment permits the
old Puritan themes to develop unchecked in an atmosphere of symbolic openness. Bunyan and Milton both wrote fictions that were un-
compromisingly tied to Christian doctrine, and although at many
points they test the limits of doctrinal explanation, the official censor
is always ready to rebuke the imaginative inventor. "May I express
thee unblamed?" Milton asks in *Paradise Lost*. In Richardson's time
religion had become largely a matter of ethics rather than dogma, and
I think it unlikely that he realized how deeply he was exploring some
of the central symbols of the Christian myth. For this very reason, he
was able to let them develop according to their own inner logic, in
which submission to Providence accords very uneasily with assertion
of the importance of the self, and in which the force of desire threatens to overwhelm any possible structure of discipline or sublimation.

Clarissa escapes the cycle of desire and guilt by electing death, but
this solution is not necessarily compatible with an assertion of desire
that is embodied not just in Lovelace, but also in the Lovelace element
in Clarissa. A traditional Puritan would be much more skeptical than
Richardson is about Clarissa's "perfection," and about the extent to
which she has the right to assert the purity of her unblemished will.
Moreover, the Lovelace interpretation of reality stands ready to reas-
sert itself if one should doubt for a moment the metaphysical basis of
Clarissa's election of death: that is, the promise of another and happier world to which the soul must journey. Lacking that basis, it would
be simply a suicidal impulse, though still perhaps a noble one, and the
Lovelace interpretation would take on a disturbing authority. It is well
to conclude by observing that every Puritan fiction rests finally on its
act of faith, and if many of us cannot share its answers, there is much
in Richardson's own imaginative conception that casts doubt on them
as well. But the questions, at any rate, remain our own, for desire and
guilt remain essential poles of human consciousness, and the great
Puritan narratives are a permanent contribution to understanding
them.

7

Tom Jones *and the Farewell to Providential Fiction*

Character and Desire

The greatest single literary work of the eighteenth century is Fielding's *Tom Jones* (1749), that urbane and spacious fable in which pragmatic knowledge of the world is made to harmonize with gratified desire. An omniscient and affectionate narrator acts as the disposing deity of the fictional universe, instructing the reader, by means of a plot whose coherence is only gradually revealed, to understand the operations of a Providence that subsumes all of the apparent accidents of chance or Fortune. *Tom Jones* thus triumphantly unites philosophical meaning with fictive form,[1] in ways that stand in a fascinating relation with the Puritan tradition we have been surveying. At the deepest level Fielding is in harmony with it, believing not only that life is providentially ordered (most novelists for the next century and a half believed that) but also that the shape of a fictional work can directly imitate that order. But in many ways he is unsympathetic to Puritan narrative, which indeed served as a negative stimulus when he left playwriting for fiction (*Joseph Andrews* began as a burlesque of Richardson's *Pamela*). I propose to survey two of the central themes of the present book—the idea of the self (or personality, or character), and the relation between human mimesis and God's plot—as a way of seeing the Puritan tradition in perspective while recognizing the precariousness, by the middle of the eighteenth century, of any art that claimed to unite formal principles with philosophical ones.

In Fielding's narratives, unlike those we have been considering thus far, mimesis is the work of a highly visible artist who selects and shapes the materials that life affords, in an ambiguous union of Aristotelian generalization with Platonic idealization, transforming (as Sidney said in the *Apology*) nature's brazen world into a golden one. Preoccupied with the embattled state of the self in a fallen world, Puritan narrative is often grim and always potentially tragic. Augustan narrative, even in dark satires like *Gulliver's Travels* and Pope's *Dunciad,* is often playful and always potentially comic. (I use the word "Augustan" as a convenient term for writers in the classical humanist tradition who admired the cultural values, if not the politics, of Augustan Rome.)

The absence of humor might almost provide a litmus test for identifying Puritan writing. Joan Webber, who notes that even on his deathbed Donne "puns as if his life depended on it," suggests that the Puritan avoids humor because "to the extent that art is play, he finds it hard to accept, and he often sees the conservative as someone who plays with words, because he cannot believe that such play may be serious."[2] We remember Bunyan's solemn declaration of veracity:

> I could have stepped into a style much higher than this in which I have here discoursed, and could have adorned all things more than here I have seemed to do: but I dare not: God did not play in convincing of me; the Devil did not play in tempting of me; neither did I play when I sunk as into a bottomless pit, when *the pangs of hell caught hold upon me:* wherefore I may not play in my relating of them, but be plain and simple, and lay down the thing as it was.[3]

The Puritan fear of play—both verbal wit and fictive invention—reflects a deep commitment to reading God's story rather than substituting one's own, but it also reflects a fear that the self might find freedom in play. Humor, as Erikson says of Luther's willingness to joke, "marks the moment when our ego regains some territory from oppressive conscience."[4] But Puritans were generally committed to the belief that conscience ought to be the ego's constant authority and guide. Lovelace jests constantly, Clarissa never, and although there is some grim wit in *Paradise Lost,* a Miltonic joke is no laughing matter. Dickens called *Robinson Crusoe* "the only instance of an universally popular book that could make no one laugh and could make no one cry."[5] Fielding and Richardson seem to have divided the alternatives between them.

Not all wit is affirming, of course. Hobbes's account of laughter as "sudden glory" at another's expense is disturbingly apt to Augustan satire, and in Pope—not to speak of Swift, who was never seen to laugh—there is always an edge of bitterness and scorn. Fielding had plenty of disappointed bitterness in his life, but *Tom Jones* stands immortally as a supremely Apollonian invention, sunlit and serene, in which evil is mastered, Dionysian energies harmonized, and the self liberated to fulfill its own best impulses. Seeing man as embattled amid fearful dangers, Puritan fiction was drawn to the image of the prison: Christian in Doubting Castle and Vanity Fair, Crusoe on his island, Clarissa in her locked rooms. For Fielding the central image is the road, that scene of unpredictable openness in picaresque fiction which he transforms into a confirmation that we should keep moving, onward not inward, until we get to a happy ending. At the end of *Tom Jones* he describes his narrative as a "long journey."[6] In a narrow sense this is a plot device, since the road permits Tom to meet the people who can rescue him from undeserved disgrace,[7] but more than that it is a fundamental principle of affirmation, life seen as possibility rather than as threat.

Puritan fiction was born of the individual's quest for a counter-*nomos*, Augustan fiction of the need to restore the old *nomos* and protect it from the unpredictableness of the separate individual. In the search for truth, Dryden wrote, we do well to curb our private notions if they threaten to disturb public peace, for "common quiet is mankind's concern."[8] Dryden was a relentless satirist of Puritan individualism, and like Pope and Swift after him he supported the social hierarchy which Puritanism was committed to extirpating. If all men are radically corrupt, then as Haller says "the absolute levels all relatives; all men are born equal."[9] Fielding knows that many of the rich and powerful are unworthy of their position, but all the same he believes in an aristocracy of goodness that overlaps to some extent with social status.

Allworthy is modeled on the philanthropist Ralph Allen of Bath, whom Pope also eulogized, in accordance with a social ethic that encourages the prosperous to integrate their inferiors into a comfortable *nomos*.

> His house is not quite a mile from this place. . . . There, I say, thou mayest be eased of thy burden, and if thou art not minded to go back to thy former habitation, as indeed I would not wish thee, thou mayest send for thy wife and children to thee to this village, where there are houses [that] now stand empty, one of which thou mayest have at reasonable rates; provision is there also cheap and good, and that which will make thy life the more happy is, to be sure there thou shalt live by honest neighbours, in credit and good fashion.

This idyllic proposal would not be out of place in *Tom Jones*, but it is in fact an account of Mr. Legality as delivered by Worldly-Wiseman.[10] Fielding of course abhors hypocrisy and regularly satirizes worldliness, but there is no denying that he would be at home in the village

of Morality, as is apparent in his frequent denunciations of sects like
the Methodists that favor faith over works. In Kierkegaard's terms he
is ethical whereas the Puritans were religious, and celebrates the sympathy that unites the group rather than the existential leap that isolates the rare individual:

> The knight of faith is obliged to rely upon himself alone, he feels
> the pain of not being able to make himself intelligible to others,
> but he feels no vain desire to guide others. . . . The true knight
> of faith is a witness, never a teacher, and therein lies his deep
> humanity, which is worth a good deal more than this silly par-
> ticipation in others' weal and woe which is honored by the name
> of sympathy, whereas in fact it is nothing but vanity.[11]

Fielding would find this formulation inexplicable if not diabolical. In
Tom Jones he satirizes something very like it in the misanthropic hermit the Man of the Hill.

For all its criticism of specific abuses, *Tom Jones* is deeply committed
to ratifying the social order, and is thus a "double theodicy" of the
kind Weber and Berger describe, providing the poor with an explanation of their poverty and the rich with an explanation of their wealth.
"The result is one of world-maintenance and, very concretely, of the
maintenance of the particular institutional order."[12] Society is the vast
structure into which one happens to be born, rather than a special
subgroup voluntarily entered by the elect, and one's place in it is confirmed by one's nature and one's actions together. Blifil is the legiti-
mate son of Bridget Allworthy, Tom the illegitimate son, but Tom
deserves to live at Paradise Hall while the vicious Blifil must be ejected
from it. It is a question both of deserving and of choosing to fit in, as
Locke indicates with (very likely) a backward glance at the Puritans:
"He must be of a strange and unusual constitution, who can content
himself to live in constant disgrace and disrepute with his own particular society."[13]

This social orientation governs the conception of character. It is no
longer a question of the unique individual confronting an alien world,
but rather of the typical character developing in accordance with the
pressures of a particular time and place. Puritan autobiographers
sought to find conventional patterns in their lives just because they
felt their individuality so keenly, and the Calvinist tradition leads directly to Rousseau with his boast that nature broke the mold after
forming him.[14] The Augustan attitude is closer to S. J. Perelman's:
"Before they made me they broke the mold." All men are defective,
but that is a familiar fact of the human condition, not an occasion for
obsessive self-hatred. And whereas the Puritan individual must learn
like Clarissa to strip away all ties of family and society, the Augustan
individual grows freely, like a living plant, under the influence of the

multiple relationships that Locke describes: "One single man may at once be concerned in, and sustain all these following relations, and many more, viz. father, brother, son, grandfather, grandson, father-in-law, son-in-law, husband, friend, enemy, subject, general, judge, patron, client, professor, European, Englishman, islander, servant, master, possessor, captain, superior, inferior, bigger, less, older, younger, contemporary, like, unlike, etc., to an almost infinite number."[15] Tom Jones is neither an isolated soul nor a human being in the abstract; he is Bridget's son, Allworthy's nephew, Blifil's half-brother, Sophia's lover, Partridge's friend, and so on. One function of the plot of *Tom Jones* is to dispel false versions of these relationships while demonstrating that the true ones are congruent with Tom's essential character.

The idea of an interior and mysterious self has little relevance for Fielding, whose neoclassical conception of character assumes that the people we meet in life are in fact types. As he says in *Joseph Andrews*, contrasting his fictions with the "romances" of ostensibly objective historians,

> I declare here once for all, I describe not men, but manners; not an individual, but a species. Perhaps it will be answered, Are not the characters then taken from life? To which I answer in the affirmative; nay, I believe I might aver, that I have writ little more than I have seen. The lawyer is not only alive, but hath been so these 4000 years.[16]

What is wanted is not mimicry but verisimilitude, as Fielding comments in *Tom Jones:*

> Vanbrugh and Congreve copied nature; but they who copy them draw as unlike the present age, as Hogarth would do if he was to paint a rout or a drum [i.e., fashionable parties] in the dresses of Titian and of Vandyke. In short, imitation here will not do the business. The picture must be after nature herself. (XIV.i, p. 742)

Types are not stereotypes, since the type will always be shaped and specialized by the details of time and place, but individuality is not individualism. Rather than postulating a unique and hidden consciousness at the heart of the self, Fielding sees character as the sum of visible actions and decisions. If these sometimes remain hidden, that is only because a mask has successfully concealed them, not because they lurk in a deep and torchlit cavern. Moreover, one does not enter the world with a fully realized self, but instead one gradually builds up and revises it, as is described in the autobiographical writings of Hume, Gibbon, and Franklin.

Whereas the Puritans defined unwanted impulses as no part of the self, or at least as ebullitions from a lower and contemptible part, Fielding is interested in the whole person and sees even the oddest behavior as expressive of a person's real nature. This is the tradition that leads to Dickens, the comic or satiric vision that interprets quirks of character as deeply chosen self-caricature—Wemmick with his postbox grin, Jaggers' compulsive hand-washing. For as Ferenczi remarks, "Character is from the point of view of the psychoanalyst a sort of abnormality, a kind of mechanization of a particular way of reaction, rather similar to an obsessional symptom."[17] When an apparently simple type-character in Fielding suddenly reveals "human" complications, for example when the philosopher Square is discovered undressed in Molly Seagrim's bedroom, the point is not that Fielding has switched literary modes but rather that an unpredictable aspect of a character is suddenly revealed. Motives are additive in Fielding's world, sometimes visible at a glance, sometimes revealed over a period of time, sometimes hidden forever. But they are never *necessarily* hidden: it is a question of what one happens to find out, not of intrinsic limitations upon knowing. In Richardson's world, motives are obscure and disturbing, not a collection but an abyss.

Just as motive is unmysterious, so the behavior of good characters like Tom and Sophia is instinctively right, directed by what Fielding repeatedly calls "Good Nature." For a Puritan there can be no such thing as good nature. Nature is the enemy, to be combatted by grace. Fielding's outward-looking, benevolist ethic is at the farthest remove from Puritan soul-searching, as is his tendency to excuse Tom's blunders because his heart is good. We remember the bitterness with which Clarissa learns the duplicities of her heart, and the misplaced confidence with which the doomed Lovelace boasts that he himself is "honest" and "ingenuous."[18] Tom Jones may not always know exactly what his real motives are, but his heart is in the right place. For persons possessed of Good Nature, sentiment or feeling becomes a guide to conduct, whereas Puritans like Bunyan feared it as a villainous tempter: "There was, moreover, one Mr. Feeling; but he was no captain, but a great stickler to encourage Mansoul to rebellion."[19]

Johnson wrote tartly in a sermon, "There is no topic more the favorite of the present age, than the innocence of error accompanied with sincerity."[20] It is no wonder that hypocrisy was so central a theme in the fiction of his contemporaries, for if moral feeling has instinctive goodness as its inner form, it has sincerity as its outward sign, and this is easily imitated. Lovelace's role-playing is in effect normal in a culture that sees itself in dramatic terms and likes to peer, as Fielding puts it in *Tom Jones,* "behind the scenes of this greater theater of Nature" (VII.i, p. 327). Tom is sincere while Blifil only seems sincere, but even the judicious Allworthy gets the two confused. No doubt inspired by the Tom/Blifil contrast, Sheridan found the perfect theatrical analogue, the fallen screen in *The School for Scandal* that exposes the villainy of Joseph Surface and vindicates his worthy brother Charles. The part of Joseph Surface was written expressly for John Palmer, an actor popularly known as Plausible Jack. Palmer later seceded from Sheridan's company, fell on hard times, and tried to return; when he protested "If you could but see my heart, Mr. Sheridan," the playwright replied, "Why, Jack, you forget I wrote it."[21]

However shrewdly the comic writers see through hypocrisy, they persist in regarding it as an aberration that can be detected and put to rout. What they will not concede is the full pessimism of a position like Pascal's:

> Man is nothing but disguise, lies and hypocrisy, both in himself and in relation to others. Therefore he does not want truth to be spoken to him, and avoids speaking it to others; and all of these dispositions, so remote from justice and reason, have a natural root in his heart.[22]

There is an unbridgeable gulf between Fielding's Good Nature and Pascal's *racine naturelle dans son coeur,* and although Fielding despises lying he does not abhor it with the violence of Puritans like Defoe: "It is the concealing of all other crimes; it is the sheep's clothing hung upon the wolf's back, it is the Pharisee's prayer, the whore's blush, the hypocrite's paint, the murderer's smile, the thief's cloak; 'tis Joab's embrace and Judas's kiss; in a word, it is mankind's darling sin and the devil's distinguishing character."[23]

Fearing fallen nature as they did, the Puritans—and severe moralists like Johnson—could sternly denounce error excused by sincerity. Johnson detested *Tom Jones*. Fielding finds himself in a more awkward if also a more genial position, insisting that character is expressed in action but discounting many of the particular actions that characters perform.

> A single bad act no more constitutes a villain in life, than a single bad part on the stage. The passions, like the managers of a playhouse, often force men upon parts, without consulting their judgment, and sometimes without any regard to their talents. Thus the man, as well as the player, may condemn what he himself acts. (VII.i, pp. 328–29)

In classical ethics morality attaches to choices rather than personality, because only in the act of choice, as Aristotle explains in the *Ethics,* is the moral individual visible. The entire plot of *Tom Jones,* like other fictions in the tradition of the *Odyssey,* is a series of choices, so that it is as Aristotelian in its ethical conception as in its artistic plan. But as a

Christian, Fielding could hardly remain at ease with such an ethics. Though he hated Methodism for preferring faith to works, on a deeper level he was committed to the idea of the moral personality as a continuous state of being rather than acting. The Tom who acts is making his moral nature visible to other people, but his good nature precedes all of his actions and remains unblemished by his erroneous ones. For this reason Empson is able to say, surprisingly but persuasively, that Tom's innate goodness resembles the right acting of the Calvinist elect, no doubt because both Calvin and Fielding "had seriously puzzled their heads over the Gospel, and tried to give its paradoxes their full weight."[24] Where Fielding differs from the Calvinists is in the degree to which he is willing to overlook or forgive human fallibility. Again and again Tom does those things which he ought not to have done, and yet there is health in him.

What defines Fielding's distance from Puritan writers most profoundly is his openness to the attractions of desire. "Reason is but choosing," Milton declares in *Areopagitica,* and God the Father concurs in *Paradise Lost:* "Reason also is choice."[25] Like nearly everyone in his time Fielding affirms that reason should direct passion, but he affirms also that choice is emotional as well as rational. We choose what we long for, and if Allworthy has a fault it is the temperateness of his feelings and his tendency to translate them into rational categories. The embattled Puritan self retreats into its island or inner castle; Fielding's characters commit themselves to the open road, a world full of possibilities for pleasure as well as for action and choice.

In Defoe pleasure is a disease or drug that lulls the conscience asleep: "So possible is it for us to roll ourselves up in wickedness, till we grow invulnerable by conscience; and that sentinel, once dozed, sleeps fast, not to be awakened while the tide of pleasure continues to flow, or till something dark and dreadful brings us to ourselves again."[26] Anything that deranges the reason is, in this tradition, a betrayal of the true self, as Augustine says ruefully of sexual intercourse: "So intense is the pleasure that when it reaches its climax there is an almost total extinction of mental alertness; the intellectual sentries, as it were, are overwhelmed."[27] Fielding, very differently, maintains that physical hunger is inseparable from the highest forms of love (VI.i). Sex in *Tom Jones* is wonderfully various and not reducible to any single code, however much we are supposed to approve Allworthy's solemn lectures on the subject. Tom is wrong but excusable to sleep with Molly, less wrong to sleep with the mammalian Mrs. Waters, more wrong to sleep with the reptilian Lady Bellaston. In *Clarissa* sex is defiling; in *Tom Jones* it is good in itself though capable, like other good things, of being badly misused (there are glances at sadism in Northerton and Blifil). In Richardson's world you are either defiled or pure. In Fielding's world there are a few great sinners, not many saints, and a wide range of mortals in between.

A similar point can be made about a less inflammatory subject: drunkenness, that abomination in the eyes of Puritans, which Defoe startlingly represents as releasing inadmissible Oedipal impulses.

> That was a good story, whether real or invented, of the devil tempting a young man to murder his father. "No," he said, "that was unnatural." "Why then," says the devil, "Go and lie with your mother." "No," says he, "that is abominable." "Well then," says the devil, "if you will do nothing else to oblige me, go and get drunk." "Ay, ay," says the fellow, "I'll do that;" so he went and made himself drunk as a swine, and when he was drunk, he murdered his father, and lay with his mother.[28]

Alcohol is far less alarming in Fielding's world, where "it was Mr. Western's custom every afternoon, as soon as he was drunk, to hear his daughter play on the harpsichord" (IV.v, p. 169). *In vino veritas,* but not a Puritan *veritas;* Western drunk is much like Western sober. In Defoe drunkenness produces an abdication of the best self, in Fielding an intensification of it, and we despise Blifil when he exploits the joy with which Tom gets drunk to celebrate Allworthy's recovery from illness.

The point is not just that Fielding was more tolerant than the Puritans, or that he understood love and pleasure while they did not. Milton at least had nothing to learn about the imaginative power of love, with his Eve who tells Adam "With thee conversing I forget all time."[29] What is at stake is Fielding's refusal to see life as an all-or-nothing test, with sex the principal arena in which the individual stands or falls.[30] This in turn implies a radical disagreement with the Puritans about fallen life and about the degree to which one can afford to give in to desire. Allworthy is perhaps absurd when he calls love oxymoronically a "rational passion" (I.vii, p. 52), especially since he is addressing the wrong audience, earnestly rebuking Jenny Jones for a lapse she has not committed. But in a digression in *Amelia,* his last novel, Fielding himself maintains that the intoxication of desire can be resisted if love is "nicely watched, pruned, and cultivated."[31] This is what the Puritans rejected as impossible. In their terms Fielding has sold out to the love of creatures, and his comic fiction is an abdication of the writer's duty to represent the realities of human life.

Mimesis and Artifice

The eighteenth century was committed to mimesis, but the question was whether mimesis should assert or conceal its artificiality. Augustan neoclassicism marks the absolute ending of the Renaissance, during which it had been normal to claim that art and nature both

imitate a higher reality. In such a theory there is no question of inferior imitation, for as Lewis says, "Art and nature become rival cop-
ies of the same supersensuous original, and there is no reason why art
should not sometimes be the better of the two."[32] By the eighteenth
century the old harmony between microcosm and macrocosm was fast
disappearing, and the Romantic idea of an imaginative heterocosm
had not yet arrived. Aesthetic theory now depended on a more literal
and less idealizing interpretation of mimesis. Its function was to generalize "philosophically" from the otherwise chaotic data of experience, which in practice tended to mean selection of certain details and
omission of others.

But selection, in turn, might seem arbitrary even if obligatory, as
Johnson indicates in the *Preface to Shakespeare* with his conflicting
claims that Shakespeare mirrors the complexity of real life yet fails to
depict life in a morally instructive way.[33] In the year following the
publication of *Tom Jones,* Johnson criticized contemporary fiction in
terms that reject mere mimesis:

> It is justly considered as the greatest excellency of art to imitate
> nature, but it is necessary to distinguish those parts of nature
> which are most proper for imitation; greater care is still required
> in representing life, which is so often discoloured by passion or
> deformed by wickedness. If the world be promiscuously de-
> scribed, I cannot see of what use it can be to read the account, or
> why it may not be as safe to turn the eye immediately upon man-
> kind as upon a mirror which shows all that presents itself with-
> out discrimination.[34]

Yet it is Fielding, after all, who glories in the selecting and shaping
power of art, and Johnson who says gruffly at another time, "I had
rather see the portrait of a dog that I know, than all the allegorical
paintings they can show me in the world." Art must generalize from
the actual, not escape into fantasy, for "a story is a picture either of an
individual or of human nature in general; if it be false, it is a picture
of nothing." Johnson disliked his friend Goldsmith's *Vicar of
Wakefield,* with its ironic romance conventions, and told Fanny
Burney that "there is nothing of real life in it, and very little of nature.
It is a mere fanciful performance."[35]

Fielding, to whom Johnson's position must seem both literalizing
and morally heavy-handed, believes as Ehrenpreis says "that art reveals the truth through seeming, while life misleads us through
artfulness."[36] His attraction to comedy is therefore more than merely
temperamental. Comedy is the genre that celebrates its own art while
exposing the artful behavior of our fellow men—the mannerisms and
deceptions which, in Horace Walpole's words, "have rendered man a

fictitious animal."[37] The genre most congenial to Puritanism was tragedy, which attributes art to the supreme dramatist or at least to the
inherent order of things. Since its goal is to represent the inexorable
connection of events, a tragedy has every reason to plant clues that
will later be shown to reveal structure; *Tom Jones* is far from unique in
this regard, and it is no accident that Coleridge praised its plot in the
same breath with Sophocles' *Oedipus*.[38] But as Nietzsche points out, a
tragic plot must seem to unwind inevitably, not to be manipulated into
place. "Aeschylean-Sophoclean tragedy employed the most ingenious
devices in the initial scenes to place in the spectator's hands, as if by
chance, all the threads necessary for a complete understanding—a
trait proving that noble artistry which, as it were, masks the *necessary*
formal element and makes it appear accidental."[39] The comedy of
Tom Jones does exactly the opposite. Though it does mount an immense structure of relationships among events, many of them remain
the effects of pure chance, and the function of the plot is therefore to
make accidents seem necessary.

These considerations tend toward the metaphysical implications of
Fielding's story, which must be postponed for the moment while we
continue to consider the relation between imitation and artifice. That
Tom Jones is an artifact is made clear throughout. It is a "history"—
that is, a narrated story, as in the double meaning of the French *his-
toire*—"which hath employed some thousands of hours in the compos-
ing" (XI.i, p. 571). Puritan fiction, committed to an illusion of literal
veracity, presents itself as first-person memoir or as letters written "to
the moment," but history requires a *histor* to shape and interpret its
myriad details, whether it is Fielding presenting an imagined tale or
Gibbon recounting the fall of Rome.[40] In repeated playful references
to the special powers that authors are endowed with, Fielding pays
homage to the multiple ironies of Cervantes. When Sancho is amazed
that the narrator of his adventures could know about events he never
saw, Quixote explains, "I promise you, the author of our history will
be some sage enchanter, for to such as they nothing they choose to
write about is hidden."[41]

The Puritan *narrator absconditus* has to pretend not to exist at all,
ascribing all authority to Almighty God and evading the question of
narrative authority. Fielding insists on the specialized role of an author who creates a book, and boasts indeed that he has created a new
kind of book with its own "laws." But it is also true that whereas Defoe
must pretend to be the real Crusoe, the real Fielding stays distinct
from the narrator whom he has "created" to conduct the story.

> As I am, in reality, the founder of a new province of writing, so I
> am at liberty to make what laws I please therein. And these laws,
> my readers, whom I consider as my subjects, are bound to be-

lieve in and to obey; with which that they may readily and cheerfully comply, I do hereby assure them that I shall principally
regard their ease and advantage in all such institutions: for I do
not, like a *jure divino* tyrant, imagine that they are my slaves or
my commodity. I am, indeed, set over them for their own good
only, and was created for their use, and not they for mine. (II.i,
pp. 77–78)

The time will come, as Fielding remarks in his affecting "Farewell to
the Reader," when he himself must die (XVIII.i), but the narrator of
Tom Jones is a permanent presence, an idealized and specialized projection of the author, whose voice will forever invite new readers to
join in compact with him. What that narrator offers is a fictional
equivalent of the social contract, in which he and his readers agree
upon an artificial construction (the novel, the state) that is designed to
afford mutual satisfaction.

In this as in other ways, Fielding is more like Milton than like the
authors of the fictions that came later. *Paradise Lost* is the most impersonal of poems but is controlled by a narrator who comments on the
action, addresses and warns the characters, and confesses his relation
to the blind and isolated John Milton in Restoration London. But that
commanding figure, speaking with the inspired voice of a prophet, is
always forbidding, and Johnson confessed that we lay *Paradise Lost*
down and forget to take it up again—"We read Milton for instruction, retire harassed and overburdened, and look elsewhere for recreation; we desert our master, and seek for companions."[42] Fielding,
comparing his tale to stagecoach travel and to festive banqueting
(XVIII.i, I.i), promises to supply that recreation and be that
companion.

The narrator of *Tom Jones* is a guide who keeps encouraging the
reader to pursue his own way, often supplying misleading hints that
get him lost in order to find him again.[43] But this is altogether different from Bunyan's "Wouldest thou lose thyself,"[44] because Bunyan
proposes a radical opening up of the reader's consciousness, while
Fielding invites the reader to join in a game. Like Bunyan, Fielding
aspires to teach, but what he teaches is knowledge of the world, not
knowledge of the self, much as Locke (that essayistic philosopher) says
that the understanding's "searches after truth are a sort of hawking
and hunting, wherein the very pursuit makes a great part of the pleasure."[45] Moreover, the hidden clues are all visible on a second reading
of the novel, during which the reader is divided into two parts, the
hoodwinked victim of the first reading and the enlightened spectator
who now knows what really happened. Sometimes these clues take a
general form, as in Bridget Allworthy's repeated shows of fondness to
young Tom; once we know she is his mother, we realize that the

fondness is real and not feigned (as the narrator had tempted us to believe). Sometimes the clues expose turning points where the plot might have taken a different course, for example when the lawyer Dowling very nearly lets slip the information that Tom is Allworthy's nephew, and realizes just in time that Tom doesn't know it (XII.x, p. 657)—a discovery which, as we later perceive, enables Dowling to blackmail Blifil as the price for keeping the secret. And sometimes the clues uncover unexpected depths, as when Blifil, having just learned who Tom's parents were, insults him by observing that Tom does *not* know it (V.ix, p. 254). Here, on second reading, we know what Tom cannot possibly know, and our knowledge allows us to see that Blifil's cruelty is diabolical.[46]

In this way *Tom Jones* becomes a kind of thought experiment that offers a simplified version of the complexity of life, whereas Puritan narrative insists on retaining that complexity in all its mysteriousness. If in Kermode's terms we are all outsiders when we read the old kind of providential narrative, then a fiction like *Tom Jones* allows us to be outsiders and insiders simultaneously. What holds it together is the narrator's ability to make us believe that he is experienced and wise. He is no mere device for getting the story told, but the essential medium through which it makes sense, so that the essayistic element in this kind of novel is its absolute sine qua non.[47] And in this Fielding is deeply traditional, just as the Puritan fiction of nonfictional veracity is modern, for as Benjamin says, "Counsel woven into the fabric of real life is wisdom. The art of storytelling is reaching its end because the epic side of truth, wisdom, is dying out."[48]

Since the narrator rejoices in his role instead of concealing it, he is at liberty to declare which facts shall count as significant instead of accumulating them without apparent art in the expectation that they will interpret themselves. In Puritan narrative, details have a twofold function. First, they are clues that need to be carefully scanned in a universe where everything may carry significance, since it is God who has planted the clues to his hidden plot. We can never be certain which bits of data will turn out to be essential. And second, they provide the necessary illusion of reality, since so much depends on persuading the reader that the story is not merely *like* life but in an absolute sense (even if allegorical) is *identical with* life. Whether by instinct or design, Defoe superbly captures the indecision of a man fussing over minute details: "By and by I saw a great fowl like a hawk sit upon a tree within shot; so to let Friday understand a little what I would do, I called him to me again, pointed at the fowl which was indeed a parrot, though I thought it had been a hawk, I say pointing to the parrot. . . ."[49] Having no use for this kind of verisimilitude, Fielding enjoys making fun of it: "He accordingly ate either a rabbit or a fowl, I never could with any tolerable certainty discover which."[50]

The Man of the Hill in *Tom Jones* is a kind of parodic Crusoe, with his animal-skin clothes and retreat from the life of his fellow men. And the story he tells, with its youthful crimes and later disgust with human nature, is a version of the Puritan first-person narrative, imprisoned within the narrowness of an obsessive point of view. Formal realism is thus embedded, by way of counter-example, in the middle of Fielding's comic epic, and proves (of course) no match for Fielding's medley of literary devices in presenting an image of truth. The old man himself is lamentably feeble at drawing conclusions from his own experience. When he generalizes about others he is merely reductive—"In France a knave is dressed like a fop, and in the northern countries like a sloven. But human nature is everywhere the same, everywhere the object of detestation and scorn" (VIII.xv, p. 482)— and when he is faced with an actual chance to help another person he remains unmoved while Tom rushes to the aid of a woman in distress. Imprisoned within a dreadful privacy, the old man badly needs a comic narrator to tell his story for him and to liberate him into the complexities of social existence. The other first-person story-teller in *Tom Jones*, Harriet Fitzpatrick, is (like Moll Flanders) one of those persons whom experience has taught to be cunning rather than good, and both ethically and aesthetically she is an unreliable narrator. But her life rapidly gets absorbed in the great body of the host organism, *Tom Jones*, and far from continuing to be the heroine of her own story, she is compelled to take her place as a minor character in Fielding's. It is worth noting that selective omission of embarrassing facts is common even to the best characters; both Tom and Sophia do it (VIII.v, p. 420; XI.viii, p. 602).

The ambiguous relationship between art and life is superbly imagined in the episode in which Partridge goes with Tom to see *Hamlet,* and naively praises the crude Claudius while dismissing Garrick's Hamlet as unremarkable. " 'He the best player!' cries Partridge with a contemptuous sneer, 'why I could act as well as he myself. I am sure if I had seen a ghost, I should have looked in the very same manner, and done just as he did' " (XVI.vi, pp. 856–57). Jones has looked forward to seeing in Partridge "the simple dictates of nature, unimproved indeed, but likewise unadulterated by art" (p. 852), and that is exactly what he gets. Partridge does his best to remember that "it is only a play" (p. 855), but unlike the bombastic performances he has seen in the country, this one is so brilliantly acted that he keeps forgetting its artifice (especially when it touches on his personal obsession, ghosts). His reaction *is* natural, and is the highest possible tribute to Garrick, whose acting is so accomplished that it doesn't look like acting.

Life, like art, has its consummate actors. The very next chapter in *Tom Jones* is devoted to that expert hypocrite Blifil, whose acting is mistaken for nature by nearly everyone.[51] But that does not mean that acting is always wicked, only that we have to learn to interpret an actor's motives. The same principle holds true for any artificial form, which is to say for any human pursuit ("Art is man's nature," Burke memorably said). What Barthes describes in professional wrestling is just as true of *Tom Jones:*

> What the public wants is the image of passion, not passion itself. There is no more a problem of truth in wrestling than in the theatre. In both, what is expected is the intelligible representation of moral situations which are usually private. This emptying out of interiority to the benefit of its exterior signs, this exhaustion of the content by the form, is the very principle of triumphant classical art.[52]

To put it less provocatively, content may well be significant but is impotent without form, while form can be effective even if the content it conveys is wholly artificial (Garrick has not seen a ghost and is only simulating fear). We know that Fielding was fascinated throughout his life with the puppet theatre, which also appears in *Tom Jones,* and liked to insist that life itself was like a puppet show. In fiction as in life, one develops a critical intelligence that can see behind the performance and judge it.[53]

For all of its headlong concatenation of events, *Tom Jones* is offered to the reader as a running commentary on human life, with moments of dialogue and memorable scenes held in suspension like tableaux.[54] Yet the impression persists that these moments are selected by the narrator from a stable reality larger than himself, rather than being generated arbitrarily for the purpose of giving amusement and instruction. Whereas Puritans tended to see life emblematically as a collection of nodal points that emerge from the flux of time, Fielding sees life as a structure of causality that has to be appreciated as a whole, which may not be possible in actual experience, but can be achieved in imagination on a second reading of his novel. Kermode has said that the epistolary method allows Richardson to merge *chronos* with *kairos,* extracting supreme significance from particular events;[55] Fielding insists on a *chronos* that embodies meaning in its totality, rather than yielding up meaning by a breakthrough into *kairos.* The Puritan novel need not construct a coherent chronology, since it is enough to suggest the stream of experience within which (as in Augustine's *Confessions*) man lives in psychological time, seeking to identify the crucial moments among the welter of unassimilable details. So *Tom Jones* has its famously perfect plot while *Robinson Crusoe* has, in that sense, almost no plot at all. Puritan poetics requires an excess of detail as the background from which significant detail can emerge epiphanically; Fielding's poetics finds significance in the whole, and is committed to showing how everything is interconnected. This narrative epistemology is reflected in the world of social relationships. The solitary Puritan pilgrim leaves his earthly home forever, avoids unnecessary entanglements with "creatures," and arrives at last at the promised land. The gregarious traveler in Fielding gets valuable assistance from the people he meets on the road, redefines his rightful place in the social order, and ends up where he began (in Tom's case, reunited with Allworthy of Paradise Hall).

These considerations suggest how different Fielding is from Puritan writers when he uses emblematic imagery. Emblems are planted and then revealed by the narrator as a way of making particular points, not embedded in a reality which is itself emblematic by a God who teaches man to interpret emblems. This is strikingly apparent at the very end of the book, when Tom swears eternal fidelity to Sophia by making her look at her own reflection in a mirror.

> "There, behold it there, in that lovely figure, in that face, that shape, those eyes, that mind which shines through those eyes: can the man who shall be in possession of these be inconstant?" . . . Sophia blushed, and half smiled; but forcing again her brow into a frown, "If I am to judge," said she, "of the future by the past, my image will no more remain in your heart when I am out of your sight, than it will in this glass when I am out of the room." "By heaven, by all that is sacred," said Jones, "it never was out of my heart." (XVIII.xii, p. 973)

Undoubtedly Fielding turns Sophia's reflected image into a kind of emblem, but this is closer to a conceit than to an intuition of celestial truth, and it can hardly be right to conclude that Sophia's "true identity is ideal, an abstraction."[56] The name Sophia means "wisdom," but Sophia Western is not wisdom personified as Spenser's Una is truth personified. She is a flesh-and-blood young woman, up whose skirts admiring innkeepers have peered (XI.ii, p. 574), and Tom wins her because he is learning to be wise, under her encouraging influence of course, not because she herself is wisdom. The emblem is only an emblem, an arbitrary sign whose meaning derives from the richer reality of the living Sophia Western, and she in turn derives from the reality of women like Fielding's dead wife, whom the fiction brings back to life even as it concedes that Fielding himself will soon join her in the grave.

> Come, bright Love of Fame, inspire my glowing breast. . . .
> Foretell me that some tender maid, whose grandmother is yet unborn, hereafter, when, under the fictitious name of Sophia, she reads the real worth which once existed in my Charlotte,

shall, from her sympathetic breast, send forth the heaving sigh. . . . Comfort me by a solemn assurance, that when the little parlour in which I sit at this instant, shall be reduced to a worse furnished box, I shall be read, with honour, by those who never knew nor saw me, and whom I shall neither know nor see. (XIII.i, p. 683)

It is not the narrator but Tom who allegorizes Sophia's image in the glass, pointing out her reflection as a way of guaranteeing his fidelity. He is showing her a visual earnest of their relationship, not stepping outside the narrative as Bunyan might to make a metaphysical point.

Even a Platonist would hold that the good cannot be loved abstractly, but is known in embodied form, and Tom's love for the real Sophia is essential for learning—what might seem alien to his ebullient "good nature"—the virtues of prudence and temperance. But Platonism is closer to the Augustinian tradition than to Fielding's worldly cheerfulness, for as Tuve says of Spenser, "We realize that vast influence of Augustine's discussions of temperance as rightly directed love. Guyon does not have to learn how to have just enough love of the world, a reasonable amount of lust. He is to love good *instead*."[57] No author is less likely than Fielding to denounce, as the Puritans did, the "love of creatures." A recurrent (and suggestive) emblem in *Tom Jones* is Sophia's muff, which Jones handles and kisses passionately, and which serves as the physical correlative for sexual desire when Sophia is briefly tempted to martyr herself to her father's commands. "Sophia was charmed with the contemplation of so heroic an action, and began to compliment herself with much premature flattery, when Cupid, who lay hid in her muff, suddenly crept out. . ." (VII.ix, p. 360). One should not forget that immediately after Tom shows Sophia her image in the glass, her father, reconciled to Tom by reason of his unexpected good fortune, bursts in exclaiming "To her boy, to her, go to her.—That's it, little honeys, O that's it!" When Tom politely beseeches him to not overwhelm Sophia's modesty, he retorts decisively, "Beseech mine arse" (XVIII.xii, p. 974).

While appreciating Western's sheer comic energy one ought not to overlook his meanness and cruelty, and it is an exaggeration (though a pardonable one) to call him the Atlas "on whose broad and presumably hairy back everything else rests."[58] Still it is true that Fielding's world has room in it for the Dionysian Western as well as the Apollonian Allworthy, and more than once Western manages to express what subtler characters miss, the fact that all normal human beings do indeed want the same things. (It is odd, though, that Western himself exhibits no active sexual interest. Presumably this is because Fielding is afraid he will seem a lecherous old man if he pursues women— though Hugh Griffiths, in his immortal impersonation of Western in

Tony Richardson's film, manages to include lechery among his tendencies.) No impassable gulf is fixed between Tom's "by all that is sacred" and Western's "beseech mine arse." In *Clarissa* different styles of speech reflect incommensurable versions of reality; just the opposite is true in *Tom Jones,* where no misunderstanding is ever permanent.

As always, we have to recognize that "realism" is too general a term to be used as an abstraction, and indeed is more aptly used in its adjectival form. A given work may seem "realistic" to its readers—not necessarily to later readers—but it does not contain or possess an entity called "realism."[59] In many of the familiar senses of the term, Defoe and Richardson are far more realistic than Fielding. Yet it is also true that Fielding exhibits, as they do not, what J. P. Stern admires in Dickens, signs of "the *eros* that binds him to this world."[60] For all of their mimetic detail, Defoe's novels reflect a withdrawal into the self rather than a commitment to social reality. *Tom Jones,* committed so enthusiastically to social reality, pays homage to *Don Quixote* as the great model for fictions in which reality tests and explodes every form of solipsism. The process is powerful because it forces us to admit, just as Swift's Houyhnhnms do, the unworkability of our highest ideals in the world we live in, and as Stern says the results can be painful: "The life of Don Quixote is a challenge (among the most poignant in all literature) to our customary notions of reality, but the challenge is rebutted at every point."[61]

In his study of quixotic fictions Alexander Welsh stresses the centrality of the problem of justice, which can never resolve itself into the absolute structure that the heart longs for, and forever thwarts the quixotic effort to attain it. But the impossibility of justice does not prevent us from wanting it, and quixotic action tends to accomplish more than official inaction. "The tradition of the knight errant as justicer, therefore, is not as silly as it seems; or rather it is silly, as quixotic fictions demonstrate, but there is no alternative institution."[62] Fielding the lawyer had no illusions about the law, and Abraham Adams in *Joseph Andrews* is very much a quixotic seeker of justice. Yet in the end Fielding endorses the *nomos* far more decisively than Cervantes does, tending to imply that injustice is the result of particular abuses rather than of a disturbance at the heart of things. Adams's naiveté is at once an unworldly folly which we cannot afford to imitate and a saintly criticism of the world that persecutes him, but even at his most quixotic he is more like an abnormally well-read baby than like a Cervantean visionary. "He was besides a man of good sense, good parts, and good nature; but was at the same time as entirely ignorant of the ways of this world, as an infant just entered into it could possibly be."[63] In Welsh's scheme fiction develops toward an increasing recognition of the universe itself as a cruel practical joke, in the spirit of Ortega's remark, "Surrounding culture . . . lies the barbarous, brutal, mute, meaningless reality of things."[64] Fielding, very differently, wants to come to terms with the shape of reality and with the human relationships that society ought to confirm. It is notable that in *Tom Jones* he presents a Sancho (Partridge) but no Quixote. Tom both deals out justice effectively, for instance when he thrashes the brutal Northerton, and receives it abundantly, when Blifil is exposed and Tom is restored to union with Allworthy and Sophia.

The deepest affinity of *Tom Jones* with the Quixote tradition lies elsewhere: not in putting the concept of justice into question, but in holding imaginative constructs of reality up to inspection even while endorsing, in the end, the notion of a stable and coherent universe. The Puritan novel tests the individual, but only indirectly and covertly does it ever test the universe that does the testing. Hence, as we have seen in both *Crusoe* and *Clarissa*, a heavy freight of fantasy can be passed off as mimetic veracity, since the very existence of fiction is never acknowledged. Clarissa sees herself as a tragic heroine because she *is* a tragic heroine; Lovelace is wrong to see himself as a comic hero, because life is not a comedy. Fielding's kind of novel, on the other hand, affirms the order of things even while exposing the incompleteness and private distortion of individual perceptions of it. The narrator stands behind the story to guarantee its integrity, both by admitting that he has made it up—what no narrator in Defoe or Richardson could possibly admit—and also by affirming that what he has made up corresponds to the larger coherence of things.

In his dual emphasis on romance (in story) and irony (in presentation), Fielding exposes the fantasy of naive realism and frankly acknowledges his own fantasy. As Marthe Robert says, the realistic novel rejects romance as insincere fantasizing, hence denying its own romantic elements, while the opposed kind of novel openly acknowledges that it is only "a set of figures and forms" while insisting that reality cannot be expressed without them.[65] In Fielding romance works to expose but also to reward the quixotic basis of every human imagination, so that the ironic *Tom Jones* is at the same time a superb feat of wish-fulfillment. And we may profitably conclude our long investigation, therefore, by looking once more at the implications of romance for providential fiction.

Providence and Fictional Form

Toward the end of *Tom Jones* the narrator makes a pronouncement that addresses itself, wryly and acutely, to the whole question of genre.

When a comic writer hath made his principal characters as happy as he can, or when a tragic writer hath brought them to the highest pitch of human misery, they both conclude their business to be done, and that their work is come to a period.

Had we been of the tragic complexion, the reader must now allow we were very nearly arrived at this period, since it would be difficult for the devil, or any of his representatives on earth, to have contrived much greater torments for poor Jones than those in which we left him in the last chapter; and as for Sophia, a good-natured woman would hardly wish more uneasiness to a rival, than what she must at present be supposed to feel. What then remains to complete the tragedy but a murder or two, and a few moral sentences?

But to bring our favourites out of their present anguish and distress, and to land them at last on the shore of happiness, seems a much harder task. . . . This I faithfully promise, that notwithstanding any affection which we may be supposed to have for this rogue whom we have unfortunately made our hero, we will lend him none of that supernatural assistance with which we are entrusted, upon condition that we use it only on very important occasions. If he doth not therefore find some natural means of fairly extricating himself from all his distresses, we will do no violence to the truth and dignity of history for his sake; for we had rather relate that he was hanged at Tyburn (which may very probably be the case) than forfeit our integrity, or shock the faith of our reader. (XVII.i, pp. 875–76)

Fielding freely acknowledges that fictional characters are puppets whom the author makes as happy or unhappy as he can. Genres impose expectations of comic happiness or tragic misery, and the author has the hard "task" of bringing these about in a plausible way. Neoclassical tragic theory had much to say about the *dénouement,* literally the untying of the *noeud* or knot, which at its best should seem surprising and yet inevitable, and of course this principle is also applicable to comedy. But the surprise and inevitability are contained within a structure of conventions, both in action and in what Aristotle called "thought." The standard tragic ending can be summarized as a few murders and some "moral sentences," and something similar presumably obtains in comedy.

An author is thus in the delicate position of inventing while making what he invents seem plausible, and of effecting a conventional ending while making it seem to grow naturally out of what precedes it. *Tom Jones* is among other things a mock epic but Fielding has his doubts, as he says in an earlier chapter, about the supernatural "machinery" of the classical epics (VIII.i, p. 397), and is committed to avoiding anything like it in his own art. Addison observes that *Paradise Lost* contains incidents which, "though they are very astonishing in themselves, are not only credible, but actual points of faith."[66] But what is believed on faith in Christianity—and a skeptic like Hume would read Addison's remark ironically as referring to what could not be believed *without* faith—cannot be a model for fiction, where "the faith of the reader" that Fielding invokes is belief in plausible events, not miracles. As we have seen in Puritan narrative, a fictional miracle is all too easy for an author to create; the difficulty is in persuading the reader that God has created it. With his open admission of artificiality, Fielding does not have to worry about that, but the connections in his story still need to make sense. Indeed the rules of the game require that they should seem surprising *and yet* make sense. The harmonies of art will always surpass the confusions of life, and one of Fielding's categories is "the marvellous." In Aristotelian terms it is enough to make the reader believe that what happens "is neither impossible nor probable, but merely possible."[67]

Happy endings are of course the common staple of comic fictions. The problem for Fielding is to keep the happy ending from seeming grossly contrived. Dark comedies often play ironically with such expectations, for example Molière's *Tartuffe* in which the villain seems triumphant until he is arrested for a hitherto-unmentioned crime in another province. Even Gay's cheery *Beggar's Opera* ends happily only because the Beggar stops the action and forces it to do so. *Tom Jones*, on the other hand, is certain to end happily. In part, as Crane says, this is a function of plot: the more Tom escapes disaster, the more likely it seems that he always will.[68] But beyond that it is a function of the narrator's presence, regarding human affairs with amusement and assuring us by tone of voice that they will remain amusing even when there is an undertone of bitterness and scorn.

If some authors write tragedies because they are "of the tragic complexion," then Fielding is of the comic complexion. His story is comic not just because it obeys certain formal principles, but also because it is suffused with a spirit of affectionate mockery. Surely this explains how it can get away with unrealistic wish-fulfillment: the romance is held in suspension as an ideal that is admitted to be an ideal, qualified and distanced by the surrounding atmosphere of irony and humor. What Ehrenpreis says of the book's moral argument can thus be extended to its generic implications: "So caustic an observer is the most persuasive recommender of a soft-hearted morality."[69]

The whole question of genre is complicated since *Tom Jones* is a knowingly literary work, and gets many of its effects from invoking or subverting the available genres. Fielding presents it as an epic or at least mock-epic, and its breadth of subject matter is certainly epic in scope. But most of what goes on in the story is closer to romance than to epic, especially if romance is defined in post-Renaissance rather than classical terms.[70] The narrator's playful style confirms the romance connection even while making fun of it, as is apparent from the very outset: "In that part of the western division of this kingdom which is commonly called Somersetshire, there lately lived (and perhaps lives still) a gentleman whose name was Allworthy, and who might well be called the favourite of both Nature and Fortune; for both of these seem to have contended which should bless and enrich him most" (I.ii, p. 34). The nature/fortune idea is commonplace in Renaissance writing, and Miller notes a striking resemblance to the first sentence of Lodge's *Rosalynde* (1590): "There dwelt adjoining to the city of Bordeaux a knight of most honorable parentage, whom Fortune had graced with many favours, and Nature honored with sundry exquisite qualities, so beautified with the excellence of both, as it was a question whether Fortune or Nature were more prodigal in deciphering the riches of their bounties."[71] Fielding's playful tone veers back and forth between romantic elegance and mimetic frankness. On the one hand, the story—though set in 1745, only four years before the date of publication—is allowed to recede into an ideal past and an ideal Somerset: "there lately lived (and perhaps lives still)." On the other hand, Fortune is no abstract goddess, but only a polite name for exactly what it would be in Jane Austen's no-nonsense world, decreeing to Allworthy "the inheritance of one of the largest estates in the county" (p. 34).

To many eighteenth-century readers the new novels, far from rising to new heights of realism, were not nearly realistic enough. A remarkable number of writers deplored the tendency of fiction to be read in solitude by persons (usually young) inclined to romantic fantasy.[72] But Johnson's point in *Rambler* 4 was that the fantasy normal to romance was made dangerous by a purportedly realistic setting; what had formerly resembled "beings of another species" were now "levelled with the rest of the world." In Frye's terms the plot may retain its romance elements, but the characters descend to the low mimetic mode, and are no longer heroes for whom the laws of nature and probability are magically suspended. "If superior neither to other men nor to his environment, the hero is one of us: we respond to a sense of his common humanity, and demand from the poet the same canons of probability that we find in our own experience. This gives us the hero of the low mimetic mode, of most comedy and of realistic fiction."[73] As critics since Coleridge have constantly repeated, the world of romance is timeless and strange. The world of *Tom Jones* is in every sense familiar, both in alluding to historically real people and events, and in tracing a firm structure of causality that accounts for every important movement of the story. Frye says elsewhere that romance is built up of unconnected "and then" episodes, contrasted with the "hence" of realism.[74] *Tom Jones* is outstandingly a "hence" narrative, whose chief glory is the ability to transform every apparent "and then" into a "hence."

More profoundly, *Tom Jones* is not fully a romance because although its hero is tested, the test consists of encouraging him to be himself while avoiding imprudent actions that will allow others to misrepresent him. Romance heroes have darker and more mysterious lessons to learn, and they find themselves by withdrawing from society, not by immersing themselves in it. When Gawain, in *Sir Gawain and the Green Knight,* returns to Arthur's court after the eerie fairy-tale experience at the Green Chapel, his society cannot really understand what has happened to him. Wherever Tom Jones goes he is still in society, which is seen as a structure that embraces everything, including (as in *The Beggar's Opera*) different but parallel levels of "high" and "low" life. In this respect Puritan narrative is closer to romance, insisting that you can and should separate yourself from the social *nomos* even if like Milton you end up a church of one, or like Crusoe a nation of one. "Romance," Frye says, "has no continuing city as its final resting place."[75] Fielding rejects the city—his urbanity is nostalgically rural, in reaction against the new suburbanity—but his novel comes to rest very much in a communal place.

All of these considerations suggest that *Tom Jones* is really more comedy than romance. It is not only that comedy tends to endorse an aggressively antiromantic realism. (Richardson wrote contemptuously of "inn-frequenting Sophia" and said of Fielding that "his brawls, his jarrs, his gaols, his spunging-houses, are all drawn from what he has seen and known.")[76] In addition comedy refuses to enter the demonic night-world of romance in which evil is felt to be genuinely evil. Lovelace is satanic, Blifil ridiculous. Lovelace expresses egocentric desires which even the noblest persons harbor in some form, while Blifil is shown to be an exception to the standard of "good nature," doomed to lose out in the end to those who embody it. In a way, therefore, Fielding's comedy is profoundly antirealistic, and the realism of Defoe and Richardson raises disturbing issues that are revived in earnest by (for example) the atheist and political radical Godwin in *Caleb Williams.*

But it would obviously be absurd to accuse Fielding, of all writers, of failing to appreciate the complexity of life. Rather, one should say that he offers comedy as an idealized and happier *version* of the life we know, with the affectionate narrator spreading a safety net beneath the narrative tightrope, ready to catch any character who falls. And the wish fulfillment is by no means simple. Consider the foundling motif, which in *Joseph Andrews* amounted to a simple fantasy of finding the desirable parents one would like to have had. In *Tom Jones* the lost parents turn out to be disappointing, the featureless clergyman Summers and the unappealing Bridget Blifil, née Allworthy. So we come to understand that Allworthy's affection—Tom has always called him "father"—responds to Tom's intrinsic worth rather than to the hidden ties of consanguinity that romance exploits. In a deep way

Tom Jones therefore contradicts the comforting satisfactions of the foundling motif. If Tom is unworthy, then Bridget's blood (which Blifil also bears) cannot make him worthy. If he is worthy, then illegitimacy cannot damage him. Hence the poignancy of his temporary loss of Allworthy's esteem, by contrast with the cynical assumption in the countryside that Allworthy had encouraged him only because he was secretly Tom's father. As we eventually find out, Bridget did indeed encourage him for such motives, just as Western's renewed approval depends on his newfound status, but the relation between Tom and Allworthy is of a different kind and contradicts the easy rewards of the fairy tale that *Tom Jones* may appear to be.

One year before *Tom Jones*, Smollett published his first novel, *Roderick Random*, an utterly un-Aristotelian work that looks back to Elizabethan rogue narratives, puts its unlovable hero through a series of disasters and recoveries that are as random as the title suggests, and ends by conferring wealth, a wife, and a long-lost father he has done nothing to deserve. The tale eventually gets somewhere, but not for any good reason; the hero eventually learns something, but not much. Smollett's novel is deeply paranoid. The most memorable passage is a frame-up on shipboard where Roderick's diary in Greek is misrepresented as a spy's cipher; this incident, unlike the analogous episode concerning Adams's copy of Aeschylus in *Joseph Andrews*, carries a real threat of fatal consequences. Roderick inhabits a Lucretian universe of ceaseless change that is at once random and determined: random in that it responds only to the swerving and rebounding of atom against atom in their fall through the void; determined in that every rebound leads to another rebound, and there is thus plenty of causation even though no presiding principle organizes the whole.

Fielding's universe, on the other hand, is the providential one described by Boethius, in which chance may still be chance but is compelled by God to take its place in the great design: "We can define chance as an unexpected event brought about by a concurrence of causes which had other purposes in view. These causes come together because of that order which proceeds from the inevitable connection of things, the order which flows from the source which is Providence and which disposes all things, each in its proper time and place."[77] Strictly speaking Fortune is nonexistent, if by that one means a capricious goddess who smiles upon her favorites, and we are rightly reminded that Fortune in Fielding's novels always turns out to be a mask for divine Providence. In his gambling days Mr. Wilson suffered disastrously for entrusting himself to Fortune, but he later learns to acknowledge the one power that governs all things: "'Sir,' says Adams, 'Fortune hath I think paid you all her debts in this sweet retirement.' 'Sir,' replied the gentleman, 'I am thankful to the great Author of all things for the blessings I here enjoy.'" No blessings,

Wilson adds, are unmixed in this world, for long ago he lost his eldest son. Adams piously replies, "We must submit to Providence, and consider death is common to all."[78] In a comic romance like *Joseph Andrews*, Providence, or the great Author, can do anything, and the long-lost son unexpectedly appears in the person of Joseph Andrews. But this does not mean that Fortune is nonexistent, only that it obeys the dictates of a higher power.

In Dante as in Boethius, C. S. Lewis observes, Fortune does indeed govern the sublunary world, because that world is fallen and God therefore permits it. "That contingency should reign in the fallen world below the Moon is not itself a contingent fact."[79] Anglican divines whom Fielding admired argued that unpredictableness is a proof of the existence of Providence, since a "mixture of contingency" is what distinguishes a personal God from a mechanical and Hobbesian determinism. Thus Archbishop Tillotson:

> For if there be a God and a providence, it is reasonable that things should be thus, because a providence does suppose all things to have been at first wisely framed and with a fitness to attain their end; but yet it does also suppose that God hath reserved to himself a power and liberty to interpose, and to cross as he pleases, the usual course of things; to awaken men to the consideration of him, and a continual dependence upon him; and to teach us to ascribe those things to his wise disposal, which, if we never saw any change, we should be apt to impute to blind necessity.[80]

In such a theology nothing is finally accidental, but that is because God forces accidents to play into his hands; and it is crucial to see that from the human point of view, much will always remain impenetrable.

In a sermon entitled "All Contingencies under the Direction of God's Providence," Robert South (a particular favorite of Fielding's) insisted on the alarming contingency of events and near-events which fulfill God's unknowable will. No one could have predicted that Cromwell, entering the House of Commons "with a threadbare torn cloak and a greasy hat," would presently usurp the place of a judicially murdered king. And if that king's son had been discovered when hidden in a tree, all subsequent history would have been different.

> There was but an hair's breadth between him and certain destruction, for the space of many days: for had the rebel forces gone one way rather than another, or come but a little sooner to his hiding place, or but mistrusted something which they passed over (all which things might very easily have happened), we had not seen this face of things at this day; but rebellion had been still enthroned, perjury and cruelty had reigned, majesty had

been proscribed, religion extinguished, and both church and
state thoroughly reformed and ruined with confusions, mas-
sacres, and a total desolation.[81]

In pondering *Clarissa* we noted that in Christian tragedy the outcome
might always have been different; so also in Christian comedy. But
the ending, when it does come, is always conformable to providential
design. At the moment when Tom has been expelled from Paradise
Hall, the narrator remarks, "*The world*, as Milton phrases it, *lay all
before him;* and Jones, no more than Adam, had any man to whom he
might resort for comfort or assistance" (VII.ii, p. 331). But the allusion to *Paradise Lost* cries out for completion:

> The world was all before them, where to choose
> Their place of rest, and providence their guide.
>   (XII.646–47)

The narrator of *Tom Jones*, as Booth has memorably observed, is a
comic analogue of Providence,[82] but that is not the same thing as a
demonstration of Providence in noncomic experience. "The world
may indeed be considered," the narrator declares at the moment when
Tom saves Sophia's muff from the fire, "as a vast machine, in which the
great wheels are originally set in motion by those which are very minute, and almost imperceptible to any but the strongest eyes" (V.iv, p.
225). Comedy strengthens our eyes, and allows Fielding to show in
detail those connections which in life must often remain hidden. "Here
an accident happened of a very extraordinary kind; one indeed of
those strange chances, whence very good and grave men have concluded that Providence often interposes in the discovery of the most
secret villainy, in order to caution men from quitting the paths of
honesty, however warily they tread in those of vice" (XVIII.iii, p. 920).
The special pleasure of neoclassical art is to imitate the interconnected-
ness of things, as in Dryden's translation of Boileau:

> Till, by a curious art disposed, we find
> One perfect whole of all the pieces joined.[83]

But it would be presumptuous to imagine that we can always, or even
often, detect the points of connection, and even more presumptuous
to assume that chance is not chance just because God bends it to his
will.

The role of accidents in *Tom Jones* is exactly suggested by a line in
Spenser, "It chaunst (eternall God that chaunce did guide)."[84] Obviously what holds all of this together is an act of faith, for the idea of
providential chance comes perilously close to the ironies of Butler in

Erewhon: "I had indeed a hairbreadth escape; but as luck would have it, Providence was on my side."[85] When Defoe asserts providential pattern we may protest that we see his hand behind the arras, planting the coincidences that he later triumphantly reveals. But Fielding openly admits that his hand is behind the arras, and offers the great structure of *Tom Jones* as an analogue of God's structure, not as a literal instance of it. An omniscient narrator is always prepared to give us, as Braudy says, "the extra piece of information that may change everything,"[86] but that is a luxury that we cannot count on in life, where Blifils may prevail and where Sophia—like Fielding's Charlotte—may find an untimely grave. The marvel of *Tom Jones* is that it balances so perfectly between determinism of plot and freedom of character. Within the large patterns of causality that God ordains, human beings remain free to improvise and change. Like Bunyan and Richardson, Fielding is a Christian, and like them he therefore asserts a providential universe, but fallen life looks altogether different to him, and his mode of fiction stands in permanent opposition to theirs.

A *Digression on* Tristram Shandy

In the long run, or at any rate for the next century and a half, the future of the English novel lay in mimetic realism. Jane Austen based her fictions firmly in the contemporary social order, Walter Scott in historical process, and George Eliot in both. Even writers who made overt use of narrative artifice, Thackeray for instance, sought to convey the illusion of a unified and completed world. Social coherence is mirrored by chronological structure: nineteenth-century fiction tends to imitate the biographical course of individual life and to base its realism upon the serial presentation of temporal experience.[87] But it is notable that in many novels the metaphysical dimension of eighteenth-century fiction all but disappears. Grounded upon the immediate experience of social place and personal time, the novel stopped asking the questions about God's plot that had once seemed fundamental.

Eventually the Victorian order broke down and its fictions broke down with it. Among other consequences the literature of the past came in for new consideration, and at the beginning of the twentieth century Laurence Sterne's *Tristram Shandy* unexpectedly emerged, as if from an obscuring mist, as the eighteenth-century work that most anticipates the modern world. As early as 1776, less than a decade after Sterne's last volume appeared, Johnson declared roundly, "Nothing odd will do long. *Tristram Shandy* did not last."[88] But *Tristram Shandy* did last after all, and if Austen and Eliot and Dickens develop certain implications of eighteenth-century fiction, Sterne's peculiar anti-narrative suggests other implications that were for a long time too disturbing to be easily faced. This is not to say that modernism is necessarily good in itself, or (which would be absurd) that *Tristram Shandy* is a greater novel than *Great Expectations* or *Middlemarch*. Rather it is to suggest the abyss of undesired possibility that lay just beyond the world view of the 1740s, and to emphasize the urgency with which the fictions of that time strove to hold the future at bay.

Presented as connected series of events, novels of every sort offered themselves as "histories," including *Clarissa, or, The History of a Young Lady* and *The History of Tom Jones, A Foundling*. Sterne too makes his narrator speak of "the history of myself," but he specifies that it is "a history-book, Sir, (which may possibly recommend it to the world) of what passes in a man's own mind."[89] Psychology and epistemology were central eighteenth-century concerns; Sterne's interest in Locke and his affinities with Hume have been well documented, and *Tristram Shandy* can fairly be called an exploration of the phenomenology of experience.[90] What we read is a literary artifact which—just as much as Fielding's fictions—selects its details in order to present an imitation of reality. What is offered is an invented image of truth rather than, as Defoe and Richardson pretend, truth itself.

"Writers of my stamp have one principle in common with painters. Where an exact copying makes our pictures less striking, we choose the less evil; deeming it even more pardonable to trespass against truth, than beauty" (II.iv, pp. 69–70). For all its jokiness this pronouncement confirms the Aristotelian view that truth is not just the mass of factual detail in which we all live, but the imaginative shaping that detects patterns in the detail, or else imposes patterns upon it. Where Sterne parts from Fielding is in focusing his imitation on connections between mental data instead of on connections between external events, juxtaposing his materials in a spirit of playful *bricolage* rather than causal explanation. The "historiographer," Tristram says,

> . . . will moreover have various
>   Accounts to reconcile:
>   Anecdotes to pick up:
>   Inscriptions to make out:
>   Stories to weave in:
>   Traditions to sift:
>   Personages to call upon:
>   Panegyricks to paste up at this door:
>   Pasquinades at that. . . . (I.xiv, p. 28)

Like Fielding, Sterne compares his work to a complex machine and boasts of the "good cookery and management" of his materials, but unlike Fielding he glories in connections that can exist nowhere beyond his highly individual imagination, and declares that "Digressions, incontestably, are the sunshine;—they are the life, the soul of reading" (I.xxii, pp. 54–55). For Fielding as for Aristotle, plot was the soul of a literary work (*Poetics*, ch. 6); for Sterne its soul is the imaginative unity in *reading* that is forged by the incorrigibly digressive mind. *Tristram Shandy*, indeed, can be read as a kind of exploded *Tom Jones*.

Insofar as a subtle understanding of the self was a Puritan preoccupation, one might argue that the idiosyncratic shape of *Tristram Shandy* is a direct outcome of Defoe's narratives, attempting "to create a fictional form that grows out of, instead of being imposed upon, what it contains."[91] But it would be truer to say that *Tristram Shandy* is phenomenological in the sense that traditional philosophy, seeking to understand man's place in the world, had always been so, and that Sterne owes much of his apparent novelty to the tradition of essayists like Montaigne. Anthony Wilden argues that there is a special modernity in the way Montaigne interprets "Know thyself" to mean an endless regress into the self rather than a simple normative ideal, and in Montaigne's conclusion that self-knowledge is mediated through language and relations with other people, rather than achieved by abstract introspection.[92] As Montaigne understands the act of writing, it does not just re-present what he already is, but forms and clarifies his being in an ongoing process.

> In modeling this figure upon myself, I have had to fashion and compose myself so often to bring myself out, that the model itself has to some extent grown firm and taken shape. Painting myself for others, I have painted my inward self with colors clearer than my original ones. I have no more made my book than my book has made me—a book consubstantial with its author, concerned with my own self, an integral part of my life; not concerned with some third-hand, extraneous purpose, like all other books.[93]

The Puritan self, though complex and hidden, tended to remain rigidly fixed, and Puritan writing aspired to be transparent (avoiding playfulness at all costs) while seeking earnestly to decipher the messages of the Almighty. *Tristram Shandy*, very differently, insists upon the ceaseless reconstitution of the self in the flux of time, and upon the obligation of writing to shape that experience, not just to report it. There is more than frivolity involved when Tristram remarks, "But this is neither here nor there——why do I mention it?——Ask my pen, —it governs me, —I govern not it" (VI.vi, p. 316). Swearingen comments, "There is a perfectly accurate sense in which he may be said not to understand what he says until after he has said it."[94]

Like the other novelists we have been considering, Sterne came late to his literary vocation. His actual profession, which he followed dutifully if not always respectably, was that of a clergyman in the Church of England, and the existential games of *Tristram Shandy* take on a special interest from their grounding in an orthodox view of religious truth.

> Of all the several ways of beginning a book which are now in practice throughout the known world, I am confident my own way of doing it is the best——I'm sure it is the most religious—— for I begin with writing the first sentence——and trusting to Almighty God for the second. (VIII.ii, p. 415).

This is something very different, however, from Fielding's artist-God whom the human artist emulates. This God connects each separate moment with the others, but we live at the cliff-edge of the latest moment, not knowing what will come next, whereas the harmonious shape of *Tom Jones* encourages a retrospective vision of totality. In earlier novels, including those as different as Richardson's and Fielding's, life is felt to be intelligible even if its causal structure is often mysterious. In Sterne, reality itself is mysterious, and this is felt to be perplexing but also liberating. We now get consciousness rather than story, and what God furnishes is the presiding context for human existence rather than a connected narrative of human actions.

Within *Tristram Shandy* the ingenuous Toby constantly proclaims the goodness of Providence, but this is an act of faith, not a practical demonstration which the narrative enacts. A genuine sermon by Sterne is inserted into the novel and is commented on by a group of characters who nevertheless pay no attention at all to its message (II.xvii). And that *is* its message—that conscience is routinely ignored because we routinely deceive ourselves. Our art forms are no exception: we translate experience into terms that gratify ourselves, whether these are Walter's syllogisms, Toby's innocent war-games, or Tristram's game of writing. It follows that no work of art can hope to be, as *Tom Jones* aspires to be, objective and whole. Like Fielding's God, Sterne's delights in bringing order out of contingency, absorbing chance into Providence;[95] but unlike Fielding's God, he neglects to show us how he does it.

To put it another way, Puritan writers insisted on the interpenetration of this world by the next: Fielding keeps his gaze on this world but claims that comic art can imitate the patterns that are hidden in it by the divine artificer. Sterne, just as much as Fielding, asserts the existence of those patterns, but he implicitly denies that a work of art can reproduce them. In its this-worldly emphasis *Tristram Shandy* is certainly a concord fiction. It brilliantly expresses the ability of the imagination to give meaning to chance occurrences, and to extract pleasure from the most thwarting experiences.[96] And it suggests that although individual persons may act solipsistically, language and consciousness are profoundly social, affirming a stable reality in which even solitary reflection is conditioned by a lifetime of *being with* others.[97] But each of these positions may seem little more than an extenuation: we need not behave solipsistically but we usually do; life can be made bearable by seeing it as play, but the playing cannot neutralize suffering for long. "What a jovial and a merry world would this be, may it please your worships, but for that inextricable labyrinth of debts, cares, woes, want, grief, discontent, melancholy, large jointures, impositions, and lies!" (VI.xiv, p. 329).

In choosing Yorick for his persona Sterne has in mind not only the jester who sets the table on a roar, but also the unclean skull that the gorge rises at. Tristram is a fictional author writing a real book, but Sterne, dying of consumption and telling us so, is a real author writing a fictional book, or at any rate a fictional narrator coughing real blood. Many pages ago we noticed Lukács's observation that the early novel broke down into lyric subjectivity, and Lukács speaks also of a mode of irony that is nostalgic and reductive in tone, even when it continues to affirm the existence of providential meaning. "Irony, with intuitive double vision, can see where God is to be found in a world abandoned by God; irony sees the lost, utopian home of the idea that has become an ideal, and yet at the same time it understands that the ideal is subjectively and psychologically conditioned, because that is its only possible form of existence."[98] For all its comic joy, Sterne's irony is unsettlingly different from the massively stable irony of Fielding's hearty narrator, and both are remote from the certitude of the supreme ironist, Milton's God who laughs his enemies to scorn.

Many readers have sensed something anxious if not unpleasant in Sterne's wit, which is a good deal less joyous than recent critics make it out to be. Some things, but above all the last thing, defy the powers of the imagination to comprehend them. Johnson makes a correspondent in the *Rambler* say that at a friend's deathbed "I felt a sensation never known to me before; a confusion of passions, an awful stillness of sorrow, a gloomy terror without a name."[99] What cannot be named must nevertheless be faced, and Sterne's edgy jokes imply a recognition that conventional literary deaths (Clarissa's for instance) are simply unbelievable, while language balks and makes fun of itself in the face of death.

Nature instantly ebb'd again, ——the film returned to its place,
——the pulse fluttered——stopp'd——went on——throb'd——
stopp'd again——moved——stopp'd——shall I go on?——No.
(VI.x, p. 324)

The death that matters most, of course, is one's own, and philosophers and preachers alike have always encouraged the contemplation of it. Augustine says, in remarkably Shandean language, "The whole of our lifetime is nothing but a race towards death, in which no one is allowed the slightest pause or any slackening of the pace."[100] *Tristram Shandy,* in which the race with death is literalized in the seventh volume, ends unfinished (as does *A Sentimental Journey*) because its author has died.

Postponing Tristram's moment of birth is more than a joke about narrative. If you haven't been born then you can't die, and the future is held at bay. By reanimating the dead Yorick, Sterne indulges (like Tom Sawyer and Huck Finn at their funeral) in the fantasy of being posthumous to oneself:

> Alas, poor YORICK!
> Ten times in a day has Yorick's ghost the consolation to hear his monumental inscription read over with such a variety of plaintive tones, as denote a general pity and esteem for him;——a foot-way crossing the church-yard close by the side of his grave, ——not a passenger goes by without stopping to cast a look upon it, ——and sighing as he walks on,
> Alas, poor YORICK!
>
> (I.xii, p. 24)

But immediately after this feat of self-resurrection come the famous black pages, empty and voiceless, that mark the bourn from which no traveller returns.

Seen in this light, wit is only wit. To be sure, Sterne's wit has successfully created *Tristram Shandy,* but that is only consolation of a sort. When an interviewer asked Woody Allen if he hoped to achieve immortality through his work, he replied magnificently, "I don't want to achieve immortality through my work. I want to achieve it through not dying." And if humor can serve as a means of reconciliation with unpalatable reality, it can also, as Freud urges, serve as an escape from it.

> The grandeur in it clearly lies in the triumph of narcissism, the victorious assertion of the ego's invulnerability. The ego refuses to be distressed by the provocations of reality, to let itself be compelled to suffer. . . . Humor is not resigned; it is rebellious. It signifies not only the triumph of the ego but also of the pleasure principle, which is able here to assert itself against the unkindness of the real circumstances.[101]

Something like this is surely the deepest explanation for the Puritan distrust of humor.

Tristram Shandy abounds in jokes, whether verbal or practical or both at once. One need not be humorless (though perhaps it helps) to sense something obsessive and unpleasant in much of Sterne's joking, especially about sex. In Fielding sex is a field of activity, in Sterne a field of inactivity, but one which so pervades the imagination that literally nothing is incapable of being sexualized. What is discouraging is the consistency with which this insight is connected with frustration and disappointment.

> Brightest of stars! thou wilt shed thy influence upon some one——
> ——The deuce take her and her influence too——for at that word I lose all patience——much good may it do him!——By all that is hirsute and gashly! I cry, taking off my furr'd cap, and twisting it round my finger——I would not give sixpence for a dozen such!
> ——But 'tis an excellent cap too (putting it upon my head, and pressing it close to my ears)—and warm—and soft; especially if you stroke it the right way—but alas! that will never be my luck——(so here my philosophy is shipwreck'd again)
> ——No; I shall never have a finger in the pye. . . . (VIII.xi, p. 423)

Sophia's muff served as an objective correlative for Sophia's deep attraction to Tom, a sexual joke denoting a human reality, as a hostile critic reluctantly admitted:

> The little incident of the muff, on which Mrs. Honour, or the author, so profusely wantons, is at the same time a great one against Sophia's delicacy, who could value it the more for Mr. Jones's egregious fooling with it; and conveys to young gentlemen and ladies admirable instructions in the art of toying. But whether these instructions contain *nothing inconsistent with the strictest rules of decency,* according to the author's early declaration, must be left to the *chaste eye* of the reader, and need not be further dwelt upon here.[102]

Tristram's cap is an occasion for sexual wordplay that invariably, in the world of the Shandys, substitutes for the thing itself:

> All womankind, continued Trim, (commenting upon his story) from the highest to the lowest, an' please your honour, love jokes; the difficulty is to know how they chuse to have them cut; and there is no knowing that, but by trying as we do with our artillery in the field, by raising or letting down their breeches, till we hit the mark.——
> ——I like the comparison, said my Uncle Toby, better than the thing itself—— (IX.viii, p. 468)

Language itself becomes a form of involuntary sexual expression, or at least of obscene relief; no wonder then that when Diego scribbles graffiti "he eased his mind against the wall" (IV, p. 202).

Rather than celebrate the comic triumph of Sterne's vision, we would do well to recognize its pathos. He has committed himself fully to the flux of experience which the providential novel, whether Puritan or Augustan, had held at a comfortable distance. In *Tom Jones* the narrator's mastery of chronology reflects an imitation of divine omniscience. In *Tristram Shandy* temporal sequence gives way to the simultaneity of mental impressions, in which psychological order often conflicts with chronological—"A cow broke in (to-morrow morning) to my uncle Toby's fortifications" (III.xxxviii, p. 175). Whereas the novels of Richardson and Fielding offer simulacra of perfected memory, in which nothing is forgotten and everything fits together, *Tristram Shandy*—whose sequence of details is impossible to recollect—compels us to immerse ourselves in the strangeness of the ever-unrolling present. But it can only do this because its narrator is reconstructing the data of his own memory, and when he stops, the narrative must stop with him.

The radical and unrelenting arbitrariness of *Tristram Shandy* does amount to a kind of philosophical statement, but it is one whose implications must vary in proportion to one's own beliefs about the arbitrary. A recent critic has well observed,

> Plot and metaphor suggest a triumph of the artist over time. It is not surprising that aestheticians, concerned to replace religion by art, have made so much of these things. *Tristram Shandy* enacts the effort to achieve them and the failure of that effort. The book is all extension and no meaning, all analogy and metonymy and no metaphor or plot.[103]

Seen from this angle, *Tristram Shandy* stands in an interesting relation to an allegory like *The Pilgrim's Progress,* which abounds in metaphor, indeed *is* metaphor, but is notably deficient in plot. Sterne can no longer believe, as the earlier novelists did, that the world is pregnant with emblematic meanings which art can reproduce, but his refusal to impose a narrative pattern looks back to Bunyan's world as much as it looks forward to Beckett's. For it would be fair to say that Sterne really does rely on God for the next sentence, and beyond that for the benign control that joins each moment securely with the rest even if human beings are helpless to predict how this will happen. Poring over the hidden connections and implications in his memories, Tristram has much in common with the old Puritan diarists who scrutinized the shifting and mysterious data of their fragmented experience. And for all of Sterne's undoubted interest in *durée*, his book gives an impression finally of existing always in the present moment, even when each present moment is superimposed upon others that lie ahead of it or behind it. In this too *Tristram Shandy* has affinities with the old Puritan narratives, in which urgent attention to the significance of each moment is more important than retrospective display of causal structure. If Defoe struggles to impose pattern upon a mode of experience that resists patterning, then Sterne goes back beyond Defoe.

At the end of the short chapter that began with Trim's analogy of the artillery and their breeches, Sterne abruptly abandons his narrative, wonders about the posthumous fate of his book, and then eloquently concludes,

> I will not argue the matter: Time wastes too fast: every letter I trace tells me with what rapidity Life follows my pen; the days and hours of it, more precious, my dear Jenny! than the rubies about thy neck, are flying over our heads like light clouds of a windy day, never to return more——every thing presses on—— whilst thou art twisting that lock, ——see! it grows grey; and every time I kiss thy hand to bid adieu, and every absence which follows it, are preludes to that eternal separation which we are shortly to make.——
> ——Heaven have mercy upon us both! (IX.viii, p. 469)

That is indeed Sterne's faith, that heaven will have mercy, but his imagination has moved to a vision of impermanence that is more like Shakespeare's than like the stable fictions of his immediate predecessors.

> Sometime we see a cloud that's dragonish,
> A vapor sometime like a bear or lion,
> A towered citadel, a pendant rock,
> A forkèd mountain, or blue promontory
> With trees upon't that nod unto the world
> And mock our eyes with air. Thou hast seen these signs:
> They are black vesper's pageants. . . .
> That which is now a horse, even with a thought
> The rack dislimns, and makes it indistinct
> As water is in water.[104]

Meanwhile we have our fictions, which are real enough as feats of imagination, but all too unreal as embodiments of reality. Of course if the religious basis is secure enough, this power may be felt to be exhilarating. "All the world is full of inscape," Hopkins wrote, "and chance left free to act falls into an order as well as purpose: looking out of my window I caught it in the random clods and broken heaps of snow made by the cast of a broom."[105] That is precisely what is at issue in eighteenth-century narrative: the chance and randomness which are perceived as falling into order.

Those signs and footsteps which Michael promised Adam are now very faint indeed, and many readers have seen in *Tristram Shandy* a potential skepticism very similar to Hume's. Flux may conceal divine purpose, or it may not, and in the latter case one might conclude with Sterne's contemporary Diderot that the ever-changing whole is the only unity there is. "Tout change, tout passe, il n'y a que le tout qui reste."[106] But Sterne himself resists the lure of skepticism, and his final position is the one that he poignantly expresses in a sermon: "Wherever thy Providence places me, or whatever the road I take to get to thee——give me some companion in my journey, be it only to remark to, How our shadows lengthen as the sun goes down."[107]

The End

In the psychologized world of *Tristram Shandy*, the past survives only in memory and the self invents its fictions in order to bear the continual disappointments of life. Wit is a defense against a world that remains indifferent to it, whatever may be the psychic relief it affords.

> By some neglect or other in Obadiah, it so fell out, that my father's expectations were answered with nothing better than a mule, and as ugly a beast of the kind as ever was produced.
> My mother and my uncle Toby expected my father would be the death of Obadiah—and that there never would be an end of the disaster.——See here! you rascal, cried my father, pointing to the mule, what you have done!—It was not me, said Obadiah.— How do I know that? replied my father.
> Triumph swam in my father's eyes, at the repartee—the Attic salt brought water into them—and so Obadiah heard no more about it. (V.iii, pp. 266–67)

In *Tom Jones* reality is resolutely de-psychologized: it is presented as a world capable of satisfying man's deepest desires, and the noble symmetry of the artifact is offered as an analogue for the symmetry of God's creation. In Sterne's fiction, words flow past and vanish like the blowing clouds; in Fielding's, they form themselves into a completed order.

> Words move, music moves
> Only in time; but that which is only living
> Can only die. Words, after speech, reach
> Into the silence. Only by the form, the pattern,

> Can words or music reach
> The stillness, as a Chinese jar still
> Moves perpetually in its stillness.[108]

That is the classic ideal, whereas Sterne fully accepts the temporality of language as of experience, and models his fiction on the ever-vanishing notes of a musical improvisation, in which certain themes recur memorably but the whole can never be apprehended at once.[109]

If *Tom Jones* is a Chinese jar, one must not forget that it is a *funny* jar. Still, the humor—unlike Sterne's volatile and unpredictable wit— is inseparable from a deep sense of the harmony of things, and all of the devices of narration are designed to give pleasure within that larger certainty. "This work," the narrator says at one point, "may, indeed, be considered as a great Creation of our own" (X.i, pp. 524–25). That is why *Tom Jones* looks back so fondly to romance: rather than accepting the purely psychological status of reality, in which the past is lost except as memory can revive it, it seeks to fold the past into an ever reinvigorated present, and to perfect a fiction that can re-create a fulfilled order as often as one cares to reread it.

As Johnson perceived, the achievement of *Tom Jones* is to combine the familiar world of mimesis with the impossible gratifications of romance. It thus unites two genres which, as Clara Reeve defined them not long after Fielding's time, might logically seem distinct:

> The novel is a picture of real life and manners, and of the times in which it is written. The romance, in lofty and elevated language, describes what never happened nor is likely to happen. The novel gives a familiar relation of such things as pass every day before our eyes, such as may happen to our friend, or to ourselves; and the perfection of it is to represent every scene in so easy and natural a manner, and to make them appear so probable, as to deceive us into a persuasion (at least while we are reading) that all is real, until we are affected by the joys or distresses of the persons in the story as if they were our own.[110]

But of course Fielding never permits us for long to imagine that his story is "really" taking place. The reader is an audience to be addressed and amused, not a participant who suspends all disbelief.

In fact Fielding's mode of comic narration is so old-fashioned as to be timeless, resembling that of Cervantes of course, but for that matter Chaucer's as well.

> And therfore, whoso list it nat yheere,
> Turne over the leef and chese another tale;
> For he shal fynde ynowe, grete and smale.[111]

When the Monk has exhausted the company's patience with his tedious tragic *exempla,* the Knight begs him to stop and the Host calls
upon the obscure Nun's Priest to tell a story. The Priest responds with
a masterfully controlled narrative that begins with a sympathetic account of a humble widow, moves from describing her barnyard stock
to the beast fable of the cock and the fox, and then presents a tale that
moves along the whole range between burlesque and tragedy. No
reader can fail to be moved by the story of the man who sees his dead
friend in a dream and later finds his body, and indeed the story is told
so effectively that one forgets that the teller is a comic rooster. Likewise the brief sketch of Andromache and Troy is potentially far more
moving than the Monk's labored *exempla;* the line that tells how Hector met his forewarned doom could be an Arnoldian touchstone—
"He wenté for to fighté natheles."[112] Arnold thought that Chaucer
lacked high seriousness. Fielding, like Chaucer, knew that seriousness
and humor can be mutually reinforcing.

　　Tom Jones contains plenty of references to the "real" world—the
1745 rebellion, Mrs. Whitefield, Fielding's dead Charlotte—and it
contains alternative narratives, like those of the Man of the Hill and
Mrs. Fitzpatrick, that remain trapped in a realm of frustration and
bitterness. With its press-gangs and sadistic soldiers, the novel does
not ignore the darker aspects of a culture which moderns sometimes
over-idealize, and of which a historian has said, "There was an edge to
life in the eighteenth century which is hard for us to recapture. In
every class there is the same taut neurotic quality—the fantastic gambling and drinking, the riots, brutality and violence, and everywhere
and always a constant sense of death."[113] But *Tom Jones* is a comic
romance that rises above suffering and transcends death. In effect it
elaborates an imaginary world that intersects the real one at various
points. It is not reality, but it is *congruent with* reality—not a direct
mimesis of it like the leave-nothing-out Puritan novel, but a perfected
interpretation of it in the classical mode that Addison recommends:
"It is the part of a poet to humour the imagination in its own notions,
by mending and perfecting nature when he describes a reality, and by
adding greater beauties than are put together in nature where he
describes a fiction."[114] Or as John Dennis expressed it in explicitly
religious terms, "The great design of arts is to restore the decays that
happened to human nature by the Fall, by restoring order."[115]

　　Tom Jones is thus—as has been said of Joyce's *Ulysses*—a terminal
moraine, the comprehensive ending of an old tradition rather than
the herald of a new one. The nineteenth-century British novel (with
certain exceptions, such as *Wuthering Heights*) is notable for the absence of an explanatory metaphysical dimension. Whether or not religious faith is assumed, it no longer dictates the particular shape of
narrated events. This is most striking in the novelist whose comic

mode most resembles Fielding's, Jane Austen. In *Emma*, for example, the theme of detection and revelation has little to do with the problem of the structure of reality, as it would in both Fielding and Sterne, but rather with the limits of individual awareness, especially when distorted by the fantasies of Emma the "imaginist."[116] On a second reading of *Tom Jones* one admires the skill with which the godlike narrator has planted clues that one could not possibly have detected. On re-reading *Emma* one sees more clearly how different characters detect the clues at different times (Knightley recognizes that Frank Churchill and Jane Fairfax are lovers well before Emma does, and individual readers will figure it out at different points, there being no single decisive clue but rather an accumulated body of evidence). The role of the ironist-narrator is to lead us through the stages of Emma's education, seeing it both from inside and from outside, rather than to tease us with the limits of possible knowing. "Mr. Knightley was hard at work upon the lower buttons of his thick leather gaiters, and either the exertion of getting them together, or some other cause, brought the colour into his face" (p. 288). Phrases like "or some other cause" are frequent in Fielding, where they often imply "a cause which you can't guess, though I as creator may know it." In Austen the phrase means "a cause which you should well be able to guess," and the ironic formula is a means of alerting the reader to it.

Emma is a true *Bildungsroman*, concerned with learning to accommodate oneself to the world as it is, whereas *Tom Jones* is a romance that accommodates the world to human desires, altering apparent relationships and economic facts in order to define a new unity and restore the lost paradise. In the modern world, not even comic fictions can claim to do that, but many of them contain nostalgic tributes to a time when it could still seem possible. Thus the toast proposed by that magnificent impostor, Augustus Fagan, M.D. (formerly Ph.D.):

> When you get to my age, if you have been at all observant of the people you have met and the accidents which have happened to you, you cannot help being struck with an amazing cohesiveness of events. How promiscuously we who are here this evening have been thrown together! How enduring and endearing the memories that from now onwards will unite us! I think we should drink a toast—to Fortune, a much-maligned lady.[117]

But the outrageous coincidences of the plot, in which characters are indeed promiscuously thrown together, are openly presented as the novelist's arbitrary inventions. There is no longer any question of demonstrating the ultimate order of things, or of proving that Fortune is really Providence after all, as another author's protagonist has occasion to reflect:

Standing on the pavement was a big fat man whom Dixon recognized as his barber. . . . At that moment two rather pretty girls
stopped at a pillar box a few yards away. The barber, his hands
clasped behind his back, turned and stared at them. An unmistakable look of furtive lust came over his face; then, like a
courtly shopwalker, he moved slowly towards the two girls.
Welch now accelerated again and Dixon, a good deal shaken,
hurriedly switched his attention to the other side of the road,
where a cricket match was being played and the bowler was just
running up to bowl. The batsman, another big fat man, swiped
at the ball, missed it, and was violently hit by it in the stomach.
Dixon had time to see him double up and the wicket keeper
begin to run forward before a tall hedge hid the scene. Uncertain whether this pair of vignettes was designed to illustrate the
swiftness of divine retribution or its tendency to mistake its tar-
get, Dixon was quite sure that he felt in some way overwhelmed. . . .[118]

It is not so much a question of religious belief dying out, as of belief
becoming specialized and losing its ability to encompass the whole of
lived experience. Frye observes that "classical mythology became fabulous, a branch of secular literature, in Christian times, and biblical
mythology, as such, is rapidly becoming fabulous now."[119] For Milton
the biblical story was the one true story of which all others were reflections. For Fielding it guaranteed a universal order which comic fiction
could imitate, even if lived experience might not always disclose it.
Since Fielding's time it has proved impossible to recreate that order in
fictive form, however much individuals might still accept it as doctrine
or ethical code.

By the end of the eighteenth century the split between experience
and doctrine, in religion as in every other aspect of living, was well
under way. Meanwhile *Tom Jones* survives as the final brilliant achievement of a conservative culture, aware that paradise is lost but willing
to perceive an ideal harmony in the universe that survives it. In Pope's
lovely lines, alluding to *Paradise Lost,*

> The groves of Eden, vanish'd now so long,
> Live in description, and look green in song.[120]

The gap between presence and absence is a sign of the recreative
power of art, not of a deconstructive abyss, and if art like water inverts
what it mirrors, the mirror remains a faithful one.

> Oft in her glass the musing shepherd spies
> The headlong mountains and the downward skies,
> The watry landskip of the pendant woods,
> And absent trees that tremble in the floods;

In the clear azure gleam the flocks are seen,
And floating forests paint the waves with green.
                                                    (211–16)

Yet absence remains absence after all, and Hegel means something very different from Pope when he refers to art as an inverted world, *die verkehrte Welt*.[121] *Tom Jones* can still give intense pleasure, but that is not to say that we can enter its world in earnest and make it ours.

Notes

Chapter One: Doctrine and Fiction

1. *God's Plot: The Paradoxes of Puritan Piety, Being the Autobiography and Journal of Thomas Shepard,* ed. Michael McGiffert (Amherst, Mass., 1972). Shepard uses the phrase on pp. 119, 141, and 181.

2. "Technique as Discovery," *Hudson Review* 1 (1948), often reprinted.

3. Thomas Babington Macaulay, "Milton," *The Works of Lord Macaulay* (New York, 1897), V, 23.

4. *Allegorical Imagery: Some Medieval Books and Their Posterity* (Princeton, 1966), p. 179.

5. The phrase is Zevedei Barbu's, in *Problems of Historical Psychology* (New York, 1960), p. 154.

6. *The Sense of an Ending: Studies in the Theory of Fiction* (New York, 1967), p. 67.

7. "Tertullian's Paradox," in *New Essays in Philosophical Theology,* ed. Antony Flew and Alasdair MacIntyre (New York, 1964), p. 207.

8. *The Symbolism of Evil,* tr. Emerson Buchanan (Boston, 1967), esp. pp. 3–10, 164–71.

9. *Epistle to Arbuthnot,* line 341.

10. *Deceit, Desire, and the Novel: Self and Other in Literary Structure,* tr. Yvonne Freccero (Baltimore, 1966), p. 29.

11. *Radical Monotheism and Western Culture* (New York, 1970), pp. 31, 50.

12. *Das Philosophenbuch,* quoted by Edward Said, *Beginnings: Intention and Method* (Baltimore, 1975), p. 38.

13. Hampshire, "Commitment and Imagination," in *The Morality of Scholarship,* ed. Max Black (Ithaca, 1962), p. 46; Said, *Beginnings,* pp. 12–13.

14. *The Act of Reading: A Theory of Aesthetic Response* (Baltimore, 1978), p. 73.

15. Ian Watt, *The Rise of the Novel: Studies in Defoe, Richardson, and Fielding* (Berkeley, 1957), ch. 1, "Realism and the Novel Form."

16. "Fiction, History, Myth: Notes Toward the Discrimination of Narrative Forms," in *The Interpretation of Narrative: Theory and Practice*, ed. Morton W. Bloomfield (Cambridge, Mass., 1970), p. 283.

17. *English Literature in the Sixteenth Century, Excluding Drama* (Oxford, 1954), p. 319.

18. *Paradise Lost* V. 620–24. Throughout this book I quote from the text in *The Poems of John Milton*, ed. John Carey and Alastair Fowler (London, 1968).

19. Northrop Frye, "Dickens and the Comedy of Humours," in *The Stubborn Structure* (Ithaca, 1970), p. 240.

20. *The Secular Scripture: A Study of the Structure of Romance* (Cambridge, Mass., 1976), p. 47.

21. "Manners, Morals, and the Novel," in *The Liberal Imagination* (New York, 1953), pp. 199–215.

22. Daniel Defoe, *Robinson Crusoe*, opening sentence.

23. *The Theory of the Novel* (1916), trans. Anna Bostock (Cambridge, Mass., 1971), p. 41.

24. See M. H. Abrams, *The Mirror and the Lamp: Romantic Theory and the Critical Tradition* (New York, 1958), pp. 272–85.

25. Denis Diderot, *Eloge de Richardson*, quoted (in French) by Watt, *The Rise of the Novel*, p. 235.

26. *The Denial of Death* (New York, 1975), p. 191.

27. See Alan MacFarlane, *The Origins of English Individualism: The Family, Property and Social Transition* (Oxford, 1978).

28. "Religious Affections," in *Jonathan Edwards: Selections*, ed. Clarence H. Faust and Thomas H. Johnson (New York, 1962), p. 254.

29. *Beyond Belief: Essays on Religion in a Post-Traditional World* (New York, 1970), ch. 2.

Chapter Two: Puritan Experience and Art

1. See J. Sears McGee, *The Godly Man in Stuart England* (New Haven, 1976).

2. C. H. and Katherine George, *The Protestant Mind of the English Reformation, 1570–1640* (Princeton, 1961), p. vii.

3. Walzer, *The Revolution of the Saints: A Study in the Origins of Radical Politics* (New York, 1974), pp. 310–11.

4. See Robert Jay Lifton, *Thought Reform and the Psychology of Totalism: A Study of "Brainwashing" in China* (New York, 1963), p. 455.

5. Peter L. Berger, *The Sacred Canopy: Elements of a Sociological Theory of Religion* (New York, 1967), p. 21.

6. See Paul Delany, *British Autobiography in the Seventeenth Century* (London, 1969), pp. 28–29.

7. *Natural Symbols: Explorations in Cosmology* (New York, 1973), pp. 40, 181.

8. See Keith Thomas, *Religion and the Decline of Magic* (New York, 1971), esp. pp. 75–76.

9. Louis Althussser, *For Marx*, tr. Ben Brewster (London, 1977), p. 233.

10. See Peter L. Berger, *The Precarious Vision: A Sociologist Looks at Social Fictions and Christian Faith* (Garden City, N.Y., 1961), p. 59.

11. John Bunyan, *The Pilgrim's Progress*, ed. Roger Sharrock (Harmondsworth, 1965), p. 79.

12. See Gordon Campbell, "The Theology of *The Pilgrim's Progress*," in *The Pilgrim's Progress: Critical and Historical Views*, ed. Vincent Newey (Liverpool, 1980), pp. 251–52.

13. Berger, *The Precarious Vision*, p. 148 (following Max Weber).

14. *The Varieties of Religious Experience* (New York, 1929), p. 8.

15. William Haller, *The Rise of Puritanism* (New York, 1938), p. 91. On conventional patterns see Robert Middlekauff, "Piety and Intellect in Puritanism," *William and Mary Quarterly*, 3rd ser., 22 (1965), 457–70.

16. *The Symbolism of Evil*, tr. Emerson Buchanan (Boston, 1969), pp. 8, 102.

17. *The Gospel of Suffering*, tr. David F. Swenson and Lilliam M. Swenson (Minneapolis, 1948), p. 67.

18. *The Symbolism of Evil*, p. 41.

19. *The Rise of Puritanism*, pp. 156–57.

20. Quoted by Philip Greven, *The Protestant Temperament: Patterns of Child-Rearing, Religious Experience, and the Self in Early America* (New York, 1977), p. 77.

21. *Diary of Cotton Mather*, ed. Worthington C. Ford (New York, 1957), I, 237, entry for 16 Oct. 1697.

22. *The Estate of Damnation, or . . . Grace*, quoted by Barbara K. Lewalski, *Protestant Poetics and the Seventeenth-Century Religious Lyric* (Princeton, 1979), p. 101.

23. As translated by Joshua Sylvester (1607), quoted by Owen C. Watkins, *The Puritan Experience; Studies in Spiritual Autobiography* (New York, 1972), p. 12. See also Sacvan Bercovitch, *The Puritan Origins of the American Self* (New Haven, 1975), pp. 19–20.

24. Posthumous papers published as *The Life of Dr. Thomas Goodwin* (1704), quoted by Watkins, *The Puritan Experience*, p. 85.

25. Franz Kafka, *The Trial*, tr. Willa and Edwin Muir, rev. E. M. Butler (New York, 1964), p. 51.

26. "Remorse—is Memory—awake," in *The Complete Poems of Emily Dickinson*, ed. Thomas H. Johnson (Boston, 1960), no. 744, p. 365.

27. Gerard Manley Hopkins, "I wake and feel the fell of dark, not day."

28. See Greven, *The Protestant Temperament*, pp. 32–43.

29. John Bunyan, *Saved by Grace*, in *Miscellaneous Works*, ed. Roger Sharrock et al. (Oxford, 1976––), VIII, 203.

30. See Zevedei Barbu, *Problems of Historical Psychology* (New York, 1960), p. 183, and Greven, *The Protestant Temperament*, pp. 109–24.

31. *The Complete Works of Thomas Brooks*, ed. Alexander Grosart (Edinburgh, 1866), II, 347. Aceldama is the "field of blood" bought with Judas's thirty pieces of silver (Acts 1:19); for Magor-missabib see Jer. 20:3.

32. See Vernon J. Bourke, *Will in Western Thought* (New York, 1964).

33. See my article "Hobbes as Reformation Theeologian: Implications of the Free-Will Controversy," *Journal of the History of Ideas* 40 (1979), 339–52.

34. *Confessions,* tr. John K. Ryan (New York, 1960), VIII.v, pp. 188–89.

35. Eugène Portalié, *A Guide to the Thought of St. Augustine,* tr. Ralph J. Bastian (Chicago, 1960), p. 108.

36. *Of Grace and Free Will,* XV.xxxi, quoted by Etienne Gilson, *The Christian Philosophy of Saint Augustine,* tr. L. E. M. Lynch (New York, 1960), p. 164.

37. John Donne, Holy Sonnet 14, "Batter my heart, three-person'd God."

38. Martin Luther, *The Bondage of the Will,* tr. Philip S. Watson and Benjamin Drewery, in *Luther's Works* (Philadelphia, 1972), XXXIII, 288–89.

39. "Of the Spirit of Grace" (sermon on Rom. 8:9–10) in *The Whole Works of the Right Rev. Jeremy Taylor,* ed. Reginald Heber (London, 1847), IV, 335.

40. *Young Man Luther: A Study in Psychoanalysis and History* (New York, 1962), p. 135.

41. *On the Predestination of the Saints,* trans. R. E. Wallis, in *Basic Writings of Saint Augustine,* ed. Whitney J. Oates (New York, 1948), I. 810–12.

42. *The City of God,* tr. Henry Bettenson (Harmondsworth, 1972), XVIII, xlix, p. 831.

43. *The Bondage of the Will,* p. 294.

44. John Calvin, *Institutes of the Christian Religion,* tr. John Allen (Philadelphia, 1936), III.xxiii. 8.

45. G. W. F. Hegel, *The Phenomenology of Mind,* tr. J. B. Baillie (New York, 1967), p. 245.

46. William Cowper, "Lines Written During a Period of Insanity" (ca. 1774, pub. 1816).

47. See John Morris, *Versions of the Self* (New York, 1966), pp. 139–60.

48. *Memoir of William Cowper,* ed. and introduced by Maurice J. Quinlan, in *Proceedings of the American Philosophical Society,* 97 (1953), p. 376, and "Lines Written on a Window Shutter at Weston" (1795). See also Morris, *Versions of the Self,* pp. 139, 158–60.

49. See D. P. Walker, *The Decline of Hell: Seventeenth-Century Discussions of Eternal Torment* (Chicago, 1964).

50. *The Soules Humiliation* (1638), quoted by Edward K. Trefz, "Satan as the Prince of Evil: The Preaching of the New England Puritans, " *Boston Public Library Quarterly* 7 (1955), p. 11.

51. *Tractatus in Johannis,* quoted by Peter Brown, *Augustine of Hippo: A Biography* (Berkeley, 1967), p. 156.

52. *Confessions* VIII.iv; Burke, *The Rhetoric of Religion: Studies in Logology* (Berkeley, 1970), p. 109.

53. *City of God* XX.xxi, p. 939.

54. *The Gospel of Suffering,* p. 71.

55. See B. A. Gerrish, " 'To the Unknown God': Luther and Calvin on the Hiddenness of God," *Journal of Religion* 53 (1973), p. 274.

56. *Thus Spake Zarathustra,* trans. Thomas Common, in *The Philosophy of Nietzsche,* ed. W. H. Wright (New York, 1954), p. 66.

57. "Sinners in the Hands of an Angry God, " in *Jonathan Edwards: Representative Selections,* ed. Clarence H. Faust and Thomas H. Johnson (New York, 1962), pp. 163–64.

58. *Institutes* III.ii.7.

59. Preface to Romans in Luther's translation of the Bible, in *Martin*

Luther: Selections from his Writings, ed. John Dillenberger (New York, 1961), p. 32.

60. *The Complete Works of Richard Sibbes*, ed. Alexander Grosart (Edinburgh, 1862), I, 72.

61. *Jerusalem and Albion: The Hebraic Factor in Seventeenth-Century Literature* (London, 1964), p. 101. The quoted phrase comes from Calvin's *Institutes*, II.xii.

62. *The Poetical Fragments of Richard Baxter* (London, 1821), p. 63.

63. See Boyd Berry, *Process of Speech: Puritan Religious Writing and Paradise Lost* (Baltimore, 1976), pp. 11, 24–34, 38–40, 102.

64. Meditation 23, First Series (on Song of Songs 4:8, "Come with me from Lebanon, my spouse"), in *The Poems of Edward Taylor*, ed. Donald E. Stanford (New Haven, 1960), p. 39.

65. Bunyan, *A Few Sighs from Hell*, in *Miscellaneous Works*, I, 285.

66. On the conventional stages, see Edmund S. Morgan, *Visible Saints: The History of a Puritan Idea* (New York, 1963), and Norman Pettit, *The Heart Prepared: Grace and Conversion in Puritan Spiritual Life* (New Haven, 1966).

67. Jonathan Swift, *A Tale of a Tub*, sec. xi (first and third quoted passages), and *The Mechanical Operation of the Spirit*, sec. ii.

68. *Autobiography*, in *A Collection of the Works of Grace* (ca. 1700), quoted by Delany, *British Autobiography in the Seventeenth Century*, p. 97.

69. Erich Auerbach, *Dante: Poet of the Secular World*, tr. Ralph Manheim (Chicago, 1961), p. 14.

70. Quoted by John R. Knott, Jr., *The Sword of the Spirit: Puritan Responses to the Bible* (Chicago, 1980), p. 58.

71. *The Trial*, p. 161.

72. *Institutes* III.ix.4.

73. Robert Cushman (1622), quoted by Larzer Ziff, *Puritanism in America: New Culture in a New World* (New York, 1973), p. 41.

74. *Confessions* IX.iv, p. 212. Quotations from the Latin text are taken from the Loeb Classical Library edition: *St. Augustine's Confessions*, ed. W. H. D. Rouse (London, 1912).

75. *Beyond Good and Evil*, sec. 47, in *The Philosophy of Nietzsche*, pp. 434–35.

76. Brown, *Augustine of Hippo*, p. 177.

77. *Jonathan Edwards*, ed. Faust and Johnson, pp. 64, 69.

78. *Autobiography of Mary Countess of Warwick* (ca. 1671), ed. T. Crofton Croker, Percy Society vol. XXII (London, 1848), pp. 22, 24.

79. *Thoughts of a Dying Man*, quoted by David E. Stannard, *The Puritan Way of Death: A Study in Religion, Culture, and Social Change* (Oxford, 1977), p. 89.

80. Quoted by Lewalski, *Protestant Poetics*, p. 43.

81. *Reliquiae Baxterianae* (1696), I, 124 (written ca. 1664).

82. Richard Rogers, in *Two Elizabethan Puritan Diaries*, ed. M. M. Knappen (Chicago, 1933), p. 72.

83. *Confessions* IV.i; I quote Peter Brown's eloquent translation in *Augustine of Hippo*, p. 164.

84. *Confessions* VIII.xii, p. 202.

85. Cited by Frank Kermode, *The Genesis of Secrecy: On the Interpretation of Narrative* (Cambridge, Mass., 1979), p. 16.

86. *Cotton Mather: The Young Life of the Lord's Remembrancer, 1663–1703* (Cambridge, Mass., 1978), p. 5.

87. William C. Spengemann, *The Forms of Autobiography: Episodes in the History of a Literary Genre* (New Haven, 1980), p. 7.

88. Lucy Hutchinson, *Memoirs of the Life of Colonel Hutchinson,* ed. James Sutherland (New York, 1973), p. 5.

89. *Institutes* III.ix.4.

90. *The Life of the Reverend Mr. George Trosse,* ed. A. W. Brink (Montreal, 1974), p. 48.

91. Fulke Greville, *Caelica,* Sonnet 100.

92. *Jonathan Edwards,* ed. Faust and Johnson, p. 83.

93. Edward Johnson, *The Wonder-Working Providence of Sions Saviour in New-England* (1654), ed. J. F. Jameson (New York, 1910), p. 107.

94. *God's Plot,* ed. McGiffert (see p. 305 above, note 1), p. 40.

95. Quoted by Perry Miller, *The New England Mind: The Seventeenth Century* (Boston, 1961), p. 374.

96. *Autobiography,* August 2, 1671, quoted by David Levin, *Cotton Mather,* p. 21.

97. Alan MacFarlane, *The Family Life of Ralph Josselin: A Seventeenth-Century Clergyman* (Cambridge, 1970), pp. 173–76, 167.

98. *Right Thoughts in Sad Hours, Representing the Comforts and the Duties of Good Men under all their Afflictions; and Particularly, That One, the Untimely Death of Children* (1689), quoted by Levin, *Cotton Mather,* p. 140.

99. T. B. Macaulay, "Milton," in *The Works of Lord Macaulay* (New York, 1897), V, 38–39.

100. See G. R. Cragg, *From Puritanism to the Age of Reason* (Cambridge, 1966).

101. Matthew Sylvester's preface to *Reliquiae Baxterianae,* sec. viii of the unpaginated preface.

102. *The New England Mind,* p. 57.

103. *The Practical Works of the Rev. Richard Baxter* (London, 1830), XVII, 254, 267, 271.

104. *The Eloquent "I": Style and Self in Seventeenth-Century Prose* (Madison, 1968), p. 123.

105. *Reliquiae,* I, 2.

106. John Bunyan, *Mr. Badman,* in *Grace Abounding and The Life and Death of Mr. Badman,* ed. G. B. Harrison (London, 1928), p. 157.

107. Letter to John Durie, quoted by Geoffrey Nuttall, *Richard Baxter and Philip Doddridge: A Study in a Tradition* (London, 1951), p. 8.

108. *Practical Works,* VII, 355.

109. See Knott, *The Sword of the Spirit,* pp. 83–84.

110. "A Breviate of the Life of Margaret Baxter," quoted by Frederick J. Powicke, *The Reverend Richard Baxter under the Cross (1622–1691)* (London, 1927), p. 108.

111. John Tillotson, letter to M. Sylvester, 3 Feb. 1692, in Powicke, p. 292.

112. See John F. Wilson, *Pulpit in Parliament: Puritanism During the English Civil Wars* (Princeton, 1969), esp. pp. 145–46.

113. *Institutes* I.xvi.9.

114. "Transition in Renaissance Ideas of Time and the Place of Giordano Bruno," *Neophilologus* 55 (1971), p. 5.

115. Georges Poulet, *Studies in Human Time,* tr. Elliott Coleman (Baltimore, 1956), p. 18.

116. *Thus Spake Zarathustra,* sec. 42, in *The Philosophy of Nietzsche,* p. 153.

117. Nicholas Noyes (1698), quoted by Sacvan Bercovitch, *The American Jeremiad* (Madison, Wisc., 1978), p. 15.

118. Mircea Eliade, *Images and Symbols: Studies in Religious Symbolism,* tr. Philip Mairet (New York, 1961), p. 170.

119. *Process of Speech,* pp. 69–70, 126. See Kermode, *The Sense of an Ending.*

120. *Thus Spake Zarathustra,* sec. 25, p. 94.

121. *The Revolution of the Saints,* p. 100, quoting Knox's *A Godly Letter of Warning or Admonition to the Faithful in London, Newcastle and Berwick* (1554).

122. Quoted by Walzer, p. 258.

123. Quoted by William Haller, *Liberty and Reformation in the Puritan Revolution* (New York, 1955), p. 129.

124. "The Fatal Influence of Words and Names Falsely Applied," *Sermons Preached upon Several Occasions* (London, 1737), VI, 26. (For Aceldama, see note 31, p. 307 above.)

125. *Confessions* X.vi, p. 233.

126. Knott, *The Sword of the Spirit,* pp. 36, 39 (quoting Hooker's *The Preparation of the Heart,* 1640).

127. See Kenneth Burke, *The Rhetoric of Religion,* p. 143.

128. *A Disputation on Holy Scripture* (1588), quoted by Knott, *The Sword of the Spirit,* p. 34.

129. See Stephen Greenblatt, *Renaissance Self-Fashioning from More to Shakespeare* (Chicago, 1980), ch. 2.

130. *A Relation of the Imprisonment of Mr. John Bunyan,* in *Grace Abounding,* ed. Sharrock, pp. 111, 123.

131. Thanckful Owen and James Barron, eulogy on Thomas Goodwin (1681), quoted by Haller, *The Rise of Puritanism,* p. 94.

132. "Grace," in *The Poetical Fragments of Richard Baxter,* p. 122.

133. See Larzer Ziff, "The Literary Consequences of Puritanism, " in *The American Puritan Imagination: Essays in Revaluation,* ed. Sacvan Bercovitch (Cambridge, 1974), 34–44.

134. Samuel Butler, *Hudibras* (1663), I.i.51–52, 81–82, 161–64 (aiming at the Presbyterians).

135. Brown, *Augustine of Hippo,* pp. 261, 262 (quoting Sermon 22.7).

136. *Confessions* XIII.xv, p. 346.

137. *Institutes* IV.xvii.21.

138. See Raymond Firth, *Symbols Public and Private* (Ithaca, 1973), pp. 414–26.

139. *A Disputation on Holy Scripture,* quoted by William G. Madsen, *From Shadowy Types to Truth: Studies in Milton's Symbolism* (New Haven, 1968), p. 34.

140. William Perkins, *The Art of Prophesying,* quoted by U. Milo Kaufmann, *The Pilgrim's Progress and Traditions in Puritan Meditation* (New Haven, 1966), p. 35.

141. Quoted by Ronald S. Wallace, *Calvin's Doctrine of the Word and Sacrament* (Grand Rapids, 1957), p. 3n.

142. *The Trial*, pp. 272–73.

143. Jonathan Edwards, sermon: "True Grace Distinguished from the Experience of Devils, " in *The Whole Works of President Edwards* (London, 1817), VIII, 105.

144. *The Pilgrim's Progress*, ed. Sharrock, p. 114.

145. Sermon on Matthew 15 (in the Weimar *Werke*, XVII.ii), quoted by Roland Bainton, "Psychiatry and History: An Examination of Erikson's *Young Man Luther*," *Religion in Life* 40 (1971), pp. 451–52.

146. See Erich Auerbach, *Literary Language and Its Public in Late Latin Antiquity and the Middle Ages*, tr. Ralph Manheim (New York, 1965).

147. See Hans W. Frei, *The Eclipse of Biblical Narrative: A Study in Eighteenth and Nineteenth Century Hermeneutics* (New Haven, 1974).

148. Erich Auerbach, *Mimesis: The Representation of Reality in Western Literature*, tr. Willard R. Trask (Princeton, 1953), p. 15.

149. See Robert Adolph, *The Rise of Modern Prose Style* (Cambridge, Mass., 1968), p. 275.

150. *The Complete English Tradesman* (1725), Letter III, quoted by Adolph, p. 277.

151. *Wordsworth and the Poetry of Sincerity* (Cambridge, Mass., 1964), p. 5.

152. Jonathan Edwards, sermon: "A Divine and Supernatural Light," in *Works*, VIII, 7.

153. Henry Smith, "The Trumpet of the Soul Sounding to Judgement," in *Four Sermons* (1598), reprinted in *English Puritanism from John Hooper to John Milton*, ed. Everett H. Emerson (Durham, N.C., 1968), p. 125.

154. *Johannes Climacus*, or *De Omnibus Dubitandum Est*, quoted by Walter Lowrie, *Kierkegaard* (New York, 1962), I, 32.

155. *Paradise Lost* IX.366.

156. Harold Bloom, *The Anxiety of Influence: A Theory of Poetry* (London, 1973), p. 85.

157. *The Trial*, p. 193.

Chapter Three: Art and Truth in Paradise Lost

1. *Paradise Lost* VII.27–28. All quotations from *Paradise Lost* are taken from *The Poems of Milton*, ed. John Carey and Alastair Fowler (London, 1968).

2. *A Reading of Paradise Lost* (Oxford, 1965), p. 25.

3. Paul Ricoeur, *The Symbolism of Evil*, tr. Emerson Buchanan (Boston, 1967), p. 240.

4. Bronislaw Malinowski, *Myth in Primitive Psychology* (London, 1923), p. 21.

5. *Life of Milton*, in *Lives of the English Poets*, ed. G. B. Hill (Oxford, 1905), I, 155.

6. Frank Kermode, *The Sense of an Ending* (London, 1967), p. 39.

7. John Calvin, *Institutes of the Christian Religion*, tr. John Allen (Philadelphia, 1936), I.xiv.16.

8. *Life of Milton*, I, 183.

9. *The Logical Epic: A Study of the Argument of Paradise Lost* (Cambridge, Mass., 1967), pp. 53–56.

10. *Complete Prose Works of John Milton* (New Haven, 1953–) I,566.

11. See H. R. MacCallum, "Milton and Figurative Interpretation of the Bible," *University of Toronto Quarterly* 31 (1962), 397–415.

12. *De Doctrina Christiana* [*Christian Doctrine*], trans. John Carey, I.ii, in *Complete Prose Works*, VI, 136.

13. *The Reason of Church Government* I.i, *Complete Prose Works*, I, 753.

14. *De Doctrina* I.xxx, *Complete Prose Works*, VI, 589.

15. See Anne Davidson Ferry, *Milton's Epic Voice: The Narrator in Paradise Lost* (Cambridge, Mass., 1963), pp. 106–7.

16. *Milton's Epic Voice*, pp. 131–32.

17. Henri Bergson, *Les Deux Sources de la Morale et de la Religion* (Paris, 1932), p. 137.

18. Louis Martz, *Poet of Exile: A Study of Milton's Poetry* (New Haven, 1980), p. 79.

19. Harold Bloom, "Visionary Cinema of Romantic Poetry," in *The Ringers in the Tower: Studies in Romantic Tradition* (Chicago, 1971), p. 40.

20. Northrop Frye, *The Return of Eden* (Toronto, 1965), p. 48.

21. Sonnet XIX.

22. *De Doctrina* I.vii, *Complete Prose Works*, VI, 299.

23. See Ernest Becker, *The Denial of Death* (New York, 1975), p. 166.

24. See Michael Murrin, *The Allegorical Epic: Essays in Its Rise and Decline* (Chicago, 1980), p. 16.

25. Frank Kermode, "Adam Unparadised," in *The Living Milton: Essays by Various Hands*, ed. Kermode (London, 1960), p. 89.

26. See Ernst Cassirer, *The Philosophy of Symbolic Forms*, vol. II, *Mythical Thought*, tr. Ralph Manheim (New Haven, 1955), p. 203.

27. Andrew Marvell, "On Paradise Lost."

28. *The Symbolism of Evil*, Part II, ch. 2.

29. *Divine Dialogues*, quoted by D. P. Walker, *The Decline of Hell* (Chicago, 1964), p. 147.

30. *De Doctrina* I.ii, *Complete Prose Works*, VI, 131; William Empson, *Milton's God* (London, 1965), p. 203.

31. *Hobbes* (London, 1904), p. 157.

32. *Milton*, plate 2, lines 16–18, in *The Poetry and Prose of William Blake*, ed. David V. Erdman (New York, 1965), p. 95.

33. H. Richard Niebuhr, *Radical Monotheism and Western Culture* (New York, 1970), pp. 44, 38.

34. *De Doctrina* I.iii, *Complete Prose Works*, VI, 166.

35. See Dennis Danielson, *Milton's Good God: A Study in Literary Theodicy* (Cambridge, 1982), chaps. 3 and 5.

36. See the essays collected in *Bright Essence: Studies in Milton's Theology*, ed. W. B. Hunter et al. (Salt Lake City, 1971), particularly Hunter's essay, "Milton's Arianism Reconsidered," pp. 29–51, and J. H. Adamson, "Milton's 'Arianism,'" pp. 53–61.

37. Empson, *Milton's God*, p. 128; Berry, *Process of Speech: Puritan Religious Writing and Paradise Lost* (Baltimore, 1976), p. 57.

38. See Gary D. Hamilton, "Milton's Defensive God: A Reappraisal," *Studies in Philology* 69 (1972), p. 99.

39. Paul Ricoeur, *Freud and Philosophy: An Essay on Interpretation,* trans. Denis Savage (New Haven, 1970), p. 251.

40. *The Doctrine of the Law and Grace Unfolded,* in *The Miscellaneous Works of John Bunyan,* ed. Roger Sharrock et al. (Oxford, 1976–), II, 108.

41. See Harold Fisch, "Hebraic Style and Motifs in *Paradise Lost,*" in *Language and Style in Milton,* ed. Ronald D. Emma and John T. Shawcross (New York, 1967), pp. 30–64.

42. Quoted by Gerald Strauss, *Luther's House of Learning: Indoctrination of the Young in the German Reformation* (Baltimore, 1978), p. 215.

43. David Hume, *Dialogues Concerning Natural Religion* (1779), ed. Norman Kemp Smith (New York, 1947), Part X, p. 198.

44. *Institutes* I.xiv.17, III.xxiii.8.

45. *Complete Prose Works,* II, 658.

46. *The Symbolism of Evil,* p. 146n.

47. *The Idea of the Holy,* trans. John W. Harvey (London, 1958), pp. 106n.

48. Quoted by Keith Thomas, *Religion and the Decline of Magic* (New York, 1971), p. 472.

49. *Confessions,* trans. John K. Ryan (New York, 1960). III.vii, p. 85; VII.xvi, p. 175; X.xxxvi, p. 267. In the Latin text, Satan says "Well done!" in Greek ("Euge, euge"), acting as usual as a rhetorician.

50. *The Holy War,* ed. James F. Forrest (New York, 1967), p. 10.

51. See the very full documentation in Stella Purce Revard, *The War in Heaven: Paradise Lost and the Tradition of Satan's Rebellion* (Ithaca, 1980).

52. *Milton's God,* p. 24.

53. "Milton's Satan and the Theme of Damnation in Elizabethan Tragedy," *Essays and Studies,* 1 (1948), repr. in *A Reading of Paradise Lost,* pp, 99, 120.

54. See J. M. Evans, *Paradise Lost and the Genesis Tradition* (Oxford, 1968), p. 229.

55. R. J. Z. Werblowsky, *Lucifer and Prometheus: A Study of Milton's Satan* (London, 1952), p. 11.

56. *Milton and His Epic Tradition* (Seattle, 1979), p. 124.

57. "Creation and the Place of the Poet in *Paradise Lost,*" in *The Author in His Work,* ed. Louis L. Martz and Aubrey Williams (New Haven, 1978), p. 65.

58. Arnold Stein, *Answerable Style: Essays on Paradise Lost* (Minneapolis, 1953), p. 11.

59. C. S. Lewis, *A Preface to Paradise Lost* (London, 1942), p. 95.

60. *Life of Milton,* I, 157.

61. See Joan S. Bennett, "God, Satan, and King Charles: Milton's Royal Portraits," *PMLA* 92 (1977), 441–57.

62. *The Works of President Edwards* (London, 1817), III, 293, 300.

63. See Harold Bloom, *The Anxiety of Influence* (London, 1973), ch. 1.

64. W. H. Auden, "The Christian Tragic Hero," *New York Times Book Review,* 16 Dec. 1945, p. 1; repr. in *Tragedy: Modern Essays in Criticism,* ed. Laurence Michel and Richard B. Sewall (Englewood Cliffs, N.J., 1963), p. 234.

65. *Poet of Exile,* p. 106.

66. *De Doctrina* I.x, *Complete Prose Works,* VI, 351–52.

67. *Caelica,* sonnet 102.

68. *Complete Prose Works,* II, 514.

69. *Schöpfung, Vernunft und Gesetz in Luthers Theologie* (Uppsala, 1971), pp. 303–5.

70. *Memoirs of the Life of the Rev. Thomas Halyburton* (Princeton, 1833), p. 89.

71. See Christopher Hill, *Milton and the English Revolution* (Harmondsworth, 1979), p. 397.

72. Danielson, *Milton's Good God,* p. 145.

73. *Institutes* III.xxiii.7.

74. Jonathan Edwards, *Freedom of the Will,* ed. Arnold S. Kaufman and William K. Frankena (New York, 1969), pp. 248–49.

75. *Milton's God,* p. 151.

76. *Institutes* II.v.5.

77. *Milton's Good God,* pp. 119–25.

78. Paul Ricoeur's term in "The Hermeneutics of Symbols and Philosophical Reflection," in *The Conflict of Interpretations: Essays in Hermeneutics,* ed. Don Ihde (Evanston, Ill., 1974), p. 295.

79. *The Conflict of Interpretations,* pp. 295, 306.

80. The classic statement of the first position is that of Millicent Bell, "The Fallacy of the Fall in *Paradise Lost,*" *PMLA* 68 (1953), 863–83. Replies from the second group have been legion; see esp. Wayne Shumaker's exchange with Bell in *PMLA* 70 (1955), 1185–1202, and H. V. S. Ogden, "The Crisis of *Paradise Lost* Reconsidered," *Philological Quarterly* 36 (1957), 1–19.

81. John S. Diekhoff, "Eve's Dream and the Paradox of Fallible Perfection," *Milton Quarterly* 4 (1970), p. 6. See also William B. Hunter, Jr., "Eve's Demonic Dream," *ELH* 13 (1946), 255–65.

82. *The Return of Eden,* p. 75.

83. *The Symbolism of Evil,* p. 250.

84. "Eve's Dream," *Milton Studies* 12 (1978), p. 28.

85. "The Example of Adam and Eve," from *Prototypes, or the Primary Precedent Presidents out of the Book of Genesis* (1640), in *English Puritanism from John Hooper to John Milton,* ed. Everett H. Emerson (Durham, N.C., 1968), p. 276.

86. See Burden, *The Logical Epic,* ch. 5.

87. See A. B. Chambers, "The Falls of Adam and Eve in *Paradise Lost,*" in *New Essays on Paradise Lost,* ed. Thomas Kranidas (Berkeley, 1969), 118–30.

88. See Evans, *Paradise Lost and the Genesis Tradition,* pp. 266–68.

89. See Mary Douglas, *Purity and Danger: An Analysis of the Concepts of Pollution and Taboo* (London, 1966), p. 153.

90. See Thomas F. Merrill, "*Paradise Lost* and the Hazards of Semantic Idolatry," *Neuphilologische Mitteilungen* 77 (1976), 387–410.

91. As Stein observes: *Answerable Style,* p. 110.

92. William Madsen, *From Shadowy Types to Truth: Studies in Milton's Symbolism* (New Haven, 1968), p. 69.

93. *The Symbolism of Evil,* p. 246.

94. *Milton's God,* p. 188.

95. Laurence Sterne, *Tristram Shandy,* ed. Watt (Boston, 1965), introduction, p. xliv.

96. See Stein, *Answerable Style,* p. 66; Christopher Ricks, *Milton's Grand Style* (Oxford, 1963), p. 110; and Fish, *Surprised by Sin,* p. 135.

97. *Milton's Epic Voice*, p. 71.

98. See Peter A. Fiore, *Milton and Augustine: Patterns of Augustinian Thought in Paradise Lost* (University Park, Pa., 1981), pp. 28–33.

99. *Answerable Style*, p. 117.

100. See Danielson, *Milton's Good God*, ch. 7.

101. See Joseph H. Summers, *The Muse's Method: An Introduction to Paradise Lost* (New York, 1968), p. 173.

102. See Burden, *The Logical Epic*, pp. 35–36, and Danielson, *Milton's Good God*, p. 154.

103. *Frankenstein, Or, The Modern Prometheus*, ed. James Kinsley and M. K. Joseph (Oxford, 1980), p. 100.

104. Isabel MacCaffrey, *Paradise Lost as Myth* (Cambridge, Mass., 1959), p. 26. See also Summers, *The Muse's Method*, ch. 3.

105. See Frye, *The Return of Eden*, p. 17.

106. See Mary Anne Radzinowicz, *Toward Samson Agonistes: The Growth of Milton's Mind* (Princeton, 1978), p. 294.

107. Barbara K. Lewalski, "Structure and the Symbolism of Vision in Michael's Prophecy, *Paradise Lost*, Books XI–XII," *Philological Quarterly* 42 (1963), 25–35.

108. Stanley Fish, *Surprised by Sin: The Reader in Paradise Lost* (Berkeley, 1971), p. 317.

109. Joseph A. Wittreich, Jr., *Visionary Poetics: Milton's Tradition and His Legacy* (San Marino, Cal., 1979), pp. 34, 50.

110. *The Protestant Ethic and the Spirit of Capitalism*, tr. Talcott Parsons (New York, 1958), p. 88.

111. *Allegory: The Theory of a Symbolic Mode* (Ithaca, 1964), p. 66.

112. Robert Martin Adams, *Milton and the Modern Critics*, foreword to the second edition (Ithaca, 1966), p. ix.

113. *A Preface to Paradise Lost*, p. 39.

Chapter Four: Experience and Allegory in Bunyan

1. Life of Bunyan in *Pilgrim's Progress*, Part III (1693), quoted by William York Tindall, *John Bunyan: Mechanick Preacher* (New York, 1934), p. 105.

2. Samuel Butler, *Hudibras*, I.ii.535–40.

3. Anonymous poem quoted by Richard L. Greaves, "The Nature of the Puritan Tradition," in *Reformation, Conformity and Dissent*, ed. R. B. Knox (London, 1977), p. 270.

4. Introduction to *The Puritans: A Sourcebook of their Writings*, ed. Perry Miller and Thomas H. Johnson (New York, 1938), I, 14, 15.

5. *A Relation of the Imprisonment of Mr. John Bunyan*, in Bunyan, *Grace Abounding to the Chief of Sinners*, ed. Roger Sharrock (Oxford, 1962), p. 108.

6. Lawrence Stone, *The Causes of the English Revolution, 1529–1642* (London, 1972), p. 96–97.

7. Christopher Hill, *Milton and the English Revolution* (Harmondsworth, 1979), p. 274.

8. *Instruction for the Ignorant* (1675), in *The Miscellaneous Works of John Bunyan*, ed. Roger Sharrock *et al.* (Oxford, 1976–), VIII, 19.

9. Monica Furlong, *Puritan's Progress: A Study of John Bunyan* (London, 1975), p. 16.

10. *The Varieties of Religious Experience* (New York, 1919), pp. 154, 184.

11. *Grace Abounding,* ed. Sharrock, p. 6.

12. Josiah Royce, "The Case of John Bunyan," in *Studies of Good and Evil* (New York, 1898), p. 55.

13. *The Marriage of Heaven and Hell,* plate 14, in *The Poetry and Prose of William Blake,* ed. David V. Erdman (New York, 1965), p. 38.

14. *The Life of the Reverend Mr. George Trosse,* ed. A. W. Brink (Montreal, 1974), p. 88. See Margaret Bottrall, *Every Man a Phoenix: Studies in Seventeenth-Century Autobiography* (London, 1958), p. 102, and Barrett John Mandel, "Bunyan and the Autobiographer's Artistic Purpose," *Criticism* 10 (1968), p. 237.

15. Thomas Shepard, *God's Plot* (see above, p. 305, note 1), p. 195.

16. See Paul Delany, *British Autobiography in the Seventeenth Century* (London, 1969), pp. 63, 66, and Rebecca S. Beal, *"Grace Abounding to the Chief of Sinners:* John Bunyan's Pauline Epistle," *Studies in English Literature* 21 (1981), 147–60.

17. *Miscellaneous Works,* VI, 47.

18. See Keith Thomas, *Religion and the Decline of Magic* (New York, 1971), pp. 166–73.

19. Tindall, *John Bunyan: Mechanick Preacher,* pp. 16, 17.

20. *A Discourse Concerning Trouble of Mind and the Disease of Melancholy* (1691), pp. vi, 364.

21. *The Cure of Melancholy and Overmuch Sorrow by Faith and Physic* (1683), in *The Practical Works of the Rev. Richard Baxter* (London, 1830), XVII, 244–46.

22. Quoted by Delany, *British Autobiography in the Seventeenth Century,* p. 85.

23. Sigmund Freud, *The Ego and the Id,* tr. Joan Riviere, rev. James Strachey (New York, 1960), p. 39.

24. Charles Baudouin (quoting Laforgue), *Psychanalyse du Symbole Religieux* (Paris, 1957), p. 109.

25. See the trenchant critique by David E. Stannard, *Shrinking History: On Freud and the Failure of Psychoanalysis* (Oxford, 1980).

26. Roy D. Waldman, *Humanistic Psychiatry* (New Brunswick, N.J., 1971), p. 124.

27. Ernest Becker, *The Denial of Death* (New York, 1975), p. 197.

28. See Karl Holl, "Martin Luther on Luther," trans. H. C. E. Midelfort, in *Interpreters of Luther,* ed. Jaroslav Pelikan (Philadelphia, 1968), 9–34.

29. *Light for Them That Sit in Darkness* (1675), in Bunyan's *Miscellaneous Works,* VIII, 156–57.

30. Carl Gustav Jung, *Psychology and Religion* (New Haven, 1938), p. 17.

31. T. B. Macaulay, "John Bunyan" (the 1854 essay), in *The Works of Lord Macaulay* (New York, 1897), VII, 302.

32. *The Compulsion to Confess* (New York, 1966), p. 316.

33. *God's Plot,* ed. McGiffert, p. 94.

34. Quoted by Stone, *The Causes of the English Revolution,* p. 101.

35. Richard Marius, *Luther* (Philadelphia, 1974), p. 107.

36. See above, p. 102.

37. See Peter J. Carlton, "Bunyan: Language, Convention, Authority," *ELH* 51 (1984), 17–32.

38. *Two Types of Faith,* tr. Norman P. Goldhawk (New York, 1961), p. 161.

39. See Richard L. Greaves, *John Bunyan* (Grand Rapids, Michigan, 1969), esp. pp. 29, 156.

40. *The Eloquent "I": Style and Self in Seventeenth-Century Prose* (Madison, Wis. 1968), p. 52.

41. See above, pp. 13–14.

42. Harold Bloom, "Ruskin as Literary Critic," in *The Ringers in the Tower: Studies in Romantic Tradition* (Chicago, 1971), p. 179; Wordsworth, "Resolution and Independence," line 54.

43. *Process of Speech: Puritan Religious Writing and Paradise Lost* (Baltimore, 1976), p. 196.

44. Roger Sharrock, *John Bunyan* (London, 1968), p. 157.

45. See Tindall, *John Bunyan: Mechanick Preacher*, p. 151, and Bunyan, *The Holy War*, ed. Roger Sharrock and James F. Forrest (Oxford, 1980), p. 254.

46. *The Holy War*, ed. James F. Forrest (New York, 1967), pp. 57–58. (My quotations are all from this edition.)

47. See Barbara K. Lewalski, *Protestant Poetics and the Seventeenth-Century Religious Lyric* (Princeton, 1979), p. 92, and Michael Walzer, *The Revolution of the Saints* (New York, 1974), p. 65.

48. Lionel Trilling, *The Opposing Self* (New York, 1959), p. 129.

49. Downame, *The Christian Warfare* (1604), p. 3. Baxter, *The Reformed Pastor*, quoted by John R. Knott, Jr., *The Sword of the Spirit: Puritan Responses to the Bible* (Chicago, 1980), p. 73.

50. *The Revolution of the Saints*, p. 150.

51. Stephen Greenblatt, *Renaissance Self-Fashioning* (Chicago, 1980), p. 9.

52. *Beyond Good and Evil*, sec. 76, trans. Helen Zimmern, in *The Philosophy of Nietzsche* (New York: Modern Library, 1954), p. 453.

53. See for instance Tindall, *John Bunyan: Mechanick Preacher*, ch. 7, and the Oxford edition of *The Holy War*, ed. Sharrock and Forrest, pp. xx–xxxiv.

54. *Antichrist in Seventeenth-Century England* (London, 1971), p. 171.

55. Quoted by E. M. W. Tillyard, *The English Epic and Its Background* (London, 1954), p. 380.

56. "A Difficulty in the Path of Psycho-Analysis," in *The Standard Edition of the Complete Psychological Works*, ed. James Strachey (London, 1955), XVII, 142.

57. Paul Ricoeur, *The Symbolism of Evil*, trans. Emerson Buchanan (Boston, 1969), p. 156.

58. Holy Sonnet no. 14, "Batter my heart, three-personed God."

59. Roger Sharrock in the Oxford edition, p. xxx.

60. *Of Liberty and Necessity* (1654), in *The English Works of Thomas Hobbes*, ed. William Molesworth (London, 1839), IV, 54.

61. Peter Berger, *The Sacred Canopy: Elements of a Sociological Theory of Religion* (New York, 1967), p. 39.

62. *Natural Symbols: Explorations in Cosmology* (New York, 1973), p. 169.

63. Angus Fletcher, *Allegory: The Theory of a Symbolic Mode* (Ithaca, 1964), pp. 23, 225, 286–87.

64. Rosemond Tuve, *Allegorical Imagery: Some Mediaeval Books and Their Posterity* (Princeton, 1966), p. 44.

65. See Knott, *The Sword of the Spirit*, p. 156.

66. Gerd Birkner, *Heilsgewissheit und Literatur: Metapher, Allegorie und Autobiographie im Puritanismus* (Munich, 1972), pp. 118–28.

67. See Fletcher, *Allegory,* p. 151.

68. "John Bunyan," p. 305.

69. See De Man, "The Rhetoric of Temporality," in *Interpretation: Theory and Practice,* ed. Charles S. Singleton (Baltimore, 1969), pp. 173–209, and "Pascal's Allegory of Persuasion," in *Allegory and Representation,* ed. Stephen J. Greenblatt (Baltimore, 1981), 1–25.

70. Stephen A. Barney, *Allegories of History, Allegories of Love* (Hamden, Conn., 1979), p. 22.

71. *The Allegory of Love* (London, 1953), p. 45.

72. *Two Concepts of Allegory* (London, 1967), pp. 17–19.

73. *The Language of Allegory: Defining the Genre* (Ithaca, 1979), p. 24.

74. See D. W. Robertson, Jr., *A Preface to Chaucer: Studies in Medieval Perspectives* (Princeton, 1962), p. 56, and Quilligan, *The Language of Allegory,* p. 28.

75. See the facsimile title page in the Penguin edition of *The Pilgrim's Progress,* ed. Roger Sharrock (Harmondsworth, 1965), from which all of my quotations are taken.

76. *Some Gospel-Truths Opened, Miscellaneous Works,* I, 13.

77. *Miscellaneous Works,* I, 344, 354. The smith's dog seems to have been proverbial; Larzer Ziff cites a similar passage in Roger Williams (*Puritanism in America* [New York, 1973], p. 55).

78. On resemblances betwee art and daydreaming (rather than dreaming), see Meredith Anne Skura, *The Literary Use of the Psychoanalytic Process* (New Haven, 1981), pp. 126–27.

79. *Allegory,* p. 349.

80. John Donne, *Devotions upon Emergent Occasions* (Ann Arbor, 1965), Expostulation XIX, p. 125.

81. William Tyndale, *A Prologue into . . . Leviticus,* quoted by William G. Madsen, *From Shadowy Types to Truth: Studies in Milton's Symbolism* (New Haven, 1968), pp. 77–78.

82. Frank Kermode, *The Genesis of Secrecy: On the Interpretation of Narrative* (Cambridge, Mass., 1979), p. 81.

83. See above, p. 63.

84. See Knott's excellent discussion of this point: *The Sword of the Spirit,* pp. 152–53.

85. "To the Reader," *The Holy War,* pp. 5–6.

86. *Grace Abounding,* p. 3.

87. Paul J. Korshin, *Typologies in England, 1650–1820* (Princeton, 1982), p. 391.

88. Mark Twain, *Adventures of Huckleberry Finn,* ed. Leo Marx (New York, 1967), ch. 17, p. 120. The propositional quality of *The Pilgrim's Progress* is suggested by Huck's further observation that "The statements was interesting, but tough."

89. Luke 14:26; see p. 54 of *The Pilgrim's Progress.* The Penguin edition omits many of Bunyan's glosses, which may be seen in the Oxford *Pilgrim's Progress* (1960), ed. James B. Wharey, rev. Roger Sharrock.

90. Søren Kierkegaard, *Fear and Trembling,* in *Fear and Trembling and The Sickness unto Death,* trans. Walter Lowrie (Princeton, 1954), pp. 82, 85.

91. Captain Roger Clap (1731), quoted by Herbert W. Schneider, *The Puritan Mind* (Ann Arbor, 1958), p. 33.

92. *Farewell Sermon,* in *Jonathan Edwards: Representative Selections,* ed. Clarence H. Faust and Thomas H. Johnson (New York, 1962), p. 192.

93. Stanley Fish, *Self-Consuming Artifacts: The Experience of Seventeenth-Century Literature* (Berkeley, 1972), p. 249.

94. *Schöpfung, Vernunft und Gesetz in Luthers Theologie* (Uppsala, 1971), pp. 52–60, with copious quotations from Luther's writings.

95. *Ibid.,* pp. 63–64.

96. *Some Gospel-Truths Opened, Miscellaneous Works,* I, 58.

97. C. S. Lewis, "The Vision of John Bunyan," in *Bunyan: The Pilgrim's Progress: A Casebook,* ed. Roger Sharrock, p. 198.

98. Blake's picture may be seen in Milton Klonsky, *William Blake: The Seer and His Visions* (New York, 1977), p. 121.

99. See A. Richard Dutton, "'Interesting, but Tough': Reading *The Pilgrim's Progress," Studies in English Literature,* 18 (1978), 439–56.

100. *John Bunyan,* p. 70.

101. See Susan Snyder, "The Left Hand of God: Despair in Medieval and Renaissance Tradition," *Studies in the Renaissance* 12 (1965), 18–59.

102. *The Freedom of a Christian,* p. 348.

103. Charles Wesley, "Wrestling Jacob," lines 43–44, in *Eighteenth-Century English Literature,* ed. Geoffrey Tillotson, Paul Fussell, and Marshall Waingrow (New York, 1969), p. 1536.

104. See Harold Golder, "Bunyan's Giant Despair," *JEGP* 30 (1931), 361–78.

105. See James Turner, "Bunyan's Sense of Place," in *The Pilgrim's Progress: Critical and Historical Views,* ed. Vincent Newey (Liverpool, 1980), p. 100.

106. See Janet Warner, "Blake's Figures of Despair: Man in His Spectre's Power," in *William Blake: Essays in Honour of Sir Geoffrey Keynes,* ed. Morton Paley and Michael Phillips (Oxford, 1973), pp. 219–21.

107. Northrop Frye, *The Secular Scripture: A Study of the Structure of Romance* (Cambridge, Mass., 1976), p. 134.

108. *Literary Remains,* in *The Complete Works of Samuel Taylor Coleridge,* ed. W. G. T. Shedd (New York, 1884), V, 262.

109. *Miscellaneous Works,* I, 7–8.

110. *The Doctrine of the Law and Grace Unfolded, Miscellaneous Works,* II, 107.

111. *A Declaration of the True Manner of Knowing Christ Crucified,* quoted by Madsen, *From Shadowy Types of Truth,* p. 176.

112. W. H. Auden, "Postscript: Christianity and Art," in *The Dyer's Hand and Other Essays* (New York, 1968), p. 457.

113. Quoted by Sacvan Bercovitch, *The Puritan Origins of the American Self* (New Haven, 1975), p. 14; and see Bercovitch's interesting note (pp. 214–15) on the metaphor of the *figura* as a sketch or sculptor's model.

114. On possible iconographical implications of Mercy's humility, see James F. Forrest, "Mercy with Her Mirror," *Philological Quarterly* 42 (1963), 121–126.

115. Wolfgang Iser, *The Implied Reader: Patterns of Communication in Prose Fiction from Bunyan to Beckett* (Baltimore, 1974), p. 28.

116. *Milton and the English Revolution,* p. 458.

117. *The Holy War,* p. 46.

118. As Knott comments in connection with this passage: *The Sword of the Spirit,* p. 156.

119. *Self-Consuming Artifacts*, p. 243.

120. See Turner, "Bunyan's Sense of Place."

121. See Knott, *The Sword of the Spirit*, p. 144.

122. Erich Auerbach, *Mimesis: The Representation of Reality in Western Literature*, trans. Willard R. Trask (Princeton, 1953), p. 49.

123. *The Life and Death of Mr. Badman*, in *Grace Abounding and The Life and Death of Mr. Badman*, ed. G. B. Harrison (London, 1928), p. 155.

124. Harold Golder long ago documented the extent of Bunyan's imaginative debt to the chapbook romances he had devoured in his youth: "Bunyan's Valley of the Shadow," *Modern Philology* 27. (1929), 55–72, and "Bunyan and Spenser," *PMLA* 45 (1930), 216–37. See also Nick Davis, "The Problem of Misfortune in *The Pilgrim's Progress*," and Nick Shrimpton, "Bunyan's Military Metaphor," both in *The Pilgrim's Progress: Critical and Historical Views*, ed. Newey, pp. 182–204, 205–24.

125. See Furlong, *Puritan's Progress*, p. 47.

126. *A Few Sighs from Hell*, in *Miscellaneous Works*, I, 333.

127. Tyndale, *The Obedience of a Christian Man*, quoted by Greenblatt, *Renaissance Self-Fashioning*, pp. 101, 112. On the increasing tendency to identify the allegorical with the literal sense, see Victor Harris, "Allegory to Analogy in the Interpretation of Scriptures," *Philological Quarterly* 45 (1966), 1–23.

128. Review of Southey's edition of *The Pilgrim's Progress* in the *Quarterly Review* (1830), repr. in *Bunyan: The Pilgrim's Progress: A Casebook*, ed. Sharrock, p. 65.

129. *The Secular Scripture*, p. 47.

130. *Anatomy of Criticism* (Princeton, 1957), pp. 304–5.

131. See Hans W. Frei, *The Eclipse of Biblical Narrative: A Study in Eighteenth and Nineteenth Century Hermeneutics* (New Haven, 1974).

132. See for instance Fletcher, *Allegory*, pp. 7–8.

133. *Allegorical Imagery*, p. 222n.

134. See Katherine Koller, "The Puritan Preacher's Contribution to Fiction," *Huntington Library Quarterly* 11 (1948), 321–40.

135. "The Vision of John Bunyan," p. 196.

136. John N. Morris, *Versions of the Self* (New York, 1966), p. 91.

137. Charles Dickens, *Great Expectations*, ed. Angus Calder (Harmondsworth, 1965), ch.1, p. 36.

138. *Self-Consuming Artifacts*, pp. 227–28.

139. See esp. Fish's chapter on Bunyan in *Self-Consuming Artifacts;* also Fletcher, *Allegory*, pp. 292–93, and Gay Clifford, *The Transformations of Allegory* (London, 1974), ch. 1.

140. See David J. Alpaugh, "Emblem and Interpretation in *The Pilgrim's Progress*," ELH 33 (1966), p. 311.

141. "*The Pilgrim's Progress* and Allegory," in *The Pilgrim's Progress: Critical and Historical Views*, ed. Newey, pp. 134, 136.

142. *Allegorical Imagery*, pp. 159–60.

143. Robert Bell, "Metamorphoses of Spiritual Autobiography," *ELH* 44 (1977), p. 115.

144. Philip Edwards makes this point: "The Journey in *The Pilgrim's Progress*," in *The Pilgrim's Progress: Critical and Historical Views*, ed. Newey, p. 114.

145. Henri Talon, "Space and the Hero in *The Pilgrim's Progress, Etudes Anglaises* 14 (1961), p. 129.

146. *Personal Narrative,* in *Jonathan Edwards: Representative Selections,* ed. Faust and Johnson, p. 67.

147. William Whittingham, quoted by Owen Chadwick, *The Reformation* (Harmondsworth, 1972), p. 186.

148. *Miscellaneous Criticism,* ed. Raysor, p. 33.

149. As Quilligan notes: *The Language of Allegory,* pp. 129–30.

150. *Two Concepts of Allegory,* p. 39.

151. "John Bunyan" (the earlier essay of 1830), in *Works,* V, 450.

152. Dorothy Van Ghent, *The English Novel: Form and Function* (New York, 1961), p. 30.

153. *Mr. Badman,* pp. 216, 183.

154. See Maurice Hussey, "John Bunyan and the Books of God's Judgements," *English,* 7 (1949) 165–67.

155. Paul Fussell, *The Great War and Modern Memory* (New York, 1975), pp. 99, 137–44.

156. *Self-Consuming Artifacts,* p. 262.

157. A. C. Charity, *Events and Their Afterlife: The Dialectics of Christian Typology in the Bible and Dante* (Cambridge, 1966), p. 153.

158. George Herbert, "The Pilgrimage," stanza 4.

Chapter Five: Myth and Fiction in Robinson Crusoe

1. *The Life and Strange Surprizing Adventures of Robinson Crusoe,* ed. J. Donald Crowley (London, 1972), p. 137. Further references to *Crusoe* are to this edition.

2. *Serious Reflections during the Life and Surprising Adventures of Robinson Crusoe,* in *Romances and Narratives of Daniel Defoe,* ed. George A. Aitken (London, 1895), III, 101.

3. Michael Walzer, *The Revolution of the Saints* (New York, 1974), p. 15.

4. *Defoe's Review,* ed. in facsimile by A. W. Secord (New York, 1938), VI, 341 (22 Oct. 1709).

5. *Defoe's Narratives: Situations and Structures* (Oxford, 1975), p. 63.

6. Richard Stauffer, *Dieu, la Création et la Providence dans la Prédication de Calvin* (Berne, 1978), p. 268.

7. John Wesley, quoted by Keith Thomas, *Religion and the Decline of Magic* (New York, 1971), p. 640; see Thomas's discussion of this point on pp. 639–40.

8. *Moll Flanders,* ed. G. A. Starr (London, 1976), pp. 274, 279.

9. *A General Martyrologie* (1677), quoted by J. Paul Hunter, *The Reluctant Pilgrim: Defoe's Emblematic Method and Quest for Form in Robinson Crusoe* (Baltimore, 1966), p. 76.

10. *The Letters of Daniel Defoe,* ed. G. H. Healey (Oxford, 1969), p. 17. See Paula R. Backscheider, "Personality and Biblical Allusion in Defoe's Letters," *South Atlantic Review* 47 (1982), 1–20.

11. See Paul J. Korshin, *Typologies in England, 1650–1820* (Princeton, 1982), pp. 218–21.

12. Paul K. Alkon, *Defoe and Fictional Time* (Athens, Ga., 1979), pp. 61, 146.

13. *Serious Reflections,* pp. 2–3.

14. René Descartes, *Discours de la Méthode,* final sentence of Part III.

15. *Personal Narrative,* in *Jonathan Edwards: Representative Selections,* ed. Clarence H. Faust and Thomas H. Johnson (New York, 1962), p. 60.

16. From Forster's *Life of Charles Dickens,* reprinted in the Norton Critical Edition of *Robinson Crusoe,* ed. Michael Shinagel (New York, 1975), p. 295.

17. *The Pilgrim's Progress,* ed. Roger Sharrock (Harmondsworth, 1965), p. 56.

18. See Maximillian E. Novak, *Defoe and the Nature of Man* (Oxford, 1963), ch. 2.

19. Richard Baxter, *The Divine Life,* III.iii, in *Practical Works* (London, 1838), III, 868.

20. David Riesman, *The Lonely Crowd,* abridged ed. (New Haven, 1961), p. 44.

21. Novak, *Defoe and the Nature of Man,* p. 133; Martin Price, *To the Palace of Wisdom: Studies in Order and Energy from Dryden to Blake* (New York, 1965), p. 275.

22. Angus Fletcher, *Allegory: The Theory of a Symbolic Mode* (Ithaca, 1964), p. 53.

23. G. A. Starr, "Defoe's Prose Style: 1. The language of Interpretation," *Modern Philology* 71 (1974), p. 292.

24. John Locke, *An Essay Concerning Human Understanding,* III.ii.1; David Hume, *A Treatise of Human Nature,* ed. L. A. Selby-Bigge (Oxford, 1888), II.ii, p. 340.

25. See esp. Homer O. Brown, "The Displaced Self in the Novels of Daniel Defoe," in *Studies in Eighteenth-Century Culture,* vol. IV, ed. Harold E. Pagliaro (Madison, 1975), pp. 69–94; and Everett Zimmerman, *Defoe and the Novel* (Berkeley, 1975), ch. 2.

26. Richetti, *Defoe's Narratives,* p. 22.

27. Harold Bloom, *The Anxiety of Influence* (London, 1973), p. 64.

28. "On General Councils" (1676), in *The Complete Works of Andrew Marvell,* ed. A. B. Grosart (New York, 1875), I, 125.

29. See Novak, *Defoe and the Nature of Man,* pp. 16–18.

30. *Grace Abounding,* ed. Roger Sharrock (Oxford, 1962), p. 76.

31. *Spectator* 411. There are two similar uses of "secret" in no. 412.

32. See Martin J. Greif, "The Conversion of Robinson Crusoe," *Studies in English Literature* 6 (1966), 553–55.

33. Samuel Taylor Coleridge, *Complete Works* (New York, 1884), IV, 312.

34. See Novak, *Defoe and the Nature of Man,* ch. 3.

35. *Colonel Jack,* ed. Samuel Holt Monk (London, 1965), p. 161.

36. *Defoe and Casuistry* (Princeton, 1971).

37. *The Rise of the Novel: Studies in Defoe, Richardson, and Fielding* (Berkeley, 1957), ch. 3.

38. Thomas Hobbes, *Leviathan,* ed. Michael Oakeshott (Oxford, 1946), II.xxiv, p. 161.

39. G. A. Starr, *Defoe and Spiritual Autobiography* (Princeton, 1965), pp. 185–97.

40. *Civilization and Its Discontents,* tr. James Strachey (New York, 1962), p. 42.

41. Max Weber, *The Protestant Ethic and the Spirit of Capitalism,* tr. Talcott Parsons (New York, 1958), p. 54.

42. *The Gulf: Poems by Derek Walcott* (New York, 1970), pp. 27–28.

43. William Haller, *The Rise of Puritanism* (New York, 1938), p. 108; José Ortega y Gasset, *The Dehumanization of Art* (New York, 1956), p. 11.

44. "Defoe, Richardson, Joyce, and the Concept of Form in the Novel," in William Matthews and Ralph W. Rader, *Autobiography, Biography, and the Novel* (Los Angeles, 1973), p. 46.

45. *The George Eliot Letters*, ed. Gordon S. Haight (New Haven, 1954–55), I, 22–23.

46. See Maximillian E. Novak, "Defoe's Theory of Fiction," *Studies in Philology* 61 (1964), 650–68.

47. T. B. Macaulay, "John Dryden," in *The Works of Lord Macaulay* (New York, 1897), V, 90.

48. "The Displaced Self in the Novels of Daniel Defoe," pp. 85, 92.

49. "Robinson Crusoe's Preface," *Serious Reflections*, pp. ix, xii, xi.

50. *Robinson Crusoe Examin'd and Criticis'd* (1719), ed. Paul Dottin (London and Paris, 1923), p. 94.

51. See Maximillian E. Novak, *Economics and the Fiction of Daniel Defoe* (Berkeley, 1962), pp. 20–21, 104, 114.

52. *Defoe's Narratives*, p. 60.

53. Paul Ricoeur, *Freud and Philosophy: An Essay on Interpretation*, tr. Denis Savage (New Haven, 1970), pp. 333–34.

54. See Michael Seidel, "Crusoe in Exile," *PMLA* 96 (1981), 363–74.

55. *On Realism* (London, 1973), p. 68.

56. See above, pp. 13–14.

57. *Origins of the Novel*, trans. Sacha Rabinovitch (Bloomington, Indiana, 1980), p. 83.

58. Northrop Frye, *The Critical Path: An Essay on the Social Context of Literary Criticism* (Bloomington, Ind., 1973), p. 120.

59. Edward M. Said, *Beginnings: Intention and Method* (Baltimore, 1975), p. 197.

60. Roland Barthes, quoted by Said, p. 202 (from (*S/Z*).

61. Walter R. Reed, *An Exemplary History of the Novel: The Quixotic versus the Picaresque* (Chicago, 1981), p. 111.

62. Georg Lukács, *The Theory of the Novel*, trans. Anna Bostock (Cambridge, Mass., 1971), p. 38.

63. *Roxana, The Fortunate Mistress*, ed. Jane Jack (London, 1964), p. 44.

64. Zimmerman, *Defoe and the Novel*, p. 187.

65. Letter to Max Brod, 12 July 1922, in Franz Kafka, *Letters to Friends, Family, and Editors*, trans. Richard and Clara Winston (New York, 1977), p. 340.

Chapter Six

1. This is the edition from which my quotations are taken: Samuel Richardson, *Clarissa*, in four volumes, with an introduction by John Butt (London, 1962).

2. James Boswell, *Boswell's Life of Johnson*, ed. G. B. Hill, rev. L. F. Powell (Oxford, 1934), II, 175.

3. See T. C. Duncan Eaves and Ben D. Kimpel, *Samuel Richardson: A Biography* (Oxford, 1971), pp. 550–56.

4. See R. H. Tawney, *Religion and the Rise of Capitalism* (New York, 1926), p. 209.

5. *Paradise Lost* I.679–84.

6. Alexander Pope, *The Rape of the Lock*, II.117–20.

7. Michael Walzer, *The Revolution of the Saints: A Study in the Origins of Radical Politics* (New York, 1974), p. 49.

8. James Harrington, *A System of Politics* (published posthumously in 1737), quoted by J. G. A. Pocock, *Politics, Language and Time: Essays on Political Thought and History* (New York, 1973), p. 112.

9. See Darrett Rutman, *American Puritanism: Faith and Practice* (Philadelphia, 1970), ch. 3, "Children of Tradition."

10. See John Allen Stevenson, "The Courtship of the Family: *Clarissa* and the Harlowes Once More," *ELH* 48 (1981), 757–77.

11. Samuel Johnson, *Rambler* 148 and 149 (1751).

12. See Boswell, *Life of Johnson*, II, 49; for Diderot see above, p. 14.

13. John Calvin, *Institutes* II.iii.2, in *Institutes of the Christian Religion*, trans. John Allen (Philadelphia, 1936).

14. Penguin edition of Ian Watt, *The Rise of the Novel* (Harmondsworth, 1963), p. 182; *fouler* ought to read *fuller*, as in the first edition (Berkeley, 1957, p. 176).

15. *Johnsonian Miscellanies*, ed. G. B. Hill (Oxford, 1897), I, 297; Mark Kinkead-Weekes, *Samuel Richardson: Dramatic Novelist* (Ithaca, 1973), pp. 167–68.

16. Robert Scholes and Robert Kellogg, *The Nature of Narrative* (London, 1966), p. 202.

17. William Beatty Warner, *Reading Clarissa: The Struggles of Interpretation* (New Haven, 1979), p. 237.

18. See Cynthia Griffin Wolff, *Samuel Richardson and the Eighteenth-Century Puritan Character* (Hamden, Conn., 1972), ch. 2.

19. See James H. Maddox, Jr., "Lovelace and the World of Ressentiment in *Clarissa*," *Texas Studies in Literature and Language* 24 (1982), p. 276.

20. *Conjectures on Original Composition* (1759), in *Eighteenth-Century English Literature*, ed. Geoffrey Tillotson et al. (New York, 1969), p. 883.

21. Max Beerbohm, *Zuleika Dobson* (New York, 1938), p. 20.

22. Simone de Beauvoir, *The Second Sex*, trans. H. M. Parshley (New York, 1953), p. xxix.

23. Warner, *Reading Clarissa*, p. 22.

24. Frederick Garber, *The Autonomy of the Self from Richardson to Huysmans* (Princeton, 1982), p. 10.

25. *Reading Clarissa*, p. xii.

26. *The Rise of the Novel*, p. 218.

27. See David E. Stannard, *The Puritan Way of Death: A Study in Religion, Culture, and Social Change* (Oxford, 1977), esp. pp. 128–29, and also the letter in which Jonathan Edwards's daughter joyfully welcomes death (pp. 149–50).

28. Letter of 15 Dec. 1748, in *Selected Letters of Samuel Richardson*, ed. John Carroll (Oxford, 1964), pp. 108–9.

29. *An Argument to Prove that the Abolishing of Christianity in England, May as*

Things Now Stand, Be Attended with Some Inconveniences, and Perhaps Not Produce Those Many Good Effects Proposed Thereby (1708), in *Eighteenth-Century English Literature*, ed. Geoffrey Tillotson et al. (New York, 1969), p. 418.

30. See Leo Braudy, "Penetration and Impenetrability in *Clarissa*," in *New Approaches to Eighteenth-Century Literature*, ed. Phillip Harth (New York, 1974), 177–206.

31. Pope, *The Rape of the Lock*, III.139–44.

32. *Purity and Danger: An Analysis of the Concepts of Pollution and Taboo* (London, 1969), p. 158.

33. Paul Ricoeur, *The Symbolism of Evil*, tr. Emerson Buchanan (Boston, 1969), pp. 118–39.

34. John Locke, *An Essay Concerning Human Understanding* (1690), II.i.16.

35. See Margaret Anne Doody, *A Natural Passion: A Study of the Novels of Samuel Richardson* (Oxford, 1974), ch. 7.

36. See John A. Dussinger, "Conscience and the Pattern of Christian Perfection in *Clarissa*," *PMLA* 81 (1966), 236–45.

37. "Mary Moody Emerson," in *The Complete Works of Ralph Waldo Emerson* (Boston, 1904), X, 399, 404, 432.

38. Letter of 29 Dec. 1740, in *The Works of the Late Aaron Hill, Esq.*, 2nd ed. (London, 1754), II, 130.

39. Samuel Richardson, *Meditations Collected from the Sacred Books, and Adapted to the Different Stages of a Deep Distress; Gloriously Surmounted by Patience, Piety, and Resignation. Being Those Mentioned in the HISTORY OF CLARISSA as Drawn up by Her for Her Own Use* (London, 1750), p. 44.

40. José Ortega y Gasset, *The Revolt of the Masses* (New York, 1957), p. 157.

41. Erik Erikson, *Young Man Luther: A Study in Psychoanalysis and History* (New York, 1962), p. 195.

42. Peter L. Berger, *The Sacred Canopy: Elements of a Sociological Theory of Religion* (New York, 1969), p. 43.

43. Terry Eagleton, *The Rape of Clarissa: Writing, Sexuality and Class Struggle in Samuel Richardson* (Minneapolis, 1982), p. 76.

44. Quoted by Edmund S. Morgan, *The Puritan Family* (New York, 1966), p. 106.

45. *Confessions*, tr. John K. Ryan (New York, 1960), XIII.xxxviii, p. 370. (Latin text from the Loeb Classical Library edition.)

46. *Pagan and Christian in an Age of Anxiety: Some Aspects of Religious Experience from Marcus Aurelius to Constantine* (New York, 1965), p. 20.

47. *Confessions* III.vi.

48. *Christian Directory*, quoted by G. A. Starr, *Defoe and Casuistry* (Princeton, 1971), p. 45.

49. Frank Kermode, *The Genesis of Secrecy: On the Interpretation of Narrative* (Cambridge, Mass., 1979).

50. *Reading Clarissa*, p. 41.

51. IV, 136; on the rich implications of this dream see Warner, *Reading Clarissa*, pp. 14–17, and Eagleton, *The Rape of Clarissa*, pp. 62–63.

52. *The Symbolism of Evil*, p. 257.

53. Anonymous, *Critical Remarks on Sir Charles Grandison, Clarissa, and Pamela* (1754), quoted by Warner, *Reading Clarissa*, p. 139.

54. *Paradise Lost* IV.306.

55. "Richardson, Milton, and the Status of Evil," *Review of English Studies* 19 (1968), p. 264.

56. *A Natural Passion*, pp. 101–2.

57. David Daiches, "Samuel Richardson," in *Literary Essays* (Edinburgh, 1966), p. 42.

58. *Troilus and Cressida*, III.ii.

59. Andrew Marvell, "A Dialogue between the Soul and Body," lines 41–42.

60. John Traugott, *"Clarissa*'s Richardson: An Essay to Find the Reader," in *English Literature in the Age of Disguise*, ed. Maximillian E. Novak (Berkeley, 1977), p. 181.

61. "'An Exemplar to Her Sex': Richardson's *Clarissa*," *Yale Review*, 67 (1977), 30–47.

62. See especially Doody, *A Natural Passion*, ch. 5.

63. See Watt, *The Rise of the Novel*, pp. 242–48.

64. *A Tale of a Tub*, sec. ix.

65. "Richardson's Lovelace: Character and Prediction," *Texas Studies in Literature and Language* 14 (1972), pp. 60–61.

66. *"Clarissa*'s Richardson," p. 204.

67. W. H. Auden, "Postscript: The Frivolous and the Earnest," in *The Dyer's Hand and Other Essays* (New York, 1968), p. 430.

68. "Richardson's Lovelace," p. 70.

69. *Leviathan*, ed. Michael Oakeshott (Oxford, 1946), I.xi, p. 64.

70. *Human Nature*, ch. 9, in *The English Works of Thomas Hobbes*, ed. William Molesworth (London, 1839), IV, 53.

71. *Leviathan*, I.viii, p. 46.

72. Ch. 5, sec. 194, of *Beyond Good and Evil*, tr. Helen Zimmern, in *The Philosophy of Nietzsche* (New York: Modern Library, 1954), p. 484.

73. On the relevance of such theories to *Clarissa* see Braudy, "Penetration and Impenetrability in *Clarissa*."

74. Blaise Pascal, *Pensées*, no. 167 (Lafuma numeration), 323 (Brunschvicg).

75. *The Holy War*, ed. James F. Forrest (New York, 1967), p. 138.

76. *Paradise Lost* IV.75.

77. *The City of God*, tr. Henry Bettenson (Harmondsworth, 1972), XIV.xv, p. 575.

78. *The Symbolism of Evil*, p. 30.

79. To Aaron Hill, 7 Nov. 1748, in *Selected Letters*, p. 99.

80. See Wolff, *Samuel Richardson and the Eighteenth-Century Puritan Character*, pp. 136–39.

81. G. Wilson Knight, "The Embassy of Death: An Essay on *Hamlet*," in *The Wheel of Fire* (London, 1949), ch. 2.

82. Edward W. Said, *Beginnings: Intention and Method* (Baltimore, 1975), p. 73.

83. *Adventurer* 120.

84. *Oedipus*, Act III, in *Dryden: The Dramatic Works*, ed. Montague Summers (London, 1932), IV, 397–98.

85. Quoted by W. H. Auden in "A Poet of the Actual," in *Forewords and Afterwords* (New York, 1973), p. 267.

86. *The Sacred Canopy,* pp. 94–95.

87. A. C. Bradley, *Shakespearean Tragedy* (London, 1904, repr. 1967), ch. 1.

88. Georg Lukács, *The Theory of the Novel,* trans. Anna Bostock (Cambridge, Mass., 1973), p. 45; see also above, p. 15.

89. John Orr, *Tragic Realism and Modern Society: Studies in the Sociology of the Modern Novel* (London, 1977), p. 12.

90. Lucien Goldmann, *Le Dieu Caché: Etude sur la Vision Tragique dans les Pensées de Pascal et dans le Théâtre de Racine* (Paris, 1959), p. 41.

91. Letter to Aaron Hill, 29 Oct. 1746, in *Selected Letters,* p. 71; and see Edward Copeland, "Allegory and Analogy in *Clarissa*: The 'Plan' and the "No-Plan,'" *ELH* 39 (1972), 254–65.

92. Goldmann's aphoristic summation: *Le Dieu Caché,* p. 46.

93. This is the central theme of my *Samuel Johnson and the Tragic Sense* (Princeton, 1972).

94. See William J. Farrell, "The Style and the Action in *Clarissa*," *Studies in English Literature* 3 (1963), 365–75.

95. See Jonathan Loesberg, "Allegory and Narrative in *Clarissa*," *Novel* 15 (1981), 39–59. On Clarissa's disillusionment with language considered as transparent and stable, and on the devious ways in which Lovelace exploits this issue, see Terry Castle, *Clarissa's Ciphers: Meaning and Disruption in Richardson's Clarissa* (Ithaca, 1982).

96. Northrop Frye, *The Secular Scripture: A Study of the Structure of Romance* (Cambridge, Mass., 1976), pp. 85–86, 88.

97. See John Preston, *The Created Self: The Reader's Role in Eighteenth-Century Fiction* (London, 1970), pp. 47–48.

98. See Watt, *The Rise of the Novel,* p. 193.

99. See Elizabeth R. Napier, "'Tremble and Reform': The Inversion of Power in Richardson's *Clarissa*," *ELH* 42 (1975), p. 221.

100. *The Borderers,* III.v. Coleridge quotes these lines in "The Character of Hamlet," in his *Shakespearean Criticism,* ed. T. M. Raysor (London, 1960), I, 34.

101. *The Created Self,* pp. 39–41, 51.

102. *The Screwtape Letters: Letters from a Senior to a Junior Devil* (London, 1942, repr. 1977), p. 77.

103. Letter to Sophia Westcomb, ca. 1746, *Selected Letters,* p. 65.

104. See above, p. 47.

105. *Language and Logos in Boswell's Life of Johnson* (Princeton, 1981), pp. 57–58.

106. Letter to Lady Bradshaigh, 14 Feb. 1754, *Selected Letters,* p. 286.

107. *Language and Logos in Boswell's Life of Johnson,* p. 69.

108. René Girard, *Deceit, Desire, and the Novel: Self and Other in Literary Structure,* tr. Yvonne Freccero (Baltimore, 1965), p. 300.

Chapter Seven

1. See esp. Martin C. Battestin, "Fielding: The Argument of Design," in *The Providence of Wit: Aspects of Form in Augustan Literature and the Arts* (Oxford, 1974), 141–63.

2. *The Eloquent "I": Style and Self in Seventeenth-Century Prose* (Madison, Wis. 1968), pp. 48, 9.

3. *Grace Abounding*, ed. Roger Sharrock (Oxford, 1962), pp. 3–4.

4. Erik Erikson, *Young Man Luther* (New York, 1962), p. 169.

5. John Forster, *The Life of Charles Dickens* (Philadelphia, 1874), III, 135n.

6. Henry Fielding, *The History of Tom Jones, A Foundling*, ed. Martin C. Battestin and Fredson Bowers (Middletown, Conn., 1975), XVIII.i, p. 913. All further references will be to this edition.

7. See R. S. Crane, "The Concept of Plot and the Plot of *Tom Jones*," in *Critics and Criticism, Ancient and Modern*, ed. Crane (Chicago, 1952), pp. 627–28.

8. *Religio Laici* (1682), lines 446–50.

9. William Haller, *The Rise of Puritanism* (New York, 1938), p. 153.

10. Bunyan, *The Pilgrim's Progress*, ed. Roger Sharrock (Harmondsworth, 1965), p. 50.

11. Søren Kierkegaard, *Fear and Trembling*, in *Fear and Trembling and the Sickness unto Death*, tr. Walter Lowrie (Princeton, 1968), p. 90.

12. Peter L. Berger, *The Sacred Canopy: Elements of a Sociological Theory of Religion* (New York, 1969), p. 59.

13. John Locke, *An Essay Concerning Human Understanding*, II.xxviii.12.

14. Jean-Jacques Rousseau, *Confessions*, second paragraph.

15. *Essay Concerning Human Understanding*, II.xxv.7.

16. Henry Fielding, *Joseph Andrews*, ed. Martin C. Battestin (Middletown, Conn., 1967), III.i, p. 189.

17. Sandor Ferenczi, "The Adaptation of the Family to the Child," in *Final Contributions to the Problems and Methods of Psycho-analysis* (London, 1955), p. 66.

18. Richardson, *Clarissa*, ed. Butt (London, 1962), II, 49, 70.

19. *The Holy War*, ed. James F. Forrest (New York, 1967), p. 94.

20. Samuel Johnson, *Sermons*, ed. Jean Hagstrum and James Gray (New Haven, 1978), Sermon 7, p. 79.

21. Quoted by Christian Deelman, "The Original Cast of *The School for Scandal*," *Review of English Studies* 13 (1962), p. 258.

22. *Pensées*, no. 99 (Lafuma), 100 (Brunschvicg).

23. "Of the Immorality of Conversation, and the Vulgar Errors of Behaviour." in *Serious Reflections of Robinson Crusoe* (see above, p. 322, note 2), p. 97.

24. William Empson, *"Tom Jones,"* in *Fielding: A Collection of Critical Essays*, ed. Ronald Paulson (Englewood Cliffs, N.J., 1962), p. 129.

25. *Complete Prose Works of John Milton* (New Haven, 1953–), II, 527; *Paradise Lost* III.108.

26. *Roxana: The Fortunate Mistress*, ed. Jane Jack (London, 1964), p. 69.

27. *City of God*, tr. Henry Bettenson (Harmondsworth, 1972), XIV.xvi, p. 577.

28. *Colonel Jack*, ed. Samuel Holt Monk (London, 1965), p. 241.

29. *Paradise Lost* IV.639.

30. See Robert Alter's excellent discussion of this point in *Fielding and the Nature of the Novel* (Cambridge, Mass., 1968), esp. pp. 8–10, 16–17.

31. *Amelia*, Everyman ed. (London, 1930), I, 260–61.

32. C. S. Lewis, *English Literature in the Sixteenth Century* (Oxford, 1954), p. 320.

33. I discuss the ambiguities of Johnson's position in *The Uses of Johnson's Criticism* (Charlottesville, Va., 1976), ch. 5.

34. *Rambler* 4.

35. *Boswell's Life of Johnson*, ed. G. B. Hill, rev. L. F. Powell (Oxford, 1934), I, 364n; II, 433; I, 415n.

36. Irvin Ehrenpreis, *Fielding: Tom Jones* (London, 1964), p. 40.

37. "Thoughts on Comedy," written ca. 1775–76, published in Walpole's *Works* (1798), and reprinted in *Essays in Criticism*, 15 (1965), 165.

38. *Coleridge's Miscellaneous Criticism*, ed. T. M. Raysor (Cambridge, Mass., 1936), p. 437.

39. Friedrich Nietzsche, *The Birth of Tragedy*, sec. 12, in *The Birth of Tragedy and the Case of Wagner*, tr. Walter Kaufmann (New York, 1967), p. 84.

40. On Fielding as *histor* see Robert Scholes and Robert Kellogg, *The Nature of Narrative* (London, 1968), pp. 265–68; on the resemblances between Fielding and Gibbon (who greatly admired Fielding) see Leo Braudy, *Narrative Form in History and Fiction* (Princeton, 1970), Part V.

41. Miguel De Cervantes, *Don Quixote*, tr. Joseph R. Jones and Kenneth Douglas (New York, 1981), II.ii, p. 437.

42. Samuel Johnson, *Life of Milton*, in *Lives of the English Poets*, ed. G. B. Hill (Oxford, 1905), I, 183–84.

43. As Ehrenpreis comments in *Fielding: Tom Jones*, p. 65.

44. *The Pilgrim's Progress*, ed. Sharrock, p. 37.

45. *Essay Concerning Human Understanding*, "Epistle to the Reader," first paragraph. See Fielding's address to the reader at the end of Book XI, ch. ix, of *Tom Jones*.

46. See John Preston, *The Created Self: The Reader's Role in Eighteenth-Century Fiction* (London, 1970), pp. 108–9.

47. See Thomas Lockwood, "Matter and Reflection in *Tom Jones*," *ELH* 45 (1978), 226–35.

48. Walter Benjamin, "The Storyteller," in *Illuminations*, tr. Harry Zohn (New York, 1968), pp. 86–87.

49. *Robinson Crusoe*, ed. J. Donald Crowley (London, 1976), p. 211.

50. *Joseph Andrews*, I.xv, p. 68.

51. As Preston notes, *The Created Self*, p. 120.

52. Roland Barthes, *Mythologies*, tr. Annette Lavers (New York, 1972), p. 18.

53. See Anthony J. Hassall, "Fielding's Puppet Image," *Philological Quarterly* 53 (1974), 71–83.

54. See Andrew Wright, *Henry Fielding: Mask and Feast* (Berkeley, 1966), ch. 3.

55. Frank Kermode, *The Sense of an Ending* (New York, 1967), p. 51.

56. Martin Battestin, "Fielding: The Definition of Wisdom," in *The Providence of Wit*, p. 185.

57. Rosemond Tuve, *Allegorical Imagery* (Princeton, 1966), p. 131.

58. Alter, *Fielding and the Nature of the Novel*, p. 89.

59. See Marshall Brown, "The Logic of Realism: A Hegelian Approach," *PMLA* 96 (1981), p. 226.

60. *On Realism* (London, 1973), p. 5.

61. *On Realism*, p. 144.

62. *Reflections on the Hero as Quixote* (Princeton, 1981), p. 64.

63. *Joseph Andrews*, I.iii, p. 23.

64. José Ortega y Gasset, *Meditations on Quixote*, quoted by Welsh, *Reflections on the Hero as Quixote*, p. 89.

65. Marthe Robert, *Origins of the Novel*, tr. Sacha Rabinovitch (Bloomington, Ind., 1980), p. 35.

66. *Spectator* 315. Battestin cites this in connection with the passage just quoted from *Tom Jones* (p. 397n of his edition).

67. Robert V. Weiss, "The Probable and the Marvelous in *Tom Jones*," *Modern Philology* 68 (1970), p. 44.

68. "The Concept of Plot and the Plot of *Tom Jones*," p. 635.

69. *Fielding: Tom Jones*, p. 11.

70. See Henry Knight Miller, *Henry Fielding's Tom Jones and the Romance Tradition* (Victoria, B.C., 1976), and Sheridan Baker, "Fielding's Comic Epic-in-Prose Romance Again," *Philological Quarterly* 58 (1979), 63–81.

71. Quoted in *Henry Fielding's Tom Jones and the Romance Tradition*, p. 25.

72. See J. Paul Hunter, "The Loneliness of the Long-Distance Reader," *Genre* 10 (1977), 455–84.

73. Northrop Frye, *Anatomy of Criticism* (Princeton, 1957), p. 34.

74. *The Secular Scripture: A Study of the Structure of Romance* (Cambridge, Mass., 1976), pp. 47–48.

75. *The Secular Scripture*, p. 172.

76. Letters to Frances Grainger (22 Jan. 1749/50) and Anne Donnellan (22 Feb. 1752), in *Selected Letters of Samuel Richardson*, ed. John Carroll (Oxford, 1964), pp. 143, 197.

77. *The Consolation of Philosophy*, tr. Richard Green (Indianapolis, 1962), Book V, Prose 1, p. 102.

78. *Joseph Andrews*, III.iii, p. 224.

79. *The Discarded Image: An Introduction to Medieval and Renaissance Literature* (Cambridge, 1964), p. 140.

80. John Tillotson, Sermon 36, "Success not always answerable to the probability of second causes," in *Works* (1820), III, 98–99. On Fielding's esteem for such preachers as Tillotson and South, see Martin C. Battestin, *The Moral Basis of Fielding's Art: A Study of Joseph Andrews* (Middletown, Conn., 1959).

81. *Sermons Preached upon Several Occasions* (London, 1737), I, 294, 296.

82. Wayne C. Booth, *The Rhetoric of Fiction* (Chicago, 1961), p. 217.

83. *The Art of Poetry*, I, 179–80.

84. *The Faerie Queene* I.xi.45.

85. See Wayne Booth's discussion of this passage in *A Rhetoric of Irony* (Chicago, 1974), p. 19.

86. *Narrative Form in History and Fiction*, p. 163.

87. See Stevan Cohan, "Narrative Form and Death: *The Mill on the Floss* and *Mrs. Dalloway*," *Genre* 2 (1978), 109–29; and Elizabeth Ermarth, "Realism, Perspective, and the Novel," *Critical Inquiry* 7 (1981), 499–520.

88. *Boswell's Life of Johnson*, ed. Hill and Powell, II, 449.

89. Laurence Sterne, *The Life and Opinions of Tristram Shandy, Gentleman*,

ed. Ian Watt (Boston, 1965), I.iv, p. 6; II.ii, p. 66. All subsequent references are to this edition.

90. See especially James E. Swearingen, *Reflexivity in Tristram Shandy: An Essay in Phenomenological Criticism* (New Haven, 1977).

91. Leo Braudy, "The Form of the Sentimental Novel," *Novel* 7 (1973), p. 10.

92. "Par Divers Moyens On Arrive à Pareille Fin: A Reading of Montaigne," *Modern Language Notes* 83 (1968), 577–97. This position closely resembles Sterne's as developed by Swearingen.

93. "Of Giving the Lie," in *The Complete Essays of Montaigne*, tr. Donald M. Frame (Stanford, 1965), II.xviii, p. 504.

94. *Reflexivity in Tristram Shandy*, p. 93.

95. See Michael Rosenblum, "Shandean Geometry and the Challenge of Contingency," *Novel* 10 (1977), 237–47.

96. See Richard Lanham, *Tristram Shandy: The Games of Pleasure* (Berkeley, 1973).

97. See Swearingen, *Reflexivity in Tristram Shandy*, pp. 81–82, 87; and see also p. 256, contrasting this position with the solitude of Crusoe.

98. Georg Lukács, *The Theory of the Novel*, tr. Anna Bostock (Cambridge, Mass., 1973), p. 92; and see above, pp. 13–14.

99. *Rambler* 54.

100. *City of God* XIII.x, p. 518.

101. "Humour" (1927), in *The Standard Edition of the Complete Psychological Works of Sigmund Freud*, ed. James Strachey (London, 1961), XXI, 162–63.

102. "Orbilius," *An Examen of the History of Tom Jones, a Foundling* (1749), in *Henry Fielding: The Critical Heritage*, ed. Ronald Paulson and Thomas Lockwood (London, 1969), p. 201.

103. Gabriel Josipovici, *Writing and the Body* (Princeton, 1982), p. 29.

104. *Antony and Cleopatra*, IV.xiv.2–11.

105. *The Journals and Papers of Gerard Manley Hopkins*, ed. Humphry House (London, 1959), p. 230.

106. "Le Rêve de d'Alembert," in *Oeuvres Philosophiques*, ed. Paul Vernière (Paris, 1956), pp. 299–300.

107. Sermon XVIII, in *The Sermons of Mr. Yorick*, ed. Wilbur L. Cross (New York, 1904), I, 290.

108. T. S. Eliot, "Burnt Norton," sec. V.

109. See William Freedman, "*Tristram Shandy:* The Art of Literary Counterpoint," *Modern Language Quarterly* 32 (1971), 268–80.

110. *The Progress of Romance* (Colchester, 1785, repr. New York, 1930), I, 111.

111. *The Miller's Prologue*, A3176–78, in *The Works of Geoffrey Chaucer*, ed. F. N. Robinson (Boston, 1961), p. 48.

112. *The Nun's Priest's Tale*, VII 3147, p. 202.

113. J. H. Plumb, *England in the Eighteenth Century* (Harmondsworth, 1950), p. 95.

114. *Spectator* 418.

115. *The Grounds of Criticism in Poetry* (1704), in *The Critical Works of John Dennis*, ed. Edward N. Hooker (Baltimore, 1939), I, 336.

116. Jane Austen, *Emma,* ed. Ronald Blythe (Harmondsworth, 1966), ch. 39, p. 331.

117. Evelyn Waugh, *Decline and Fall* (Boston, 1956), p. 277.

118. Kingsley Amis, *Lucky Jim* (New York, 1958), p. 182.

119. *The Secular Scripture,* p. 14.

120. *Windsor-Forest* (1713), lines 7–8.

121. See Marshall Brown, "The Logic of Realism: A Hegelian Approach," pp. 237–38.

Index

NOTE: It has proved impractical to index those terms and concepts that appear most frequently, e.g., allegory, autobiography, determinism, evil, narrative, novel, psychology, symbolism, Christ, God, Providence, Satan.